THEOLOGY
WITHOUT
BORDERS

Peter C. Phan
Photograph courtesy of Phil Humnicky, Georgetown University

THEOLOGY WITHOUT BORDERS

Essays in Honor of Peter C. Phan

LEO D. LEFEBURE, EDITOR

FOREWORD BY THOMAS BANCHOFF

GEORGETOWN UNIVERSITY PRESS / WASHINGTON, DC

The publisher is not responsible for third-party websites or their content. URL links were active at time of publication.

Library of Congress Cataloging-in-Publication Data

Names: Phan, Peter C., 1943– honouree. | Lefebure, Leo D., 1952– editor.
Title: Theology without Borders: Essays in Honor of Peter C. Phan / Leo D.
  Lefebure, editor
Description: Washington, DC: Georgetown University Press, 2022. | On March 30
  and 31, 2017, the late Gerard Mannion convened a symposium at Georgetown
  University to discuss "Theology without Borders: Celebrating the Legacy of
  Peter C. Phan." Scholars from across the globe gathered to explore a wide range
  of theological issues relating to Phan's contributions, especially his pioneering
  work on religious pluralism, migration, and Christian identity.—Introduction |
  Includes bibliographical references and index.
Identifiers: LCCN 2021027081 (print) | LCCN 2021027082 (ebook) |
  ISBN 9781647122409 (hardcover) | ISBN 9781647122416 (paperback) |
  ISBN 9781647122423 (ebook)
Subjects: LCSH: Phan, Peter C., 1943– | Christianity—Asia—Congresses. |
  Theology—Asia—Congresses. | Christianity and culture—Asia—Congresses. |
  Christianity and other religions—Congresses. | Emigration and immigration—
  Religious aspects—Christianity—Congresses. | Eschatology—Congresses.
Classification: LCC BR1065.T44 2022 (print) | LCC BR1065 (ebook) |
  DDC 275—dc23
LC record available at https://lccn.loc.gov/2021027081
LC ebook record available at https://lccn.loc.gov/2021027082

♾ This paper meets the requirements of ANSI/NISO Z39.48-1992 (Permanence of Paper).

23 22   9 8 7 6 5 4 3 2   First printing

Printed in the United States of America

Cover design by Nathan Putens. Cover photo © Thomasgehmacher | Dreamstime.com
Interior design by BookComp, Inc.

CONTENTS

Foreword   vii
Thomas Banchoff

Introduction: Celebration and a Memorial   1
Leo D. Lefebure

PART I: WORLD CHRISTIANITY AND MIGRATION

1 Peter C. Phan and the Reconstruction of World Christianity   11
Dale T. Irvin

2 Being Church among Asians: Perspective and Insights
of the Asian Theology of the FABC   29
Anh Q. Tran, SJ

3 Between "Memory and Imagination": Reimagining World
Christianity without Borders   47
Jonathan Y. Tan

4 Christian Resilience and Vulnerable Migrants   65
Gemma Tulud Cruz

5 Wives Submitting to Husbands: Domestic Violence, Women,
and the Christian Faith   83
Cristina Lledo Gomez

PART II: CHRISTIAN IDENTITY
AND RELIGIOUS PLURALISM

6 Dialogue and Reconciliation in the Renaissance and in Vatican II   109
John W. O'Malley, SJ

7 Interfaith Christology? Some Dogmatic Prolegomena   118
   William P. Loewe

8 Interreligious Marriage as a Way of Being
   Religious Interreligiously   128
   Chester Gillis

9 Peter Phan and Ecclesiology Beyond Borders   145
   Brian P. Flanagan

10 Dialogue in a Multireligious and Political Ecosystem: Understanding
    Catholic Relations with Other Religions in Mainland China   157
    Stephanie M. Wong

PART III: ESCHATOLOGY

11 Migration and Eschatology in Hebrews   175
    Alan C. Mitchell

12 Waiting Outside Time? The Intermediate State   183
    Brian M. Doyle

13 On Religions, Peter Phan, and Christian Expansivism   201
    Keith Ward

PART IV: THE LEGACY OF PETER C. PHAN

14 Decentralizing Theology: Peter Phan and
    the Second Vatican Council   219
    Debora Tonelli

15 Peter Phan and the Congregation for the Doctrine of the Faith   235
    Charles E. Curran

16 Being Honestly Pluralistically Religious   249
    John Borelli

17 Counting the Uncountable: The Contributions of Peter Phan   264
    Leo D. Lefebure

Epilogue   273
   Peter C. Phan

Appendix: Curriculum Vitae of Peter C. Phan   279

Contributors   299

Index   305

FOREWORD

Theology Without Borders, the title of this volume, aptly evokes the seminal contributions of Peter Phan, a remarkably productive and creative scholar who challenges us to make global humanity the starting point for theological reflection. The title also captures our historical reality. Christian reflection on God and the world today no longer unfolds within clearly demarcated ecclesial, national, or cultural spaces. Religious and cultural pluralism, reinforced by accelerating transborder communications, mobility, and exchange, are our shared point of departure. We cannot think theology without them.

In pathbreaking ways, Peter has explored the theological possibilities and imperatives opened up by our global era. Over several decades, he has persuaded us that the collapse of established, bounded frameworks—especially those of a European Christianity with a monopoly on truth—is not to be feared but celebrated. The titles of some of his most important books make the point succinctly: *Christianity with an Asian Face*; *Being Religious Interreligiously*; and, most colorfully, *The Joy of Religious Pluralism*.

Peter's scholarly adventures beyond established borders mirror both his personal pilgrimage and that of the Catholic Church. In 1968 he left his native Vietnam for doctoral study in theology in Rome, before being ordained and emigrating to the United States in 1975. There, his career took him from the University of Dallas to the Catholic University of America and finally to Georgetown University, where he holds the Ignacio Ellacuría, SJ, Chair of Catholic Social Thought. Peter's personal journey coincided with the opening of the Church to the modern world unleashed by the Second Vatican Council (1962–65). With the council, the Church endorsed interreligious dialogue and the principle of religious freedom and embraced a global horizon, identifying fully with "the joys and the hopes, the griefs and the anxieties" of all humanity.

On his academic odyssey accompanying the postconciliar Church, Peter has written and edited more than thirty books and published more than one hundred journal articles as well as innumerable book chapters and encyclopedia entries (see the appendix for his curriculum vitae). His work has been translated into ten languages, from Italian to Chinese and Indonesian. His prodigious output has contributed to and enriched literatures in ecclesiology, Christology, missiology, patristics, and other fields.

In all his impressive scholarship, Peter has embodied the idea of dialogue. With a self-effacing manner and sly sense of humor, he has put forth his ideas not just to persuade but to engage—to elicit the views of others, to listen and learn, and to move the conversation along. It is Peter's style, as well as his superb scholarship, that have won him so many grateful colleagues, from the former students he has mentored to so many scholars influential in the academy today.

This volume, ably edited by Peter's Georgetown colleague Leo Lefebure, is testimony to the intellectual community that Peter has fostered. It brings together the contributions from fifteen friends and collaborators, leading scholars in their own right, and engages systematically with Peter's ideas across a range of vitally important topics, from global Christianity and migration to religious pluralism, the legacies of the Second Vatican Council, and eschatological controversies. Taken together, the essays provide an overview of Peter's scholarly contributions and a road map for better understanding theology without borders in our contemporary world.

Most of the essays presented here were originally prepared for a conference at Georgetown in 2017 organized by Peter's close friend and colleague Gerard Mannion. This volume is dedicated to the memory of Gerard, who passed away in 2019. In him Georgetown University and the academic community lost a brilliant and caring colleague whose life and work continue to inspire.

—Thomas Banchoff
Vice President for Global Engagement and
Professor of Government and Foreign Service
at Georgetown University

Celebration and a Memorial

Leo D. Lefebure

Since coming to the United States of America as a refugee from Vietnam in 1975, Peter C. Phan has contributed significantly to our understanding of many areas of Christian theology, including the relatively new fields of world Christianity, migration, religious pluralism, and Christian theology in Asia; to the traditional topics of Pneumatology, Christology, and eschatology; as well as to the specialized study of Paul Evdokimov, Karl Rahner, Alexandre de Rhodes, and countless more figures. On March 30 and 31, 2017, the late Gerard Mannion convened a symposium at Georgetown University to discuss "Theology without Borders: Celebrating the Legacy of Peter C. Phan." Scholars from around the globe gathered to explore a wide range of theological issues relating to Phan's contributions, especially his pioneering work on religious pluralism, migration, and Christian identity.

The omnipresent Mannion played his familiar role of impresario, organizing conversations, making introductions, and animating dialogue. He treasured the theme of theology without borders, and he took special pride in facilitating explorations of Christian theology in dialogue with peoples, religious traditions, and cultures from around the world. He valued personal connections, he knew that often the most important exchanges occur outside the organized program, and he took great pleasure in the informal discussions over coffee or wine that he repeatedly facilitated. He had intended to edit the essays presented at this conference into a volume in honor of Peter Phan's legacy. But to our great surprise and dismay, Mannion departed this world on September 21, 2019, leaving many bereaved family members, friends, and admirers. We dedicate this volume to the memory of Gerard Mannion, who enriched our world with his tireless energy, restless questioning, and creative inquiry. This volume is both a celebration of the theological legacy of Peter

Phan and also a memorial to the endearing friendship and tireless activity of Gerard Mannion in crossing borders and bringing people together.

Part I of this volume, chapters 1 through 5, explores themes of world Christianity and migration, which are central to the work of Peter Phan. Phan knew firsthand the widespread suffering during the war in Vietnam and came to the United States in 1975 as a refugee; this life-altering experience has shaped his long-standing concern for refugees and for all migrants. In wide-ranging chapter 1, Dale T. Irvin reminds us how strongly this personal experience of migration has shaped all aspects of Phan's groundbreaking theology of world Christianity. Having lived in many places around the world, Phan repeatedly learned to make himself at home in new, unfamiliar settings. Irvin emphasizes the polycentric character of Phan's theology that prods us to move beyond thinking of any one particular center of Christianity. Irvin points out that Phan shapes a cosmopolitan theology based on the multiple ecumenes in which he dwells. Irvin holds up Phan as a model of how a cosmopolitan theology can inhabit multiple contexts.

One of Phan's most influential contributions is his mentoring of younger scholars; two of his former students, Anh Q. Tran and Jonathan Y. Tan, explore dimensions of Christian identity in Asia. In chapter 2, Anh Q. Tran explores how Asian Christian theologies have developed new forms of reflection and practice, especially in the wake of the Second Vatican Council: Asian Christian theology is inductive, in solidarity with the poor, open to dialogue with followers of other religions, and centered not on the inner life of the Church but on relations with the world. These theologians draw on Asian cultural and religious traditions creatively, exploring the significance of the Gospel in Asian contexts; they focus especially on pastoral practice and ponder the significance of the ancient mystical and apophatic traditions for practitioners today. Tran agrees with Phan in stressing that the Church has a mission among the peoples, not merely toward them.

In chapter 3, Jonathan Y. Tan takes inspiration from Phan's project of doing theology with memory and imagination; he poses the question of what a theology without borders would look like in a world of migration, a topic very dear to his mentor. Tan explores the factors that shape emerging religious identities, including online communities, hybridity, and ecclesial dual belonging; he pays particular attention to those who dwell on the border of Christianity and other traditions, variously Islamic, Hindu, or Buddhist. He points out the coexistence of local Christian communities in Asia with migrants who bring their own forms of Christian practice and often encounter suspicion and even xenophobia. Tan notes the profound implications for ecclesiology of all these experiences.

In chapter 4, Gemma Tulud Cruz explores migration, a theme that is central to the theology of Phan. Evoking Phan's image of Deus Migrator (God the Primordial Migrant), Cruz proposes that Christian hope can inspire the practice of empathy and solidarity in a time of great tension, leading to resilience for both migrants and their advocates. And in chapter 5, Cristina Lledo Gomez, who migrated from the Philippines to Australia and has worked extensively with women's advocacy groups, explores the tragedy of domestic abuse that so often afflicts vulnerable women in new situations. Building on Phan's scholarship and going beyond it, she examines the interrelationship between traditional Christian attitudes and practices and the unbearable suffering of women, and she recommends important changes that could improve the lives of those who are vulnerable.

Part II, chapters 6 through 10, explores the relationship between Christian identity and religious pluralism, another issue that is central to the work of Phan. In chapter 6, John W. O'Malley reminds us that interreligious awareness and the inclusion of religious figures from other traditions is not new in the history of the Catholic Church. In a fascinating tour of Renaissance Catholic thought and the Sistine Chapel, O'Malley reflects on Michelangelo's placing of the pagan mantic priestesses known as sibyls alongside the prophets of ancient Israel on the chapel's ceiling. Without claiming direct influence, O'Malley shows how the attitudes of Catholic Renaissance humanists and their creative practice of dialogue anticipated the openness of the Second Vatican Council to dialogue with followers of other religious paths.

Noting that perspectives on the identity and work of Jesus Christ are of crucial importance for assessing the relation between Christian identity and religious pluralism, in chapter 7, William P. Loewe responds to Phan's constructive proposal for an interreligious Christology that considers Jesus Christ among the many faiths. Phan has proposed a correlation between Christian understandings of Christ and analogous images and concepts in other traditions, stressing the critical importance of Pneumatology: the Spirit that is at work in Jesus Christ is active in other traditions as well. Loewe reflects on the significance of Phan's perspective both appreciatively but also critically, posing questions concerning the meaning of correlation, the basis for making normative judgments, and the tension between a truly interfaith reflection and the project of Christian theology. Noting that Phan presents his proposal as tentative and exploratory, Loewe suggests that it contains unresolved tensions that call for further reflection; Loewe also acknowledges that the Catholic dogmatic tradition offers space for creative interreligious exploration, especially in relation to the activity of the Holy Spirit.

In chapter 8, Chester Gillis explores the intimate area of interreligious relations in marriages between practitioners of different religious traditions. Based on his study of interfaith marriages in the United States today, Gillis discusses the challenges and possibilities that interreligious married couples negotiate. He notes the widely differing attitudes toward interreligious marriage, including the difficult debate within the Jewish community concerning marriage to those of other faiths. He also notes the close relationship between the religious issues in a marriage and the familial, social, cultural, and personal factors in play.

In chapter 9, Brian P. Flanagan presents Phan as a theologian of the Church, who is personally grounded in the complex context of Church life and who is also constantly pondering the ecclesiological dimension of theology, even when this is not the explicit focus of attention. Flanagan stresses the methodological contributions of Phan as a contextual theologian, particularly his pointing out how strongly religious, cultural, and historical contexts shape our perspectives. Following Phan's lead, Flanagan warns that the temptation to conform to our contemporary consumerist society can lead the Church to cling to a secure sense of identity and neglect the mission to proclaim the Kingdom of God to those outside. He notes that Phan proposes a vision of the Church that centers on proclaiming the Kingdom in dialogue with others and that is kenotic, or self-emptying, in service to the world, especially the poor and the marginalized. Flanagan relates Phan's vision of a regnocentric Church to the leadership of Pope Francis: Phan's call for the Church to decenter itself and focus on service to others resonates with Pope Francis's warning against the danger of a Church that is preoccupied with its own internal problems to the neglect of the world. Both Pope Francis and Phan call the Church away from self-absorption to mission.

In chapter 10, Stephanie Wong finds the sociological models of the religious market and religious ecology helpful in exploring the complex situation of Catholics in China today with regard to interreligious relationships. She notes both Catholic magisterial teaching and also the various ways in which the Chinese state seeks to influence and shape Catholic interreligious relations in relation to its own goals, such as stability and social harmony. In light of this complex and ever-changing context, Wong describes various challenges and possibilities for Catholics living as a minority in multireligious China.

Part III, chapters 11 through 13, explores another enduring concern of Peter Phan: Christian eschatology. In chapter 11, Alan Mitchell accepts Phan's interpretation of the Church as an institutional migrant since the time of the Acts of the Apostles. From this angle of vision, Mitchell reads the Epistle to the Hebrews in relation to migration and eschatology, bringing together two themes that have occupied Phan's attention across the decades. Mitchell interprets Hebrews as a homily or sermon that presents a word of exhortation or encouragement (Heb. 13:22), originally addressed to the community in Rome after the destruction of Jerusalem by the Roman Army in 70 CE. As we have seen, Phan experienced the social dislocation of leaving Vietnam and coming to the United States as a refugee; Mitchell stresses the social dislocation of the original audience of Hebrews, citing the author's self-description as "we who have taken refuge" (Heb. 6:18). Mitchell points out that Hebrews presents eschatological hope to those in dire need of encouragement; Hebrews also praises two virtues modeled by Abraham that are dear to Phan: hope and *philoxenia*, "love of the stranger," or hospitality.

In chapter 12, Brian Doyle notes the perplexing character of eschatological questions, especially what happens to a deceased person in "the intermediate state"—that is, the time between personal death and the final judgment. Observing that Phan has returned again and again to discussions of eschatology, Doyle relates Phan's work to the writings of Karl Rahner and the debate between Gisbert Greshake and Joseph Ratzinger. After an overview of the biblical passages cited in this debate, Doyle proposes that Phan's perspectives, informed as they are by Eastern Christianity and dialogue with other religions, can help move the discussion forward. Doyle notes that Phan emphasizes the mutuality of relations in forming human identity, which means the Communion of Saints is the vital context for eschatological reflection. Doyle explains that Phan follows Rahner in interpreting death in relation to human freedom; but Phan expands the Western discussion by exploring the Eastern Christian tradition's witness in the early Church and beyond. Phan also proposes an interreligious horizon that includes dialogue with the Buddhist and Hindu traditions that affirm rebirth, and also with liberation, feminist, ecological, and process theologians.

In chapter 13, Keith Ward poses a provocative challenge to religious pluralists by noting that the directly conflicting eschatological predictions of differing religious traditions cannot all be true; it is likely that all humans are at least in part mistaken in their eschatological expectations; and it may be that none of our predictions is true. After a brief survey of the history of changing Catholic attitudes toward the salvation of non-Catholics, Ward reflects on what is necessary for Christian salvation and hopes that all humans will be able finally to learn the truth and come into proper relationship with ultimate reality after death. Given the uncertainty of our current state of knowledge, he proposes what he calls Christian expansivism—that is, the recognition that his beliefs could be expanded by knowledge of other religious and philosophical views. Christian expansivism frames his dialogue with Phan's eschatology: while Ward hopes that persons holding false beliefs can nonetheless experience a transforming relationship with ultimate reality, he also believes there are limits to this expansion, and he poses critical questions for Phan's position. Ward acknowledges the metaphorical or analogical character of language about God and the afterlife, and he recognizes that statements that contrast sharply may not actually contradict each other if taken in a metaphorical or analogical manner. He closes by hoping that followers of different religious paths can learn from each other through creative and respectful exchange.

Part IV, chapters 14 through 17, turns to consideration of certain aspects of the legacy of Peter Phan. In chapter 14, Debora Tonelli describes Phan's contribution to decentralizing theology in the post–Vatican II context as moving from a Eurocentric, colonial past into a multicultural, multireligious present and future. Tonelli stresses that after many centuries during which European philosophical categories dominated the interpretation of Christian faith, the Second Vatican Council encouraged contributions from all the cultures of the world. She notes the intertwining of theological and political issues both in the historic European centralization of Christian faith and also in the recent broadening of horizons to welcome non-European perspectives with greater respect. She questions the traditional narrative of Christianity as an allegedly "Western" religion and laments the effects of imperialism and colonialism on the history of Christian mission. She presents Phan as one of the leading interpreters of the new challenges and possibilities opened up by the Second Vatican Council. And she highlights Phan's praise of "foolish wisdom," which breaks open the old plans and introduces new perspectives, drawing together the wisdom of the Christian tradition and Asian cultures. In this foolish wisdom, she suggests, Phan points a path to the future.

One of Phan's most important contributions is his example of how to respond to critical questioning by ecclesial officials. In chapter 15, Charles E. Curran assesses Peter Phan's impact on the Church, especially the theological community, in his exchange with the Congregation for the Doctrine of the Faith (CDF). Curran, who had earlier had personal experience with the CDF, maps out the process used by the CDF in investigating Phan's work. He then reflects on the question of why the CDF abruptly ended its process and transferred it to the US Conference of Catholic Bishops, and he concludes with an ethical reflection on the requirements of justice in such cases. After the CDF directed that Phan write an essay addressing its concerns regarding religious pluralism, Phan replied that this would require him to take a leave from his academic position for six months, and he required financial compensation from the congregation for this period as a matter of justice. Curran praises Phan's astuteness in requiring financial remuneration and notes the difficult choice that this presented to the Roman officials. Rather than reply to Phan's requirement of funding, the CDF transferred the process to the Committee on Doctrine of the US Conference of Catholic Bishops. Curran speculates on possible reasons why the CDF adopted this course of action. After reviewing a number of investigations of other Catholic theologians, Curran judges that the procedures used by the CDF do not meet the requirements of justice.

In chapter 16, John Borelli places Peter Phan's contributions to our understanding of religious pluralism in the context of recent developments in the theology of religions, especially Pope Francis's signing of the "Document on Human Fraternity for World Peace and Living Together," together with the grand imam of Al Azhar University, Ahmed el-Tayeb, in February 2019. The assertion of Pope Francis and Imam el-Tayeb that God wills religious pluralism aroused the concern of a number of Catholic leaders, but it converges with Phan's affirmations. In tracing the development of Catholic attitudes toward other religions, Borelli emphasizes that for both Pope Francis and Phan, acknowledging the authentic values present in other religions does not in any way diminish one's commitment to one's own tradition. He also notes the theme of joy that is repeatedly emphasized by Pope Francis in *The Joy of the Gospel* and *The Joy of Love* and in his apostolic exhortation *Rejoice and Be Glad*; the pope's invocation of joy converges strongly with Phan's presentation of *The Joy of Religious Pluralism*. In chapter 17, my concluding retrospective seeks to pay tribute to the many-sided character of Peter Phan's contributions.

In the epilogue, Phan offers the final word in this conversation, reflecting on the variety of perspectives on his work. In honoring his work, we also pay homage to memory of our dear friend, Gerard Mannion, who made this celebration possible. Phan's curriculum vitae is included as an appendix.

PART I

WORLD CHRISTIANITY AND MIGRATION

CHAPTER 1

Peter C. Phan and the Reconstruction of World Christianity

Dale T. Irvin

The man who finds his homeland sweet is still a tender beginner; he to whom every soil is as his native one is already strong; but he is perfect to whom the entire world is as a foreign land.

—Hugh of Saint Victor

Over the past half century, one has often heard a lament in the halls of theological schools that the "age of the theological giants" has past.[1] Any one making such a claim today has obviously not yet encountered the work of Peter C. Phan. Phan is without question a theological giant, with many of us already happily perched upon his shoulders.[2] His scholarship covers an enormous theological range, from earliest Christianity to contemporary culture, engaging the ecumenical spectrum of Orthodox, Roman Catholic, Protestant, and Pentecostal traditions and perspectives. Along the way, he has touched constructively on almost every major area of Christian doctrine in the various traditions, from creation to eschatology. His work defies any easy classification. He is at much at home in Rome as he is in Washington or Hong Kong. Although acknowledging that all theologies are grounded in the particular context of their production and reflect a location, he has nevertheless demonstrated that one is never bound to a particular location or school of theological thought. In short, he embodies both polycentrism and multivocality.

The multiplicity that is found in his thought is in part a result of his experience of migration. Human beings migrate, both physically and intellectually. But such migration does not necessarily result in erasure of memory and identity. One of Phan's great contributions to world Christianity has been to both study and undertake such migration, physically and intellectually, in multiple directions.[3] He has done so while maintaining all his previous identities and commitments. As a result, he is someone who engages not only in what Thomas Tweed calls "crossing." Phan equally embodies Tweed's other kinetic religious moment, that of "dwelling."[4] Phan is someone who simultaneously moves through and inhabits what Arjun Appadurai calls multiple ecumenes,[5] practicing what Namsoon Kang calls cosmopolitan theology.[6] In this regard, it is not only that he is one of the world's most important and influential Christian theologians of the past century. Unlike many of us who are, in the words of Hugh of Saint Victor, either still tender beginners or already strong, Phan is truly a world Christian theologian whose work approaches what Saint Victor called perfection, or completion. I will return to the theme of Phan being a world Christian practicing cosmopolitan theology in multiple ecumenes at the end of this chapter. But first I would like to locate him in the framework of the study of world Christianity.[7]

WORLD CHRISTIANITY
AS A FIELD OF STUDY

Phan's contributions to the field of study known as world Christianity have been enormous. His intellectual sojourn that brought him to the field has been as much a story of migration as the story of his life's journey. A Roman Catholic who was born in Vietnam, he studied in Rome, where he obtained his first doctorate with a dissertation on the theology of the icon in the thought of a Russian Orthodox theologian, Paul Evdokimov, which brought him expertise in patristics and into dialogue with the Eastern Orthodox tradition.[8] He obtained his second doctorate with a thesis on Karl Rahner's eschatology, which secured his reputation as a significant contemporary systematic theologian.[9] His third doctorate, the "higher doctorate," was granted by the University of London on the basis of his works on mission, inculturation, and interreligious dialogue. It was his 1988 book on the impact of Alexandre de Rhodes on the development of Christianity in seventeenth-century Vietnam,[10] followed by a trilogy of books on Asian American and Asian theology published by Orbis Books in an eighteen-month period in 2003 and 2004,[11] that brought him into prominence in the field of world Christianity.

He entered a field in which ironically there is a considerable lack of consensus in understanding what exactly is being studied. This lack of agreement is evident in a 2005 volume edited by Lamin Sanneh and Joel Carpenter,

The Changing Face of Christianity: Africa, the West, and the World. Patricia Harkens-Pierre, in a chapter titled "Religion Bridge: Translating Secular into Sacred Music—A Study of World Christianity Focusing on the US Virgin Islands," writes: "Within the wide-flung geographical and cultural region of the Caribbean, a dynamic concept of world Christianity is revitalizing the twenty-first-century church. This reality is becoming increasingly evident in one Caribbean community—the US Virgin Islands—where Christianity in its Western colonial form has been rejected by much of the population."[12]

From this, it would appear that world Christianity is something other than Christianity in its European or Western colonial form, which world Christianity is intent on rejecting. Yet further on in the same volume, in another chapter titled "Shall They Till with Their Own Hoes? Baptists in Zimbabwe and New Patterns of Interdependence, 1950–2000," Isaac Mwase writes, "The case I wish to argue is that world Christianity implies interdependence. Mutual reliance, not unilateralism and isolationism, has to win the day in cross-cultural Christian relations and inform mission policy."[13] In this case world Christianity is not something that is set over against Western Christianity, but would seem to entail the possibility at least of mutual reliance and interdependence between Christians from all parts of the globe, including its Western colonial form.

In a brief essay posted on the web page of the Center for Global Christianity and Mission at the Boston University School of Theology, Gun Cheol Kim writes, "Simply speaking, the phrase [world Christianity] describes the global presence of Christians from diverse backgrounds, including race, nationality, culture, gender, etc."[14] It would seem from this definition that world Christianity includes the study of Christianity on six continents.[15] Yet the web page for the Centre for the Study of World Christianity at the University of Edinburgh explains its mission to be "advancing scholarship in Christianity outside the Western Hemisphere."[16] What this means is not exactly clear. The *Encyclopedia Britannica* defines "the Western Hemisphere" as consisting of the continents of North and South America and the surrounding waters.[17] This would not seem to be the definition that the Edinburgh center has in mind, because this would mean that the center is not concerned with advancing scholarship regarding Christianity in Latin American, which it has done. The *Encyclopedia Britannica* also acknowledges that the Western Hemisphere could be defined as that part of the Earth west of the Greenwich borough of London to roughly the 180th meridian on the globe, but that would include some areas of Europe, Africa, and Oceania. Is world Christianity the study of Christianity in Asia, and in parts of Europe, Africa, and Oceania? Some of the history behind the Centre for the Study of

World Christianity helps clarify the issue a bit. It was founded in 1982 at the University of Aberdeen, and its original name was the Centre for the Study of Christianity in the Non-Western World. But even this remains somewhat confusing. Is Latin America "non-Western"? Are Australia, New Zealand, and even Hawaii part of the "West"?[18]

This divide can become even more confusing when it is seen from the North American side of the Atlantic. In 1997 the American Theological Library Association established the World Christianity Interest Group. According to its web page, this group "provides a forum for discussion and research related to World Christianity. This group defines 'World Christianity' as Christianity practiced outside of the United States and Canada. Also included in this definition is Christianity practiced within the United States and Canada whose participants worship or otherwise express their faith in languages other than English."[19] Christianity in this case is reduced to English-speaking North America, while world Christianity is everything else, including French-speaking Quebec and the Spanish-speaking South Bronx.

In all these descriptions, what emerges as a common theme is the assumption or assertion that there is a global geographical divide, often mounting to the ranks of opposition, between Christianity in something called "the West" and Christianity in what Stuart Hall termed "the rest."[20] The roots of this divide are easily located in the modern world's colonial configuration, in which, beginning in the fifteenth century, European nations that were predominantly Christian in their religious identities to varying degrees colonized other regions and peoples of the world politically, socially, and culturally. The colonial project of the modern era was launched from Iberia, where Catholic Christianity dominated. The Northern European nations of the Netherlands, which was predominantly Reformed, and England, in which the Anglican Church was established but where other branches of Protestantism were flourishing, joined the endeavor early in the seventeenth century. By the eighteenth century, these Northern European powers were dominating the global colonial landscape. At the end of the nineteenth century, the United States, which was predominantly Protestant, joined the ranks of colonial powers, thereby entering into membership in the colonial club called "the West."

Catholic, Anglican, and Protestant churches rode the colonial waves of the modern era to send first chaplains and then missionaries to the regions of the world where European and then North American colonial reach extended. By this means, Christianity in its modern European cultural forms of Catholics, Anglicans, or Protestants was spread to other regions of the world. In the process, the power imbalance between colonizer and colonized was reinscribed in terms of church and mission or, in more general cultural terminology, between "Christian lands" and "mission lands." The construction was not without its own precedents in Latin Christendom that reached back centuries. J. Kameron Carter has argued that the origins of modern racism, which is corollary to the construction of the West versus the rest, can be found in the anti-Judaism that arose in early Christianity.[21] The construction took on new overtones at the end of the eleventh century in the Latin West, with the launch of the First Crusade against heretics and infidels (Islam) in the original "clash of civilizations."[22]

Already the divide is in view in the twin *Summas* of Thomas Aquinas, the *Summa Theologiae*, and the *Liber de veritate catholicae fidei contra errores infidelium* ("Book on the Truth of the Catholic Faith against the Errors of the Unbelievers"), better known as the *Summa contra Gentiles*. The purpose of the former book was "to propound the things belonging to the Christian religion in a way consonant with the education of beginners (*incipientium*)."[23] The purpose of the latter was setting forth "the truth that the Catholic faith professes, and of setting aside the errors that are opposed to it (*contrarios*)" held by those who are not Christian—that is, Jews, Muslims, and "gentiles," or in later terms, "pagans."[24] Taken together, the two *Summas* construct an inside/outside world of Christian truth, effectively drawing a boundary between the "beginners" being taught within the Church, and the contrarians or infidels outside and beyond the sacred boundaries of Christendom.

Aquinas drew no firm territorial lines in making his distinction. The contrarians and infidels to whom his first *Summa* was addressed were as much within the territorial boundaries of Western lands as they were beyond. The *reconquista* of Iberia was still under way as Aquinas was composing the *Summa contra Gentiles*, as was the crusade against the Cathars in Southern France. The territorial divide began to come more clearly into view in the fifteenth century, with the launch of the explorations of Portuguese ships along the coast of Africa in search of a sea passage to India. In his papal bull of 1455, *Romanus Pontifex*, Nicholas V explicitly identified the location of knowledge that he and others in Europe shared. The voyages toward southern and eastern shores (*versus meridionalis et orientalis plagas navigari*) had exposed an absence in the knowledge held by "those of us of the west" (*nobis occiduis*), he said. "We occidentals" have no certain knowledge of these other peoples, Nicholas admits (*nullam de partium illarum gentibus certam notitiam haberemus*). They are unknown, incognito, *incognitum*. Here we begin to see clearly the early contours of Edward Said's "orientalism."[25]

The sixteenth century saw this divide between believers and contrarians, and the correlating divide between the West and the rest (South and East, "*meridionalis et orientalis*") become that of Church and mission. The Jesuits in the sixteenth century are commonly identified as having been the first to name efforts that the Church directs against outsiders (both heretical Protestants and unbelieving "pagans") as being "missions," thereby constituting mission as being "beyond" Christendom.[26] The nomenclature of Church and mission quickly took hold among Western Europeans. What happened in the West was Church, while what happened in the rest was missions. The Church was by definition the center of this theological construction, while missions (plural) constituted the periphery.

This construction of the world dominated Christian theology globally into the twentieth century. It was not simply a matter of dominant numbers, but also a matter of dominant political and social power that allowed Western peoples to impose cultural knowledge, including religious cultural knowledge, upon colonized peoples.[27] Anticolonial forces were never entirely absent, of course. There is a continuous history of anticolonialism through the modern era. But it was not until the middle of the twentieth century that anticolonial movements for political liberation and self-determination were able to succeed to a significant degree globally. In the 1950s the revolutionary currents of independence became caught up in the politics of the "Cold War" between the United States and the Soviet Union. The term "Third World" was coined to name the nations of Asia, Africa, and Latin America that were not aligned politically with either the North Atlantic Treaty Organization or the Soviet Bloc.[28] "Third World" was also used almost interchangeably with "developing nations" or "developing world," terms that referred to nations whose material economy was not predominantly industrialized and whose social infrastructures were measured at the lower end of what is now called the Human Development Index of the United Nations Development Program.[29]

A significant number of those who were part of the twentieth-century ecumenical movement, which was the main precursor to what is now being called "world Christianity," had by the 1960s come to embrace the anticolonial revolutionary theological currents sweeping the globe.[30] M. Richard Shaull was a US missionary teaching in Brazil when he published *Encounter with Revolution* in 1955.[31] Eleven years later, in Geneva at the World Conference on Church and Society sponsored by the World Council of Churches, his plenary presentation was titled "The Revolutionary Challenge to Church and Theology."[32] In 1968 the Uppsala Assembly of the World Council of Churches affirmed the council's commitment to supporting revolutionary movements around the world.[33] In 1969 the council launched the Program to Combat Racism in response to a mandate from the Uppsala assembly.[34]

Despite the strong support found within the World Council of Churches for revolutionary movements around the globe, the council itself continued to be identified as being Western-dominated in both its theological commitments and its administrative structures. The emergence of self-consciously identified "liberation theologies" in the 1960s drew even more forcefully upon the global revolutionary political, social, and cultural streams in the so-called underdeveloped or developing nations in Latin America, Asia, Africa, and Oceania, and among oppressed communities in both North America and Europe, to create distinctive expressions of "Third World theologies." The formation of the Ecumenical Association of Third World Theologians (EATWOT) in 1976 was a landmark in bringing these efforts into conversation with one another. Through a series of conferences and publications operating under the EATWOT name, theologians from Asia, Africa, Latin America, and oppressed communities in North America sought to articulate the convergences and divergences of the various liberation and contextual theologies that they were constructing.[35] A new kind of world Christianity was being articulated.

The apparent end of the Cold War brought with it a rethinking of the terminology of "Third World" in theology. There was a growing sense among many that the phrase was outdated, inaccurate, or reinscriptive of the very geopolitical power imbalance that so-called Third World theologies were seeking to address. By the end of the 1980s, the phrase "Two-Thirds World" had emerged as an alternative to "Third World."[36] It quickly gained acceptance, notably among evangelicals but also among those who were leery of the more radical theological positions being staked out by those who called themselves "Third World theologians."[37] There was also a growing awareness among Christian observers of the shift in global Christian demographics. Most of the world's Christians no longer lived in the North Atlantic world that constituted the center of the West. They now inhabited the global rest. In line with this awareness of a new majority status in terms of demographics, members of the Two-Thirds World Church issue group at the 2004 Forum for World Evangelization convened by the Lausanne Committee for World Evangelization in Pattaya, Thailand, "unanimously decided that we should use the expression 'Majority World Church' instead of Two-Thirds World Church."[38] Along these same lines, the phrase "the Global South" has also become a popular alternative to identify what was once called "the non-Western World."[39]

All these efforts continue to one degree or another to reinscribe the territorial divide in Christianity that has been part of the last five hundred years between the West and the rest, the modern and the colonial, church and mission, or what as late the 1970s were still being called "older churches" and "younger churches."[40] As they do so, they often continue to reproduce the colonial divide of church and mission along territorial lines. For many, the field of world Christianity is just another name for mission studies.[41] To the degree that world Christianity gets reduced to being the continuation of missiology and not ecclesiology or theology proper, it reproduces the power dynamic that makes European history the center and the histories of other regions of the globe peripheral.[42] Those on the periphery are defined only in relation to the center, as its "other" ("non-Western," "rest"). Those in the center on the other hand self-define in a manner that does not require that they acknowledge the periphery. Lalsangkima Pachuau, in his recently published work *World Christianity: A Historical and Theological Introduction*, against his own best intentions, unwittingly continues this dynamic. Early in the text he writes, "This study largely presumes basic knowledge of the better-known— some would say dominant—Western Christianity, and focuses on Christian faith in the majority world to present a new portrait of world Christianity. Although world Christianity has become a popular topic in some Christian circles, the larger body of Christian academia and churches is not aware of or meaningfully engaged with this reality."[43] Western Christianity appears to be one thing and world Christianity another. Even more astounding, after asserting several times that the majority of Christians now live in the Global South and East, which is the domain of world Christianity, he states that "the larger body" of churches is not aware of world Christianity. The conclusion would be that the churches that occupy world Christianity lack self-awareness.

My own formulation of world Christianity has followed the work of the contemporary postcolonial theorist Walter Mignolo.[44] Mignolo poses the divide in terms of a "modern/colonial" border that cuts through every location on the globe today.[45] This border gives rise to the various forms of double-consciousness or double-mindedness that are part of the experience of those who have been colonized and continue to experience oppression. Mignolo calls it "border thinking." He writes, "Border thinking can only be such from a subaltern perspective, never from a territorial (e.g., from inside modernity) one."[46] Along these lines I argue that world Christianity does not refer to some sectors of the globe and not others. Rather, it is a way of seeing Christianity in every place through a lens of double-consciousness or double-mindedness that characterizes the experience of the subaltern or oppressed.

I see my own perspective as lining up with that of Lamin Sanneh, who argues for a distinction between global Christianity and world Christianity.[47] Sanneh's distinction comes close to that of Mignolo, who differentiates in Spanish between *globalización* and *mundialización*.[48] *Globalización* names those processes and forces that seek to reinscribe global colonial power, while *mundi-alización* names those processes and forces that seek to articulate what Mignolo refers to as the "colonial difference" that is constituted through local histories.[49] For Sanneh, global Christianity "is the faithful replication of Christian forms and patterns developed in Europe. . . . It is, in fact, religious establishment and the cultural captivity of faith." World Christianity, on the other hand,

> is the movement of Christianity as it takes form and shape in societies that previously were not Christian, societies that had no bureaucratic tradition with which to domesticate the Gospel. In these societies Christianity was received and expressed through the cultures, customs, and traditions of the people affected. World Christianity from this perspective is not one thing, but a variety of indigenous responses through more or less effective local idioms, but in any case without necessarily the European Enlightenment frame.[50]

For Sanneh, one of the tasks of world Christianity as an intellectual field of study is to challenge the tribalism that too often characterizes the academy.[51] The "telltale signs" of this tribalism, he argues, are found today in "the efforts in the West to define the West out of world Christianity." He continues:

> The fight about what name to give to the subject is really a fight of the West and its surrogates to contest the right of Christians elsewhere to consider themselves as equals in the religion. . . . The West is happy to yield on the quantitative argument of numerical growth elsewhere without budging on the qualitative ground of its intellectual and economic superiority despite evidence of religious recession and retreat. . . . In this argument, Christianity will lose its gains and standing without the European achievement. Yet anywhere else in the world such a cultural entitlement to the faith would be considered tribal and syncretist. The counter-move with the inclusive title "world Christianity" is intended to force a reckoning with this "tribal" view. In its historical core and course, the religion has been diverse in different and plural societies with styles, forms, and practices that are breathless in their variety and complexity. It is no different today except in scale and direction, and perhaps, too, in the challenge to Western proprietorial claims.[52]

Sanneh's analysis is both affirmed and then deepened by Phan, who argues, "There is not, nor has there ever been, one Christianity; rather, there exist Christianities (in the plural), all over the world and all the time."[53] Phan does not deny the power exercised from Rome or other centers of European or Western Christian life. One need only to read the opening chapters of his recent book, *The Joy of Religious Pluralism: A Personal Journey*, where he details the effect of his notification from the Congregation for the Doctrine of the Faith on his life and work.[54]

Along these lines, Klaus Koschorke and his colleagues in what has been called the "Munich School of World Christianity" have made a strong methodological case for a more polycentric understanding of our subject.[55] Koschorke argues, "In order to understand the polycentric history of world Christianity, one has to take into account the variety of regional centers of expansion, plurality of actors, multiplicity of indigenous initiatives, and local appropriations of Christianity."[56] Sebastian Kim and Kirsteen Kim likewise argue for a more polycentric understanding of Christianity as a world religion.[57] They emphasize as well the need to keep the West integrated in the overall picture in ways that neither privilege nor dismiss it: "In our view, the strength of world Christianity is that it provides an integrated understanding of global Christian dynamics from which the West cannot be excised. It draws attention to the currents of Christianity globally, its transnational ties and movements. . . . Our study suggests that the destinies of the Christianities of North and West and the South and East are linked in very many respects."[58]

These polycentric conceptions and models of world Christianity have sought with various degrees of success to emphasize local or regional experiences, on one hand, and the connecting factors among them that make for "world" Christianity, on the other hand. In this regard they resonate with Roland Robertson's concept of "glocalization," a concept that seeks to hold together the global and local, or universal and particular dimensions, of human social experience in a single but complex structure.[59] Over against simpler theories of "globalization" that emphasized the growing social and cultural homogenization of the world, Robertson argued for greater attention to the processes of renewed indigenization or *dochakuka* in Japanese that he says he first began to notice in Japanese business practices in the 1990s.[60] At the same time, he argued against essentializing the local as a reality unto itself.[61] Local realities are always connected socially with other local realities on a global scale, even when the connections are not immediately apparent or acknowledged. They have been for centuries. Robertson notes the global/local puzzle has come into view as a general theme or problematic in the modern era, but it is not unique to modernity. He writes:

> It is clear that for a long, long time what is now called globalization has involved the adaptation of panlocal developments to local

circumstances. Perhaps the history of the Roman Catholic church—as well as other "world religions"—illustrates this particularly well. Indeed, one might "heretically" go so far as to say that the differentiation of the idea of the supernatural into not merely distinctive monotheistic, Abrahamic religions (e.g., Judaism, Christianity, Islam) but also, in Weber's sense, into "Oriental" religions (e.g., Hinduism, Confucianism, Buddhism, Taoism) has involved a long process of glocalization. Moreover, it is not only with respect to religion that one can historically apply the idea of glocalization. One could readily apply the idea to a very large spectrum of sociocultural practices—ranging from particular institutions, such as the educational and the military, to genres, such as music, the visual arts, sexuality and eroticism, and so on.[62]

What is being called "the global" in this discussion of Robertson turns out to be not simply an enlarged "local." Rather, what is "global" is the interconnectedness, the relationality, among them that gives rise to the "trans" dimensions that make for a global or world reality. Local realities link up in complex and diverse ways, because goods, services, bodies, and ideas all travel. Attending to the local—and the manner in which translocal, transregional, and/or transnational connections are made—is at the heart of our work in world Christianity.

A WORLD CHRISTIAN THEOLOGIAN

I noted above that over the course of the past several decades, Peter Phan has been a major figure bringing about a shift in our thinking about Christianity, from being one thing to being many things. In no small part because of his work, it is becoming more common for many of us to think not of there being something called "Christianity" spread throughout the world, but rather there being "Christianities." It is more than simply a deeper refinement of the historical analysis that sees Christianity as branching off into four major global trajectories of Orthodox, Catholic, Protestant, and, more recently, Pentecostal streams over its past one thousand years, as scholars such as David Barrett, Todd Johnson, and Douglas Jacobson have argued.[63] It is also more than the usual regional or continental survey of Christianity.[64] Phan has moved us beyond older center/periphery models of thinking to a more polycentric way of thinking.

He has done so by working on multiple themes simultaneously. Over the past several decades, he has published volumes on Asian Christianities,[65]

Asian-American Christianities,[66] and theology of migration.[67] He has edited a major handbook on the doctrine of the Trinity,[68] while his recent volume, *The Joy of Religious Pluralism: A Personal Journey*, offers a short systematic theology. He has even published texts on pastoral matters.[69] What emerges from his enormous body of scholarship is not only a major voice in the study of world Christianity but also a major world Christian who, as I noted at the beginning of this chapter, moves through and inhabits multiple ecumenes, practicing cosmopolitan theology.

I have borrowed the concept of multiple ecumenes from Arjun Appadurai, from his 1996 publication *Modernity at Large: Cultural Dimensions of Globalization*. Appadurai argues that the twin factors of mass migration and mass-mediated images have combined to create "a new order of instability in the production of modern subjectivities."[70] The manner in which migration and media have joined forces to become "massively globalized, that is to say, active across large and irregular transnational terrains,"[71] has challenged the monopoly of the modern territorial nation-state "over the project of modernization."[72] In the past, time and distance worked like a gravitational force to keep culturally separated groups spatially apart, hampering the formation of what he calls "large-scale ecumenes." That began to change over the last several centuries, however, as "an overlapping set of ecumenes began to emerge."[73] These ecumenes go beyond Benedict Anderson's "imagined communities."[74] They are deterritorialized, overlapping, swirling cultural flows that interact to produce multiple new formations around the globe. They are not fixed in number, but are broadly reflective of the "ethnoscapes" that make up the modern world.[75] They are not organized according to a center/periphery model but are multicentric, with forces flowing in multiple directions from one to another at any given time.

Navigating the swirling interaction among multiple ecumenes requires a new kind of ecumenism, what Appadurai calls "cosmopolitanisms" (plural).[76] "Cosmopolitanism," writes Namsoon Kang, "invites one to radically rethink the relationship between particularity and universality."[77] It moves beyond the binary to embrace them both at once, something she later calls "*situated universalism*" (emphasis in the original).[78] Cosmopolitan theology is not about boundary-making so much as it is boundary-embracing and transcending at the same time.[79] It is antitribal and calls for multiple attachments.[80] Cosmopolitan theologians practice "hospitality, solidarity, justice, and neighbor-love."[81] They are characterized by their compassion. They are, in Kang's words, theologians without passports: "*Theologians without passports* intentionally dissociate themselves from the dominant power practice, or discourse that totalizes, categorizes, and classifies an individual person into a stereotypical box of numbers and data. *Theologians without passports* commit themselves to 'make a contribution to the universal community,' to the Kingdom of God. . . . 'The word *beyondness* captures the spirit of cosmopolitan theologians'" (emphasis in the original).[82]

Phan fits the definition of being a cosmopolitan theologian better than anyone else living and working today in the academic world. He has been able to articulate a constructive theology that is cosmopolitan in scope and yet grounded in his own historical identity. His work on the various Asian Christianities, including Asian American Christianities, has opened the door to new ways of understanding theology, Church, and mission. As a Catholic theologian, he has articulated a theology in which Asian Catholic churches exists alongside the Roman Catholic Church, not necessarily replacing it but also not simply amending it.[83] Furthermore, in his persistent theology of pluralism and interreligous dialogue, he has articulated a dialogue of life that moves Christians out of their own space and into the common world with their neighbors.

In his final chapter of *The Joy of Religious Pluralism*, Phan argues for a "kingdom-centered" ecclesiology. He calls here for an "ecclesiological kenosis" that moves the Church beyond itself:[84] "This ecclesiological kenosis is predicated upon the theological conviction that at the heart of the Christian faith and practice, there lies not the Church and its institutional elements but the reign of the Triune God. . . . To be truly the Church, the Asian Church, paradoxically, must cease to be "church," that is, it must "empty" itself and cease to exist for its own sake for the service of a higher reality, namely, the Kingdom of God."[85]

Overcoming the hierarchical ordering that places the Church at the center and others on the periphery is as important for Phan as is overcoming the hierarchical ordering that places European history and identity over Asian history and identity, helping in effect to bring about the end of what Robin H. S. Boyd in 1974 so elegantly termed the "Latin captivity of the Church."[86]

Both in terms of relations among churches globally, and the relationship between the church and other religions, Phan calls for a new configuration to emerge, "a communion of communities."[87] The intended result is a true fellowship that is both grounded in and gives rise to radical practices of mutuality, compassion, and solidarity. He refers to this as the "*dialogue of life*" and the "*dialogue of action*" (emphasis in the original).[88] The result is a cosmopolitan theologian who is keenly attuned to world Christian realities, lives in multiple ecumenes, and understands well that theology in the end must be "a recommendation for life."[89]

NOTES

Hugh of Saint Victor, *The Didascalicon: A Medieval Guide to the Arts*, trans. Jerome Taylor (New York: Columbia University Press, 1961), 101.

1. David Tracy, "Theology as Public Discourse," *Christian Century*, March 19, 1975, 284.

2. I am of course referring to the famous phrase attributed to Bernard of Chartres that we see much further when we are perched on the shoulders of giants. See Richard W. Southern, *The Making of the Middle Ages* (New Haven, CT: Yale University Press, 1952), 203.

3. See Peter C. Phan, "Betwixt and Between: Doing Theology with Memory and Imagination," in *Journeys at the Margin: Toward an Autobiographical Theology in American-Asian Perspective*, ed. Peter C. Phan and Jung Young Lee (Collegeville, MN: Liturgical Press, 1999), 113–34; Elaine Padilla and Peter C. Phan, eds., *Contemporary Issues of Migration and Theology* (New York: Palgrave Macmillan, 2013); Elaine Padilla and Peter C. Phan, eds., *Theology of Migration in the Abrahamic Religions* (New York: Palgrave Macmillan, 2014); Elaine Padilla and Peter C. Phan, eds., *Christianities in Migration: The Global Perspective* (New York: Palgrave Macmillan, 2016); Peter C. Phan, "Deus Migrator: God the Migrant—Migration of Theology and Theology of Migration," *Theological Studies* 77, no. 4 (2016): 845–68; Peter C. Phan, "The Experience of Migration in the United States as a Source of Intercultural Theology," *Center for Migration Studies* 18 no. 2 (2003): 143–69; and Peter C. Phan, "Migration in the Patristic Era: History and Theology," in *A Promised Land, A Perilous Journey: Theological Perspectives on Migration*, ed. Daniel G. Groody and Gioacchino Campese (Notre Dame, IN: University of Notre Dame Press, 2008), 35–61.

4. Thomas A. Tweed, *Crossing and Dwelling: A Theory of Religion* (Cambridge, MA: Harvard University Press, 2008).

5. Arjun Appadurai, *Modernity at Large: Cultural Dimensions of Globalization* (Minneapolis: University of Minnesota Press, 1996), 128.

6. See Namsoon Kang, *Cosmopolitan Theology: Reconstituting Planetary Hospitality, Neighbor-Love, and Solidarity in an Uneven World* (Saint Louis: Chalice Press, 2013).

7. For a brief introduction to the term "world Christianity" in the US context, see James Strasburg, "Creating, Practicing, and Researching a Global Faith: Conceptualizations of World Christianity in the American Protestant Pastorate and Seminary Classroom, 1893 to the Present," *Journal of World Christianity* 6, no. 2 (2016): 217–36.

8. Peter C. Phan, *Culture and Eschatology: The Iconographical Vision of Paul Evdokimov* (New York: Peter Lang, 1985).

9. Peter C. Phan, *Eternity in Time: A Study of Karl Rahner's Eschatology* (Selinsgrove, PA: Susquehanna University Press, 1988).

10. Peter C. Phan, *Mission and Catechesis: Alexandre de Rhodes and Inculturation in Seventeenth-Century Vietnam* (Maryknoll, NY: Orbis Books, 1998).

11. Peter C. Phan, *Christianity with an Asian Face: Asian American Theology in the Making* (Maryknoll, NY: Orbis Books, 2003); Peter C. Phan, *In Our Own Tongues: Perspectives from Asia on Mission and Inculturation* (Maryknoll, NY: Orbis Books, 2003); Peter C. Phan, *Being Religious Interreligiously: Asian Perspectives on Interfaith Dialogue* (Maryknoll, NY: Orbis Books, 2004).

12. Patricia Harkens-Pierre, "Religion Bridge: Translating Secular into Sacred Music—A Study of World Christianity Focusing on the US Virgin Islands," in *The Changing Face of Christianity: Africa, the West, and the World*, ed. Lamin Sanneh and Joel A. Carpenter (Oxford: Oxford University Press, 2005), 22.

13. Isaac M. T. Mwase, "Shall They Till with Their Own Hoes? Baptists in Zimbabwe and New Patterns of Interdependence, 1950–2000," in *Changing Face*, ed. Sanneh and Carpenter, 63.

14. Gun Cheol Kim, "An Implication of World Christianity," paper for Center for Global Christianity and Mission of Boston University School of Theology, www.bu.edu/cgcm /annual-theme/an-implication-of-world-christianity/.

15. The seven continents that geographers identify as making up the land mass of the globe are Asia, Africa, Europe, North America, South America, Australia, and Antarctica. Antarctica has never been home to permanent human habitation other than for research purposes and thus is not included in the continents on which Christianity has found a home. Those who consider Australia to be part of Asia and not a free-standing continent on its own refer to Christianity as being located on five, not six, continents.

16. See the web page of the Centre for the Study of World Christianity, www.ed.ac.uk /divinity/research/centres/world-christianity.

17. "Western Hemisphere," in *Encyclopedia Britannica*, www.britannica.com/place/Western -Hemisphere.

18. For a brief genealogy of the modern conception of the "West" and its problematic usage in world Christianity, see Dale T. Irvin, "What Is World Christianity?" in *World Christianity: Perspectives and Insights*, ed. Jonathan Y. Tan and Anh Q. Tran (Maryknoll, NY: Orbis Books, 2016), 15–16.

19. See its web page, www.atla.com/Members/divisions/interest/Pages/World-Christianity .aspx.

20. Stuart Hall, "The West and the Rest: Discourse and Power," in *The Formations of Modernity*, ed. Stuart Hall and Bram Gieben (Oxford: Blackwell, 1992), 275–332.

21. J. Kameron Carter, *Race: A Theological Account* (New York: Oxford University Press, 2008), 4–5, 42–45.

22. Samuel P. Huntington, *The Clash of Civilizations and the Remaking of World Order* (New York: Simon & Schuster, 1996).

23. Thomas Aquinas, *Summa Theologiae*, "Prologue" to part I.

24. Thomas Aquinas, *Summa contra Gentiles*, book I.1.2.

25. Edward W. Said, *Orientalism* (New York: Random House, 1978).

26. Thomas Ohm, *Machet zu Jüngern alle Völker: Theorie der Mission* (Freiburg: Erich Wewel Verlag, 1962) 37–39; followed by Bosch and Bevans.

27. Walter D. Mignolo, *The Darker Side of Western Modernity: Global Futures, Decolonial Options* (Durham, NC: Duke University Press, 2011).

28. The term was first used in print by the French historical economist Alfred Sauvy in an article titled "Trois Mondes, une Planète," published in the newspaper *L'Observateur*, no. 118 (August 14, 1952). For its theological genealogy, see Giancarlo Collet, "Third World Theology," *Religion Past and Present*, http://dx.doi.org/10.1163/1877-5888_rpp_COM_03906.

29. For a formative critique of the "theology of development," see Gustavo Gutierrez, "Liberation and Development," in *Theology of Liberation: History, Politics, and Salvation* (Maryknoll, NY: Orbis Books, 1988), 13–27.

30. See Dale T. Irvin, "World Christianity: A Genealogy" (Special Edition of *Journal of World Christianity*, ed. Afe Adogame, Raimundo César Barreto Jr., and Richard Fox Young) 9, no. 1 (2019): 5–22.

31. M. Richard Shaull, *Encounter with Revolution* (New York: Haddam House, 1955).

32. M. Richard Shaull, "The Revolutionary Challenge to Church and Theology," *Theology Today* 23, no. 4 (1967): 470–80.

33. Norman Goodall, ed., *The Uppsala Report 1968: Official Report of the Fourth Assembly of the World Council of Churches, Uppsala July 4–20, 1968* (Geneva: World Council of Churches, 1968), 41.

34. Goodall, 241.

35. See M. P. Joseph, *Theologies of the Non-Person: The Formative Years of EATWOT* (New York: Palgrave Macmillan, 2015).

36. David Wemple wrote: "Looking at the two maps [Mercator and Peters] side-by-side, for example, who could resist asking why the Third World actually occupies two-thirds of the globe?" David Wemple, "Third (or Two-Thirds) World," *Washington Report on Middle East Affairs*, November 1987, 14, www.washingtonreport.me/1987-november/third-or -two-thirds-world.html on 8/15/2017.

37. For a fuller discussion of this shift, see Vinay Samuel and Chris Sugden, eds., *Sharing Jesus in the Two Thirds World: Evangelical Christologies—The Papers of the First Conference of Evangelical Theologians from the Two Thirds World, Bangkok, Thailand, March 22–25, 1982* (Grand Rapids: Wm. B. Eerdmans, 1984).

38. David D. Ruiz, "The Two-Thirds World Church: Lausanne Occasional Paper No. 44," in *A New Vision, a New Heart, a Renewed Call, Volume 2: Lausanne Occasional Papers from the 2004 Forum for World Evangelism*, ed. David Clayton (Pasadena, CA: William Carey Library, 2005), 118.

39. Douglas Jacobsen, *Global Gospel: An Introduction to Christianity on Five Continents* (Grand Rapids: Baker Books, 2015), 11, writes: "In recent years, a new pairing of terms has emerged. The world Christian movement is now frequently described as consisting of a global Christian North and a global Christian South. North and South in this usage do not correspond to the equator but instead to a slanted line that runs from Central America to Siberia and separates Europe and North America from Africa, Asia, and Latin America." See also Philip Jenkins, *The New Faces of Christianity: Believing the Bible in the Global South* (Oxford: Oxford University Press, 2006).

40. See, e.g., the usage in Georg F. Vicedom, ed., *Christ and the Younger Churches: Theological Contributions from Asia, Africa and Latin America* (London: SPCK, 1972) and Walbert Buhlmann, *The Coming of the Third Church* (Maryknoll, NY: Orbis Books, 1976). Lalsangkima Pachuau, *World Christianity: A Historical and Theological Introduction* (Nashville: Abingdon Press, 2018), 19, continues this practice under the terminology of "older Christians" and "newer Christians." He writes: "We locate the hub of world Christianity in the relation between the older Christianity of the West, or more accurately the North and West, and the newer Christianity of the so-called global South, or more accurately global South and East."

41. See, e.g., John G. Flett, "Method in Mission Studies: Comparing World Christianity and Intercultural Theology," *Theologischen Literaturzeitung* 143 (2018): 717–31; and David Maxwell, "Historical Perspectives on Christianity Worldwide: Connections, Comparisons and Consciousness," in *Relocating World Christianity: Interdisciplinary Studies in Universal and Local Expressions of the Christian Faith*, ed. Joel Cabrita, David Maxwell, and Emma Wild-Wood (Leiden: Brill, 2017), 49.

42. See Dale T. Irvin, "From One Story to Many: An Ecumenical Reappraisal of Church History," *Journal of Ecumenical Studies* 28, no. 4 (1991): 537–54; and Irvin, "World Christianity."

43. Pachuau, *World Christianity*, 18–19.

44. Walter D. Mignolo, *Local Histories / Global Designs: Coloniality, Subaltern Knowledges, and Border Thinking* (Princeton, NJ: Princeton University Press, 2000).

45. See Ramón Grosfoguel, "Colonial Difference, Geopolitics of Knowledge, and Global Coloniality in the Modern/Colonial Capitalist World-System," *Review (Fernand Braudel Center)* 25, no. 3 (2002): 203–24.

46. Mignolo, *Local Histories / Global Designs*, 45.

47. Lamin Sanneh, *Whose Religion Is Christianity? The Gospel beyond the West* (Grand Rapids: Wm. B. Eerdmans, 2003), 22.

48. Mignolo, *Local Histories / Global Designs*, 278–310.

49. Mignolo, 279.

50. Sanneh, *Whose Religion Is Christianity?*, 22.

51. From a conversation held during a consultation of the history of the World Christian Movement project on January 6, 2003 at the Divine Word Conference Center, Techny, IL. In an email to me on October 26, 2017, Sanneh confirmed my recollection of our conversation and added, "I certainly concur with the sentiments you report of me."

52. Personal email, October 26, 2017.

53. Peter C. Phan, "World Christianity: Its Implications for History, Religious Studies, and Theology," *Horizons* 39, no. 2 (2012): 175. See also Peter C. Phan, ed., *Christianities in Asia* (Malden, MA: Blackwell, 2011); and Elaine Padilla and Peter C. Phan, eds., *Christianities in Migration: The Global Perspective* (New York: Palgrave Macmillan, 2016).

54. Peter C. Phan, *The Joy of Religious Pluralism: A Personal Journey* (Maryknoll, NY: Orbis Books, 2017).

55. See Adrian Hermann and Ciprian Burlacioiu, "Introduction: Klaus Koschorke and the 'Munich School' Perspective on the History of World Christianity," *Journal of World Christianity* 6, no. 1 (2016): 4–27.

56. Klaus Koschorke, "Transcontinental Links, Enlarged Maps, and Polycentric Structures in the History of World Christianity," *Journal of World Christianity* 6, no. 1 (2016): 34.

57. Sebastian Kim and Kirsteen Kim, *Christianity as a World Religion: An Introduction*, 2nd edition (London: Bloomsbury Academic, 2016), 271.

58. Kim and Kim, 273.

59. Roland Robertson, *Globalization: Social Theory and Global Culture* (Thousand Oaks, CA: Sage, 1992).

60. Roland Robertson, "The Conceptual Promise of Glocalization: Commonality and Diversity," in *Art-e-fact* 4 (2004), http://artefact.mi2.hr/_a04/lang_en/theory_robertson_en.htm.

61. Robertson, "Conceptual Promise," writes: "To subscribe to the idea of 'the local in itself'—without contextualization or framework—makes no sense."

62. Robertson, "Conceptual Promise."

63. See David B. Barrett, George Thomas Kurian, and Todd M. Johnson, eds. *World Christian Encyclopedia*, 2 vols. (New York: Oxford University Press, 2001); and Douglas Jacobsen, *The World's Christians, Who They Are, Where They Are and How They Got There* (Chichester, UK: Wiley-Blackwell, 2011). The distinction of Pentecostalism from Protestantism as a separate historic stream of Christianity is often traced to Henry P. Van Dusen, "The Third Force in Christendom," *Life*, June 9, 1958, 113–24.

64. See Jacobsen, *Global Gospel*; Charles E. Farhadian, ed., *Introducing World Christianity* (Malden, MA: Wiley-Blackwell, 2012); and Sebastian Kim and Kirsteen Kim, *Christianity as a World Religion: An Introduction*, 2nd ed. (London: Bloomsbury Academic, 2016). It should be noted that Kim and Kim explicitly acknowledge the internal pluralism of the "Christianities" that exist in each region. In the introduction to their second edition they explicitly acknowledge Peter Phan's influence on this decision when they write: "Second,

by using the plural 'Christianities,' we signal that the faith is not defined by territory. Although there are common geopolitical factors that influence the development of Christianity in different regions, there are a variety of expressions of Christian faith in each continent as a result of both historical and ecclesial factors (Phan 2011:1-6)." The reference is to Peter C. Phan, ed., *Christianities in Asia* (Chichester, UK: Wiley-Blackwell, 2011).

65. In addition to the various volumes already cited, see Peter C. Phan, *Asian Christianities: History, Theology, Practice* (Maryknoll, NY: Orbis Books, 2018).

66. In addition to the various volumes already cited, see Peter C. Phan, *Vietnamese-American Catholics* (Mahwah, NJ: Paulist Press, 2005).

67. In addition to the various volumes already cited, see Peter C. Phan and Jung Young Lee, *Journeys at the Margin: Toward an Autobiographical Theology in American-Asian Perspective* (Collegeville, MN: Liturgical Press, 1999).

68. Peter C. Phan, *The Cambridge Companion to the Trinity* (Cambridge: Cambridge University Press, 2011).

69. Peter C. Phan, *Living into Death, Dying Into Life: A Christian Theology of Death and Life Eternal* (Hobe Sound, FL: Lectio, 2014).

70. Appadurai, *Modernity at Large*, 4.

71. Appadurai, 9.

72. Appadurai, 10.

73. Appadurai, 28.

74. Benedict R. Anderson, *Imagined Communities: Reflections on the Origin and Spread of Nationalism* (London: Verso, 1991).

75. Appadurai, *Modernity at Large*, 48, writes: "The landscapes of group identity—the ethnoscapes—around the world are no longer familiar anthropological objects, insofar as groups are no longer tightly territorialized, spatially bounded, historically unselfconscious, or culturally homogeneous. . . . The ethnoscapes of today's world are profoundly interactive."

76. Appadurai, 49.

77. Kang, *Cosmopolitan Theology*, 49.

78. Kang, 181.

79. Kang, 33.

80. Kang, 21, 35.

81. Kang, 126.

82. Kang, 187.

83. For a recent self-assessment of his intellectual migration from European to Asian theology and how this resulted in the positive embrace of multiple ecumenes, see Peter C. Phan, "Take and Read: An Asian Theology of Liberation," *National Catholic Reporter*, March 7, 2016, www.ncronline.org/blogs/ncr-today/take-and-read-asian-theology-liberation.

84. Phan, *Joy of Religious Pluralism*, 132.

85. Phan, 133.

86. Robin H. S. Boyd, *India and the Latin Captivity of the Church* (Cambridge: Cambridge University Press, 1974).

87. Phan, *Joy of Religious Pluralism*, 127.

88. Phan, *In Our Own Tongues*, 19.

89. I have borrowed this phrase from Sarah Coakley, *God, Sexuality, and the Self: An Essay "On the Trinity"* (Cambridge: Cambridge University Press, 2013), 18.

CHAPTER 2

Being Church among Asians: Perspective and Insights of the Asian Theology of the FABC

Anh Q. Tran, SJ

Christian theology, especially in its historical development, is often associated primarily with the contributions of Western authors, starting with the Greek and Latin fathers, continuing with the Scholastic theologians of the Middle Ages, and then into modern times with famous figures like Karl Barth, Yves Congar, Karl Rahner, Hans Urs von Balthasar, and Paul Tillich—to name a few. Indeed, we cannot fail to acknowledge and appreciate their great contributions to the history of theology and the work of interpreting the faith for their generations.

Before there were books written in the mother tongues, Asian students had to study philosophy and theology using one or more European languages, such as Greek, Latin, French, German, English, Italian, and Spanish. This is no surprise, because Western Christianity has been introduced to Asia since the early sixteenth century. Thus, Western theological thought has contributed significantly to building and shaping theological thinking in Asian countries. The same can be said of Asian professors who received their advanced degrees from European and American centers of higher learning. Upon returning and staffing local seminaries and theological centers, these members of theology faculties design the curriculum in the models they have learned, instead of using indigenous cultural categories to express faith. This is evidenced by the fact that until recently, most theological books in native Asian and African languages have been works of translation and ideological syntheses of Western theologians.

Nevertheless, sometimes we find that research articles or books are rooted in Asian and African experiences and ideas. After World War II, when the peoples of Asia and Africa declared their independence, indigenous theologians, although most of them were trained in the West, began to share their theological reflections on the cultural, historical, economic, and political factors in which they live. This way of theological thinking based on the background and cultural reference frame outside the West has a new name: *contextual theology*.

Meanwhile, the influence of North Atlantic theology is still so wide and strong that many people consider contextual theology to be the specific reflections of theological currents from Asia, Africa, and South America in the context of postcolonialism. The theology of Europe and America, it is said, has a universal character, playing a leading role in thinking and practicing the faith for all Christians. Yet we must also ask ourselves a question, in the words of Saint Vincent of Lérins, Is there such a universal theology, that is valid "for all times, all places and all people" (*quod ubique, quod semper, quod ab omnibus creditum est*)?[1]

Theologians such as Peter Phan have long challenged the monopoly on theological thinking by the dominant North Atlantic authors. He has persuasively argued that the fifth-century Vincentian triple criteria were only applied to the Christian domain of the Roman Empire and applied much less to other forms of Christianity, both in times and spaces. The need to maintain orthodoxy and uniformity of the Constantine Era gave rise to such a formulation, which was once obvious but now seems problematic in world Christianity.[2] Stephen Bevans even goes further. In his *Models of Contextual Theology*, he declares that *all* theologies are contextual theologies. By "contextual," he means that theological reflection is always done in context, taking the experience and situation of individuals and communities as *locus theologicus*.[3]

This chapter offers an argument in continuity with Phan, Bevans, and others: that theology developed out of the Asian experiences should not be viewed only as a localized variation of some universal theology. It should be valued as a theological method and a contribution to the renewal of the way of thinking, learning, and teaching theology, not only in Asia but also for the universal Church in the global scene today. In what follows, I first review the historical context of Asian Catholic theology as promoted by the Federation of Asian Bishops' Conferences (FABC) in the 1970s, and subsequently celebrated by the Synod of Asian Bishops in 1998. Then I present some features of this particular form of contextual theology. I offer an updated assessment of the triple dialogue mandated by the FABC, as well as adding two more forms of dialogues that are essential for the twenty-first century. Finally, I give reflections on the Church of Asia. In doing so, I hope to continue the trend that Peter Phan has begun in many of his writings, to address the multi-ethnic, multicultural, and multireligious realities that are shaping the future of the worldwide Church.[4]

WHAT IS CONTEXTUAL THEOLOGY?

The reception of "indigenization," "localization," or "inculturation" has been a key model for theological reflection in the context of culture and society, and the religion of Asia. On the Catholic side, since the Second Vatican Council (1962–65), the liturgical celebration in the native language, as well as the construction of the local Church, have led to the promotion of local contextual theology. The switch from Latin to vernacular languages in liturgy proved significant for the Asian faithful. In the subsequent decades, instead, they were encouraged to read, reflect, and exchange in the local language.

On the Protestant side, the Taiwanese Protestant theologian Shoki Coe (Ng Chiong-hui, 1914–88) soon realized the limitations of this localization method in theological thinking. In a short but influential article published in *Theological Education* in 1973, Coe and his colleagues, James Burtness and Aharon Sapsezian of the Theological Education Fund of the World Council of Churches, presented a new method of theological reflection.[5] Coe was the first Asian to promote the term "contextualization" in place of the typical "indigenization" model used in teaching and learning Asian theology. For him the concept of "indigenization" is outdated because it is backward-looking, referring to the past instead of the present as the starting point.[6] Localization assumes that it is sufficient to integrate biblical categories and traditional beliefs into indigenous culture. Coe showed that theological currents at that time (1950–70) in Latin America, Africa, and Asia were nothing more than a shift of European theology to the indigenous culture. The message of the Gospel is only "translated" in the traditions of the peoples of Asia, Africa, or Latin America. In a sense, doing theology in this way is akin to digging up an old tree and transplanting it to a new location.

But theology for Asians is not just a cultural copy of European theology. Coe and his associates devised another method of theological reflection based on contemporary elements that are "open to change" and "future-oriented" (forward-looking).[7] Contextualization, for Coe, means that theology must begin with "missiological *discernment of the times*, seeing where God is at work and calling us to participate in it."[8] Contextual theology is a reflection on how God is interacting with people in the particular historical, cultural, social, religious, economic, and political circumstances of each local community. Coe called on Christian churches in Asia in general, and on Taiwan in particular, to do theology and preach the Gospel in their particular circumstances. The study and teaching of theology in Asia must be based on the experience of the Asian people, and not merely mechanically apply the categories of Western theology.

DEVELOPING A CONTEXTUAL
THEOLOGY FOR ASIA

The Second Vatican Council (1962–65) marked a new turning point for the Catholic churches in Asia. Although the presence of the Catholic bishops from Asian countries at Vatican II was small—some 300 out of 2,500 participants, and many were missionary bishops from the West—their voices were not insignificant. Not only did they make some modest but important contributions at the council, but they also were instrumental in founding a pan-Asian conference of bishops in the years after Vatican II.[9] At the council, the bishops were looking for a practical adaptation of the Christian faith in the Asian setting, especially in the areas of inculturation, mission, and dialogue. It is not an exaggeration to claim that the Asian bishops were pioneers in fostering a "contextual" or "inculturated" approach to theological, educational, and pastoral innovation. The shared experience of fraternity was so positive that the bishops would look for the opportunity to gather again.

Five years after the closing of the council, more than 180 Asian bishops gathered in Manila on the occasion of the Eucharistic Congress presided over by Pope Paul VI. Besides meeting the pope, the Asian bishops came to share pastoral experience and "to search for new ways through which [they] could be of greater and more effective service, not to [the] Catholic communities only but also to all the people of Asia."[10] They realized that the Church must accompany and engage in dialogue with people and social institutions in the unique circumstances of Asia so that the Church can become the Church of the poor, of young people, and ethnic communities living in diverse cultures and religions in Asia. Indeed, the Asian Church has embraced the mode of dialogue proposed by Pope Paul VI in *Ecclesiam suam* (1964) as its modus operandi.

Inspired by the Federation of Latin American Bishops' Conferences (Consejo Episcopal Latinoamericano), which was founded in 1968, the Asian bishops felt the need to work together to build churches on this continent.

Twelve bishops' conferences in South Asia and Southeast Asia have progressed to establishing the Federation of Asian Bishops' Conferences.[11] Coming together as a voluntary association of the episcopal conferences of Asia, the Asian bishops and their theologians pledge "to foster among its members solidarity and co-responsibility for the welfare of Church and society in Asia."[12] The bishops decided to hold a rotating plenary assembly every four years to discuss a particular theme that is relevant to the churches of Asia: evangelization (Taiwan, 1974), prayer (Calcutta, 1978), Church (Bangkok, 1982), laity (Tokyo, 1986), toward the third millennium (Bandung, Indonesia, 1990), discipleship (Manila, 1995), mission of love and service (Bangkok, 2000), family (Daejong, South Korea, 2004), Eucharist (Manila, 2009), new evangelization (Xuan Loc, Vietnam, 2012), and the Catholic family in Asia (Colombo, 2016).[13] Besides, during the interval years, specialized offices of the FABC organized seminars, training courses, and regional meetings on issues and challenges for the churches in Asia.

For more than four decades since its founding, the FABC has chaired discussions on the realities of the Asian Church. Unsurprisingly, most of the topics presented and discussed have not mentioned much of the emerging controversial issues in the West such as the Church's magisterium, sexual morality, liturgical language, the ordination for women, and reform of governance and canon law. Instead, the FABC promotes an "ecclesiological kenosis," that is, the Church goes out of its internal interests to work toward the service of the Kingdom of God. In other words, the Asian Church is more concerned with the external dimension (*ecclesia ad extra*) than the inner (*ecclesia ad intra*). Not that the issues within Church life in Asia are unimportant, but because most are missionary countries, the FABC is more concerned with the role and responsibility of the Church in Asian societies, in many places where Catholics are still a minority. The direction of the FABC continues the spirit of Vatican II, especially of the pastoral constitution *Gaudium et spes*, a document that emphasizes encounter, dialogue, and cooperation with the outside world.

SYNOD OF ASIA: CELEBRATION OF ASIANNESS

In 1998, the Synod of Asian bishops was convened by Pope John Paul II as a part of a series of synods of bishops in preparation for the Holy Year of 2000. It also marked twenty-five years of collaboration between the Asian bishops. Unlike the other synods of Africa, Oceania, America, or Europe,

the Asian synod received quite a bit of coverage in the press and even produced several books on the history and impact of the synod.[14] If the voices
of the bishops from Asia were marginal at Vatican II, this time they came
with their own agenda. In the months of preparation before the synod,
tensions were felt at times between certain episcopal conferences and the
Roman Curia. The Asian bishops unanimously demanded respect for their
contribution. This was an Asian synod for Asian bishops who had worked
among themselves in a collegial atmosphere to build up their vision for the
Church, not only *in* Asia but *of* Asia. It was finally the coming of age of the
Asian Church.

At the synod, the Asian bishops delivered their concerns to the whole
Church, communicating the vision and pastoral practices of the FABC with
which they had wrestled for a quarter of a century. The bishops continued to
emphasize the necessity of the threefold dialogue that has been characteristic
of the mission of the Church in Asia: with the poor and marginalized Asians,
with their cultures, and with their religious traditions. Asian values and ways
of being were voiced at the meetings: "love of silence and contemplation,
simplicity, harmony, detachment, non-violence, discipline, frugal living, the
thirst for learning and philosophical inquiry, . . . respect for life, compassion
for all beings, closeness to nature, filial piety towards parents, elders, and
ancestors, and highly developed sense of community."[15] The bishops urged
a radical decentralization of the Church and genuine respect for the local
churches. They tried to overcome the inherent bias of "older churches" (the
European Church) versus "younger churches" (the missionary churches)
that at times was the on the mind and attitude of some Roman curial officials. Instead, the Asian bishops have spoken of the Church primarily as a
"communion of communities," where the "discipleship of equals" takes place
in a dialogical spirit.

In addition to its minority status, the Church in Asia is also characterized
by ecclesial diversity, so it is more accurate to talk about the Churches of
Asia than the Church in Asia. Not only are Catholicism and Protestantism
treated like two different religions, but there is also a diversity of ecclesial
histories, canonical structures, liturgical traditions, and theological orienta-
tions, even within the Roman Church.[16] Ecumenical dialogue and collaboration, although encouraged by Church officials, still takes a secondary place
in comparison with interreligious dialogue. In today's era of globalization, no
particular churches can stay isolated from one another. Asian churches, while
trying to assert their own Asianness, still need to network with the universal
Church in the context of living the Church as a communion. Because of this
reality, an Asian ecclesiology is still in the making.

FEATURES OF ASIAN THEOLOGY

As the Asian Catholic bishops began to renew local churches based on the spirit of the Second Vatican Council, they also realized the need to renew the theology and preaching of the Gospel in an Asian way. When the FABC met for the first time in Taipei in 1974, the bishops promoted a contextual theology, even if they did not use the term "contextual theology" like Shoki Coe. For bishops, churches in Asia must go into their specific circumstances. At the FABC I (1974), the bishops agreed on a pastoral orientation in Asia: the Church must accompany the poor in conversation with Asian cultures and religions. Asian theology must be a theology closely related to Asian realities, both practical and pastoral, rather than an unrealistic rational theology. Asian theology begins from concrete circumstances, contemplated in the light of the Gospel, in the tradition of the Church, but always open to dialogues with economic, social, and political elements, and with culture and religion, which are the living conditions of the Asian people.

It should be noted that the FABC was established to help Catholic churches in Asia share the experience of applying the spirit of Vatican II to the local situation. Although the FABC is an advisory body without juridical binding on the Asian bishops' conferences, the guidelines provided by the FABC bring practical ideas to the churches in Asia. In other words, the FABC's theology is consultative, but it includes the contributions of theological thought from all members of the Church—bishops, clergy, religious, and lay people—in their particular body. Its influence on the thinking and praxis of Catholicism in Asia is due to its radical openness to a "new way of being Church," a Church that is committed to becoming a "community of communities" and "a credible sign of salvation and liberation."[17]

In the following paragraphs, I offer briefly but not exhaustively some characteristics of Asian theology inspired by the vision of FABC. Asian theology should be a theology for dialogue, using an inductive and praxis approach, focusing on pastoral response, and leading people to the building of the reign of God.

First, Asian theology is of and for dialogue: The term "dialogue" appears many times in FABC documents. Dialogue is the focal point of how the FABC expresses the solidarity between the Church and the peoples and Asian society. When it comes to the Church choosing the path of dialogue and reconciliation as the way of proceeding, many people think that dialogue is nothing more than negotiation or compromise. Yet dialogue and negotiation are two different categories for different purposes. Dialogue is first of all the spirit of wanting to listen, to understand the world and the people in the living situation. Negotiation is about exchanging, discussing, or arguing to find a consensus or to come to a general conclusion. Negotiations always have specific goals and results. Dialogue does not necessarily lead to any consensus. It is simply listening and talking to understand each other better. But there can be no negotiations without a spirit of dialogue.

In the FABC's vision, dialogue frees the Church from its inner concerns (*ad intra*). The dialogues envisioned by the bishops are open to whatever concerns the Asian peoples: their economic and political realities, class consciousness, social movements, cultural traditions, regional customs, religious heritages, popular piety, historical legacies, ecological concerns, and world affairs, to name a few. These realities are both raw materials for theological reflection as well as pastoral direction. In other words, the Asian theological method must be in dialogue with the realities and living situations of Asian believers. In the general context of sociocultural and religious affairs on the continent, the three main concerns of the Church are human liberation, cultural integration, and religious dialogue. For the FABC, these are not three separate activities, but three dimensions of the same evangelizing mission of the Church, a mission of service and presence. This mission is only possible in today's world through dialogue.

Second, Asian theology is inductive and praxis-oriented: If in traditional theology, theological reflection is the interpretation of the truth of the Gospel and doctrine based on philosophical categories—a kind of theology "from the top down" (theology from above; deductive theology) that begins with theoretical propositions and formulas—then contextual theology, particularly the FABC's theology, is "from the grassroots" (theology from below; inductive theology), and is based on Asian people's concerns. In addition to biblical revelation and ecclesiastical tradition, Asian theology also uses materials from cultural lifestyles, religious traditions, Asian wisdom, folk festivals, customs and practices, and economic, social, political, and even global events. In general, there is nothing in life that cannot be the starting point for theological reflection. The search for the truth of faith through life experience itself, not merely applying some teachings to life but the totality of Asian life in dialogue with Scripture and Christian tradition. Thus, this means that the Asian theological approach pursues a multidisciplinary approach, which involves a dialogue between revelation and traditional doctrine with the branches of history, language, art, culture, anthropology, sociology, economics, politics, music, and other fields of interest.

Third, Asian theology is pastorally focused: Unlike traditional academic theology, contextual theology is closer to human life. Asian theologians are trying to restore the way of thinking of the ancient Asian Christian tradition, which emphasizes the mystical, contemplative, and apophatic dimension that is played and described in the hymns and parables of the Syriac Church. These parables and images are very close to the Asian mind. Examples are the narrative theology of Kokuye Koyama and Choan-Seng Song and the parables of Anthony de Mello. The narrative theology uses the folk wisdom of Asian peoples to express the Christian faith through thoughtful stories like Zen *koans* (riddles).

The questions for Asian theologians are: How should theology meet the spiritual needs of Asian people? How to talk about God in a common language that everyone can understand? How can theology not be a strange, mysterious discipline with abstract words and concepts of Western philosophy? How to show people that Christ is not only Christian but also for Asian peoples, whether they join the Church or not? How does Christ not become alien to Asians but become a child of Asia? Furthermore, the existence of so-called religious conflicts in some parts of Asia in recent years (e.g., India, Indonesia, and Myanmar) makes it urgent for theologians to dig into the roots of such tragic conflicts. Are there nonreligious factors embedded in ethnic tensions or political interests? How to address religious violence? How can we teach and speak about God amid a conflictual and distrustful atmosphere? Contextual theology demands an analysis and pastoral response to the sociocultural, economic, religious, and political situations of the locals.

Fourth, Asian theology directs people to the reign of God: The usage of the cultural and religious experiences of others as sources for theological reflection is neither to extract some common core of religious experience that is supposed to undergird all religious traditions nor to erect a universal religion and theology based on allegedly common wisdom. Instead, Asian theologians are working toward a realistic pluralism in which diversity is embraced and promoted but that does not fall into either indifferentism on one hand or exclusivism on the other hand. This pluralism is not about toleration of difference but a realization that the final objective of Christians is not about gaining Church membership or social influence but building a society and world in accord with Gospel values.

Evangelization continues to be a major concern of the churches of Asia. Nevertheless, the "making of disciples of all nations" (Mt. 28:20) takes on a new meaning of "being present with the people, responding to their needs, with sensitivity to the presence of God in cultures and other religious traditions, and witnessing to the values of God's Kingdom through presence, solidarity, sharing and word."[18] In other words, this new evangelization must take on a spirit of "*missio inter gentes,*" mission among the peoples and not just toward them. The existence of the Church in Asia is to preach the Gospel of the Kingdom of God everywhere and at all times, not necessarily to entice or compel people to become religious and to join the Church to enjoy a certain right. Today, people find their way to the Church for spiritual needs, not just to be "rice Christians."

The reality of the Church in Asia exists in small churches, with the role of making salt, yeast, and catalysts. Despite being a small percentage of the population in many parts of mainland Asia (excluding the Philippines, East Timor, and the countries of the former Soviet Union), Catholicism is of modest size—from 0.5 percent in Nepal to 7 percent in Vietnam to 29 percent in South Korea), Asian churches have contributed much to education, health care, and social charity in many countries. The object of service is those people in need, not just Christians.

UPDATES ON THE TRIPLE DIALOGUES
OF THE ASIAN CHURCHES

Keep in mind that as a response to Vatican II's impetus on dialogue, the FABC's theology has gotten off to a good start by conducting three dialogues on society, culture, and religion. The triple dialogue envisioned by the FABC is still valid today, but with some modifications.

First, the dialogue with the poor of Asia is now about engaging the Asian displaced people. Politically, Asia in the aftermath of the Vietnam War still harbors several military conflicts. There is still a threat of war between North Korea and South Korea, and between Pakistan and India. There are tensions on the land and sea borders between China and neighboring countries, ethnic cleansing in Sri Lanka and Myanmar, and separatist movements in the southern Philippines, Xinjiang, and Tibet. All have made the Asian continent unstable. In many places, people face constant stress because of violence, conflict, and the threat that war can break out at any time. This has created a sizable number of refugees and victims of conflicts.

Furthermore, economic hardship leads to a vast migration in Asia, both within a country (internal migration) and across Asia (external migration). Despite the economic achievements of the 1990s and 2000s in East and Southeast Asia, the gulf between rich and poor has not diminished but has increased. Only a small part of the Asian population has a decent and stable life, enjoying a comprehensive education, while the majority still live in poverty, malnutrition, and illiteracy, especially children in rural regions and remote mountainous areas. Though it is a huge continent that is home to two-thirds of the world's population, Asia is facing chronic victims and uneven distribution of resources and populations. Although most Asian countries are agricultural, residents of rural areas are flocking to urban and industrial areas to make a living. At the same time, a large proportion of young people export their labor to more developed countries. Many young people who are tempted by the material life of the consumer culture flee the country in search of a way to change their lives. Women and children, in particular, are at greater risk of becoming victims of human trafficking, forced labor, or sex slavery. Not to mention that in many parts of Asia, the preference for boys over girls results in many female embryos being discarded. As a result, because of the disproportional gender imbalance, millions of young Chinese and Indians cannot find wives. This has led to the abduction and trafficking of brides from neighboring countries. All these issues call Asian theologians to a renewed understanding of the complexity of migration, which are driven by many political and economic factors, not to mention environmental ones.

Second, the dialogues with Asian cultures have resulted in haphazard results, with strong resistance in some Christian circles. For a very long time, Christianity in Asia—both Catholicism and Protestantism—was viewed with suspicion. With the exception of small pockets of native Asian Christians in the Middle East, Armenia, Iraq, and South India, most Asians have received the Good News of Jesus Christ through Western missionaries associated with European colonial powers. The major expansion of Christianity on Asian soil since the sixteenth century, perhaps except in the Philippines, has not resulted in any numerical significance. To the majority of Asians, Christians seemed to live in their own world, being strangers in their own homelands.

The challenge for Asian faithful and their leaders is how to find a way to nurture their faith without the trappings of European Catholicism, as well as how to effectively introduce Jesus to nonbelievers in a nonthreatening way. This task is further complicated by the fact that many older Asian Catholics were accustomed to European images and devotional practices promoted by missionaries of an earlier era. They are often alien to the cultural and religious minds around them. This unfortunate attitude is a result of centuries of being taught that their native cultural and religious expressions are inferior to those of the Christian West. Thus, it is difficult for many Asian Christians to shake off this indoctrination of an "inferiority complex" about using the native cultural and religious expressions. Consequently, the efforts to indigenize the Catholic faith in images, statues, architecture, music, dance, and rituals have met a mixed reception. It is hard to change the pietistic practices to which people have been accustomed.

The dialogue with Asian cultures is not simply a return to the past or an embrace of the traditional heritage of Asia. At the speed of modern communication through the media and smartphones, Asian people are more affected by modern cosmopolitanism and a lifestyle not much different from that of the West. Young people are into games, social media, and the digital culture. Traditional ways of life and religious sentiments are eroding quickly. Families are getting smaller in the city, and many couples decide against having children. Consumerism and individualism are on the rise. This should be a cause of concern for Asian theologians to find an effective way to speak of God to a generation that has little regard for anything or anyone but themselves.

Third, there is the question of interreligious dialogue: Given the reality of religious pluralism in Asia, dialogue is the preferred mode of evangelization. Interreligious dialogue has become a constitutive aspect of the Church's missionary activities. Note that for the vast majority of Asians, dialogue does not primarily take the form of intellectual exchange between experts of various religions, as it often does in the West. Rather, of the four models of interreligious dialogue suggested by the Pontifical Council for Interreligious Dialogue in 1991,[19] the dialogue of *shared life* (common living as good neighbors) and the dialogue of *common action* (collaboration for development and liberation) take precedence over the other two; only after friendship and mutual respect are fostered can the dialogue of sharing *religious experiences* (sharing spiritual richness) and *theological exchanges* (understanding other beliefs and practices) be effectively carried out in daily encounters. In seeking a deeper understanding and appreciation of other heritages, the challenge for Asian Christians is to find an appropriate way to proclaim Jesus Christ to the Asian people without denying the fundamental Christian belief that "Christ is the way and truth and life" (Jn. 14:6).

Furthermore, due to political situations in some countries like India, China, and Vietnam, many Christian communities have been isolated, and believers have been harassed. As a result, the main concern of many churches is how to survive without being destroyed by hostile forces. This leads to only caring for their community instead of engaging in religious dialogue with the rest of society. Interreligious dialogue seems to be on the surface and has not materialized into any deeper change of attitude, either for Christian believers or for their dialogue partners. At best, it is an attitude of tolerance of difference. Christians are remaining foreign both culturally and religiously in the eyes of their compatriots.

NEW FORMS OF DIALOGUES
IN THE ASIAN CHURCH

In addition to the triple dialogues spelled out by the FABC more than forty years ago, contemporary situations necessitate two more types of dialogue for the twenty-first century. They are the dialogue with science and technology, and the dialogue with the state authority.

The *technical dialogue between science and theology* is essential for the present day, when people put a lot of faith in the progress of science and technology. Especially in developed countries in Asia, religion is at risk of being left behind and losing influence on society if it fails to harmonize with the discoveries of modern science. If the contradictions and antagonisms between science and religion in previous centuries revolved around cosmology and the origins of all things, it is no longer a big controversial issue between theology and science today. The concerns of both theology and science today revolves around biological and environmental issues, especially the harmful effects of technology on human life and the Earth. If theological thinking is for the sake of a human being, then theologians must learn and use biological, environmental, and psychosocial knowledge in theological thinking and reasoning. In Asia's religiously pluralistic environment, we can also learn how other religions harmonize science in their beliefs. Also, deforestation, the construction of hydroelectric dams, the indiscriminate discharge of chemicals, and nonbiodegradable plastic waste have caused many environmental effects—including floods, droughts, famines, and water pollution—and have been detrimental to the lives of millions of people. The Asian Church is just beginning to deal with environmental crises.

Political dialogue between the Church and the state authority is a major challenge for the Church in Asia today. From geopolitical and economic perspectives, Asian countries such as China, India, Japan, and South Korea are playing a significant role on the global stage in the twentieth-first century.[20] In addition, several Central Asian countries (the former Soviet territories) have experienced new growth in Christianity. Asian Church leaders cannot afford to ignore these new realities, especially in the area of the Church–state relationship. Culturally and religiously, perhaps except for the Philippines and East Timor, Catholicism and Protestantism have never been the majority in Asian countries. Christianity in Asia is still considered a Western religion, even though Christians have been present in India since the first century, and in China since the eighth century. This foreign factor is a hindrance for Asian Christians.

In many regions of Asia, Christians have been living in fear of persecution and restrictions by a hostile national or local government. Freedom of religion is not a reality in these regions, although it may exist on the books and in government propaganda. Some governments, due to religious or political concerns, see the Church as a challenge to their ruling authority and power. Historically, Christian churches do not want to be subjected to regulation and control by any temporal power. Many misunderstandings and doubts about Catholics still exist because many people believe that Catholics are loyal to a foreign power (the pope), not their government. This mispercep-tion leads to unfortunate conflicts and misunderstandings that have resulted in the persecution of Christians in Qing China, Choson Korea, and Nguyen Vietnam in the past, and the perception of Western cultural dominance felt by political leaders in contemporary India and China. Furthermore, since the Asian Churches often champion human rights and oppose state policy in the area of social justice, tensions naturally arise. How the Church can effectively carry out a dialogue with a hostile government is a looming question.

Another crucial factor for the survival of Christians in such a place as India or China is the relationship between the Vatican and a particular gov-ernment. Among the great religions of the world, only the Catholic Church has a particular organization, that is, the Vatican State. The Holy See is both a religious organization and a civil state, with the pope as the head of state and government structures like any other nation in the world. The political role of the Holy See concerns countries with a Catholic population, and how to meet the need of the local Church there. In Sino-Vatican relations, for example, both sides try to address the appointments of bishops, an issue that has brought a lot of tension and division among Chinese Catholics themselves. Church and state dialogue is a slow process with many rounds of negotiations and, sometimes, compromises. Still, the dialogue between the Church and the state is essential to eliminate the common suspicion that reli-gion wants to dominate the state or wants to replace it. The Kingdom of God is not aimed at any political reality on Earth. Therefore, the Church does not aim at politics or steering the policy of the state. If the Church has spoken out about inadequacies in society, it is because of respect for human dignity. In fact, the Church wants to collaborate with governments to build a more equal and compassionate society and world.

CHALLENGES AND OPPORTUNITIES FOR ASIAN THEOLOGY

The main developments in this chapter are to show that contextual theology is not a "trend of fashion," as we still perceive it, but rather a theological method based on personal experience and society. It is a dialogical theology between faith and experience, doctrine and situation. This method dates back to the early Church's time, when the Gospel was proclaimed by the disciples of Jesus in ancient Greece and beyond, to neighboring civilizations. Not only valuable in the past, contextual theology is also an appropriate theological method in the reality of the social, cultural, and religious pluralities of today's globalization and digitalization.

Indeed, in the digital age, the world has come more closely together, thanks to globally interconnected information technology. Thanks to modern communication networks, billions of people have reached each other easily and quickly in all forms. Personal and community news spread like lightning, especially through social media. The richness and diversity in the information flow require people today to practice multidimensional thinking, even for the question of faith. In a way, contextual theology can be viewed as a way of theological reflection to meet this new situation. This is because Asian theology is empirical, is rooted in concrete situations, and is done through dialogue between the subject and the different agents on a journey of experience in seeking the truth.

Asian contextual theology is not a new theology, in the sense of giving new doctrinal content. What is new is that it offers a theological approach capable of responding to the challenges of modern people. It is a theology that brings joy to the Gospel, hope for those who are distressed and disappointed, and concern for the spiritual and social needs of Asian peoples. It is a theology that wants to shed light on God's presence and love through Jesus Christ—a man of Asia—for today's Asian people.

In the decades to come, the churches in Asia are still growing, as the sociologist Philip Jerkins predicted.[21] But their impact on Asian societies might not be as significant as in the past. In the twentieth century, even though the Asian Christians are a minority (less than 10 percent of any country's population, except for the Philippines, East Timor, Kazakhstan, and Kyrgyzstan[22]), they contributed greatly in fields of education, health care, and social services. At present, many of these functions have been taken over by nongovernmental organizations and government agencies. In terms of solidarity with the poor and marginalized, one of the perennial problems for Asian Christians is how to effectively fight local corruption and politics, escalated by a globalized economy and often unjust trade policies. Conscience building, demand for transparency, and empowerment of marginalized men and women to speak up for their causes are among the ongoing tasks for the churches in Asia today.

Furthermore, the backlash from Muslim, Hindu, and Buddhist fundamentalist groups that view Christian social works as undercover proselytism may deter many Asian Christians from providing educational, medical, and social services in areas that might need them the most—rural and impoverished regions across Asia. Many Asian Christians have personally suffered the effects of violence incited by fundamentalist extremists in India, Pakistan, Indonesia, Malaysia, Sri Lanka, and the Philippines.[23] Faced with violence and difficulties, the temptation of Asian Christians today is to retreat, turn inward, and be complacent about social realities. More than ever, Asian Catholics need to continue following the spirit of *Gaudium et spes*, reaching out to all people to build a more just, more peaceful, and more harmonious world for themselves and their offspring. The call to collaborate with men and women of goodwill still rings true today, as it did half a century ago: "We do not wish to turn a blind eye to the spiritual and moral values of the various non-Christian religions, for we desire to join with them in promoting and defending common ideals in the spheres of religious liberty, human brotherhood, education, culture, social welfare, and civic order."[24]

Although the future of Asian churches is, of course, not predictable, one thing remains clear from the last fifty years: the pastoral nature of Vatican II, exemplified in *Gaudium et spes* and related documents, forever changed the shape and orientation of Asian churches. Without the inspiration from Vatican II, the Asian bishops would not have formed the FABC, giving shape to the Asian Churches as they are today. At the same time, in the process of reception of the council, the Asian Churches also contribute to the universal Church with their theological vision, missionary zeal, and vibrant communities.[25] In the eloquent words of the Asian American theologian Peter Phan, "The gift that Rome gave to Asia 50 years ago is now brought back to Rome, enlarged, enhanced, enriched."[26]

NOTES

1. See Vincent of Lérins, *Commonitory*, 2.6.
2. Peter C. Phan, *Asian Christianities: History, Theology, Practices* (Maryknoll, NY: Orbis, 2018), xvii, 156–67.
3. Stephen B. Bevans, *Models of Contextual Theology* (Maryknoll, NY: Orbis, 1992/2002), 4.
4. Since the late 1990s, Peter Phan has written or edited several works on the Asian theological method, and the theology of the Federation of Asian Bishops' Conferences (FABC). His significant works on the subject include *The Asian Synod: Texts and Commentaries* (1998); *In Our Own Tongues: Perspectives from Asia on Mission and Inculturation* (2003); *Christianity with an Asian Face: Asian American Theology in the Making* (2003); *Being Religious Interreligiously: Asian Perspectives on Interfaith Dialogue in Postmodernity* (2004); and *Asian Christianities: History, Theology and Practice* (2018)—all published by Orbis Books.
5. Shoki Coe, "In Search of Renewal in Theological Education," *Theological Education* 9 (1973): 237–43.
6. Coe, "In Search," 240.
7. Coe, 241.
8. Coe, 241. Note that his "discernment of the times" echoed the "reading the signs of the times" advocated by Vatican II's document *Gaudium et spes* (1965).

9. One can see names of Asian bishops in the list of contributors and committee members, especially on liturgy (*Sacrosanctum Concilium*), interreligious dialogue (*Nostra aetate*), and mission (*Ad Gentes*).

10. Asian Bishops' Meeting, 1970, art. 2, in *For All the Peoples of Asia*, I: 3–10. The documents of the FABC and its institutions and offices have been collected in a five-volume work, *For All the Peoples of Asia*: *Volume I* (1974–91), edited by Gaudencio Rosales and C. G. Arevalo (Manila: Claretian Publications 1997); *Volume II* (1992–96), *Volume III* (1997–2001), and *Volume IV* (2002–6), all edited by Franz-Josef Eilers and published by Claretian Publications in 1997, 2002, and 2007, respectively; and *Volume V* (2007–12), edited by Vimal Tirimanna and published by Claretian Publications in 2014. Since 2006, many FABC documents and papers have been available online at www.fabc.org.

11. At present (2020), there are nineteen full member bishops' conferences: Bangladesh, India (four), Indonesia, Japan, Kazakhstan, South Korea, Thailand, Timor-Leste, Laos-Cambodia, Malaysia-Singapore-Brunei, Myanmar, Pakistan, Philippines, Sri Lanka, Taiwan, and Vietnam. Eight territories that do not have full episcopal conferences enjoy associate membership: Hong Kong, Macau, Mongolia, Nepal, Kyrgyzstan, Tajikistan, Turkmenistan, and Uzbekistan. On the history and structure of the FABC, see Miguel Marcelo Quatra, *At the Side of the Multitudes* (Manila: Claretian, 2000), 5–21; and see the journalistic account of Thomas Fox in *Pentecost in Asia* (Maryknoll, NY: Orbis, 2002), 22–37.

12. FABC mission statement, www.fabc.org/about.html.

13. FABC XII met in Samphran, Thailand, during November 2020.

14. James H. Kroeger and Peter C. Phan, eds., *The Future of the Asian Churches: The Asian Synod & Ecclesia in Asia* (Quezon City: Claretian, 2002); Peter C. Phan, ed., *The Asian Synod* (Maryknoll, NY: Orbis, 2000); Thomas C. Fox, *Pentecost in Asia*: A New Way of Being Church (Maryknoll, NY: Orbis, 2002), esp. chaps. 11–12 (pp. 149–84).

15. *Ecclesia in Asia*, no. 6. This is a postsynodal apostolic exhortation by Pope John Paul II that incorporates many ideas proposed by the Asian bishops at the synod. For the full text, see http://w2.vatican.va/content/john-paul-ii/en/apost_exhortations/documents/hf_jp-ii_exh_06111999_ecclesia-in-asia.html.

16. See Peter C. Phan, *Christianities in Asia* (Oxford: Wiley-Blackwell, 2011).

17. Cf. FABC VI (1995), art. 3, in *For All the Peoples*, II: 2.

18. FABC V, art. 3.1.2, in *For All the Peoples*, I: 279.

19. Cf. Congregation for the Evangelization of Peoples and the Pontifical Council for Interreligious Dialogue, *Dialogue and Proclamation*, nos. 42–46, www.pcinterreligious.org/pcid-documents.

20. I do not include the Catholic churches in the Middle East here, not because they are not part of Asia geographically but because they have not been part of the FABC gatherings and discussions.

21. In the *Next Christendom*, 3rd ed. (New York: Oxford University Press, 2011), the sociologist of religion Philip Jerkins describes the shift of the center of the Church activities and movements from the Euro-American North to the Third-World South. The fastest and vibrant growth of the Church is taking place in Africa, Asia, and Latin America.

22. Most of the Christian population of Kazakhstan (40 percent) and Kyrgyzstan (15 percent) are Russian Orthodox who were relocated during the Soviet era. Because the present economy of those countries is now in flux, many Russian Orthodox are returning to Russia. The Christian future of these Central Asian countries is uncertain.

23. See the ongoing news and reports by nongovernmental organization groups such as Human Rights Watch (www.hrw.org) and International Christian Concern (www.persecution.org).

24. *Gaudium et spes*, 108; cf. *Nostra aetate*, 2: "The Church, therefore, exhorts her sons, that through *dialogue and collaboration* with the followers of other religions, carried out with prudence and love and in *witness to the Christian faith and life*, they recognize, preserve and promote the good things, spiritual and moral, as well as the socio-cultural values found among these men."

25. In the United States, e.g., the effects of Vietnamese and Filipino Catholics are the most obvious. Although they make up only a small percentage of the total US Catholic population, the number of Asian clergy and religious women and men is disproportionally high. For the statistics, consult the US Conference of Catholic Bishops' website (www.usccb.org).

26. Peter C. Phan, "Reception of and Trajectories for Vatican II in Asia," in *50 Years On: Probing the Riches of Vatican II*, ed. David Schultenover (Collegeville, MN: Liturgical Press, 2015), 293–312, at 312.

CHAPTER 3

Between "Memory and Imagination": Reimagining World Christianity without Borders

Jonathan Y. Tan

The title of this chapter takes its inspiration and starting point from Peter C. Phan's autobiographical essay "Betwixt and Between: Doing Theology with Memory and Imagination." In the essay's introduction, Phan writes:

> Theology betwixt and between is theology done with both memory and imagination; it is contemplating the past and creating the future at the same time. Memory anchors the theologian in the ocean of history and tradition, the Church's and one's own; but the stability and security it affords is impermanent and illusory. . . . Like powerful undercurrents, the imagination thrusts into a new world or at least a different way of being in the world. It empowers the theologian to break out of the limits of the past and bring human potentialities to full flourishing. . . . Both memory and imagination in their mutual interactions are indispensable tools for theology. Without memory, theology would be empty; without imagination, it would be blind. They are the epistemological equivalents of *yin* and *yang*, ever in movement, ever transmuting into each other, ever complementing each other, to capture reality in its wholeness.[1]

Taking the cue from Phan's insights above, if theologians and scholars could reimagine world Christianity without borders, what would that look like? How could theologizing be affected when theologians collaborate with social scientists? How do we map the social and virtual geographies of world Christianity, especially when we talk about going beyond the boundaries and borders that are established by Eurocentric Christianity? How do we pay attention to developments in the daily lives of Christians around the globe, especially those who are on the move across the world, in online and virtual communities, as well as migrants, and insider movements, that is, peoples in Asia and Africa who choose to follow Jesus while choosing to remain within their own religious traditions? This chapter examines and analyzes the implications of transient migrants and insider movements for rethinking the contours of world Christianity generally, and ecclesiology in particular.

TRANSIENT MIGRANTS AND
CHRISTIANITY WITHOUT BORDERS

The Global Phenomenon of Migration
and Its Theological Implications

To say that we are living in an age of massive migration around the world is an understatement. Without a doubt, migration is a contemporary global phenomenon that is deeply embedded in, as well as shaping and transforming, the lives of not just those who are migrating but also those who interact with these migrants. According to the International Organization for Migration's *World Migration Report 2011*, about 1 billion people (or one in seven of the world's population) are migrants.[2] The *World Migration Report 2011* also notes that five of the top ten emigration countries are located in Asia—namely, India (second), China (fourth), Bangladesh (sixth), Pakistan (seventh), and the Philippines (ninth).[3] As people move, they bring with them their cultures, religious traditions, and ways of living.

In recent decades, a close nexus has been drawn between migration as a contemporary phenomenon and its important interdisciplinary implications.[4] In turn, this has generated the interest of religion scholars and theologians in exploring the religious and theological implications of migration. This has resulted in excellent critical discussions on migration and its biblical,[5] theological,[6] ethical,[7] and interreligious implications,[8] migration and gender,[9] as well as the theological implications of migration in Asia.[10] Moreover, the increasing waves of migrations by Asians around the globe have profound implications for Christian theology and identity construction in general, and the theology of Christian mission in particular.[11] In his pioneering study of ethnic migrants and the emergence of American religion, the

US historian Timothy Smith notes that migration is "often a theologizing experience."[12]

Much of the existing theological scholarship has focused on migrants who make a *permanent* and *unidirectional* move from their homelands to new countries, whether they are economic migrants who could be documented or undocumented, refugees, or asylum seekers. Hence, the principal focus has been on the pastoral outreach to, and care of, these migrants in diasporic communities, whether they are internally displaced migrants or migrants who leave their homelands because of persecution,[13] or for better economic opportunities abroad.[14] Here, the theological focus has been on responding to, as well as addressing, the marginalized status of these migrants. For example, in Roman Catholic circles, both Pope John Paul II and the Pontifical Council for the Pastoral Care of Migrants and Itinerant Peoples' 2004 Instruction *Erga migrantes caritas Christi* speak of the need for outreach to migrants as part of the task of doing Christian mission, especially the pastoral care of Christian migrants in diasporic communities globally. As the late Indian theologian Soosai Arokiasamy explained, migration "reveals the vulnerability of people's lives, their insecurity, exploitation, joblessness, uprootedness, political uncertainty and humiliating treatment as outsiders or foreigners."[15] Likewise, Stephen Bevans writes that Christian mission "done in the light of migration is a radical commitment to the marginalized."[16] The Maryknoll missioner James Kroeger points out the reality that migrants are often "not only culturally alienated, but also religiously marginalized; frequently, they are relegated to the status of belonging to a minority, 'foreign' religion" in situations where they "follow a religious tradition different from their host country."[17] Not surprisingly, both the migrants and their host communities are often ill-prepared to handle the inevitable cultural shock that arises when different social, cultural, ethical, and religious dimensions are brought together in an explosive mix. The Jesuit theologian Thomas Michel describes it thus: "There is often the culture shock of moving from a simultaneously supportive and restrictive village society; where ethical and religious values are handed on and enforced by the community, to the secularized, individualistic, highly mobile world of industrialized societies. There are hence, the difficulties of social integration, often compounded by feelings of being unwanted or unaccepted by the host societies."[18]

From Permanent to Transient Migrants

Since the beginning of the twenty-first century, sociologists have begun to pay attention to a new category of migration called "transient migrants" as distinct

from "permanent migration," and that emerges as the result of transnational
forces that shape recurrent migrations rather than a singular, linear, and unidirectional migration. In a seminal essay titled "From International Migration to Transnational Diaspora,"[19] the Korean American sociologist John Lie
argues that the classic immigration narrative of a "singular, break from the old
country to the new nation" is no longer tenable or viable in view of a world
that is becoming increasingly global and transnational.[20] Lie argues that "it
is no longer assumed that immigrants make a sharp break from their homelands. Rather pre-immigration networks, cultures, and capital remain salient.
The sojourn itself is neither unidirectional nor final. Multiple, circular, and
return migrations, rather than a single great journey from one sedentary space
to another, occur across transnational spaces. People's movements, in other
words, follow multifarious trajectories and sustain diverse networks."[21] More
important, Lie suggests that transnational and global forces subvert the "uni-
directionality of migrant passage; circles, returns, and multiple movements
follow the waxing and waning structures of opportunities and networks."[22]

It is in this context of recurrent transnational migrations that the Asian
Australian sociologist Catherine Gomes has coined the terms "transient migration" and "transient mobility" to focus attention on those "transient migrants"
who are constantly on the move and not looking to stay in a particular location
permanently or for the long term. In an essay that Gomes coauthored with
me, she uses the terms "transient migrants," "transient migration," and "transient mobility" to refer to the global and transnational movements of people
for work, study, and lifestyle, including skilled professionals and students in
pursuit of international education.[23]

On one hand, the concept of transient migrants is not new. Indeed, existing theological scholarship has rightfully focused attention on *unskilled* transient migrants, especially foreign domestic workers and discussing important
theological implications and pastoral responses to their lack of agency, ill
treatment, and poor working conditions.[24] On the other hand, theologians
have paid comparatively little attention to the growing transient migration
and mobility of educated skilled professionals and international students. In
global financial hubs like Singapore and Hong Kong, transient migrants constitute a significant proportion of the population. For example, of 1.6 million
of the 5.47 million in Singapore, that is close to 30 percent of Singapore's
population, are nonresident migrants.[25] Increasingly, transient migrant Christians are overshadowing local Christians in Hong Kong, Taiwan, and Japan,
judging from the growing number of English, Tagalog, and Bahasa Indonesia
services in these places, compared with services in local languages such as
Cantonese, Mandarin, or Japanese.

Transient Migrants and Christianity

More significantly, these educated transient migrants, whether skilled pro-fessionals or international students, comprise one of the prime drivers of the growth of world Christianity without borders as they move across cities, countries, and continents in search of the next professional job assignment or higher education prospects. In this regard, Gomes's fieldwork among tran-sient migrants in Singapore and Melbourne, who were either skilled profes-sionals or university-going international students, reveal the active role that Christianity plays in the identity constructions and social networking for many of these transient migrants.[26] Gomes herself noted that while she and her research assistants did not specifically go out to investigate Christianity among transient migrants, they discovered that "the Christian faith featured prominently in the answers of a number of respondents" in Singapore, with more than one-third—that is, thirty of eighty-eight respondents—identified as Christian.[27] In our analysis of the interviews of these respondents, we came to this conclusion:

> The results revealed that Asian foreign talent transient migrants who identified themselves as Christian turn to Christianity as a way of coping with everyday life in transience. On one level, the Christian groups they join allow them to create a sense of community while being away from the home nation. *This sense of community, however, is with other Asian foreign transient migrants, rather than with locals,* such as sharing the same nationality and ethnicity dominate. The results of this study contribute to ongoing intersecting discussions on the (transient) migration experience, community and Christianity.[28] (emphasis added)

We also noted how Christianity provided a framework for these transient migrants to develop resilience in order to cope with the various challenges of transience that they experience in their lives:

> Respondents [in Singapore] noted that they actively struck up friendships with people in order to help cope with the traumas of their voluntary uprootedness, with Christianity being a key feature in this quest. Of the thirty participants interviewed, a quarter of them alleviated these conditions by making friends with people from their respective churches. While a few participants were already Chris-tian before coming to Singapore such as the Filipino Catholics and

Indonesian Christians, others found Christianity while living in the island-state.[29]

It came as no surprise that transient migrants, whether longtime Christians or recent converts to Christianity, chose to join congregations with fellow transient migrants rather than with local Singaporeans, experiencing a "community in transience" with fellow Christian transient migrants.[30] In other words, for many, if not the majority, of the transient migrants in Singapore who embraced Christianity and made it a part of their identity constructions as transient migrants, their Christian faith becomes an important and defining aspect of who they are, affording them an opportunity to maintain their own Christian identity apart from Singaporean Christians. Gomes's ethnographic study of international students in Melbourne also reveals similar developments:

> Melbourne . . . is home to several significant churches catering to international students, including the Cross Culture Church. Situated in the heart of the city, the Cross Culture Church, which belongs to the Churches of Christ denomination, has services in English and Mandarin and one of its pastors is dedicated to ministering specifically to international students. . . . Even the serviced apartment complex Arrow on Swanston, which almost exclusively caters to international students during semester sessions, has church facilities in its basement and likewise holds regular Sunday services.[31]

Transient Migrants in the Gulf Region of West Asia

Another region that has witnessed rapid growth in transient migrant Christians is West Asia, where transient migrant professionals in the petroleum, engineering and construction, as well as hospitality sectors are contributing to the rapid growth of Christianity in a region dominated by Islam. In a 2014 article in the *Boston Globe*, the columnist John L. Allen Jr. notes that the Arab Peninsula is witnessing dramatic Catholic growth rates driven, not by Arab converts, but by transient migrants who are foreign expatriates with no rights to permanent residency or citizenship: "The result is a Catholic population on the peninsula estimated at around 2.5 million. Kuwait and Qatar are home to between 350,000 and 400,000 Catholics, Bahrain has about 140,000 and Saudi Arabia itself has 1.5 million."[32] The bulk of these Catholic transient migrants are Filipino Catholics.[33] John Allen also reported that King Hamad bin Isa Al Khalifah of Bahrain agreed to donate land for the construction of a Catholic church to be called "Our Lady of Arabia" for use by the Catholic transient migrants in Bahrain. Up to this point, there is no church, and Catholic transient migrants needed to go to one of the European embassies or gather in a private home or on the grounds of foreign-owned oil companies for masses.[34] In this vein, it is interesting to note that the largest Catholic parish church worldwide is not in Europe or North America, but in Dubai: Saint Mary's Church in Dubai has over 300,000 parishioners, all of whom are transient migrants working in Dubai, with thirty-five to forty weekend masses in twelve languages and over 80,000 hosts distributed weekly. In 2014, the nightly Simbang Gabi services at Saint Mary's Dubai leading up to Christmas drew crowds of more than 15,000 Filipino Catholics each night, resulting in the services being held in the church's parking lot.[35]

Transient Migrants and the Catholic Charismatic Renewal Movement

Unlike Dubai and Bahrain, Saudi Arabia, with the largest concentration of Catholic transient migrants, many of whom are Filipino Catholics, has not granted permission for the building of churches, whether Catholic or Protestant. In this ecclesial vacuum, the Catholic Charismatic Renewal Movement (CCRM) generally, and Gulf Catholic Charismatic Renewal Services in particular, as well as individual Catholic charismatic groups, such as the Filipino El Shaddai Catholic Charismatic movement, play a very important role for the maintenance and nourishment of the faith life of these Catholic transient migrants.[36] In this situation, charismatic prayer groups not only empower transient migrant lay Catholics as prophets, exorcists, healers, and lay leaders but also enable them to transcend political borders and circumvent legal restrictions on churches and clergy presence. This has enabled transient migrant Christian lay leaders to assume leadership and responsibility for keeping the Christian faith alive and strong among their fellow transient migrant Christians in Saudi Arabia and across the Gulf region.

Not surprisingly, the Catholic Charismatic movement's empowerment of lay leadership and participation has kindled the fire that has led to its explosive growth around the globe generally, and in Asia in particular. The Charismatic movement has swept through much of Asia, transforming Asian Christianity in general and Asian Catholics in particular. Asia joins Africa and Latin America in having a sizable number of Pentecostal and Charismatic Christians. The Roman Catholic Charismatic Renewal movement took root in Asia in the late 1960s, in the aftermath of the Second Vatican Council (1962–65) that transformed the Roman Catholic Church in general and the Asian Catholic Church in particular. Since the charismatic movement caught fire among Asian Catholics in the 1970s, it has experienced

tremendous growth throughout Asia. According to the latest statistics compiled by the Vatican-backed International Catholic Charismatic Renewal
Services (ICCRS), there are nearly 14,000 charismatic prayer groups in the
Asian Church, with an estimated 15 percent of Asian Catholics involved in
the CCRM. Indeed, Asia comes second after Latin America, which has an
estimated 16 percent of Catholics involved in the CCRM.[37]

The CCRM in Asia received a big boost in 1994 with the formation of
the Catholic Charismatic Council for the Asia-Pacific under the aegis of the
ICCRS. As a result of the efforts of various local leaders in building and promoting the CCRM within various regions of Asia, the tremendous growth of
the CCRM throughout Asia caught the attention of the ICCRS, which established the ICCRS Sub-Committee for Asia-Oceania in December 2006 at a
meeting in Singapore that drew participants from fourteen countries in the
Asia-Oceania region. The Sub-Committee for Asia-Oceania organized the
First Asia-Oceania Catholic Charismatic Renewal Leaders' Conference in
Jakarta from September 14 to 18, 2008, which drew 525 CCRM leaders from
21 countries in the Asia-Oceania region and marked an important milestone
in the awakening of the Spirit in the revival of the Asian Catholic Church.
This was followed by the establishment of the Gulf Catholic Charismatic
Renewal Services and an inaugural conference from December 7 to 9, 2008,
that drew 1,800 leaders from Bahrain, Kuwait, Oman, Qatar, Saudi Arabia,
and the United Arab Emirates under the banner "Let the Fire Fall Again." The
sizable numbers of leaders from the West Asia–Gulf Region is testimony to
how lay Catholic Charismatic leaders have organized and nourished the faith
of their Catholic transient migrants in the absence of churches and clergy
to maintain the traditional Catholic sacramental life. This 2008 conference
paved the way for Asia to have the honor of hosting the International Catholic Charismatic Leaders' Conference in Seoul from June 2 to 9, 2009. This
was the first time that this global conference was held outside Italy in Asia.
Drawing participants from forty-three countries around the world, this conference culminated in a charismatic prayer rally that drew about fifty thousand participants. This was an important milestone and coming of age for the
CCRM in Asia, enabling Asia to take its place alongside Latin America and
Africa as regions where the CCRM is growing and thriving.[38]

Transient Migrants and Online Communities:
A New Way of Being Church?

In response to the restrictions on churches and clergy, transient migrant
Christians in the Gulf region of West Asia are also breaking boundaries
when they create online communities and form "cyberchurch" to circumvent

legal restrictions on churches and clergy. Digital presence and online communities that are shaped by social media and mediated by livestreaming and messaging apps are redefining the traditional boundaries of Christianity and paving the way for a global and transnational world Christianity that is also being realized in virtual and online communities.

Agnes M. Brazal and Randy Odchigue's exploratory essay, "Cyberchurch and Filipin@ Migrants in the Middle East,"[39] describes how Filipino transient migrants create online faith communities and utilize Facebook,[40] YouTube videos, livestreaming of the Sunday Eucharist and other liturgies, email lists and discussion groups, and other online resources to stay in touch with fellow Christians and practice their Christian faith in the absence of churches and clergy.[41] In other words, the transient Christian identity of these Filipino transient migrants in the Gulf Region that Brazal and Odchigue surveyed are making use of social media and other online tools to create online communities of faith that transcend geographical borders and political restrictions of churches operating in those regions. This paradigm shift toward online or virtual communities of faith is redefining what it means to be Christian, as well as demonstrating a new way of being church that breaks the traditional geographical parochial boundaries and clerical leadership of such churches.

This turn by transient migrants toward online communities that define and nourish their transient migrant and Christian faith identities is not limited to transient migrants in the Gulf region of West Asia. We see the same developments in the transient migrants in Singapore and Melbourne that Catherine Gomes surveyed. For example, an Indonesian information technology professional in Singapore speaks of nourishing his Christian faith through online downloads and Christian YouTube channels featuring pastors and preachers.[42] Other examples illustrate how the transient Christian identity is often nourished and maintained by social media platforms such as Facebook and Instagram, as well as messaging apps such as Weibo, QQ, Renren, and WeChat—all of which are popular with transient migrants from mainland China—as well as WhatsApp and Line for transient migrants generally.[43]

INSIDER MOVEMENTS AND THE CHANGING BOUNDARIES OF WORLD CHRISTIANITY

The term "insider movements" was introduced by Scott Moreau in his book *Contextualization in World Missions: Mapping and Assessing Evangelical Models.* Moreau identifies insider movements as "movements to obedient faith in Christ that remain integrated with or *inside* their natural community."[44] Although insider movements are often misunderstood at best, and criticized as heretical at worst by mainstream Christian theologians and clergy, they nevertheless represent a significant development of emergent communities of faith, which by virtue of their theological hybridity and ecclesial-communal double belonging, present profound implications for rethinking theology generally, and ecclesiology and missiology in particular.[45] Examples include Chrislam in Nigeria,[46] Muslim believers in Jesus across the Islamic world,[47] Buddhist followers of Jesus in Thailand,[48] and Hindu followers of Jesus in India within Protestant/Evangelical-centric Yeshu Satsangs,[49] or Charismatic Catholic Khristbhakta movements.[50]

In India, an emerging charismatic movement with profound ecclesiological and liturgical implications is the Khristbhakta Movement. The Khristbhaktas are Indian devotees of Yesubhagavan (Christ Jesus) as their Satguru, that is, the true lord and teacher who shall lead them along the path of new life and spiritual growth. They draw spiritual nourishment from Christian ashrams, maintaining a dual belonging or hybridized identity as followers of Christ and his Gospel while not formally seeking baptism and Church membership, in order to retain their Hindu identities.[51] Although the Khristbhaktas are not, strictly speaking, Catholics, because they have neither sought baptism nor participate in the traditional Catholic sacramental life, nonetheless they demonstrate the future direction of hybridized or dual/multiple-belonging Indian Catholic Charismatic faith and practice that confounds the institutional structures and boundaries of classical forms of Christian identity and church membership that first emerged in Late Antique Europe.

The Khristbhakta movement is the vision and brainchild of Father Anil Dev, an Indian Catholic priest and missioner of the Indian Missionary Society (IMS), who started the movement in 1993 at Matridham Ashram. Founded and operated by the IMS in the midst of the Hindu heartland of Varanasi, Matridham Ashram represents a unique Indian Catholic experiment to provide a liminal space for hybridized Hindu *bhakti* (devotional) and Indian Catholic charismatic expressions of spiritual formation and faith development. Since then, the Khristbhakta movement has spread among the subaltern Dalits and Tribals in the northern region of India. According to the IMS missioner Jerome Sylvester, who undertook an ethnographical study of the Khristbhakta movement, a survey conducted between 2003 and 2007 reveals that the Scheduled Castes make up about 37.3 percent of the Khristbhaktas. Sylvester further notes that the majority of Khristbhaktas are from the subaltern communities of Dalits and Tribals in India.[52] While Matridham Ashram remains the spiritual heartland of the Khristbhakta movement, newer communities have emerged across northern India, including Jeevan Dham (Faridabad, near New Delhi), Yesu Darbar (Allahabad), Jabalpur

(Madhya Pradesh), Uttar Pradesh, Ranchi (Jharkhand), Patna (Bihar), and Haryana.[53]

Eschewing the path of baptism for membership in the Indian Catholic Church, most Khristbhaktas opt to maintain a hybridized identity, remaining in the *liminal* space of the interstices between Hinduism and Charismatic Christianity, participating in weekly charismatic prayer meetings with the laying on of hands and healings called *satsangs* that combine aspects of rituals of liturgical tradition with devotionals (*bhakti*), feasting (*melâ*), healing, and exorcisms that are led by lay leaders called *aguwas*.[54] The *satsangs* are well attended, and numbers grow as a result of testimonies of miracles and healings by participants. From his fieldwork among the Khristbhaktas, the IMS missioner Jerome Sylvester notes that the Khristbhaktas seek to combine traditional Indian devotional practices with devotional and ritual elements from the Charismatic movement.[55] Sylvester unpacks the implications of the Khristbhakta Movement: "The Khristbhaktas are trying to create a social space for themselves in different ways by affirming their experience in Christ. They have found the Khristbhakta Movement as one of the channels. Emancipation and empowerment become the driving force that draws them to the movement. They find support and shelter in features of free association in the Satsang. The movement is free in every sense of the word, no membership and no limiting structures."[56]

CONCLUSION

The two examples of transient migrant Christians and insider movements, both of which are impacting the developing of world Christianity, have profound implications for missiology and ecclesiology in the context of a rapidly changing world that is buffeted by the forces of postcolonialism, transnationalism, and globalization. The complexities of multiple belongings and hybridized identities are changing the face of world Christianity by crossing multiple boundaries and creating new convergences of multifaceted identities—personal and communal faith identities in the context of transnational networks.

In the past, the grounded geography of Christianity meant that Christianity is based on communities meeting in physical buildings that are built in specific geographical regions. Ecclesiologies and theologies have been constructed, debated, and shaped by the needs and aspirations of faith communities who gather for worship, fellowship, and communal life in those buildings in specific geographical locations. The growth of transient migrant Christian communities poses new challenges and opportunities for virtual ecclesiologies and theologies. Those transient migrants who are educated professionals and international students who move to new cities in search of jobs and educational prospects often turn to Christianity and online communities as a means of finding meaning, networking, and constructing their own faith and social identities. One could certainly argue that online communities and digital resources nourish the *resilience* of these transient migrants in the face of the many challenges of living in transience.

On one hand, the 1.5 million Catholics in Saudi Arabia cannot legally build a church or gather for a Sunday Eucharist that is presided over by an ordained priest. On the other hand, lay run Catholic Charismatic Renewal cell groups such as El Shaddai and individual transient migrant Catholics in Saudi Arabia and across the Gulf Region can turn to social media and online communities to create virtual or online church beyond the reach of Saudi law. Indeed, without social media and online communities, there is no church in Saudi Arabia. Indeed, social media and online communities are redefining the boundaries of world Christianity, reimagining ecclesiology and pastoral ministry, and posing new questions for theology on the issues of faith and identity formation in transience.

More important, though transience may be *lo cotidiano* for transient migrants, it is still an experience in uprootedness, loneliness, and a yearning for home. Historically, as a universal religion that spread throughout the world because of transnational movements, Christianity plays an important role in helping transient migrants make sense of themselves and their faith experiences in strange and unfamiliar settings.[57] Yet, just because transient migrants embrace Christianity and make Christianity a part of their identity, it does not necessarily signal their assimilation into the broader host society or acceptance by their fellow Christians in their host society. Taking transient migrant Christians in Singapore as an example, by embracing Christianity on their own terms, these transient migrants "have consciously forced religious identities in opposition to the discrimination they have encountered," despite their shared Christian faith with Singaporean Christians because they have "created institutions that reflect their concerns and cater to their own needs."[58] In other words, the world Christianity of transient migrants can and does exist alongside indigenous or local Christianity because of the differing worldviews and expectations of these transient migrants and the locals who are citizens and permanent residents. This would have profound implications for ecclesiology and catholicity, especially the tensions between a universal vision of faith and church vis-à-vis the particularity of diversity and pluralism. Indeed, Catherine Gomes and

I myself see this in the majority of the transient migrant Christians in Singapore, as we concluded:

For many, if not the majority of these Asian foreign talent transient migrants who embrace their Christian faith and make it a part of their diasporic identity in Singapore, their Christian identity becomes an important and defining aspect of who they are, enabling them to communicate with Singaporean Christians, yet affording them the opportunity to carve out a niche where they can define their own identity apart from their fellow Singaporean Christians, . . . leading to heterogenized, hybridized, and conflicting constructions of faith identity that simultaneously connect yet distance themselves from other Singaporean Christians. It is important to note that when Asian foreign talent transient migrants embrace a Christian faith identity, often with more fervour than they do in their homelands, this goes beyond mere nostalgic longing for home to encompass new opportunities for them to shape their own transnational, hybridized, and often contested multiplicity of identities in Singapore, where they are at best tolerated or at worse vilified by Singaporeans who express varying degrees of xenophobia against them.[59]

Likewise, insider movements are contributing to the growth of world Christianity outside traditional ecclesial boundaries of classical forms of Christian identity and church membership. While the per capita percentage of the population of Christians in Asia has remained stable despite ongoing intense missionary activity, the numbers of Christians increase once we factor in those followers of Jesus who, nonetheless, eschew baptism and ecclesial membership in favor of remaining within their own cultural and religious communities across Asia.

More important, insider movements within world Christianity reveal the complexities of multiple belongings and hybridized identities that challenge the homogeneity of the ecclesiological vision of Eurocentric Christianity.[60] By putting at the center of their faith life their hybridized devotional and popular ritual practices rather than Eurocentric church structures, membership, and worship practices, these subaltern Asians are challenging the hegemony of a Eurocentric institutional vision of church. This has profound implications especially as the center of Christianity has shifted away from Europe and North America to the Majority (or Two-Thirds) World.[61]

In contrast to the experiences of transient migrants who are educated professionals or international students, insider movements hail primarily from the subaltern classes across the majority world who are confronting the challenges of postcolonialism, postmodernism, and globalization that are rapidly transforming the world around them.[62] Although Jerome Sylvester made these remarks in the context of Khristbhaktas, they are pertinent to the marginal status of other subaltern groups in other insider movements, who reject official ecclesial identities for hybridized identities: "The subaltern struggle against caste and class can be well understood against the background of heterodox and antisystemic movements. Those who are at the margins negotiate the porous borders in their search of a new identity and empowerment. Khristbhaktas negotiate the borders of faith and culture for empowerment against social exclusion and marginalization from the liminal position of Hinduism and Christianity."[63]

Finally, although transient migrants and insider communities appear to be living in separate worlds, they do share much in common, in the sense that they live hybridized lives where they do not often fit neatly into the mainstream society around them. Faith in Jesus Christ becomes a *means of resilience* in the face of the challenges of everyday life "betwixt and between" in transience. As a fitting conclusion, let us return to the beginning of this chapter, which opened with Peter Phan's call to doing theology betwixt and between "with both memory and imagination."[64] Phan's clarion call for a theological imagination that "thrusts into a new world or at least a different way of being in the world"—empowering the crossing of boundaries, breaking past limitations, and bringing "human potential to full flourishing"— continues to be highly relevant as transient migrants, online communities, and insider movements transgress the borders and redefine the boundaries of world Christianity for the future ahead.[65]

NOTES

1. Peter C. Phan, "Betwixt and Between: Doing Theology with Memory and Imagination," in *Journeys at the Margin: Toward an Autobiographical Theology in American-Asian Perspective*, ed. Peter C. Phan and Jung Young Lee (Collegeville, MN: Liturgical Press, 1999), 113–33, at 114–15.
2. International Organization for Migration, *World Migration Report 2011* (Geneva: International Organization for Migration, 2011), 49.
3. International Organization for Migration, 68, citing World Bank, *Migration and Remittances Factbook, 2011* (Washington, DC: World Bank, 2011), 3.
4. See Caroline B. Brettell and James F. Hollifield, eds., *Migration Theory: Talking across Disciplines, Third Edition* (New York: Routledge, 2014); Stephen Castles, Hein de Haas, and Mark J. Miller, *The Age of Migration: International Population Movements in the Modern World, Fifth Edition* (New York: Guilford Press, 2013); and Mikkel Rytter and Karen Fog

Olwig, eds., *Mobile Bodies, Mobile Souls: Family, Religion and Migration in a Global World* (Aarhus: Aarhus University Press, 2011).

5. See Jean-Pierre Ruiz, *Readings from the Edges: The Bible & People on the Move* (Maryknoll, NY: Orbis, 2011).

6. See Elaine Padilla and Peter C. Phan, eds., *Contemporary Issues of Migration and Theology* (New York: Palgrave Macmillan, 2013); Daniel G. Groody and Gioacchino Campese, eds., *A Promised Land, A Perilous Journey: Theological Perspectives on Migration* (Notre Dame, IN: University of Notre Dame Press, 2008); and Gioacchino Campese and Pietro Ciallella, eds., *Migration, Religious Experience, and Globalization* (New York: Center for Migration Studies, 2003).

7. See Tisha M. Rajendra, *Migrants and Citizens: Justice and Responsibility in the Ethics of Immigration* (Grand Rapids: Wm. B. Eerdmans, 2017).

8. See, e.g., Elaine Padilla and Peter C. Phan, eds., *Theology of Migration in the Abrahamic Religions* (New York: Palgrave Macmillan, 2014).

9. See Glenda Tibe Bonifacio and Vivienne S. M. Angeles, eds., *Gender, Religion, and Migration: Pathways of Integration* (Lanham, MD: Lexington Books, 2010); Gemma Tulud Cruz, *An Intercultural Theology of Migration: Pilgrims in the Wilderness* (Leiden: Brill, 2010); and Rhacel Salazar Parreñas, *Servants of Globalization: Women, Migration, and Domestic Work* (Stanford, CA: Stanford University Press, 2001).

10. Fabio Baggio and Agnes M. Brazal, eds., *Faith on the Move: Toward a Theology of Migration in Asia* (Quezon City: Ateneo de Manila University Press, 2008).

11. Jeffrey M., Burns, Ellen Skerrett, and Joseph M. White, eds., *Keeping Faith: European and Asian Catholic Immigrants* (Maryknoll, NY: Orbis, 2000); Helen Rose Ebaugh and Janet Saltzman Chafetz, eds., *Religion and the New Immigrants: Continuities and Adaptations in Immigrant Congregations* (Walnut Creek, CA: AltaMira Press, 2000).

12. Timothy L. Smith, "Religion and Ethnicity in America," *American Historical Review* 83 (1978): 1155–85, at 1174.

13. See, e.g., Daniel G. Groody, "Crossing the Divide: Foundations of a Theology of Migration and Refugees," *Theological Studies* 70 (2009): 638–67.

14. For examples of the academic theological literature focusing on various dimensions and implications of these categories of migration, see Jennifer B. Sauders, Elena Fiddian-Qasmiyeh, and Susanna Snyder, eds., *Intersections of Religion and Migration: Issues at the Global Crossroads* (New York: Palgrave Macmillan, 2016); Elaine Padilla and Peter C. Phan, eds., *Christianities in Migration: The Global Perspective* (New York: Palgrave Macmillan, 2016); and Gemma Tulud Cruz, *Toward a Theology of Migration: Social Justice and Religious Experience* (New York: Palgrave Macmillan, 2014).

15. Soosai Arokiasamy, *Asia: The Struggle for Life in the Midst of Death and Destruction.* FABC Paper 70 (Hong Kong: Federation of Asian Bishops' Conferences, 1995), 9.

16. Stephen Bevans, "Migration and Mission: Pastoral Challenges, Theological Insights," in *Contemporary Issues of Migration and Theology,* ed. Elaine Padilla and Peter C. Phan (New York: Palgrave Macmillan), 157–77, at 171.

17. James H. Kroeger, "Living Faith in a Strange Land: Migration and Interreligious Dialogue," in *Faith on the Move: Toward a Theology of Migration in Asia,* ed. Fabio Baggio and Agnes M. Brazal (Manila: Ateneo de Manila University Press, 2008), 219–51, at 225–26.

18. Thomas Michel, "The Church and Migrants of Other Faiths," *Seminarium* 37, no. 4 (1985): 175–88, at 182.

19. John Lie, "From International Migration to Transnational Diaspora," *Contemporary Sociology* 24, no. 4 (1995): 303–6.

20. Lie, 303.
21. Lie, 304.
22. Lie, 305.
23. Catherine Gomes and Jonathan Y. Tan, "Christianity as a Culture of Mobility: A Case Study of Asian Transient Migrants in Singapore," *Kritika Kultura* 25 (2015): 215–44, which has been revised and expanded as "Christianity: A Culture of Mobility," by Catherine Gomes and Jonathan Tan, in *Transient Mobility and Middle-Class Identity: Media and Migration in Australia and Singapore*, ed. Catherine Gomes (Singapore: Palgrave Macmillan, 2017), 185–208. The discussion that follows in this section summarizes and discusses the key ideas and conclusions that are taken from our coauthored 2015 and 2017 essays. See also Catherine Gomes, "Liking It, Not Loving It: International Students in Singapore and Their Navigation of Everyday Life in Transience," in *The Asia-Pacific in the Age of Transnational Mobility: The Search for Community and Identity on and through Social Media*, ed. Catherine Gomes (London: Anthem Press, 2016), 87–116.
24. E.g., Cruz, *Intercultural Theology*; Cruz, *Toward a Theology of Migration*; and Parreñas, *Servants*.
25. Gomes and Tan, "Christianity," 219.
26. This fieldwork in Singapore and Melbourne provided the ethnographic data for our coauthored 2015 and 2017 essays.
27. Gomes and Tan, "Christianity," 225.
28. Gomes and Tan, 226.
29. Gomes and Tan, 228.
30. Gomes and Tan, 227.
31. Gomes and Tan, 188.
32. John L. Allen Jr., "Catholicism Growing in Heart of Muslim World," *Boston Globe*, March 8, 2014, www.bostonglobe.com/news/world/2014/03/08/catholicism-growing -heart-muslim-world/LxIiUYwSlro7Zl6ugvVQJM/story.html.
33. See Agnes M. Brazal and Randy Odchigue, "Cyberchurch and Filipin@ Migrants in the Middle East," in *Church in an Age of Global Migration: A Moving Body*, ed. Susanna Snyder, Joshua Ralston, and Agnes M. Brazal (New York: Palgrave Macmillan, 2016), 187–200.
34. Allen, "Catholicism."
35. The information and statistics on Saint Mary's Church in Dubai come from personal communication with the Filipino American theologian Ricky Manalo, who visited this church in December 2014 and observed the weekend liturgies and Simbang Gabi celebrations.
36. El Shaddai, since being established in 1981 by Mike Velarde, has spread like wildfire among Filipino Catholics in the Philippines as well as in the global Filipino diaspora, garnering a following of about 11 million within fifteen years, with chapters in nearly every province of the Philippines and more than thirty-five countries around the world. For an in-depth examination of El Shaddai, its growth, and its impact on Filipino Catholicism, see Katharine L. Wiegele, *Investing in Miracles: El Shaddai and the Transformation of Popular Catholicism in the Philippines* (Honolulu: University of Hawai'i Press, 2005).
37. The statistics are taken from a paper presented by Cyril John (vice president of the ICCRS), "Lay Movements and New Communities in the Life and Mission of the Church in Asia: Experiences from the Catholic Charismatic Renewal," Congress of Asian Catholic Laity, Seoul, August 31–September 5, 2010.

38. John, "Lay Movements."
39. Brazal and Odchigue, "Cyberchurch," 187–200.
40. Brazal and Odchigue surveyed eight Filipino transient migrants in the Gulf Region: four in Saudi Arabia, who are a graphic artist, caregiver, mechanic, and engineer; and four in the United Arab Emirates, who are an electrical engineer, company administrator, teacher, and machine operator, respectively. See Brazal and Odchigue, "Cyberchurch," 187–88.
41. Brazal and Odchigue, 190–91.
42. Gomes and Tan, "Christianity," 226.
43. See example given by and discussion by Gomes and Tan, 190.
44. A. Scott Moreau, *Contextualization in World Mission: Mapping and Assessing Evangelical Models* (Grand Rapids: Kregel, 2012), 161. Although Moreau is responsible for the term "insider movement," he is not the first to study this movement. In his groundbreaking book, *Churchless Christianity* (Pasadena, CA: William Carey Library, 2001), Herbert E. Hoefer analyzed the phenomenon of communities of believers in Jesus Christ who chose not to identify with, or join Christianity or churches, referring to these believers as "non-baptized believers in Christ" and concluding that it was possible to be a believer in Jesus without identifying as Christian and joining a church. For a more recent discussion of insider movements, see Harley Talman and John Jay Travis, *Understanding Insider Movements: Disciples of Jesus within Diverse Religious Communities* (Pasadena, CA: William Carey Library, 2015).
45. See the in-depth and nuanced discussion by William A. Dyrness, *Insider Jesus: Theological Reflections on New Christian Movements* (Downers Grove, IL: IVP Academic, 2016).
46. Abraham McLaughlin, "In Africa, Islam and Christianity Are Growing—and Blending," *Christian Science Monitor*, January 26, 2006, www.csmonitor.com/2006/0126/p01s04-woaf.html.
47. For a case study of the Magindanon believers of "Isa al-Masih" (Jesus, the Messiah/Christ) in Mindanao, the Philippines, see E. Acoba (pseud.), "Towards an Understanding of Inclusivity in Contextualizing into Philippine Context," in *The Gospel in Culture: Contextualization Issues through Asian Eyes*, ed. Melba Padilla Maggay (Manila: OMF Literature, 2013), 416–50. For broader theological discussions, see David Greenlee, ed., *Longing for Community: Church, Ummah, or Somewhere in Between?* (Pasadena, CA: William Carey Library, 2013).
48. Kang-San Tan, "An Examination of Dual Religious Belonging theology: Contributions to Evangelical Missiology" (PhD diss., University of Aberdeen, 2014), which explores the endeavors of "New Buddhists" in Thailand who are believers and followers of Jesus while retaining a dual belonging to their Buddhist religious tradition. For further discussion, see also Banpote Wetchgama, "The New Buddhists: How Buddhists Can Follow Christ," *Mission Frontiers* 36, no. 6 (2014): 28–31.
49. See Darren Todd Duerksen, *Ecclesial Identities in a Multifaith Context: Jesus Truth-Gatherings (Yeshu-Satsangs) Among Hindus and Sikhs in Northwest India* (Eugene, OR: Pickwick, 2015); and Herbert Hoefer, "Jesus, My Master: 'Jesu Bhakta' Hindu Christian Theology," *International Journal of Frontier Missions* 19, no. 3 (2002) 39–42.
50. For in-depth ethnographical and theological discussions of the *Khristbhakta* movement, see Jerome G. Sylvester, "The Khristbhakta Movement: A New Paradigm of Faith in Christ Jesus," *Vidyajyoti Journal of Theological Reflection* 27 (2013): 345–59 (part I), and 443–56 (part II); Jerome G. Sylvester, *Khristbhakta Movement: Hermeneutics of a*

Religio-Cultural Phenomenon (Delhi: ISPCK, 2013); Ciril J. Kuttiyanikkal, *Khrist Bhakta Movement: A Model for an Indian Church? Inculturation in the Area of Community Building* (Zurich: LIT, 2014); and Kerry P. C. San Chirico, "Between Christian and Hindu: *Khrist Bhaktas*, Catholics and the Negotiation of Devotion in the Banaras Region," in *Constructing Indian Christianities: Culture, Conversion and Caste*, ed. Chad Bauman and Richard Fox Young (New Delhi: Routledge, 2014), 23–44.

51. Sylvester, "Khristbhakta Movement," I, 345.
52. Sylvester, I, 348.
53. Sylvester, I, 345–48.
54. Sylvester, II, 448, 452, 453.
55. Sylvester, II, 450.
56. Sylvester, II, 448.
57. Gomes and Tan, "Christianity," 233–34.
58. Gomes and Tan, 234.
59. Gomes and Tan, 234–35.
60. On the challenges of hybridized identities, see Homi K. Bhabha, "Signs Taken for Wonder," in *The Location of Culture*, by Homi K. Bhabha (New York: Routledge, 1994), 102–22.
61. See, in particular, the excellent analysis of this paradigm shift by Wesley Granberg-Michaelson, *From Times Square to Timbuktu: The Post-Christian West Meets the Non-Western Church* (Grand Rapids: Wm. B. Eerdmans, 2013); Jehu Hanciles, *Beyond Christendom: Globalization, African Migration, and the Transformation of the West* (Maryknoll, NY: Orbis, 2008); Philip Jenkins, *The Next Christendom: The Coming of Global Christianity*, revised and expanded edition (New York: Oxford University Press, 2007); and Andrew Walls, *The Cross-Cultural Process in Christian History: Studies in the Transmission and Appropriation of Faith* (Maryknoll, NY: Orbis, 2002).
62. On the challenges posed by the subaltern classes, see Gayatri Chakravorty Spivak, "Can the Subaltern Speak?" in *Marxism and the Interpretation of Culture*, ed. Cary Nelson and Lawrence Grossberg (Urbana: University of Illinois Press, 1988), 271–313.
63. Sylvester, "Khristbhakta Movement," I, 348–49.
64. Phan, "Betwixt and Between," 114–15.
65. Phan, 115.

CHAPTER 4

Christian Resilience
and Vulnerable Migrants

Gemma Tulud Cruz

The twenty-first century has been called "the age of migration," essentially because there are more migrants in the world today than ever before.[1] Indeed, at no other point in history has the number of people on the move been at such a large scale—in fact, John Haywood describes it as "the world on the move."[2] Estimates by the International Organization for Migration even indicate that the number of migrants worldwide could rise to as much as 405 million by 2050.[3] Although the closure of international borders due to the COVID-19 pandemic has curtailed people's movements, it certainly has not stopped, nor dampened, vulnerable populations' desire, or attempts, to cross borders.[4] In fact, the global economic devastation brought by the pandemic is expected to exacerbate the swelling of the number of poor people who are desperate to move.

THE POOR ON THE MOVE:
HUMAN MOBILITY AND
"UNDESIRABLE ALIENS"

In contemporary times, the poor on the move are increasingly labelled and treated as "undesirable aliens," or unwanted migrants, and are progressively being made to experience various forms of indignities in a way that poses questions about what it means to be Christian in the context of the migration of vulnerable populations today. The immense movement of people in search of *bare life* is not only rearranging human geography but also challenging the socioeconomic, political, and religiocultural fabric of destination countries in ways that test social cohesion and people's sense of responsibility.[5] The increasing tendency by governments in transit and destination countries to focus on what are perceived as problems and burdens associated with migration create a climate in which certain segments of the population see migration not so much a gift but a threat, a peril not a promise—for example, Donald Trump's ban on immigration from what he referred to as "shithole countries."[6] The use of misleading, derogatory, and exclusionary rhetoric against migrants, often by politicians who weaponize immigration to score political points, fan the flames of simmering anti-immigrant sentiments that make life difficult not only for (potential) migrants but also for individuals and communities in transit and destination countries who take seriously not only people's need or right to move but also their responsibility for the poor and vulnerable. Former Italian interior minister Matteo Salvini's refusal to allow migrant (rescue) boats to dock at Italian ports, and the harassment of immigration activists and humanitarians rescuing distressed migrants at sea, illustrate the predicament plaguing vulnerable migrants and those who care for, or advocate, for them.[7]

Peter Phan speaks of Deus Migrator, or God the Primordial Migrant, and of "migrantness" as a mark of the Church to frame Christian faith and practice in the context of contemporary migration.[8] In this chapter, I first explore two core beliefs in Christianity that shine a light on resilience among vulnerable migrants; then I reflect on associated themes that may help Christians in transit and destination countries, especially immigration advocates, to foster resilience in their care as well as a sense of responsibility for vulnerable migrants. I argue that, from a Christian perspective, hope underpins the practice of resilience, whether one is the migrant or the advocate.

FINDING LIGHT IN THE DARKNESS: RESILIENCE AND VULNERABLE MIGRANTS

In *The Capacity to Be Displaced: Resilience, Mission and Inner Strength*, Clemens Sedmak contends that in order to deal with the stressful nature of displacement, people need to be resilient. Resilience, Sedmak posits, makes people flourish in adverse circumstances.[9] It is, in a sense, about surviving well. Early theories about resilience stressed the role of genetics. However, Judith Rodin insists that, as a skill and capacity to be robust under conditions of enormous stress and change, resilience is not an inborn individual trait or an inherent characteristic of a company or community.[10] It is something that is built and nurtured at the individual and, in particular, communal levels. It is more about a continuous effort rather than a fixed goal.

But how is resilience built and nurtured in the context of the challenges of migration today? More specifically, which key Christian beliefs and practices that figure prominently in the lives of vulnerable migrants might assist in understanding how resilience plays out, and is nurtured, amid precarious situations? Further, what theological themes arise from these beliefs and practices that may, in turn, shed light on how Christians in transit and destination countries might become (more) resilient in their care and responsibility for vulnerable migrants in the midst of increasing animosity, if not downright hostility, toward migrants?

THE CRUCIFIED GOD: EMPATHY, ENCOUNTER, AND STRATEGIC SOLIDARITY

To migrate is to cross borders. For today's migrants, however, borders are no longer just the political membranes through which goods and people must pass in order to be deemed acceptable or unacceptable. Today, borders have become the "thin porous membrane[s]" that people cross at their own peril.[11] Pepe and Maria's harrowing border-crossing experience illustrates this: "Our *coyote* [human smuggler] told us that we had to hit the ground because an (immigration) helicopter was coming overhead and we threw ourselves on the desert floor. When we got up, my wife was covered in cactus spines and for eight days I removed them from her body."[12] Others, like Fatima Dhaiwi and her two daughters, are subjected to indignities by being pushed back.[13] Some face even more tragic fate, like the Syrian boy Aylan Kurdi; Oscar Alberto Martinez and his twenty-three-month-old daughter, Valeria; the thirty-nine Vietnamese migrants found dead in a refrigerated truck in the United Kingdom in 2019; and the thousands who have perished during extremely risky land or sea border crossings.

An equally tragic condition plagues those for whom border crossing left them "suspended, awaiting the next step in their life's journey," trapping them "in a reality that is filled with human suffering, poverty, neglect, and despair,"[14] such as those in US detention centers and migrant camps in various parts of the world[15]—for example, the "jungle" camp in Calais, France,[16] and the Moria camp in Lesbos, Greece, which burned down in September 2020.[17] Borders have become, in the words of Gloria Anzaldua, an "open wound." They are gaping, bleeding wounds that serve as a testament to the violence of wars and entrenched inequalities as well as the culture of indifference

among states that are "more concerned about their sovereignty and protecting themselves from migrants than protecting migrants and refugees from
human rights abuse and ensuring that their vulnerability is not exploited."[18]

When one crosses the border, one traverses the yawning gap between
being a citizen to being an alien or a foreigner, a visitor, a guest—in short,
an outsider.[19] To cross the border is to live on the margins and be a stranger.
Xenophobia—fear of the stranger—is the curse of the migrant, for today's
migrant is today's stranger—"the image of hatred and of the other."[20] As the
document of the World Synod of Catholic Bishops, *Justice in the World*, points
out, migrants are "often forced to leave their own country to find work, but
frequently find the doors closed in their faces because of discriminatory attitudes, or, if they can enter, they are often obliged to lead an insecure life or
are treated in an inhuman manner."[21]

Daniel Groody and Gioacchino Campese posit that migrants, particularly forced and undocumented migrants, are today's "crucified peoples."[22]
This is a perspective that the Peruvian theologian Gustavo Gutierrez echoes
by referring to the contemporary immigrant as iconic of the face of the poor
in the modern globalized world.[23] Due to a combination of complex personal, social, economic, and political factors, vulnerable migrants tend to
live on the fringes of society. Hence, many migrant congregations start from
urban peripheries and are often forced to remain in these marginal places
for purposes of cheaper rents or due to government policies and initiatives.
For example, the Kingsway International Christian Center, a large church in
London that was founded by a Nigerian pastor and is composed mainly of
members with primarily West African backgrounds, had to move out of its
headquarters in an industrial park to make way for the large-scale regenera-
tion of the area in preparation for the 2012 London Olympics.

The experience of "coerced liminality" leads most vulnerable migrants to
embrace the image of the Crucified God, or the suffering God, in order to help
them deal with the various challenges they face in the context of migration.[24]
Habiba, the charismatic Eritrean leader of one the largest migrant domestic worker Pentecostal congregations in Lebanon, credits Jesus speaking to
her in and through her suffering for surviving five years of abuse as a maid.[25]
Vulnerable migrants' embrace of the suffering God to address the travails of
mobility is also reflected in the popular practice of the *Via Crucis* (Way of the
Cross) by Mexican Americans in the Pilsen and Little Village neighborhoods
of Chicago. The practice is a witness to "a theology that is also a politically
grounded concept of culture" in the way it is engaged within a space and
architecture of domination experienced by these neighborhoods.[26] A young
Mexican American refers to it as "a re-enactment of a historical event, but it

is not a play" rather a "reliving (of) that moment which is actually happening now."[27] The practice and the vulnerable migrants' life, therefore, become a *Living* Way of the Cross (emphasis added).[28] Among mixed-status Latinx families in the United States, who observe a permeable boundary between family and nonfamily such as *compadre* and *comadre* (the child's baptismal godfather and/or godmother), the sacramental responsibility, which effectively extends to fostering the well-being of a *compadre*'s or *comadre*'s family in *lo cotidiano* (ordinary life), may include facing the effects of illegality—for example, driving a *compadre* to the hospital because he does not have proper documentation or being willing to support a *comadre*'s children if she is deported.[29] Indeed, for many Christians who face unrelenting struggle as a migrant the cross, as a symbol of suffering, is both a historical event and a present reality. As mediators of the crucified, this *pueblo crucificado* summons Christians to be an *ecclesia crucis* because, as Paul makes clear,[30] "if you claim to be a disciple of the crucified one you must expect to participate in his sufferings; . . . you will have to become a community of the cross."[31] This borderland ecclesiology demands solidarity with the victims as the privileged praxis through which we demonstrate ourselves to be Church and practice resilience in our response to issues surrounding vulnerable migrants.[32]

A Christian understanding of, as well as identification with, the suffering other is often suggested as a means of insight into the paradoxical nature of human resilience. In fact, the ability and propensity to make meaning of woeful times is considered a building block of resilience. This dynamic of meaning making is often the way resilient people build bridges from present-day hardships to a fuller, better constructed future.[33] Those bridges make the present manageable, removing the sense that the present is overwhelming.

Like Jesus, migrants do not actively seek the cross. They seek the Kingdom values of justice, peace, and well-being and accept the cross as part of it. What is clear in their case is that the recognition and integration of vulnerability can be morally enriching and politically empowering for fostering resilience. Resilience born out of vulnerability becomes a social justice and theopolitical category in the lives of migrants, in two ways. First, it provides a subtle hermeneutical framework through which to interpret the perils and possibilities of contemporary life. Second, it enhances their capacity to live creatively in a complex world.

Migrants' embrace of the crucified God on account of the suffering they experience points to the practice of empathy, encounter, and strategic solidarity as a means for stimulating and nurturing resilience in Christians' care and advocacy for vulnerable migrants. Put simply, empathy is the ability to perceive accurately what another person is feeling. It is both a trait and skill that is vital for immigration advocacy and activism because it motivates people to take action when they see others who are suffering. It is different from sympathy. Whereas sympathy relates more to feeling pity for someone's pain or suffering, or the concern stimulated by the distress of another, empathy is more about looking for a common humanity. Empathy is the very fabric of Christian relationality. Emotional empathy, sometimes called compassion, is more intuitive and involves care and concern for others. Cognitive empathy, meanwhile, involves more effort and systematic thinking because it requires considering others and their perspectives and imagining what it is like to be them. Mature empathy entails reflective or active listening and the willingness or capacity to be confronted with negativity with the aim of understanding the other. When someone relates to us with true empathy, and not simply pity, they offer us a space in which we can literally be, a space where we feel safe enough to be fully present and safe enough to be heard. Participants in a study of volunteers at an immigration detention center, for instance, reported that the act of visiting and allowing the detainee to lead, shape, and control the conversation affirmed the humanity of those being held.[34] We are, first and foremost, relational beings. It is through relating, and within relationships, that we find meaning in our lives. Relationality itself is indispensable to pastoral care and ministry among migrants, as evidenced by the "relational turning point" in the field of theological and pastoral reflection on human mobility.[35] Empathy is basic not only to building relationships with, but also to passionately advocating for, vulnerable migrants.

Side by side with empathy is encounter. Mary Jo Leddy, a Canadian who is widely recognized for her work with refugees in Toronto, points to the vital role of encounter in eliciting advocacy and involvement on issues relating to vulnerable migrants: "As I have listened to frontline church workers, refugee advocates, and immigration lawyers, two realities seem to emerge as constants in their experience: the first is that many of them are rooted in some church tradition; the second, that most of them got involved in 'refugee work' through a personal encounter with a refugee or a refugee family."[36]

The witness of these people could be described as authentic solidarity born out of the power of encounter.[37] Leddy, who traces her own work for refugees to an encounter with a refugee in great need, describes this ethical moment as conversion—the change of mind and heart and moral imagination—through a personal relationship. She posits that this ethical moment is the moment when we are "summoned, addressed, and commanded— ... the time of annunciation and visitation. ... For many, the encounter with a real person called 'refugee' evokes feelings of profound compassion that lead to practical forms of kindness. It is within this reach of mercy that the necessity (and near impossibility) of justice begins to emerge."[38] African Christians in Europe, for instance, have set up evangelistic initiatives to reach out to groups of people that are rarely directly targeted by indigenous missionaries. These groups include drug addicts, alcoholics, prostitutes, victims of human trafficking, juvenile delinquents, and undocumented migrants.[39] As the document *Welcoming Christ in Refugees and Forcibly Displaced Persons: Pastoral Guidelines* [n. 58] indicates, the first point of reference should be the human person. Failure to find a reference to the human face of the migrant could result to the core issues at stake becoming lost and easily distorted. If we do not get the human face of the migrant right, a just society is not possible.[40] Thus, in the context of human dislocation, there can be no meaningful mission without costly incarnation. As Jonathan Bonk bluntly puts it:

To be a Christian entails recognizing and resisting the terrible reductionisms of all self-serving nationalisms, tribalisms, and racisms—and their ever attendant legalisms—that undervalue or even dismiss the stranger, the refugee, or the immigrant, or the enemy. When we cooperate in such systemic reductionism we subvert our own identities as men and women created in the image of God, since we yield to Caesar something to which Caesar has no ultimate claim—human beings, including ourselves. *Legality*, for Christians, can never be an acceptable substitute for *justice*.[41]

In Christian terms all sanctification, all inner transformation, is ultimately for the sake of transformative action and redemptive practice in society.[42] Action on behalf of justice and participation in the transformation of the world, therefore, is a constitutive dimension of the preaching of the Gospel, or, in other words, of the Church's mission for the redemption of the human race and its liberation from every oppressive situation (*Justice in the World*, no. 6). The multifarious suffering endured by vulnerable migrants calls for Christian witness to be more strongly linked with migrants' quest for a life with dignity. Further, certain groups of migrants are more vulnerable than others. The asylum seeker, the refugee, the undocumented, and those in insecure work are often at the receiving end of more discriminatory and dehumanizing conditions. Thus, there is a need for what may be called strategic solidarity or preferential option for the more, or most, vulnerable migrant. This strategic solidarity could be helpful in fostering resilience among immigration advocates since its targeted nature makes caring for vulnerable migrants more manageable, effective and, to a certain extent, less daunting. To be sure, the scale and complexity of the issues surrounding vulnerable migrants can be overwhelming. Solidarity can be quite demanding to the point of being a "burdened virtue."[43] Further, so-called compassion fatigue can very easily set in. Thus, refraining from having a messianic complex and choosing one's battles wisely, by focusing one's time and energy to a specific immigration-related cause or volunteer work one is passionate about, can go a long way in preventing burnout, thereby sustaining resilience, to a certain extent, among immigration advocates.

GOD IN THE EUCHARIST: COMMUNITY, HOSPITALITY, AND PRAYER

For many migrant Christians, Sunday is not complete without participating in the Eucharist. The extraordinary opening of a Catholic Church in Dubai, for example, is strongly credited to migrant workers from the Philippines, Sri Lanka, and other Asian countries.[44] Even the lack of actual church buildings does not deter them. They find or go to even the most unlikely places to celebrate the Eucharist if there is no church building available. They build their own "church" out of parks, gyms, basements, abandoned shop lots, and auditoriums. Most migrant domestic workers' churches in Lebanon—which have members from Sudan, Philippines, Eritrea, Kenya, and other East African nations—have to rent the space in which they operate.[45] Even the threat of arrest in countries like Saudi Arabia, whose religious police strictly enforce the prohibition of public display of religion other than Islam, does not dissuade some from celebrating the Eucharist. For Sudanese refugees in Egypt, "Sunday Masses became an important moment in their lives to defend their racial and cultural identity, and to access information on the situation in their original homes. The liturgical celebrations became not only the main space of expression of faith in the Lord who saves but also the occasion to rebuild communal bonds."[46]

In her comparative study of migrant women domestic workers in Hong Kong, Singapore, and Taiwan, Shu-Ju Ada Cheng specifically extols church attendance as one practice that "provides an important opportunity and space for women to establish their support system and networking, which is essential for breaking the isolation of the household."[47] Indeed, many admit to a feeling of homecoming whenever they join other domestic workers for a Eucharistic celebration. Wherever it is held, "it's another home," where they can "forget [the] misgivings induced by being a stranger in another country."[48] They do not care whether they have to stand instead of sit, kneel on a rough floor, or put up with the noise and the stares of curious passers-by. For them, it is the spirit in which one attends the Eucharist that counts.

The Filipino sociologist Randy David offers a glimpse of the role played by the Eucharist in migrants' spiritual resilience:

I recently sat through a Sunday service in one such gym in Hong Kong, and wondered what it was that drew in the participants. It could not have been the long high-pitched and thoroughly uninspiring lecture-sermon of the *pastora* [female pastor], who certainly did not deserve her audience's reverential attentiveness. I am more certain now that it was the community, and the bonding and the comfort they derived from each other's sheer presence that made them come. . . . For when it was time to sing, . . . the gym came alive. A band started to play a rousing tune and costumed dancers with ribbons and tambourines took center court. I thought for a while it was a prelude to a basketball tournament. Three thousand Pinoys, almost all of them women, stood up. With eyes closed and arms raised, they swayed their bodies to the rhythm of a prayer. They cheered, they clapped and they shouted God's name; and in that anonymous collective drone, they cried out their individual pain.[49]

There are connections between the dynamics of immigration and the structure of the Eucharist: the breaking of the bread and the breaking of migrants' bodies, the pouring of Christ's blood and the pouring out of migrants' lives for their families, Christ's death and resurrection and the migrants' own. Groody reckons that immigrants offer a new way of looking at the Eucharist; and the Eucharist, in turn, gives many immigrants a new way of understanding their struggles.[50] I posit that migrants' practice of the communal meal after the Eucharist becomes an equally potent wellspring of resilience. I have been to many such meals with various migrant communities in different parts of the world, and the experience can be evangelizing. It is like witnessing the Gospel at (the community) table. The spirit of joy, the atmosphere of warmth and affection, and the sense of community that are continually nourished and deepened are such that the experience itself becomes a God experience. It is like seeing "the substance of religion and more . . . the strength that comes from valuing the intangibles, the meanings that are continually created and understood, when human beings come together to share their lives and their fears, their meals and their memories."[51] It is the

Eucharist in the flesh rooted in the tenacity and beauty of the human spirit. In many ways such gatherings fit Eddie Gibbs and Ryan Bolger's description of emerging churches or Christian communities in postmodern cultures, which "include the outsider, even those who are different, . . . place a great emphasis on the Eucharist as a central act of worship," and where "the ethos of the service is one of hospitality."[52]

Vulnerable migrants' deployment of the Eucharist, and the shared meal after it, to deal with the pathos of the migrant condition highlights the significance of the community in fostering resilience on the part of immigration advocates. Having and working with allies and partners on multiple levels (local/national, parish/diocese, nongovernmental organization or faith-based organization), even across borders counts.[53] The multisectoral and collaborative character of many faith-based organizations working on immigration issues—whether within, between, or among Christian traditions—demonstrates this.[54] Christians are people born into a community—that is, the family—and brought into a community—that is, the Church—by the God of community, that is, the Trinity. It makes sense, therefore, that Christian faith is lived in and with a community. In practical forms, community involves relationships—connecting with others, learning from others, sharing with others, rejoicing with others, and struggling with others. Through community hermeneutics, we seek a growing understanding, if not agreement, on key issues, such as migration, that can help us test our theologies and our practices.[55] As shown in the life of the early Christians, communal meals are vital for building and nurturing community.[56] Shared meals in the Christian tradition are potent reminders that Christian life is not just about individual salvation but also about collective liberation; not just about families but also about communities; and not only marked by fasting and mourning but also with celebrations. Lawrence Cunningham and Keith Egan write: "But to celebrate the Eucharist well we must learn, first of all, how to celebrate, to make festival, to make 'Sabbath.' What does not happen outside of Eucharist will not happen at the Eucharist: we cannot become instant celebrators, festive people merely by walking through a church door. We cannot celebrate the Eucharist well if we do not celebrate elsewhere."[57]

Christian spirituality in itself cannot be limited to an exclusively individualistic "care of the soul." It is found and nourished in community. Christian spirituality maintains that the way of discipleship in community finds its highest expression in the sharing of the Eucharist and, ultimately, our task as disciples of Jesus is to invite others to share at the table. Thus, the Eucharist and the shared meal, or communal meal, after it also draw attention to the role of hospitality as a building block for resilience insofar as these provide opportunities for healing, bonding, and bridging. Sharing meals in Jesus's way helps build resilience on the part of those who care and advocate for migrants because of its various meanings and implications. From a religious perspective, sharing meals as Jesus did means overcoming exclusionary practices (Lk. 11:37–54). Socioculturally, it means relating to each other not according to status and honor, healing the shame that might exist in the one who has nothing (Lk. 19:1–10). Anthropologically, it implies the need to recognize the others in all their diversity, to give them a place at the table, and integrate them in society (Lk. 7:36–50).[58] It is without dispute that hospitable acts of the local population in transit and destination countries toward vulnerable migrants help in the latter's well-being. In the same manner, whether in the context of a meal, hospitable encounters with vulnerable migrants can also be a source of inspiration and encouragement for immigration advocates and activists. Realistically speaking, such advocacy and activism is not easy, especially in the current global sociopolitical and economic climate and in the wake of the COVID-19 pandemic. Before the pandemic, there were migrant and refugee advocates and activists who had been subjected to harassment, imprisonment, even death threats.[59] These advocates and activists are not superhumans and hence are not immune to exhaustion, dejection, or despair. Hospitable encounters with vulnerable migrants, therefore, would be like special occasions of grace that could inspire advocates and activists to persist in what they are doing, whether it is volunteering at the soup kitchen after work, helping with immigration paperwork, or organizing and joining protests. Christian advocacy and activism certainly should not hinge on such encounters. The point being made here is that, from a human perspective, such encounters matter in nourishing the soul.

Christian hospitality draws inspiration from the notion that the God in whom we believe is the God of the stranger (Deut. 10:17–18; Ps. 146:9). Thus, from a Christian perspective, all of us are strangers and God is, ultimately, the host in hospitable encounters. What happens in these encounters, therefore, is a form of hospitality rooted in solidarity among strangers. Such theology augurs well for fostering resilience among migrants, and those who care and advocate for them, because it presents both as guests and, consequently, as both strangers.[60] It is a more egalitarian way of looking at the experience of hospitality, and it is very much Christian, as exemplified in our experience of creation, grace, healing, and forgiveness as God's gifts. This means that whenever Christians receive or practice hospitality, they are actually sharing in God's hospitality, regardless of immigration or citizenship status. Such understanding of hospitality builds resilience among immigration advocates because there is something unifying and liberating in recognizing a shared calling and identity, and in seeing vulnerable migrants not only as sites of need but also as partners and gifts. It fortifies resilience, as well, because it is empowering. As Jesus shows by sending his disciples on mission in pairs (Mk. 6:7–13), one does not have to do the work alone, that one is never alone. An understanding and practice of Christian work in the context of migration as shared mission could make the load for immigration advocates a little bit lighter and, in effect, more bearable. Indeed, witnessing as "one body and one people sharing in one bread" makes the work with, and on behalf of, vulnerable migrants more possible and meaningful and, at the same time, less of an experience in the wilderness.[61]

Last but not least, the employment of the Eucharist by migrants to deal with the precariousness of migration reflects the role of prayer in fostering resilience in immigration advocacy. Because prayer taps into some of the deepest places of loneliness and longing lodged in the human heart, prayer allows us to develop that intimate conversation with Christ that enables us to abide with him and know each other as intimate friends (Jn. 15:4). As the doorway to spiritual depth, human meaning, and genuine intimacy, prayer also allows us to perceive more clearly the truths of life. Exercised in private and in community, prayer builds and nourishes relationships, because it is not just a psychological tool for self-actualization but also a spiritual grace that facilitates human transformation.[62] This makes prayer especially important for those involved in the work of care and justice for vulnerable peoples. In missionary work, action and contemplation must go together for they complement one another. Prayer and justice are two sides of the same spiritual coin: justice without prayer quickly degenerates into frenetic and exhausting social activism, but prayer without justice is hollow and empty. Jesus drives home the importance of prayer for personal spiritual nourishment, renewal, and fortification in the Agony in the Garden (Mt. 26:36–46) and when he encouraged his disciples to "Come to me, all you who are weary and burdened, and I will give you rest" (Mt. 11:28).

SHINING A LIGHT ON HOPE

All migrants know that moving across borders is never easy. It takes courage to migrate. It is a long, difficult, and potentially dangerous process that never truly and fully ends, even long after one has successfully crossed one physical border to another. What is striking is that migrants still decide to take the journey, despite being aware of the perils that await them. In the words of Julio: "We are aware of the dangers, but our need is greater. There's always the risk of dying (in the desert) but the desire to survive and keep going is even more important."[63] The enormity of the threats and dangers for migrants during their journey is such that Dante's inscription over the gates of hell—*Lasciate ogne speranza, voi ch'intrate*, "Abandon hope all who enter here"—might seem appropriate. And yet migrants never lose hope. In fact, it is their enduring weapon. They fiercely and desperately believe in the promise of a better future and continue to do so despite the odds. It is there in how countless people continue to move across borders despite the difficulties and dangers, even in the midst of a pandemic when recession-plagued destination countries become more reluctant, if not downright hostile, when it comes to accepting vulnerable migrants.[64] Hope is there in how migrants put up with, or fight against, isolation and discrimination, in how they refuse to leave and give up, and in how they continue to weave and nurture dreams for a better life. It is a courageous hope in the sense that it is a "hoping against hope," a sense of hope that continues to believe and open itself to possibilities of transformation that can never be fully spoken of.[65] As Cesar reminisces, "When I was in the desert I thought about Jesus' temptation. It was like God was testing me in some way. . . . For me the temptation was not to trust God, to give up, to admit defeat, to allow myself to die in the desert. But I couldn't do it. . . . I felt God was calling me to fight, to keep going, to suffer for my family. I did not want to let myself be conquered by death least of all."[66]

Susanna Snyder contends that mysticism and action for social justice are intimately interwoven and suggests that recognition of this could enrich Christian discussion and praxis surrounding immigration.[67] Indeed, one could argue that the same courageous hope fuels the tireless and fearless efforts of Christians who care and advocate for vulnerable migrants today. To be sure, their efforts are rarely, if not never, recognized. Some who work with people of other religions are sometimes subjected to suspicion of proselytism, while those who engage in care work in immigration detention centers face problems of access and arbitrary restrictions.[68] Ethel and her colleagues, for example, had to take political action to obtain entry.[69] As mentioned above, some face harassment along with threats of imprisonment or death. Nevertheless, these groups and individuals continue with their increasingly complex and difficult task.

Michael Downey writes that one constant or essential component in any approach to Christian spirituality is that there is a quest for personal integration in the face of forces of fragmentation and depersonalization.[70] Human authenticity, then, is the outcome of a continuous dynamism of self-transcendence toward that which is true and truly good. Migrants and tireless Christian immigration advocates reflect this dynamic orientation and struggle toward what is true and truly good, toward what is life-giving and, consequently, toward what gives hope.[71]

Indeed, this life-oriented resilience of vulnerable migrants, as well as migrant and refugee advocates and activists, shines a light on the importance of hope in building resilient Christian faith and practice in the context of the migration of vulnerable populations today. As an ethical activity, hope has a conscience and intelligence which mere optimism lacks. Moreover, hope looks beyond self-regarding satisfactions to the transcendent values that alone can nourish life and give it direction. Thus, hope refuses to see the ultimate meaning of life as simply "more of the same." It is patiently open to what is, and must be, "otherwise." It cannot rest except in the truly meaningful and the genuinely good, thereby increasing the scope and energies of the human spirit in the quest for the fullness of life. Hope, then, breathes the conviction that what is deepest in our aspirations is not ultimately worthless or self-defeating.[72] It is a conduct of life, a mode of living and acting which inspires action. It engenders a deep moral sense and points in the direction of a more passionate self-involvement in the making of the world, and risking even life itself for the greater good of oneself or others. As theological virtue, hope is not only about giving thanks for what is already given but also being open to what is beyond all imagination and control. Hope for oneself then expands to hope for others, interceding for all who are our companions in the light and shadow of the history we share.

Christians are called to embody hope in order to witness to the central tenet of Easter among vulnerable migrants. Even in death Jesus did not remain within the boundaries of what death means: failure, defeat, destruction. By his resurrection he crossed the borders of death into a new life, thus bringing hope where there was despair, victory where there was vanquishment, freedom where there was slavery, and life where there was death. In this way, the borders of death become frontiers to life in abundance.[73] The resurrection of Jesus from the dead offers Christian communities that receive vulnerable migrants hope that it is not impossible to overcome all that deters, or threatens, what is ultimately good and life-giving. As Easter people, Christians need to cling to a hope that endures and knows how to risk in order to bring about transformative ecclesial praxis no matter how long it takes.

NOTES

1. Stephen Castles and Mark Miller, *The Age of Migration: International Population Movements in the Modern World*, 4th edition (Basingstoke, UK: Palgrave Macmillan, 2009). And see Andrés Solimano, *International Migration in the Age of Crisis and Globalization: Historical and Recent Experiences* (Cambridge: Cambridge University Press, 2010).

2. Other previous great migrations have been largely based on and described according to ethnic or regional groups. John Haywood, *The Great Migrations: From the Earliest Humans to the Age of Globalization* (London: Quercus, 2009), 244–49.

3. International Organization for Migration, *World Migration Report 2010: The Future of Migration—Building Capacities for Change* (Geneva: International Organization for Migration, 2010), 3.

4. Rick Kelsey, "English Channel Migrants: Where They're From and What They're Escaping," www.bbc.com/news/newsbeat-53721146.

5. Saskia Sassen, "The Making of Migrations," in *Living (With)out Borders: Catholic Theological Ethics on the Migrations of Peoples*, ed. Agnes Brazal and Maria Teresa Davila (Maryknoll, NY: Orbis, 2016), 11–22, at 11.

6. Ibram Kendi, "The Day *Shithole* Entered the Presidential Lexicon," *Atlantic*, January 13, 2019.

7. Jason Horowitz, "Salvini's Standoff at Sea Highlights Italy's War on Rescue Ships," *New York Times*, August 16, 2019. And see Billy Perrigo, "The Far Right Lost Power in Italy Two Months Ago: So Why Are Migrant Boats Still Being Refused Entry?" *Time Magazine*, October 29, 2019.

8. Peter Phan, "Deus Migrator: God the Migrant—Migration of Theology, Theology of Migration," *Theological Studies* 77, no. 4 (2016): 845–68.

9. Clemens Sedmak, *The Capacity to Be Displaced: Resilience, Mission, and Inner Strength* (Leiden: Brill, 2017).

10. Judith Rodin, *The Resilience Dividend: Being Strong in a World Where Things Go Wrong* (New York: PublicAffairs, 2014), 6–7.

11. Daisy Machado, "The Unnamed Woman: Justice, Feminists, and the Undocumented Woman," in *Religion and Justice: A Reader in Latina Feminist Theology*, ed. Maria Pilar Aquino et. al. (Austin: University of Texas Press, 2002), 161–76, at 169.

12. Daniel Groody, *Border of Death, Valley of Life: An Immigrant Journey of Heart and Spirit* (Lanham, MD: Rowman & Littlefield, 2002), 21.

13. Gul Tuysuz et al., "Masked Men, Assault and Abandonment," CNN, September 17, 2020, https://edition.cnn.com/2020/09/17/europe/greece-migrants-turkey-intl/index.html.

14. Machado, "Unnamed Woman," 169.

15. *National Catholic Reporter*, "Editorial: Don't Look Away from the Concentration Camps at the Border," www.ncronline.org/news/opinion/editorial-dont-look-away-concentration-camps-border.

16. Kara Fox, "Calais 'Jungle' Camp in France: What You Need to Know," CNN, October 21, 2016, https://edition.cnn.com/2016/10/21/europe/calais-jungle-migrant-camp-explainer/index.html.

17. Iliana Mier and Elena Becatoros, "'Thousands of Asylum Seekers Left Homeless After Fires Destroy Overcrowded Refugee Camp in Greece," *Time Magazine*, https://time .com/5888377/fire-destroys-moria-refugee-camp-homeless/.

18. Mathias Burton Kafunda, "The Situation of Migrants/Refugees in African Context," in *Flight and Migration: Between Homelessness and Hospitality*, ed. Klaus Krämer and Klaus Vellguth (Quezon City: Claretian, 2020), 87–95, at 89.

19. Virgilio Elizondo, "'Transformation of Borders': Border Separation or New Identity," in *Theology: Expanding the Borders*, ed. Maria Pilar Aquino and Roberto S. Goizueta (Mystic, CT: Twenty-Third, 1998), 29.

20. Julia Kristeva, *Strangers to Ourselves*, trans. Leon S. Roudiez (New York: Columbia University Press, 1991), 1.

21. Synod Bishops, *Justice in the World*, 1971, no. 21, www.cctwincities.org/wp-content /uploads/2015/10/Justicia-in-Mundo.pdf.

22. See Daniel D. Groody, "Jesus and the Undocumented Immigrant: A Spiritual Geography of a Crucified People," *Theological Studies* 70 (2009): 307–16; and Gioacchino Campese, "Cuantos Más? The Crucified People at the US-Mexico Border," in *A Promised Land, A Perilous Journey: Theological Perspectives on Migration*, ed. Daniel Groody and Gioacchino Campese (Notre Dame, IN: University of Notre Dame Press, 2008), 271–98.

23. Gustavo Gutierrez, "Poverty, Migration, and the Option for the Poor," in *Promised Land*, ed. Groody and Campese, 76–86.

24. Sang Hyun Lee, "Marginality as Coerced Liminality: Toward an Understanding of the Context of Asian American Theology," in *Realizing the America of Our Hearts: Theological Voices of Asian Americans*, ed. Fumitaka Matsuoka and Eleazar Fernandez (Saint Louis: Chalice Press, 2003), 11–28.

25. Daniel Chetti, "Vulnerable and Missional: Congregations of Migrant Domestic Workers in Lebanon," in *Church in an Age of Global Migration*, ed. Susanna Snyder et al. (New York: Palgrave Macmillan, 2016), 201–16, at 207.

26. Karen Mary Davalos, "The Real Way of Praying: The Via Crucis, Mexicano Sacred Space, and the Architecture of Domination," in *Horizons of the Sacred: Mexican Traditions in US Catholicism*, ed. Timothy Matovina and Gary Riebe-Estrella (Ithaca, NY: Cornell University Press, 2002), 41–68, at 42.

27. "That moment" refers to suffering; Davalos, "Real Way of Praying," 41.

28. Gioacchino Campese, *The Way of the Cross of the Migrant Jesus* (Liguori, MO: Liguori, 2006).

29. Victor Carmona, "Mixed-Status Families, Solidarity, and *Lo Cotidiano*," in *Sex, Love, and Families: Catholic Perspectives*, ed. Jason King and Julie Hanlon Rubio (Collegeville, MN: Liturgical Press, 2020), 199–210, at 209.

30. Roberto Goizueta, "*Corpus Verum*: Toward a Borderland Ecclesiology," in *Building Bridges, Doing Justice: Constructing a Latino/a Ecumenical Theology*, ed. Orlando Espin (Maryknoll, NY: Orbis, 2009), 143–66, at 147–49.

31. Douglas Hall, *The Cross in Our Context: Jesus and the Suffering World* (Minneapolis: Fortress Press, 2003), 140.

32. Goizueta, "*Corpus Verum*," 149.

33. Diane Coutu, "How Resilience Works," *Harvard Business Review*, May 2002.

34. Susanna Snyder et al., "Immigration Detention and Faith-based Organizations," *Social Work* 60, no. 2 (2015): 165–73, at 168.

35. Gioacchino Campese, "The Responses of the Church to the Challenge of Migration," in *Flight and Migration*, ed. Krämer and Vellguth, 227–36, at 235.

36. Mary Jo Leddy, "When the Stranger Summons: Spiritual and Theological Considerations for Ministry," *New Theology Review* 20, no. 3 (2007): 6. See also Edmund Chia, "Biblical Reflection on Asylum Seekers and Refugees in Australia," *Asian Horizons* 8, no. 4 (2014): 706–18, at 709.

37. See Diego Fares, SJ, *The Heart of Pope Francis: How a New Culture of Encounter Is Changing the World and the Church* (New York: Crossroad, 2015).

38. Leddy, "When the Stranger Summons," 6–7.

39. See J. Kwabena Asamoah-Gyadu, "To the Ends of the Earth: Mission, Migration and the Impact of African-Led Pentecostal Churches in the European Diaspora," *Mission Studies* 29 (2012): 23–44, at 30–31; and Dominic Pasura, "Religious Transnationalism: The Case of Zimbabwean Catholics in Britain," *Journal of Religion in Africa* 42 (2012): 26–53, at 37.

40. Daniel Groody, "The Church on the Move: Mission in an Age of Migration," *Mission Studies* 30 (2013): 27–42, at 36.

41. Jonathan Bonk, "Whose Head Is This and Whose Title?" Presidential address delivered at International Association for Mission Studies Thirteenth Quadrennial Conference, Toronto, August 15–20, 2012.

42. Robert Egan, "The Mystical and the Prophetic: Dimensions of Christian Existence," *The Way* (Supplement, 2002): 92–106. See also Philip Sheldrake, "Christian Spirituality as a Way of Living Publicly: A Dialectic of the Mystical and Prophetic," *Spiritus: A Journal of Christian Spirituality* 3, no. 1 (2003): 19–37.

43. The concept of "burdened virtues" refers to a way of examining the reality that, under conditions of oppression, virtues do not necessarily lead to flourishing. For an exploration of how solidarity may end up as a "burdened virtue" in the context of migration, see Tisha Rajendra, "Burdened Solidarity: The Virtue of Solidarity in Diaspora," *Journal of the Society of Christian Ethics* 39, no. 1 (Spring–Summer 2009): 93–101.

44. Francisco Claver, SJ, "Philippine Migrant Labor: The Challenge to Their Religious Identity," in *Migration: Challenge to Religious Identity II, Forum Mission, Volume 5*, ed. Josef Meili, Ernstpeter Heiniger, and Paul Stadler (Lucerne: Verein zur Förderung der Missionswissenschaft, 2009), 58–67, at 63–64.

45. Chetti, "Vulnerable and Missional," 209.

46. Nader Michel, "The Sudanese Refugees in Egypt," in *Living (With)out Borders*, ed. Brazal and Davila, 25–34, at 29.

47. Shu-Ju Ada Cheng, "Migrant Women Domestic Workers in Hong Kong, Singapore, and Taiwan: A Comparative Analysis," in *Asian Women in Migration*, ed. Graziano Battistela and Anthony Paganoni (Quezon City: SMC, 1996), 119.

48. Chris Yeung, "A Building That Serves Both God and Mammon," SCMP, June 27, 1983, as quoted by Mission for Filipino Migrant Workers, *Filipino Workers: Off to Distant Shores* (Hong Kong: MFMW, 1983), 66.

49. Randy David, *Public Lives: Essays on Selfhood and Social Solidarity* (Pasig City: Anvil, 1998), 50–51.

50. Daniel Groody, "Fruit of the Vine and Work of Human Hands: Immigration and the Eucharist," in *Promised Land*, ed. Groody and Campese, 299–315, at 301.

51. David, *Public Lives*, 52.

52. Eddie Gibbs and Ryan Bolger, *Emerging Churches: Creating Christian Community in Post-modern Cultures* (London: SPCK, 2006), 119.

53. See Daniel Groody, "Migrants and Refugees: Christian Faith and the Globalization of Solidarity," *International Review of Mission* 104, no. 2 (2015): 314–23.

54. See, e.g., Robin Hoover, "The Story of Humane Borders," in *Promised Land*, ed. Groody and Campese, 160–73.

55. Paul Hiebert, "The Gospel in Human Contexts: Changing Perceptions of Contextualization," in *Missionshift: Global Mission Issues in the Third Millennium* (Nashville: B & H, 2010), 82–102, at 96.

56. See Reta Halteman Finger, *Of Widows and Meals: Communal Meals in the Book of Acts* (Grand Rapids: Wm. B. Eerdmans, 2007), 48–79, 169–82.

57. Lawrence Cunningham and Keith J. Egan, *Christian Spirituality: Themes from the Tradition* (Mahwah, NJ: Paulist Press, 1996), 185.

58. Rafael Luciani, "The Itinerant Fraternity of Jesus: Christological Discernment of the Migration Drama," in *Living (With)out Borders*, ed. Brazal and Davila, 206–12, at 210.

59. See, e.g., Rhina Guidos, "Priest Helping Migrants, Staff in Guatemala Receive Death Threats," www.ncronline.org/news/world/priest-helping-migrants-staff-guatemala-receive-death-threats.

60. For a substantive treatment of this idea, see Ross Langmead, "Refugees as Guests and Hosts: Towards a Theology of Mission Among Refugees and Asylum Seekers," *Exchange* 43 (2014): 29–47.

61. Gemma Tulud Cruz, *Toward a Theology of Migration: Social Justice and Religious Experience* (New York: Palgrave, 2014), 153–60.

62. Daniel Groody, *Globalization, Spirituality and Justice: Navigating the Path to Peace* (Maryknoll, NY: Orbis, 2007), 249–50.

63. Quoted by Groody, *Border of Death*, 23–24.

64. Tuysuz et al., "Masked Men."

65. Jennifer Drago, "Intentional Community and Displaced People: Dwelling Together in the Body of Christ," in *Church in an Age of Global Migration*, 217–26, at 220–21.

66. Quoted by Groody, "Jesus," 305.

67. Susanna Snyder illustrates this in "Looking Through the Bars: Immigration Detention and the Ethics of Mysticism," *Journal of the Society of Christian Ethics* 35, no. 1 (Spring–Summer 2015): 167–87.

68. Sarah Miller, "Faith-Based Organizations and International Responses to Forced Migration," in *The Changing World Religion Map: Sacred Places, Identities, Practices, and Politics*, ed. Stanley Brunn (Dordrecht: Springer, 2015), 3115–33, at 3126.

69. Snyder et al., "Immigration Detention," 170.

70. Michael Downey, *Understanding Christian Spirituality* (Mahwah, NJ: Paulist Press, 1997), 14.

71. See Mary Jo Leddy, *At the Border Called Hope: Where Refugees Are Neighbors* (Toronto: HarperCollins, 1997).

72. See Anthony Kelly, *Eschatology and Hope* (Maryknoll, NY: Orbis, 2006).

73. Peter Phan, "Where We Come From, Where We Are, and Where We Are Going: Asian and Pacific Catholics in the United States," *American Catholic Studies* 118, no. 3 (2007): 1–26, at 25–26.

CHAPTER 5

Wives Submitting to Husbands: Domestic Violence, Women, and the Christian Faith

Cristina Lledo Gomez

An ABC News report on domestic violence tells this story:

> Grace had already left one abusive relationship with the father of her
> daughter in the Philippines when she met a man she thought was the
> one. The man with the kind words wooed her parents as much as her,
> and she thought it would be a fresh start, . . . a chance to leave the
> slums of Manila. "He's really nice, he's like an angel to me. . . . And
> because I long for a man who protects me, that's why I say: 'Wow, I
> think I found right person,'" said Grace (not her real name). But her
> lover's behaviour changed as soon as she arrived in Australia—he was
> physically and sexually abusive and controlling.[1]

The story of "Grace" (an alias), a fifty-year-old Filipina bookkeeper, is
just one among those of many other migrant women who experience the
double difficulties of settling into a new country and dealing with domestic violence. Migrant women can experience violence through their partners who are citizens of their host countries. The men often "woo" them
into relocating to their countries and, once in the country, will abuse them
and isolate them from help. Migrant women can also experience violence
via their male partners who migrate with them and hold particular beliefs
about their dominance in the family as the male sex. The pressures of settling in; the beliefs held about men's and women's roles; and finding oneself

powerless without employment, limited English, and even clashing with a new culture—all could lead to the vulnerability of migrant women to domestic violence.

In the past year, the COVID-19 pandemic added extra vulnerabilities for migrant women who are victim-survivors of domestic violence. The closure of support charities sponsored by nongovernmental organizations, culturally specific support systems, and places of worship—along with the inability of migrant women on temporary visas to access refuges, emergency relief, and medical care, and the increased fear of deportation due to increased insecurity during the pandemic—have just been some of the many ways in which migrant women victim-survivors of domestic violence have had increased vulnerabilities during the pandemic.[2]

This chapter is concerned not only with the misuse or misunderstanding of Christian beliefs to justify violence against migrant women and girls (VAWG) but also the norms, practices, and structures that perpetuate VAWG and are reinforced by these misunderstandings and/or misuses of Christian beliefs. The beliefs include those on martyrdom, sin, forgiveness, Jesus's sacrifice, God as Father, and covenant marriage. The norms, practices, and structures include gender inequality, little or narrow discussions on healthy sexuality and relationships (if any at all), a history of violence that normalizes violence against females, and a context that enables other oppressions to exist.

This chapter begins by defining domestic violence, its prevalence, types, and risk factors. Second, it names the particularities of being a migrant and experiencing domestic violence. Third, it addresses key theological Christian concepts that have been misunderstood or misused and the norms, structures, and practices that support and perpetuate violence against women and girls. Finally, it presents ways in which the Church can address these norms, structures, practices, and beliefs through preventive and proactive community actions.

In theologizing about migration, Peter Phan has often proposed a three-fold approach: socioanalytic mediation, hermeneutical mediation, and practical mediation.[3] For Phan, socioanalytic mediation, borrowing the term from Clodovis Boff, is about telling stories from the ground, and thus providing context or location for the theologizing.[4] Phan also turns to the Latinx theologians who would call for this approach as attending to *lo cotidiano*, the daily activities and even the mundane—it is about attending to the realities, just as this chapter begins, not only to the realities of women experiencing domestic violence all over the world but also to the particular realities of migrant women experiencing domestic violence in the Australian setting.

The second, hermeneutical mediation seeks to view the sociological and historical data within the Christian tradition, turning to Christian texts, the Bible and doctrinal tradition, to give the data and the realities their proper theological mediation. By exploring the Christian texts and concepts that have been misused or misunderstood to justify VAWG, this chapter thus attends to this second part of Phan's migrational theological approach.

Finally, in presenting ways in which the Church can begin or improve its ways of resisting violence against women and girls, the chapter attends to practical mediation. For Phan, a turn to praxis is not simply attending to the preferential option for the poor to which the individual theologian is called but is also about the pistic criteriology of theology, borrowing the term again from Boff.[5] Phan explains that pistic criteriology is the "inherent capacity of faith for sociopolitical transformation."[6] If faith does not enable this transformation, then praxis questions the alleged truths of faith, the theory, and inversely the theory refines and shapes praxis—making faith praxis distinct from poiesis, a practice that has no history and no context.[7]

DOMESTIC VIOLENCE

Domestic violence is a pattern of abusive behavior carried out by a family member or other significant relationship (e.g., de facto partner) that is threatening or harmful to other members of the family or relationship. It is the use of power and control by one person over another or others, and results in fear, distress, and often isolation. Domestic violence can also result in serious physical injury. The Australian Bureau of Statistics reports that in 2019 alone "about one in three homicide offences (30% [or 125 victims]) and sexual assaults (33% [or 8,985 victims]) were family and domestic violence related."[8] Females constituted an alarming majority (83 percent, or 22,337) of victims of sexual assault.[9] In 2020, multicultural and domestic family violence specialists in New South Wales, Australia reported:

- an increase in migrant and refugee women clients since the outbreak of the pandemic;
- an escalation or worsening of violence experienced by migrant and refugee women during the pandemic;
- that migrant and refugee women were reporting violence and abuse specifically related to the COVID-19 crisis (e.g., financial pressures, having children at home, or other stresses that served as triggers for the abuse);

- an increase in migrant and refugee women experiencing escalating violence in the context of sharing childcare arrangements with an abusive partner during the pandemic lockdown; and
- that their clients' fears of deportation increased due to visa insecurity during the pandemic.[10]

On a global scale, the World Health Organization (WHO) reports that "about 1 in 3 (35 percent) of women worldwide have experienced either physical and/or sexual intimate partner violence or non-partner sexual violence in their lifetime." Further, 38 percent of all murders of women are committed by male intimate partners.[11] In terms of the COVID-19 pandemic, the Migration Data Portal reported there was a general significant increase in gender-based violence all over the world,[12] citing a report that pointed to a 90 percent increase in domestic violence in China due to the pandemic.[13] Meanwhile, the Institute for Research into Superdiversity at the University of Birmingham reports an increase in sexual and gender-based violence along with increased vulnerabilities among forced migrant survivors of sexual and gender-based violence due to the pandemic.[14]

Often, people associate domestic violence with physical and sexual violence, but other types of domestic violence can also combine with or be used as a lead up to physical and/or sexual violence: psychological abuse, verbal abuse, financial abuse, coercive control, and spiritual or religious abuse. Psychological and emotional abuse include intimidation, belittling, humiliation, and being exposed to violence toward another family member. Coercive control includes isolating victims from family and friends, controlling access to finances, monitoring their movements, and restricting access to information and assistance. Meanwhile, spiritual and/or religious abuse include misuses of Scripture or the pulpit to control behavior, requirements of secrecy and silence or pressure to conform, and the suggestion that the abuser has a "divine" position and a requirement of obedience to the abuser.[15]

The risk factors leading to the vulnerability of women experiencing domestic violence fall under four areas of influence: societal, community, interpersonal, and individual. Examples of risk factors include, at the *societal* level, an "absence or lack of enforcement of laws addressing violence against women, and gender discrimination in institutions (e.g., police, health)"; at the *community* level, "harmful gender norms that uphold male privilege and limit women's autonomy," and "high levels of poverty and unemployment"; at the *interpersonal* level, "high levels of inequality in relationships / male-controlled relationships / dependence on partner" and "men's use of drugs and harmful use of alcohol"; and, at the *individual* level, "childhood experience of violence and/or exposure to violence in the family" and "attitudes condoning or justifying violence as normal or acceptable."[16]

Some contrasting protective factors in the same areas of influence include, at the *societal* level, "laws that promote gender equality, promote women's access to formal employment, and address violence against women"; at the *community* level, norms that "support non-violence and gender equitable relationships and promote women's empowerment"; at the *interpersonal* level, intimate relationships characterized by "gender equality, including in shared decision-making and household responsibilities; and, finally, at the individual level, "secondary education for women and men and less disparity in education levels between women and men, and both men and boys and women and girls are socialized to, and hold gender equitable attitudes."[17]

Viewing the risk factors and contrasting protective factors given above, one can conclude that for WHO, gender norms, beliefs, structures, and practices play a large role in the perpetuation as well as the prevention or resistance to VAWG both inside and outside the domestic space. WHO itself points to gender inequality and the acceptability of VAWG as norms, as the root causes of violence against women.[18]

Anne Marie Choup, a professor of political science, points to no single cause of gender-based violence, but rather to three interconnecting causes: "history, gender inequality, and dramatic changes to social and economic order leading to social displacement."[19] She argues that government policy that seeks to provide services to survivors of domestic violence, rather than policies that seek to address its root causes, treats a complex and deeply rooted problem superficially and in a reactive rather than a proactive manner.

In terms of history, Choup points to the historic pattern of toleration of gender-based violence that needs to be disrupted as a major cause of violence against women. She argues that this disruption can only happen when there is a deliberate approach that takes into consideration those who benefit (namely, males with privilege) as a barrier to the disruption of the pattern.[20]

With regard to gender inequality, Choup argues that violence against women exists intersectionally—that is, alongside other inequalities, such as those based on race and ethnicity that in turn support the unequal treatment of women.[21] She proposes that "these inequalities were cultivated and institutionalized for reasons of maintaining power and specific forms of social order."[22] Although other factors, such as individual (e.g., exposure to abuse and disposition of the person) and community (e.g., economic downturn and isolation), play a role in VAWG, the presence of persistent inequality in its various forms in society creates an environment in which inequality is the norm and thus tolerates the abuse against women. By simply addressing domestic violence rather than intersectional inequality, we superficially treat "a complex and deep-rooted problem."[23]

The displacement of men within social or economic hierarchies as a result of rapid social change, stressful life events, and economic downturn, in conjunction with a history of violence against women and gender inequality, results in either new or increased violence, according to Choup. She says if the history of inequality were not present, "economic stress would most likely not trigger violence against women."[24] Citing Pickup, Williams, and Sweetman, Choup argues that "it is the loss of male dominance [that] either triggers new violence or increases levels of violence already in place."[25]

DOMESTIC VIOLENCE AND REFUGEE AND MIGRANT WOMEN AND GIRLS

According to Australia's National Research Organisation for Women's Safety (ANROWS), "the types of violence experienced by CALD [culturally and linguistically diverse] women differ to non-immigrant women including 'multi-perpetrator family violence, and the impact of violence and abuse exacerbated by immigration policy, visa status and the stressors of the migration experience generally.'"[26] For Kaur and Atkin, the research on the experience of domestic violence against women from CALD communities is unclear.[27] They argue that this nonrecognition of ethnic women in the research can be seen as "play[ing] into systemic institutional racism and white privilege," contributing thus to the upholding of "hegemonic norms," "processes of othering," and the reinforcement of factors ("race, ethnicity, social class, patriarchy, religion, immigration status, and linguistic diversity"), which intersect and lead to further vulnerabilities and oppression.[28] Thus, for migrant women and girls, the experiences of domestic violence differ from those of nonimmigrant women because of their intersectional experience.

The key experiences that emerge for migrant and refugee women in domestic violent situations are isolation and powerlessness. The contributing factors to these experiences include the type of visa on entry into host countries (the immigration context); the normalization of violence, especially of one sex over another (family and community context); the limitations of services offered and a lack of collaboration with other organizations (the service context); and the extra challenges of living in a regional area (place-based context). The four contexts mentioned above are the overarching contexts in which women experience domestic violence, seek help, and get access to information and services.[29] This chapter focuses on the familial and community context, given the possibility for influence and change in this area for the Christian community.

DOMESTIC VIOLENCE, MIGRANT WOMEN, AND THE FAMILY COMMUNITY CONTEXT

The ANROWS Aspire Project reports that in families and communities, domestic violence can be normalized.[30] A range of social, religious, and personal values in various cultural contexts can support beliefs that "men should have power over women and control the family environment," as the anecdotes below exemplify:[31]

> And even now, I'm not going to church anymore, because I feel shame to see the community people. And some people ignoring me, so I feel something bad about myself.

> Ah my mum very, she's very old thinking. . . . Always talk to my mum about my situation, about his behaviour. But she talk to me, all men are like him and it's normal.

> I think it's a power thing, because we are taught that men are the head of the family. You know, so they are the boss of the home, so whatever they say goes, . . . they can get away with anything, but in the process, women are suffering.[32]

It is often the case that women from CALD communities are pressured to prioritize their family over themselves and their family's need to settle after the difficulties of migrating, even when the women are experiencing violence:

> For women in emerging [CALD] communities, the disclosure of family violence may exacerbate their sense of isolation with the added burden of shame associated with 'failure' in the new country. Immigrant women are often under extreme pressure to keep the family together in a situation where other supports are absent, in a context where English is not a familiar language, and the culture and legal system of the new country are not well understood. Where a family has already undergone the difficulties of immigration, and where they may feel isolated because of their perceived "difference," maintaining the integrity of the family unit becomes an imperative beyond the woman's individual sense of safety.[33]

Some women are encouraged by family members not to take action against their perpetrator and have been threatened with community ostracism and/or personal harm if they were to take action. The support for this extends to family members living overseas, further increasing the isolation of CALD woman in a domestic violent situation. An asylum seeker reports her own experience of prioritizing her family over herself, even minimizing her own violence and comparing it with the immense difficulties of seeking asylum:

> Sometimes you have this big problem, you're confused and think am I gonna be able to solve it? Is it gonna come to an end? And then you have another problem, like sexual violence or maybe ah like maybe you're beaten by your partner or your husband, so your mind becomes so much occupied by this asylum seeker thing, you end up thinking these other ones are just too, they're not as serious as what you have. Because like seeking asylum, it's about like, that's your life. So, it occupies your mind and it's like a very big mountain you know, you're trying to climb, so these other ones, you tend to . . . so you're sexually abused or molested there, so you're like ok, it's not as serious as what you have at the moment."[34]

And yet there are families and communities that could be relied upon as a source of support for the woman, as a source of help to escape from the perpetrator, and as a source of help to establish new lives, to seek support services, and to inform her of her rights.

KEY THEOLOGICAL CONCEPTS USED TO JUSTIFY DOMESTIC VIOLENCE

From January 2017 to December 2018, I was the social justice coordinator for the Diocese of Broken Bay in Sydney. During this time, I had met with clergy, parish social justice groups, police, local councils, and legal and social services within the diocese to survey the top three social issues of each parish. Consistently, domestic violence appeared on the list. At the same time, I constantly heard from gatherings addressing domestic violence that Christian teachings were being used and misused to justify violence. Given my knowledge as a theologian, my experience as the social justice coordinator, and learnings about the issues for women experiencing domestic violence, including in CALD communities, I decided to create "A Catholic Response to Domestic Violence."[35] This parish resource was created in conjunction with the social service, Catholic Care Broken Bay, and the Broken Bay Diocese Safeguarding Office for the promotion of safety for both children and vulnerable adults within Catholic institutions in the diocese. The resource was created to equip priests and parishioners alike for recognizing violence in families and relationships, for denouncing and rejecting any toleration for violence, and for working toward a culture of peace, safety, and justice for all.

On one hand, the "Catholic Response" resource can be described as differing from others already published because it sought to address the root factors of domestic violence. On the other hand, it also had its limitations, given that there were constraints involved in being a diocesan publication—namely, it could not critique a critical factor in the perpetuation of domestic violence: the Church's governance structure, which excludes females from its ecclesial decision-making powers and in the building up of communities as its ordained leaders. Because of this limitation, this resource could also be accused of promoting soft complementarianism—denouncing violence on one hand but upholding patriarchy on the other hand. Another initial limitation of the resource was that it was only written in English, making it difficult for migrant and refugee women from CALD communities to access. However, it was eventually republished in Tagalog, Vietnamese, and Korean, which was very appropriate, given the high volume of domestic violence incidents occurring within these communities; but it was seen as a taboo subject leading to misinformation and further isolation for victim-survivors.

From practitioners on the ground—including social workers, local councils, and pastoral leaders—to survivors of domestic abuse and literature on Christianity and domestic violence, the common misconstruing of Christian belief to perpetuate and normalize domestic violence fall into four main areas: first, biblical proof-texting or literalistic approaches to certain Bible texts; second, and connected to the first, the imagining of God as exclusively male; third, misunderstandings of soteriological concepts, such as on forgiveness, sin and grace, and sacrifice and martyrdom; and fourth, ignorance with regard to covenant marriage and canon law.

Biblical Proof-Texting

On biblical proof-texting, perpetrators of abuse turn to the classic line from Saint Paul's household codes: "Wives submit to your husbands" (Eph. 5:28; 1 Cor. 11:3; Col. 3:18–19) in order to justify abuse against their female spouses. But Paul's uses of the household codes were about encouraging Christians to keep harmony in their households by following the structures of society. The man, as the paterfamilias, the head of his household, had such power over everyone in his household—women, children, and slaves—that civil law allowed for him to kill anyone within that household. At the same time, Saint Paul also challenged those in power, the paterfamiliae, to not abuse their power and show kindness. The domestic violence kit I had created pointed to the unequivocal statement that men and women today could equally be seen as heads of their households and the fact that civil law today clearly states it is a crime to physically or sexually harm another person.

Violence as an act of love can be justified using texts from the Bible in turn justifying domestic violence. For example, in Hebrews, chapter 12, the writer tells his audience that the suffering they are enduring is from God and that it is an act of love, where God is the loving Father and the suffering audience are his sons. Punishment is acknowledged as painful but also argued as being for the good of those loved by the male God, the divine authority. When violence is confused with being an act of love, this only serves to confuse the victim-survivor about what is the most loving and life-giving choice for themselves, their children (if any are involved), and their partner-perpetrator. For as an abuse survivor, your idea of a normal or at least familiar relationship is one marked by abuse mixed with and mistaken for love.

God as Male

The second theological justification used by perpetrators of abuse is the imagining of God as a divine male. In Genesis 2, perpetrators argue that this God not only creates the first person as a male but also creates it as *imago Dei*. Further, perpetrators argue that a woman is derived from this man, which then evidences her secondary role; like other creatures on Earth, she is also to be lorded over. The original draft of the parish kit, which sought to point out that the Adam and Eve story was a myth derived from other creation myths, was not approved by the director within my office because he believed people would not cope with the creation story as a myth. In the end, the author overcame this difficulty by simply referring to the creation by God (who is neither male nor female) of both Adam and Eve, both in God's image, as of one flesh, a unity (from Gen. 2:25) who stood side by side with each other. This is not the best exegesis of Genesis 2, and it can lead to a complementarity view justifying gender binarism; but in the least showed that it was wrong to imagine a male God as creating the first human as male.

The image of God as male is reinforced in the Eucharistic liturgy, where the lectionary uses exclusively male language referring to God as a male and referring to God's children as simply God's sons. Though the pope has recently changed canon law to allow women to officially be installed as lectors and altar servers, priesthood, leadership of the community in the Catholic tradition, remains barred from women. When women do not appear in the language of the community in their texts and their rituals, in the representation of the community as leaders and decision-makers (given that it is the ordained who make decisions for the Church community), the inferiority of women to men continues to be communicated, despite arguments by male clergy and nonclergy alike that both men and women have equal dignity but simply have separate roles—for women to give birth because of their biological makeup, and for men to lead, because they cannot give birth.

Forgiving Seventy Times Seven

Third, perpetrators and victims have used the excuse that Christians are instructed by Jesus to forgive seventy times seven (Mt. 18:22) and that the state of humanity is to be sinful, fallen. Therefore, they fall into a trap of thinking that abuse is normal, and that as long as a perpetrator shows remorse and tries to make up for his violence, it is OK to stay in a violent relationship.[36] Further, the valorization of suffering is concretized in women who have been beatified and canonized by the Catholic Church. For example, Saint Elisabetta Canori Mora of Italy endured physical and psychological violence from her husband, and even when she was advised by her confessor to leave her husband, she stayed with him because she felt God had entrusted to her her violent husband through the Sacrament of Marriage. She is canonized because of her commitment to the Christian Sacrament of Marriage at the cost of her own life. Another example is Saint Rita of Cascia, who endured domestic violence in order that her husband would eventually be transformed through her love and devotion to him. She became a saint, again for her commitment to marriage, despite the violence and threat to her life. In an indirect way, even saints such as Agnes of Rome—who was not married but endured various forms of violence from men, in order to keep her virginal purity—contributes to the valorization of the suffering of women and girls. This valorization is embedded in Catholic tradition such that on the feast of Saint Agnes, January 21, two lambs (because Agnes in Latin translates as "lamb") are brought from the Trappist Abbey of the Three Fountains in Rome so that they may be blessed by the pope and their wools can become woven into "pallias" to be presented to and worn on the feasts of Saints Peter and Paul to newly appointed metropolitan archbishops, to show their jurisdictional authority and unity with the pope. Though Saint Agnes had died in the early fourth century, this tradition only began in the sixteenth century and continues to this day.

It is inappropriate to display upon the shoulders of clergy the reminder of the abuse of a young girl (Agnes was thirteen years old at the time of her abuse and death), in light of the scandals of abuse by clergy of children and vulnerable adult women. This example shows that embedded into the Church structure and practice is the norm of valorizing the suffering of women. Yet the practice may be seen as innocuous, and it may be argued by defenders of the practice that it in fact valorizes women rather than their suffering. But such lack of insight into the insidious messages of the sacrifice of the lambs only enables the perpetuation and normalization of violence against women and girls.

Lack of insight also occurs with regard to what constitutes being in a healthy, unhealthy, or violent relationship. Often, both perpetrator and victim can be highly unaware that they are trapped in a cycle of violence (see figure 5.1). Some survivors of domestic abuse speak of encountering the image of the cycle of violence for the first time, and that this was their moment of realization that they were in a domestically violent situation. Perpetrators can also see the cycle of violence and recognize that their actions are a choice. Often, both perpetrators and victims, and their families, make excuses for the violence: for example, he was drunk and he would normally not touch his wife; or he was going through stress from work or post-traumatic stress disorder from his childhood and therefore he did not mean to hit her; or he just had a moment of violence, and he would normally not harm his girlfriend. The kit emphasized that whatever excuses one made, committing violence against another person is and will always be a personal choice. Moreover, it named domestic violence as a sin and showed some of the possible stages involved in the lead-up to and the consequences of the sin of abuse.

In order to break the cycle of violence, the "Catholic Response" resource proposed that perpetrators needed to undertake the hard work of reparation and reconciliation with God and the harmed persons (as shown in figure 5.2). Instead of seeing his remorse—and, for example, the buying of gifts—as being "good enough" to repair a relationship, the perpetrator is encouraged to undertake the processes of truth-telling, acknowledgment of the wrongdoing, reparation for the violence, and seeing ways to relate differently to the harmed spouse, a way that moved toward adult relationships that provided safety, trust, and empowerment, especially for the survivor. Survivors of domestic violence especially point to the importance of truth-telling

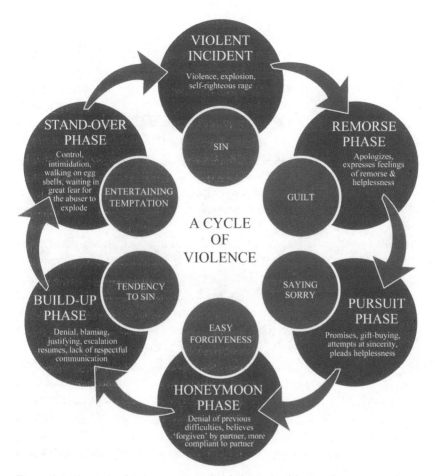

Figure 5.1 The Cycle of Violence—Aligned with the Cycle of the Sin of Domestic Violence

as the first step, because until perpetrator and victim acknowledge the truth of their situation, they can delude themselves into thinking that violence is normal, is manageable, and has no detrimental effects—and even if it does, it cannot be helped.

Further, as the stories of migrant and refugee women show, this truth-telling must also be something with which the whole community and families must engage to counter the normalization of violence and of the subjugation of women. Domestic violence can be a sign of intergenerational abuse, which makes it even more urgent to stop the endless cycle of violence using the cycle of true reconciliation.

Figure 5.2 A Cycle of True Reconciliation

Covenant Marriage

Fourth, ignorance in the area of covenantal marriages has meant that women have stayed in abusive marriages because "for better or worse, . . . in sickness and in health, till death do us part" is often interpreted as meaning that a spouse could never leave his or her marriage. Yet Canon 1055 §1 states that the marriage covenant "of its own very nature is ordered to the well-being of the spouses" alongside the "procreation and upbringing of children." When one spouse harms another, that is no longer looking after their well-being. As Canon 1153 §1 points out: "A spouse who occasions grave danger of soul or body to the other or to the children, or otherwise makes the common life unduly difficult, provides the other spouse with a lawful reason to leave, either by a decree of the local Ordinary or, if there is danger in delay, even on his or her own authority."

After delivering several talks in a few parishes within the Broken Bay Diocese on domestic violence, including the communication of the information given above from canon law and Pope Francis's own denouncing of domestic violence, the author received a number of emails and face-to-face feedback of how important these pieces of information were to Church audiences.[37] Further, some women felt comfortable enough to tell stories of their mothers and grandmothers staying within marriages or feeling shame at leaving their abusive marriages because they believed marriage was forever, no matter what, according to Church teaching.

International priests have a unique role in countering domestic violence against migrant women. By their very presence, some migrant women may find affinity with them if they are from the same country of origin and therefore are more likely to disclose domestic abuse to them. But migrant priests can also be reluctant to engage in the fight against domestic violence because they can come from cultures where patriarchy is normative. Further, given that gender inequality is at the heart of violence against women, some international priests can believe the fight against gender inequality is the fight of unreasonable and angry Catholic feminists who in the end have a single agenda, which is the ordination of women in the Catholic Church.

After a training session on domestic violence, one international priest communicated to the author: "I've been in Australia for over thirty years. We are in a crisis over our sexual identity because men do not know how to be men and women how to be women. But if you look at my father and mother, there is no abuse there because they know their place in society. My father does not ask my mother to mow the lawn because that is a man's job, and my mother likewise does not ask my father to wash the dishes because that is a woman's job." This view is not surprising in one sense, because the deeply embedded patriarchy in Christianity is not something that would simply disappear overnight; just because the surrounding culture upholds the equality of men and women, it does not mean Christianity has aligned with the surrounding culture. In another sense, this view is surprising because such views expressed in civil society would be considered ones from a long-gone era.

Looking toward another researcher, who argues for the connection between Christianity and domestic violence, we see similar findings as I have argued above.[38] Through her exploration of the power of language to either perpetuate or break the cycle of violence in Christian families, Leonie Westenberg points to three areas in which language is used to perpetuate domestic violence: (1) women's submission and male leadership; (2) the sanctity of marriage (and its unbreakable bond); and (3) the value of suffering and the virtue of forgiveness (in other literature, this is described as the valorization of suffering and the offering of cheap forgiveness or cheap grace).[39] Westenberg critiques various documents created by different Christian denominations within Australia to raise awareness of domestic violence in churches because ultimately they do not address the root factors of violence. She says of the Anglican Diocese of Melbourne's "Preventing Violence Against Women" document, "the programmes advocated . . . fail to address possible causal issues that relate to theological language concerning marriage. The programmes instead choose to focus on factors that may indicate the presence of abuse."[40] This can result in even the denial of the presence of domestic violence within congregations.

On the Catholic Bishops' Council in Victoria's pastoral statement and parish kits, Westenberg comments that they "[emphasise] responses to domestic violence" but [do] not engage in "an examination of causal factors."[41] She further comments on "Protestant and Evangelical churches that teach 'soft complementarianism' (denouncing of violence whilst upholding male headship within communities and families)—they too fail to address the root causes of violence which includes the promotion of complementarity of the sexes (equal but different)."[42] Samuel Wells makes the important point that "women have been regarded almost entirely as receivers of the Christian tradition, rather than its co-creators."[43] Therefore, in order to change the ideology, Wells says the identity of the ideologues also need to change.[44]

During Pope Francis's pontificate, he has denounced domestic violence more often than his predecessors.[45] More recently, he has named the monthly prayer intention as being for women experiencing domestic violence. Unfortunately, the language used is passive, highlighting women's victimhood rather than the male perpetrators' sin of abuse. Part of truth-telling within the cycle of reconciliation that this chapter promotes involves naming the act of sin rather than simply the victims of the sin, for naming is part of the process of ownership of sin and thus ownership of reparation and rebuilding.

CHRISTIANITY AND DOMESTIC VIOLENCE

What are we seeing here? In the Christian community, the normalization of gender inequality and lack of diversity in language and representation; the valorization of women's and girls' suffering to the point of death for the sake of evangelization and conversion of the sinner; the misuse of texts, concepts, and teachings to justify violence against women and girls; the ascribing of an exclusive gender to God—these are just some of the norms, practices, and structures existing within Christianity that communicate gender inequality and violence, abuse, and the lessening of the status of women and girls in the Church as the norm, despite the foundational Catholic social principle of human dignity, which includes the equal dignity of women to men. As paragraphs 1931 and 1935 of the *Catechism of the Catholic Church* (CCC) respectively state: "Respect for the human person proceeds by way of respect for the principle that 'everyone should look upon his neighbor (without any exception) as another self.' The equality of men [and women] rests essentially on their dignity as persons and the rights that flow from it: 'Every form of social or cultural discrimination in fundamental personal rights on the grounds of sex, race, color, social conditions, language, or religion must be curbed and eradicated as incompatible with God's design.'"

Some proponents of soft complementarianism utilize CCC paragraph 1928 to argue for "women's dignity but difference" to men according to their "nature" as the only sex able to birth: "Society ensures social justice when it provides the conditions that allow associations or individuals to obtain what is their due, according to their nature and their vocation. Social justice is linked to the common good and the exercise of authority." But as CCC paragraphs 1931 and 1935 show, equal dignity and rights belong to all persons "without exception," be it sex, race, color, social conditions, language, or religion that differentiates them from another person.

Using Choup's threefold breakdown of the cause of gender-based violence, we can see from another perspective how domestic violence can continue to be normalized and perpetuated in the Church. First, it must be acknowledged that the existence of the historic pattern of the promotion of gender inequality in the Church and that male clerics have benefited from this form of inequality for centuries. Thus, it is without surprise that often one finds the cleric who makes excuses and continues to make excuses for the barring of women from ordination and decision-making and leadership roles in the Church, citing Church tradition, biblical texts (via proof-texting), and soft complementarianism. Recently, by changing canon law so that women can be installed as lectors and acolytes in the Church,[46] and by appointing a woman as undersecretary of a Synod of Bishops, giving her voting rights,[47] Pope Francis has begun the interruption of the pattern of gender inequality in the Church.

Second, from an intersectional perspective, though racial and ethnic diversity seems to be a nonissue in the Church, with more vocations coming from non-Western countries and assisting Western churches, other injustices continue to exist within the Church and thus enable gender inequality to exist as part of an ecclesial culture of injustice and oppression. This includes nonaccountability and nontransparency still applied from within many local churches, bishops' offices, and synod of bishops' gatherings.[48] Until churches decide to examine and root out the various forms of injustices within them and their institutions, gender inequality will continue to exist as part of the culture of ecclesial injustice.

Finally, though men retain their exclusive access to ordination, their displacement from traditional male-only leadership positions in other areas of life, within the social, economic, and domestic spheres, alongside a history of female exclusion from other ministries within the Church, and the history of abuse of religious women by ordained males only serve to provide justifications for misogyny and/or gender inequality within the Church. Thus, by perpetuating gender inequality, the Church inadvertently contributes to the normalization of violence against women and girls.

A ROLE FOR CHURCHES

Churches and specifically leaders of Christian communities have the unique position of being able to address many of the difficulties named above. Changing the language used in Church from male-exclusive to female-inclusive language and the veneration of female saints not for their purity and martyrdom in marriage but for their contribution to society, by their resistance to violence, are just some of the ways gender inequality in the Church can begin to be addressed and resisted. Other practices and systemic changes that can be made within the limitations of our Church today are:

- Reeducating and realigning believing communities toward denouncing violence in any way, shape, or form; upholding a culture of dignity and respect for all; and prioritizing peace for churches and families, which is essentially partnered with justice, through the language, practices, symbols, and policies used and promoted from the pulpit to the actions of parish members (the family and community context).[49] Faith communities thus must ask the hard questions of what it means to blindly follow the same rituals that ignore women and acknowledge only males, overtly and underhandedly. Faith communities must ask what it even means to proclaim texts of violence, as in Hebrews 12; how this sends mixed messages about violence and love; how this may affect victim-survivors in the community; and how this participates in the normalization of violence.
- Encouraging the parish community to gather specifically to address the issue of vulnerable migrants on temporary visas (the immigration

context). That is, making the issue of migrants a parish priority, just as much as making disciples or faith formation, may be a priority for the parish. This prioritizing aligns with the vision of the Church as being about integral human development in all that it proclaims and performs. The Church cannot be simply concerned with faith development or making disciples because it is and should be about developing the whole person with his or her various dimensions (physical, spiritual, social, psychological, intellectual, and political development). As Pope Benedict XVI says in *Caritas in veritate*: "The whole Church, in all her being and acting—when she proclaims, when she celebrates, when she performs works of charity—is engaged in promoting integral human development."[50]

- Working in collaboration with local councils, social services, police, and legal services to communicate a consistent message of no tolerance for violence and dignity and respect for all (the service context). This is also the integral human developmental approach, which Pope Francis emphasized by creating the Dicastery for Promoting Integral Human Development and placing the Pontifical Council for Pastoral Care of Migrants and Itinerant People under this dicastery alongside the Pontifical Councils for Justice and Peace, "Cor Unum," and Pastoral Health Care Workers—signaling the approach of collaboration with regard to justice and the Church. No longer can the Church act in silos when it approaches justice or concern for all creation. The Church must work collaboratively with as many agencies as possible, toward a common good, if it will truly effect real human and societal development.[51]

- Assigning competent and professional religious leaders and workers in parishes in regional areas, particularly from CALD (culturally and linguistically diverse) communities, ideally trained in recognizing and responding to domestic violence (the place-based context). In addition, religious leaders have the unique position to educate against racism, discrimination, and cultural exclusion by speaking of and creating a culture of welcome and inclusion in the parish. This is just one way of applying Pope Francis's "Responding to Refugees and Migrants: Twenty Pastoral Action Points," in order to truly welcome, promote, protect, and integrate the migrant, refugee, and asylum seeker.[52]

Of the four contexts, churches and their leaders can make a real difference in changing the story for the family and community context. ANROWS partnered with the Victorian State government and Our Watch, aptly named its shared framework for the primary prevention of violence against women and their children in Australia, "Change the Story," because the story on the normalization of violence truly needs to be changed (as the anecdotes from migrant women experiencing domestic violence have shown above).

CONCLUSION

This chapter has shown a picture of the risk factors and protective factors against domestic violence, in particular with regard to migrant and refugee women. It has also shown that churches can respond already by creating cultures of safety and justice for all and seeking ways to address the four contexts in which migrant and refugee women experience domestic violence. Four theological arguments often used by perpetrators, victims, and their communities alike were also explored. Parish priests can reeducate their congregations by clarifying Christian teachings used to perpetuate and normalize violence. Seminary training could also ensure that priests are equipped with ways to recognize violence and create cultures of safety and justice.

International priests have a unique role in fighting against the abuse of migrant and refugee women because they appear as migrants themselves. But they too can be a block to the denouncing of domestic violence in the aversion of some to the phrase "gender inequality," which can be misconstrued as domestic violence being a "women's issue" rather than a men's issue, in that men can seek to dominate, control, and humiliate women simply for being women.

Seminary training for priests and ongoing training for priests and parishioners alike should include an awareness of the signs of domestic violence and how to respond to this issue as individuals and as a community. But more than this, it should be communicated that denouncing violence and providing practical help is not enough. Churches will need to truly ask themselves how they can continue to promote violence by promoting patriarchy and the subjugation of women, inadvertently, in the language, symbols, rituals, and texts that they use and their ways of governance and interacting within the congregation.

In Australia, in preparation for the 2021 Plenary Council, Catholic Churches have been gathering to discern and answer the question "What do you think God is asking of us in Australia at this time?"[53] One answer to this is hearing the cries of women and children experiencing domestic violence, particularly migrant and refugee women, and responding to them. They suffer in silence and isolation, and more so as CALD women, when they face the double difficulties of settling into a new country and dealing with domestic violence—because of gender inequality; because of a history of VAWG in churches, societies, and their own families; and because of the existence of other types of oppression and abuse. When the Church only attends to servicing the victims of domestic violence rather than asking how its structures and practices promote misogyny, abuse, and the protection of perpetrators, it is providing a band-aid solution to a complex problem. Patriarchy, misogyny, gender inequality, discrimination, and exclusion of women are not just "women's rights" issues; they are life-and-death issues—exacerbating the culture of abuse of women and girls, and resulting in the death of at least one woman per week in Australia and as many as 38 percent of murders of women committed by men globally.

NOTES

1. Ryma Tchier, "Domestic Violence Victims on Temporary Visas Left with No Escape Due to Legal Loophole," ABC News, March 23, 2018, www.abc.net.au/news/2018-03-23/no -escape-foreign-born-domestic-violence-victims-migration-act/9575756.

2. Hayley Foster, Beth Roman, Amani Mahmoud, and Chelsea Boyle (Women's Safety NSW, Advocating for Freedom from Violence), "Impact of COVID-19 on Migrant and Refugee Women Experiencing Domestic and Family Violence," July 31, 2020, 1–10, www .womenssafetynsw.org.au/wp-content/uploads/2020/07/31.07.20_Impact-of-COVID -on-Migrant-and-Refugee-women-experiencing-DFV_FINAL.pdf; Sandra Pertek, Jenny Phillimore, and Pip McKnight, "Forced Migration, SGBV and COVID-19: Understand- ing the Impact of COVID-19 on Forced Migrant Survivors of SGBV," May 2020, www .birmingham.ac.uk/Documents/college-social-sciences/social-policy/iris/2020/sgbv -covid-19.pdf.

3. See, e.g., Peter Phan, "The Experience of Migration as Source of Intercultural Theology," in *Contemporary Issues of Migration and Theology, Christianities of the World*, ed. Peter Phan and Elaine Padilla, 179–209 (New York: Palgrave Macmillan, 2013); and Peter Phan, "Deus Migrator: God the Migrant—Migration of Theology and Theology of Migration," *Theological Studies* 77 (2016): 845–68, at 855–57.

4. Phan, "Experience of Migration," 191–92.

5. Phan, 194.

6. Phan.

7. Phan.

8. Australian Bureau of Statistics, "Recorded Crime—Victims, Australia," July 9, 2020, www.abs.gov.au/statistics/people/crime-and-justice/recorded-crime-victims-australia /latest-release.

9. Australian Bureau of Statistics.

10. Foster et al., "Impact of COVID-19," 3–4.

11. World Health Organization (WHO), "Violence Against Women (2013)," November 29, 2017, www.who.int/news-room/fact-sheets/detail/violence-against-women.

12. Migration Data Portal, "Migration Data Relevant for the COVID-19 Pandemic," January 11, 2021, https://migrationdataportal.org/themes/migration-data-relevant-covid-19-pandemic.

13. Christina Haneef and Anushka Kalyanpur (CARE and International Rescue Committee), Global Rapid Gender Analysis for COVID-19, April 2020, https://insights .careinternational.org.uk/media/k2/attachments/CARE-IRC_Global-RGA-COVID -19_April-2020.pdf.

14. Pertek, Phillimore, and McKnight, "Forced Migration."

15. Cristina Lledo Gomez, "A Catholic Response to Domestic Violence," Catholic Diocese of Broken Bay, 2018; republished in 2020 in English, Korean, Filipino, and Chinese, www .bbcatholic.org.au/our-faith/life-marriage-and-family/social-justice/domestic-violence/ domestic-violence-response.

16. WHO, "Respect Women: Preventing Violence Against Women—A Framework for Policymakers," 2019, 1–26, at 6, www.unwomen.org/-/media/headquarters/attachments /sections/library/publications/2019/respect-women-preventing-violence-against -women-en.pdf?la=en&vs=5901.

17. WHO, "Respect Women," 7.

18. WHO, "Violence Against Women," November 29, 2017, www.who.int/news-room/fact -sheets/detail/violence-against-women; WHO, "International Day to Eliminate Violence Against Women," November 25, 2020, www.who.int/news-room/events/detail/2020/11 /25/default-calendar/international-day-to-eliminate-violence-against-women.

19. Anne Marie Choup, "Beyond Domestic Violence Survivor Services: Refocusing on Inequality in the Fight against Gender-Based Violence in the Americas," Bulletin of Latin American Research 35, no. 4 (2016): 452–66, at 455–56.

20. Choup, 458.

21. Choup.

22. Choup.

23. Choup.

24. Choup, 460.

25. Choup—citing F. Pickup, S. Williams, and C. Sweetman, Ending Violence Against Women: A Challenge for Development and Humanitarian Work (Oxford: Oxfam, 2001), 18–19, 127.

26. Cathy Vaughan, Erin Davis, Adele Murdolo, Jasmin Chen, Linda Murray, Regina Quiazon, Karen K. Block, and Deb Warr, Promoting Community-Led Responses to Violence against Immigrant and Refugee Women in Metropolitan and Regional Australia, Aspire Project Final Report (Alexandria, Australia: ANROWS, 2016), cited by Jatinder Kaur and Nina Atkin, "Nexus between Domestic Violence and Child Protection: Multidimensional Forms of Oppression Impacting on Migrant and Refugee Women in Australia," Australian Social Work 71 (2018): 238–48.

27. Kaur and Atkin, "Nexus," 243.

28. Kaur and Atkin.

29. Vaughan et al., Promoting Community-Led Responses, 3–4, at 3; more detail on the contexts can be found at 25–86.

30. Vaughan et al.

31. Vaughan et al., 4.

32. Jesuit Refugee Services Australia, Free from Violence Against Women and Girls (VAWG) Report 2018, 10, 12, https://aus.jrs.net/wp-content/uploads/sites/20/2020/11/Free -from-Violence-Against-Women-and-Girls-VAWG-Report-2018.pdf.

33. National Council to Reduce Violence Against Women and Their Children, "Background Paper to Time for Action: The National Council's Plan for Australia to Reduce Violence

against Women and their Children, 2009–2021," March 2009, 34, www.dss.gov.au/sites /default/files/documents/05_2012/background_paper_to_time_for_action.pdf.

34. Jesuit Refugee Services Australia, *Free from Violence*, 1–16, at 8.

35. Cristina "Gomez, "A Catholic Response to Domestic Violence."

36. See especially Christopher Ellison, John Bartkowski, and Kristin Andersen, "Are There Religious Variations in Domestic Violence?" *Journal of Family Issues* 20 (1999): 87–113; Sarah Wendt, "Christianity and Domestic Violence: Feminist Poststructuralist Perspectives," *Journal of Women and Social Work* 23 (2008): 144–55; and Gemma T. Cruz, "Liberating Theology: A Theological Exploration on the Challenge of Wife Battery to Christian Theology," in *Ecclesia of Women in Asia: Gathering the Voices of the Silenced*, ed. Evelyn Monteiro and Antoinette Gutzler (Delhi: ISPCK, 2005), 53–69.

37. Most recently, Pope Francis had denounced violence against women, particularly in domestic violent situations. See Cindy Wooden, "Pope Prays for Women, Especially Those Facing Domestic Violence," Catholic News Service, April 13, 2020, https:// cnstopstories.com/2020/04/13/Pope-prays-for-women-especially-those-facing -domestic-violence/#more-27098.

38. This chapter provides one example among numerous others that present the ways in which Christianity is misused to justify, perpetuate, and maintain violence against women and girls. For further insights, see Sarah Wendt, "Christianity and Domestic Violence," *Affilia* 23, no. 2 (2008): 144–55; Caroline Blyth, Emily Colgan, and Katie B. Edwards, *Rape Culture, Gender Violence, and Religion: Biblical Perspectives* (Cham: Springer International, 2018); and Andy J. Johnson, *Religion and Men's Violence Against Women* (New York: Springer, 2015).

39. "Leonie Westenberg, "'When She Calls for Help': Domestic Violence in Christian Families," *Social Sciences* 6 (2017): 71, 74. On topic areas within Christianity that promote and perpetuate violence against women, see, e.g., Cruz, "Liberating Theology"; Sharon Bowland, "Process Theology's Relevance for Older Survivors of Domestic Violence," *Journal of Pastoral Care and Counseling* 65, nos. 3–4 (2011): 1–9; and Joanne Carlson Brown, "Because of the Angels: Sexual Violence and Abuse," *Violence Against Women, Concilium 1994/1*, ed. Elisabeth Schüssler Fiorenza and Mary Shawn Copeland (London: SCM Press, 1994), 3–10.

40. Westenberg, "When She Calls," 73.

41. Westenberg.

42. Westenberg, 74.

43. Samuel Wells, "Domestic Violence," in *How Then Shall We Live? Christian Engagement with Contemporary Issues* (Norwich: Canterbury Press, 2016), 91–98, at 93.

44. Wells.

45. An example is Pope Francis, *Amoris laetitia: Post-Synodal Apostolic Exhortation on Love in the Family*, 2016, n. 54, 204, 229, www.vatican.va/content/francesco/en/apost_exhortations /documents/papa-francesco_esortazione-ap_20160319_amoris-laetitia.html.

46. Vatican News, "Pope Francis: Ministries of Lector and Acolyte to Be Open to Women," January 11, 2021, www.vaticannews.va/en/pope/news/2021-01/pope-francis-opens -ministries-lector-acolyte-women.html.

47. Gerard O'Connell, "For the First Time, Pope Francis Appoints a Woman with the Right to Vote as Undersecretary of the Synod of Bishops," *America Magazine*, February 6, 2021, www.americamagazine.org/faith/2021/02/06/pope-francis-women-synod-voting -nathalie-becquart-239941.

48. See, e.g., Catholics for Renewal, *Getting Back on Mission: Reforming Our Church Together* (Mulgrave, Australia: Garratt, 2019); and Brian Dive, *Accountability and Leadership in the Catholic Church: What Needs to Be Improved* (Cambridge: Cambridge Scholars, 2020). For a possible process of transparency in the Church, see Cristian Mendoza Ovando, "What Kind of Transparency for the Church? Proposing Operational Transparency for Processes, Solutions and Decisions in the Catholic Church," *Church, Communication and Culture* 5, no. 2 (2020): 210–34.

49. As discussed in more detail in the "Key Theological Concepts used to Justify Domestic Violence" section of this chapter.

50. Pope Benedict XVI, *Caritas in veritate*, n. 11, June 29, 2009, http://w2.vatican.va/content /benedict-xvi/en/encyclicals/documents/hf_ben-xvi_enc_20090629_caritas-in -veritate.html. See also Pope Paul VI, *Populorum progressio*, March 26, 1967, http:// w2.vatican.va/content/paul-vi/en/encyclicals/documents/hf_p-vi_enc_26031967 _populorum.html.

51. See Pope Francis, *Statutes of the Dicastery for Promoting Integral Human Development*, August 2016, http://w2.vatican.va/content/francesco/en/motu_proprio/documents /papa-francesco_20160817_statuto-dicastero-servizio-sviluppo-umano-integrale .html.

52. Pope Francis, "Responding to Refugees and Migrants: Twenty Pastoral Action Points," August 2017, https://drive.google.com/file/d/1ANaebbCUvsVItQyc3-o-EyoxSWtUA o5y/view.

53. See Australian Catholic Bishops Conference, *Plenary Council 2020*, 2018, http://plenary council.catholic.org.au.

PART II

CHRISTIAN IDENTITY
AND RELIGIOUS PLURALISM

Dialogue and Reconciliation in the Renaissance and in Vatican II

John W. O'Malley, SJ

Interreligious dialogue burst upon the Catholic Church in the aftermath of Vatican II's passage of its declaration on non-Christian religions, *Nostra aetate*. This declaration imposed upon the Church a brand-new task: being an agent of reconciliation among the religions of the world. The task fell to all Catholics, but most squarely on the popes, the leaders of the Catholic community.

INTERRELIGIOUS RELATIONS

Since the Second Vatican Council, the popes, especially Saint John Paul II and Pope Francis, have taken up the task of being agents of reconciliation with vigor and have become the major voices in the world today calling for reconciliation among the world's religions and for the end of hate-rhetoric, wars, and sometimes-unspeakable atrocities. No one needs to be told how rampant these evils are even today and how urgent is the need for the ministry of dialogue and reconciliation.

The evils we are experiencing are, therefore, the continuation of a long tradition that manifested itself in crusades and pogroms. The Holocaust was the wake-up call for the Church. It occurred in Germany, a country where some 40 percent of the population identified as Catholic and another 40 percent as Lutheran. Saint John XXIII's awareness of this scandal led him to insist that Vatican II issue a document on the relationship of the Church with the Jews, which resulted in *Nostra aetate*.

We therefore correctly interpret *Nostra aetate* as a radical break with the past and as opening for the Church a path along which it had never trod before. True though that is, we must reckon with the fact that through the ages, there was a nagging concern among some Christians that other religions were not altogether bad. We must reckon with the nagging doubt that God willed the damnation of everybody who was not a baptized Christian with faith in at least the dogmas of the Trinity and Incarnation. Would that not mean that God willed the damnation even of his holy patriarchs and prophets?

From the earliest days of the Church, therefore, some thinkers sought ways to explain how salvation for non-Christians might be possible. The Church Fathers wrestled with this problem, especially in relationship to Plato and other authors from classical Greek literature and philosophy. Some postulated that Plato had met either Jeremiah or Moses in Egypt or at least had read the Hebrew Scriptures.

A few based their reconciliation on the idea of a universal inspiration, a Logos, that God distributed to persons of goodwill who searched for him. The primary scriptural justification was a verse from the prologue to John's Gospel: the Logos was "the true light that enlightens every person" (Jn. 1:9).[1]

RENAISSANCE HUMANISM

Medieval thinkers were heirs to this tradition, but they did not give it particular prominence. That situation changed significantly with the Renaissance of the fifteenth and early sixteenth centuries. The humanists of that era were particularly concerned with the salvation of the classical authors they so admired, but some of them had broader concerns.

By far the most important visual monument to the tradition occurs in no less a place than the Sistine Chapel, in the frescoes painted by no less a person than Michelangelo.[2] Though not a humanist himself, Michelangelo was profoundly devout, moved in humanist circles, and was well read in the pertinent literature. His paintings are not simply beautiful works of art. They also convey a vision of humanity, often touched by divinity. It is too much to say that he was a theologian, but he was certainly a religious thinker.

Most visitors to the Sistine Chapel focus their attention on the central panels of the ceiling depicting episodes from the early chapters of Genesis and on the wall behind the altar depicting the Last Judgment. They pay less attention to the cycle of monumental frescos that alternate the prophets and the sibyls that run along the wall just under the central panels. Yet, the placing of Hebrew prophets and pagan sibyls on an equal basis in the popes' own chapel is certainly one of the most striking elements in that room filled with striking elements.

In the classical tradition, the sibyls were mantic priestesses who dwelt in shrines where they uttered enigmatic judgments and prophecies. A body of their supposed oracles, much of which was authored by Jews and Christians over the course of several centuries, was known to the Fathers and quoted by them. Messianic in character as many of their utterances were, they were evidently designed to help reconcile the pagan world to Jewish or Christian beliefs. In other words, they embody a three-way dialogue.

The messianic preoccupations of the sibyls were confirmed by the promise made by the Cumaean Sibyl in Virgil's eclogue of "a new progeny from heaven" that will initiate a "return of the Golden Age." Men and women of the Renaissance enthusiastically endorsed the venerable opinion that this utterance foretold the birth of Christ during the reign of Augustus, which was when Virgil wrote.

The significance of the sibyls becomes clear from the prominence Michelangelo accords the prophet Jonah. He places him at the center of the far wall, the first figure one sees when entering the chapel through the ceremonial door at the other end of the room. Why does Jonah occupy such an important space? He was, after all, only a minor prophet, not to be compared in importance with others such as Isaiah or Jeremiah.

Of the seven prophets in the Sistine Chapel, however, Jonah was the only one to have been a prophet to the Gentiles, preaching as he did to the people of Nineveh. He thus somehow unites in himself the function of both prophet and sibyl and suggests the essential identity of their messianic visions. The message of reconciliation gives visual form to an important feature of Renaissance humanism, his visual form's verbal counterpart, as will become clear below.

Contrary to what we have sometimes been led to believe, the Renaissance was a profoundly Christian era. Like every era, it had its share of sinners and rogues, some of whom wore clerical garments and held high positions in the Church. Recent scholarship has vindicated the Christian character of the Renaissance, one of whose manifestations are the religious and theological concerns of many of the humanists.

We must rid ourselves of the idea that there were both Christian humanists and pagan humanists. Scholars have not been able to find a pagan humanist, search though they will. There were of course some humanists who were not particularly interested in religious issues, but that does not make them pagan. Although the humanists defined themselves by their zeal in recovering and promoting the Greek and Roman classics, they were also keenly interested in other works from antiquity, including the Bible and the Fathers of the Church. They were also interested in exotic writings such as the Sibylline Books.

Even today, general histories of the Renaissance take little account of the religious and theological character of the humanist movement within them. This oblivion is particularly acute in histories of theology, which move seamlessly from late-medieval Scholasticism to the Reformation.[3] They do so because Luther's theology developed in part as a reaction to Scholasticism. Once the histories have established this fact, they go on to show how first, in reaction to Luther and the Reformation, Catholic theology developed a newly controversialist pattern; and second, how, independent of the Reformation, it also developed a renewed interest in the theology of Thomas Aquinas that ushered Scholasticism into a new phase in its development.

These histories invariably devote a few lines or a few paragraphs to Renaissance Humanism, especially for its contribution to the historical-critical methods applied to the Bible, as pioneered by Lorenzo Valla (1404–57) and carried forward by others, especially Erasmus (1466–1536). They might even mention Erasmus's famous clash with Luther over free will, in the years 1524–25, but that is generally the end of it.

They thus reduce to a passing mention an important chapter in the history of Western religious thought. The humanists of the Renaissance did much more than lay the groundwork for the textual criticism that the nineteenth and twentieth centuries further developed into a phenomenon with which we are so familiar today. They developed a theological vision based on sources and methodological principles that is strikingly similar to the sources and principles that animated the theological vision of Vatican II.

RENAISSANCE HUMANISM AND THE SECOND VATICAN COUNCIL

In this chapter, I describe the achievement of Renaissance humanism in that regard and point out ways in which it anticipated traits found in the Second Vatican Council, especially *Unitatis redintegratio* and *Nostra aetate*. I am not arguing a direct influence on Vatican II but simply point out how and why the two phenomena are similar. In the years preceding the council, however, a few theologians had in fact discovered and begun to appreciate the achievement of Erasmus and other humanists, and they found in them kindred souls.[4] Only to that degree was the Renaissance directly present at Vatican II.

The reassessment of the religious character of humanism that allows us to see clearly what earlier generations missed began in the 1950s, especially in Italy and North America. Between 1969 and 1972, for instance, three books appeared in Italy independently of one another showing that Valla, once considered the prince of pagan humanists, was in fact a Christian theologian of considerable merit.[5]

At about the same time, scholars celebrated the five hundredth anniversary of Erasmus's birth in 1466 with several important international conferences, which threw new light on the centrality of religious issues in his writings. By 1970, a resurgence of scholarship on religion in the Renaissance was in full swing, symbolized by the publication that year of Charles Trinkaus's two-volume book *"In Our Image and Likeness": Humanity and Divinity in Italian Renaissance Thought.*[6] This renaissance of the Renaissance climaxed a decade or so later but has continued at a reduced pace up to the present.

Humanism was essentially a cultural and educational movement that sought wisdom from the literary texts of classical antiquity, which were believed to be more authentic guides for a happy and constructive life than what was currently prevalent, especially in Scholastic philosophy and theology.

As much as the humanists admired both the wisdom and the eloquence of the ancients, they saw that the ancients' understanding of humanity was incomplete and needed fulfillment with the Christian mysteries of Creation and the Incarnation. Their respect for the ancients was so great, however, that some of them willingly accepted the tradition that hidden in ancient authors were traces of divine revelation, somehow mysteriously communicated to them. Although the humanists did not invent the tradition, they pursued it more thoroughly than earlier generations and came up with bolder expressions of it.

There are many other parallels between Renaissance humanism and Vatican II, but certainly most fundamental is the pervasive influence of epideictic rhetoric—that is, the rhetoric of praise, eulogy, and congratulation. To praise others is to extend a hand in friendship. It implies an attempt to understand the other and to do so with benign intent. It finds appropriate expression in conversation—that is, in dialogue—which emerged as a prominent and characteristic literary form in the Renaissance. In Vatican II, dialogue became so closely identified with the council as almost to define it.

In the Renaissance, the dialogue, sometimes called a colloquy, was so widespread that "it seems to represent a fundamental and innovative aspect of the intellectual life."[7] Dialogue entailed a turn to subjectivity, as the authors projected two or more voices, each expressing a different viewpoint and different persons that the authors explored within themselves.

The very process of dialogue implied an openness to the other, a mind ready to listen and learn. Dialogue does not end in resolution, as does a disputation. The speakers take their leave of one another better informed and, presumably, more accepting of the other. Erasmus, for instance, ended his colloquy "The Funeral" (*Funus*) with one of the speakers saying, "Each of these men was my friend. Perhaps I am not a fair judge of which one died in a manner more becoming a Christian."[8]

The Renaissance produced hundreds of dialogues in both Latin and the vernaculars, and virtually every major author of the period made use of them. Among the best-known works are Thomas More's *Utopia* (1516) and Baldassare Castiglione's *The Book of the Courtier* (1528), but they are only the tip of the iceberg. Erasmus wrote over sixty dialogues, largely as texts for students to provide them with models of good Latin style but at the same time to convey in interesting, sometimes humorous ways important moral or religious truths.

The intermittently persistent Christian impulse to find some way to save persons who were unbaptized and ignorant of the Gospel that resurfaced strongly in the Renaissance found in dialogue an apt medium in which to explore the beliefs of such people. The humanists of the Renaissance were particularly concerned with the great figures of classical antiquity, and they found in them wisdom and ways of expressing it that inspired them to a more Christian way of life.

In his dialogue, titled "The Godly Feast" ("Convivium religiosum"), Erasmus leaves no doubt as to what he believed in that regard. The best-known passage occurs when one of the speakers says, "I think I have never read anything in pagan writers more proper to a true Christian than what Socrates spoke to Crito shortly before drinking the hemlock." To that another replies, "An admirable spirit, surely, in one who had not known Christ and the Sacred Scriptures. And so, when I read such things, I can hardly help exclaiming, 'Saint Socrates, pray for us!'"[9]

In another passage, which is somewhat reminiscent of *Nostra aetate*, Erasmus provided a theological basis for the sanctity of such pagan authors: "Whatever is devout and contributes to an upright life should not be called profane. Of course, the Scriptures are the basic authority in everything, yet I sometimes run across ancient sayings of pagan writers—even the poets— so purely and reverently said that I cannot help believing that the authors' hearts were moved by some divine power. And perhaps the spirit of Christ is more widespread than we understand, and the company of saints includes many not in our calendar."[10]

No less a figure than Saint Antoninus of Florence (1378–1449) gave explicit approval to the principle that all truth, no matter by whom uttered, was from the Holy Spirit.[11] Few carried further the syncretistic approach to ancient philosophies and religions than Giles of Viterbo (1472–1532), who was a polymath, prior general of the Augustinian order, cardinal, and major cultural figure in Rome in the early years of the sixteenth century.[12]

Giles did not compose any dialogues, but in his quest for religious concord he pursued virtually every ancient source to be found in Mediterranean antiquity, including those we now know to be apocryphal. As he matured, he concentrated more and more on the Kabbalah, convinced that it contained a revelation of the mysteries of the Trinity and the Incarnation. To perfect his Hebrew, which was necessary for deciphering the message, he befriended the great rabbi Elijah Levita. He took Elijah and his family into his household for ten years so that Elijah might teach him Hebrew, as Giles in return taught him Greek. In 1518, moreover, Giles had a Latin translation of the Qur'an made for himself in Spain.

Jean Bodin (1529/30–96) wrote the most intriguing interreligious dialogue of the period, the *Heptaplomeres*, which in its standard English translation is presented as *Colloquium of the Seven about Secrets of the Sublime.*[13] Bodin, a Catholic and brilliant thinker during the French Renaissance, wrote important works on legal theory and political philosophy. The *Colloquium* is so different from his other works that a few scholars have questioned his authorship. Today, however, the attribution to him is generally acknowledged as correct.

Written in Latin, the *Colloquium* purported to be a conversation between a Catholic, a Jew, a Lutheran, a Calvinist, a Muslim, a skeptic, and a philosophical naturalist. It was a model of interreligious dialogue. It was an implicit but powerful call for religious understanding, which was surely the result of his living through the horrors of the French Wars of Religion, 1562–98, between Catholics and Huguenots. Living through the horrors of World War II made reconciliation with the Other an imperative for the participants in Vatican II.

CONCLUSION

In this chapter, I have tried to provide a basic introduction to a large and complex subject and to show how and why it in certain ways anticipated Vatican II. The presupposition of some authors that under the literal sense of texts there lurked a primitive revelation of Christian doctrines cannot be taken seriously today. Nonetheless, the basic impulse in them to look with kindly eyes upon others' beliefs continues to make good sense. It is perhaps our most precious inheritance from the Renaissance and from Vatican II.

Precious but delicate. It was too delicate to survive the bitterness that broke upon the scene with the Reformation. Today, Pope Francis has taken up the cause and become the major figure on the world stage calling for dialogue, understanding, and reconciliation. In this regard, he faces many obstacles and even explicit opposition. We can only pray that somehow his message—and the message of the humanists and Vatican II—prevail in a world where, despite progress in certain respects, the major religions still show themselves as antagonistic to one another.

NOTES

1. See, e.g., Paul Ciholas, "Plato: The Attic Moses: Some Patristic Reactions to Platonic Philosophy," *Classical World* 72 (1978): 217–25.
2. See, e.g., John W. O'Malley, "The Theology behind the Ceiling," in *The Sistine Chapel: The Art, the History, and the* Restoration, ed. Carlo Pietrangeli et al. (New York: Harmony Books, 1986), 92–148.
3. See, e.g., Martin Grabmann, *Storia della theologia cattolica: Dalla fine dell'epoca patristica ai tempi nostri*, trans. Giacomo di Fabio, 2nd ed (Milan: Vita e Pensiero, 1939); Jaroslav Pelikan, *Reformation of Church and Dogma (1300–1700)*, vol. 4 of *The Christian Tradition: A History of the Development of Doctrine* (Chicago: University of Chicago Press, 1984); and Roger E. Olson, *The Story of Christian Theology: Twenty Centuries of Tradition and Reform* (Downers Grove, IL: InterVarsity Press, 1999).
4. See, e.g., Louis Bouyer, *Erasmus and the Humanist Experiment*, trans. Francis X. Murphy (Westminster, MD: Newman Press, 1959); and Henri de Lubac, *Exégèse medieval: Les quatre sens de l'écriture*, 2 vols. (Paris: Aubier, 1959–64), passim in 2.2.
5. Mario Fois, *Il pensiero cristiano di Lorenzo Valla nel quadro storico del suo ambiente* (Rome: Università Gregoriana, 1969); Giovanni di Napoli, *Lorenzo Valla: Filosofia e religione nell'Umanesimo* (Rome: Storia e Letterarura, 1971); Salvatore I. Camporeale, *Lorenzo Valla: Umanesimo e teologia* (Florence: Istituto Nazionale di Studi sul Rinascimento, 1972).
6. Charles Trinkaus, *"In Our Image and Likeness": Humanity and Divinity in Italian Renaissance Thought*, 2 vols. (Chicago: University of Chicago Press, 1970).
7. Eva Kushner, "Renaissance Dialogue and Subjectivity," in *Printed Voices: The Renaissance Culture of Dialogue*, ed. Dorothea Heitsch and Jean-François Vallée (Toronto: University of Toronto Press, 2004). See also Virginia Cox, *The Renaissance Dialogue: Literary Dialogue in Its Social and Political Context, Castiglione to Galileo* (Cambridge: Cambridge University Press, 1992); and Roberta Ricci and Susan Wright, ed., *The Renaissance Dialogue* (Buffalo: Northeast Modern Language Association, 2016).
8. Erasmus, "The Funeral," in *Colloquies* (CWE 40), 1974, 763–95, at 795.
9. Erasmus, "Godly Feast," in *Colloquies*, 194.
10. Erasmus, 192.
11. See John W. O'Malley, *Giles of Viterbo on Church and Reform: A Study in Renaissance Thought* (Leiden: Brill, 1968), 20.
12. Ibid.

13. See Jean Bodin, *Colloquium of the Seven about Secrets of the Sublime*, ed. Marion Leathers Kuntz (University Park: Pennsylvania State University Press, 2008). See also Marion Daniels Kuntz, "Harmony and the Heptaplomeres of Jean Bodin," *Journal of the History of Philosophy* 12 (1974): 31–41; and Noel Malcom, "Jean Bodin and the Authorship of the 'Colloquium Heptaplomeres,'" *Journal of the Warburg and Courltauld Institutes* 69 (2006): 95–150.

CHAPTER 7

Interfaith Christology?
Some Dogmatic Prolegomena

William P. Loewe

One good turn deserves another. Several years ago, my friend and onetime colleague at the Catholic University of America, Peter Phan, was kind enough to contribute an adventurous article to a volume that some of my former students were assembling. The challenge to which Peter was responding in that article, as in much of his prodigious scholarly work, was the challenge of globalization and the new valence that globalization confers on religious pluralism. That challenge is with us still. Phan titled his piece "Christ in the Many and Diverse Religions: An Interreligious Christology."[1] Programmatic in character, the piece argued for the possibility and desirability of constructing, on the basis of authentic interreligious dialogue, what Peter called "an interfaith Christology." As a pioneer in the project, he invoked the work of Raimon Panikkar. It is to this article of Peter's that I direct my remarks here. The first section notes several of the questions that Phan's text suggests, while the second one proposes that various elements of the Christian doctrinal and theological tradition create a space for a project like that which Peter proposes.

PHAN'S PROPOSAL: SOME QUESTIONS

The goal of Phan's proposal was to arrive at an enlarged and enriched understanding of the concept, Christ. This would be achieved by critically correlating the Christian understanding of the term "with concepts and images present in other religions that exhibit significant similarities or functional analogies with it."[2] Immediately, a first question arises: how, on what basis, can such similarities or functional analogies be discerned? In reply, Peter invokes Christian usage. Citing Colin Greene's typology of premodern Christologies as cosmological, political, or anthropological,[3] he goes on to venture that "underlying these divergent Christologies . . . is the notion that somehow in Jesus, however his historical role is interpreted, humans are given the possibility of fulfilling their nature and reaching their ultimate goal."[4] Here, Phan advances a valuable insight into the character of Christian usage. The image of the Messiah or Christ proved a fit vehicle for Christian faith in Jesus precisely because of the heuristic character that Peter astutely discerns in it. Messiah, in its original historical context, had developed into a culture-specific symbol that evoked Jewish hopes for one through whom God would make everything all right, that is, would enable their fulfillment individually and as a people, and would resolve the problem of evil as they experienced it. Applied to Jesus, the symbol both articulated the salvific significance his followers found in him and left open—"somehow, in Jesus," Peter writes—the question of how that hope for salvation was fulfilled in Jesus. That further question would be resolved through the narratives his followers would compose.

At this point, Peter makes an interesting move. Noting that, in the Christian narrative context, it is at divine initiative and by divine power that Jesus fulfills his messianic function, and that Christians identify the source of that power as the Spirit of God, Peter suggests that his interfaith Christology ought to be prefaced with a pneumatology. From a Christian standpoint, I believe his suggestion corresponds to a shorthand genetic account of Christian faith: in and by the Spirit, one is moved and enlightened to recognize Jesus as the Christ and revealer of the way to the Father. From the viewpoint of Peter's project, he finds it advantageous to begin with pneumatology because, he says, the Spirit not being tied to a particular historical individual, it is easier to find analogies to the Spirit in non-Christian religions. This assertion may perhaps occasion discussion. Is it the case that, for Christians at least, the Spirit floats so freely? In what sense might one affirm this?

Let me make one more observation about Peter's article. Early on, in rehearsing the ground rules for authentic interfaith dialogue, he insists on the need to understand one's partners as far as possible on their own terms, and this requirement precludes regarding other religions "simply as various paths leading to the same religious summit (e.g., God) or merely diverse cultural expressions of the same core religious experience."[5] I take this comment to allude to the common, if perhaps inadequate, typology of Christian theologies of world religions as either exclusive, inclusive, or pluralist, and to rule out the latter. In rejecting the pluralist position, Phan joins those who have criticized it as a new, imperialist form of exclusivism. The pluralist position betrays its exclusivism, in that it requires that the various faith traditions scale back their respective truth claims. At this point, however, a question occurs to me. I would ask whether Peter finds this stricture against the pluralist position honored when, in closing his article, he proposes Raimon Panikkar as a pioneer in interfaith Christology. The stricture, to repeat, rules out the notion of the religions as "merely diverse cultural expressions of the same core religious experience."[6] Is this stricture observed when Peter writes of Pannikar that "central to Panikkar's Christophany is his belief that every being, in particular every human being . . . is a Christophany, that is, the divinization of humanity, which is the other side of the humanization of God?"[7] (When Panikkar claims that his *advaita* Christophany "is shared by Jesus and all human beings," is he proposing something like a universal core religious experience?[8])

Several more general questions about Peter's proposal for an interfaith Christology come to mind. First, it seeks a "profound and diverse understanding of the Christ on the basis of the most varied and even contradictory affirmations of different religions on what makes a particular being . . . the Christ."[9] "A profound and diverse understanding of the Christ": I am prompted to ask what is the Christ that is being understood? Is it anything over and beyond the varied and even contradictory manners in which different religions envisage the human situation, the human predicament, and its solution? Does the interfaith Christology that Peter proposes have a referent—Panikkar's certainly seems to—or does its Christ float freely in a constructed, purely conceptual realm?

A second question: In order to construct an interfaith Christology, having discerned similarities and analogies among the religions in their responses to the human situation, these similarities and analogies are to be "critically correlated."[10] Critical correlation would seem to imply a normative moment, and so I would ask whence that norm might be derived. Perhaps globalization is now raising in a new form the problem of objectivity that historical consciousness raised for the Christian West.

Third, I can see how, if "Christ" is taken in a purely heuristic sense, pursuing this heuristic can promote mutual understanding among adherents of diverse religions. I would ask, however, whether the term "Christ" itself is necessary to that end. Peter would seem to say that it is not when he recognizes that adherents of other religions might pursue an interfaith Buddhology, Krishnology, and the like, "just as Christians speak of an interfaith Christology."[11] Does the project of interfaith Christology fall after all within the realm of Christian theological discourse? There seems to be a tension here between a specifically Christian project and one that is truly interfaith.

Fourth, if one moves beyond the heuristic sense into specific similarities and analogies with concepts and images found in other religions, I see, as Phan urges, that Christian self-understanding can be enhanced, but this is a gain of what Peter terms dialogical Christologies, and he distinguishes these from a truly interfaith Christology. So also, that more substantive move can enhance the intelligibility of Christian faith among non-Christian believers, and Peter cites Panikkar to this effect: "If Christ is to have any meaning for Hindus, Andines, Ibos, Vietnamese, and others who do not belong to the Abrahamic lineage, this meaning can no longer be offered in the garb of Western philosophies."[12] There is, of course, an ambiguity in this statement. In the context of Christian missionary endeavors, it affirms the necessity of inculturation, and this necessity raises the perennial issue of the hermeneutics of tradition to a new level. Panikkar seems to imply this missionary motive when he writes: "If Christ is to have any meaning." To whom is it a concern that Christ have meaning for those outside the Abrahamic lineage? Such missionary intent is, however, foreign to the project of an interfaith Christology, which seeks the mutual understanding to be achieved by a collaboration between Christians and adherents of other faiths in constructing a concept of Christ that operates on the level of intelligibility while eschewing, or bracketing, truth claims.

This in turn suggests a final question. Peter insists that what is at issue in an interfaith Christology is strictly a matter of an intelligibility, and to make the point he cites Bernard Lonergan on the distinction between doctrines and systematics. This distinction rests in turn on a prior distinction between judgment, in which the truth about the real is grasped, and understanding, which yields a hypothetical intelligibility that may or may not be relevant to the data of experience. For Lonergan, in the ordinary course of human knowing, understanding precedes judgment; but in the mediating phase of theology, that relationship is reversed: systematics seeks to develop the intelligibility of doctrines held to be true. On one hand, Peter invokes the distinction to assign his interfaith Christology to the level of intelligibility. Yet on the other hand, he also ventures that such a Christology may be deemed "theologically inappropriate or even heterodox" from the viewpoint of Christian orthodoxy.[13] How do these two affirmations cohere? Orthodoxy concerns doctrines—that is, judgments, affirmations, not simply concepts or intelligibilities. Nor is it clear how interfaith dialogue and mutual understanding would be promoted if an interfaith Christology were to arrive at a concept, "theologically inappropriate or even heterodox," in which Christian participants could not recognize something of their own self-understanding. There seems to be a tension on this point in Peter's proposal.

Phan is up front when he acknowledges the programmatic, tentative, and exploratory character of his proposal. As he says, the project is in its infancy, so the proof will lie in the pudding. In the course of its development, it may well be that the questions and perplexity Peter's proposal can evoke will be resolved.

DOGMATIC PROLOGOMENA FROM THE CATHOLIC TRADITION

Meanwhile, as a theologian woefully unschooled in other religious traditions and unpracticed in interfaith dialogue, I appreciate the virtuosity of Peter's imaginative, ground-breaking thinking outside the box. I also believe that there are elements of the Catholic tradition—indeed, of Catholic dogma— that create a space for the kind of inquiry he suggests. Let me comment on a few of these.

First, Peter's proposal gives antecedence to pneumatology over Christology. In the theology of the Trinity, the Holy Spirit proceeds as the *vinculum amoris*, the bond of love between Father and Son. Then, economically, in the *oikonomia*, "God's love is poured out in our hearts with the gift of the Holy Spirit given to us," as Saint Paul has it in Romans 5:5. Phenomenologically, or existentially, when in my better moments I try to love the Lord my God with my whole heart and my whole soul, with my whole mind and all my strength, and my neighbor as myself, this engagement in love of God and neighbor flows in response to the gift of the Spirit at work in me.

Clearly, this gift is not restricted to Christians. Doctrinally, I am taught that God wills the salvation of all people. Several years ago, I was present as faculty adviser at a program sponsored by what was then called the National Council of Christians and Jews. The program, called Seminarians Interacting, sponsored an exchange of students among seminaries of different denominations and religions. The young men and women chosen to participate would spend a set period of time in a seminary of a different denomination or religion. Then, toward the close of the academic year, all the participants were called together, and as part of the program for the weekend each group performed a liturgy at which all were present. There were Muslims engaged in their response to the call to prayer. Young Jews danced joyously with the Torah. Pulpit Christians and altar Christians each engaged in some instance of their respective forms of worship. Watching all this, it struck me that in the fervor of their prayer, all these young people were loving the Lord their God with their whole hearts. In that loving, the gift of the Spirit was being poured forth.

These seminarians were, of course, representatives of the Abrahamic religions. Does one find similar or analogous experiences beyond that limit? This question takes me beyond my pay grade as a conventional, even in some ways conservative, Christian theologian. I am intrigued, however, by Francis Clooney's comparative readings of Christian and Hindu texts and the warm fervor that these readings manifest.[14] In addition, I recall Saint Paul's classic enumeration of the fruits of the Spirit: "love, joy, peace, patience, kindness, generosity, faithfulness, gentleness, self-control" (Gal. 5:22–23). These would seem to be precisely the characteristics that have rendered Buddhists like the Dalai Lama and Thich Nhat Hanh so attractive and prominent in the West, and I would venture to surmise that participants in the interreligious Buddhist-Christian monastic dialogue like that promoted by Abbot James Wiseman recognize these characteristics in one another as well.[15]

This line of reflection leads to a question that I would find it intriguing to discuss. Does a recognition on the part of a Christian of the gift and fruits of the Spirit operative beyond the bounds of the Christian religion, a recognition of the universality of the offer and effects of grace, imply something like the positing of a "core religious experience" that Peter eschews but Panikkar may be suggesting? Wittgenstein may remind us that experience is, of course, always constructed; but nonetheless, I wonder. I am not persuaded that our various religious language games are so hermetically isolated as to preclude communication and mutual understanding among them.

At any rate, I am endorsing Peter's suggestion that pneumatology take precedence in approaching interfaith dialogue. Christians may, of course, object, that such a course of reflection overlooks their conviction that Jesus Christ is the universal savior. This conviction in turn meets the stubborn fact that Jesus Christ plays no role in the religious life of vast numbers of the human race.

Perhaps three classical Christian dogmas can open a way beyond this apparent impasse. In 325, the Council of Nicaea defined that in his divinity, the Lord Jesus Christ is *homoousios*—one in being, consubstantial, with the Father; and Athanasius of Alexandria interpreted this to mean that whatever you can say of the Father, you can say of the Son, and vice versa, except what is proper to being Father and Son. Fifty-six years later, the First Council of Constantinople extended this dogma to include the Spirit as well. Saint Augustine in turn ventured that all the divine acts ad extra are common to the three Persons, though the manner of the respective Persons' share in that common activity may be differentiated. Third, some seventy years after the

First Council of Constantinople, in 451 the Council of Chalcedon affirmed that in Christ there come together in one Person two natures, the divine and the human, and that though these natures cannot be divided or separated, neither are they changed or confused, and that in his humanity Christ is composed of a rational soul and a body, being like us in all things except sin.

How can these classical dogmas further our inquiry? First, orthodox Christianity insists on their truth status as affirmations of what is. At the same time, it characterizes them as mysteries, that is, as truths whose full meaning and intelligibility are grasped by God alone. What is possible for Christians who profess them is, as the First Vatican Council stated, a fruitful but imperfect, analogous understanding that is always subject to development, whereas an earlier council held at the Lateran cautioned that in the case of such analogies, the difference remains always greater than the similarity. The dogmas themselves are instances of a development that begins with the symbolic mode of New Testament discourse, through the beginnings of a theoretical apprehension of the cognitive dimension of New Testament symbolism that they themselves embody, to the systematic-theoretic apprehension represented by something like the "Pars Tertia" of Aquinas's *Summa Theologiae*. Today, the new context of globalizing modernity—or, if you will, postmodernity—would make further development in this ongoing process imperative. It follows, I believe, that Christian truth claims should be advanced with humility, always recalling that now we see as in a glass, darkly.

Second, if one begins with something like a phenomenology of the gift and fruits of the Spirit, Nicaea and I Constantinople would remind us that the Spirit is always the Spirit of the Father and the Son; that the gift and fruits of the Spirit are always in some sense Trinitarian in structure; and that the Spirit is always, as Saint Paul has it, the Spirit of Christ.

Third, if this insistence on the unity in difference of the Persons of the Trinity both immanently and economically smacks of imperialism, the First Vatican Council's caution stands: how God is Triune remains a mystery of which we can have only an imperfect, analogous understanding, subject to development. The Council of Chalcedon provides another caution when it affirms that in his humanity, the Word Incarnate is composed of a rational soul and a body, like us in all things except sin. The completeness of this humanity was an issue in the debates of the fourth and fifth centuries, and if the outcome was couched in metaphysical terms—composed of a rational soul and a body—today these metaphysical terms are complemented by historical and existential terms. So, for example, in the ongoing project of the quest for the historical Jesus, the so-called New Quest was brought to a halt by the revelation that it neglected to take full account of Jesus's Jewishness.[16]

Chalcedon's "like us in all things except sin" embraces more than metaphysical constitution. It also implies cultural and historical particularity, and such particularity implies limits. Thus Frederick Crowe has suggested that we recognize a triple kenosis of the Word Incarnate: a metaphysical kenosis, in that the Word assumes a human nature; a psychological kenosis, in that the Word becomes the subject of a fully human consciousness; and finally a historical kenosis, in that the Word is born a first-century Galilean Jew.[17]

The point is, perhaps, obvious. In his ministry, Jesus proclaimed and enacted the nearness of the coming of the Kingdom of God, a symbol that bore meaning and meaningfulness to his fellow Jews to whom he directed that ministry. His earliest disciples, in turn, made sense of his ministry, death, and resurrection as setting in motion an apocalyptic scenario of final tribulations, divine vindication, and imminent, longed-for final victory. Soon, however, the Hebrew "Messiah" gave way to the Greek "Christ," and the latter became simply a proper name, while the process of inculturation into the Hellenist culture of the Roman Empire gave rise to the Logos Christologies of Justin and the apologists. The ambiguities of these Christologies led in turn to the clarifications proffered by the classical Church councils, and the latter came to find a home in medieval Christendom, a Western culture that came to understood itself in classicist terms as normative, in possession of the one true religion, the perennial philosophy, and, in the literature of ancient Greece and Rome, the highest achievements of the human spirit.[18] From the classicist viewpoint, other cultures suffered by comparison as undeveloped and inferior, while other religious traditions were written off as superstitions, perhaps the work of demons.

If Christendom shattered with the onslaught of the religious, scientific, philosophical, and political revolutions that ushered in modernity, Catholicism's first response was withdrawal into a subculture where the classicist ideal perdured well into the middle of the twentieth century. Thus, Catholic higher education continued to require immersion in Latin and Greek literature—an English major at the College of the Holy Cross who failed to study Latin was awarded a bachelor of science degree, not a bachelor of arts, to which was added a heavy dose—really, a second major area of study, Scholastic philosophy—along with a course in apologetics to arm one for life in an alien world.

Good Pope John's program of *aggiornamento* could not but precipitate a crisis, not of faith but of culture, a crisis to which the contested reception of Vatican II bears ample witness. The crisis is complex. On one hand, there is determined resistance to the need to disengage from a classicist self-understanding. On the other hand, the culture of modernity is itself highly ambiguous, a culture in which the very objectivity of meaning and value is contested.

So, "like us in all things except sin." Chalcedon's dogma points to the historical and cultural particularity of the ministry exercised by Jesus, the Word Incarnate, and of the community founded upon the meanings and values that he embodied. This particularity is a limit, but never simply a limit. The redemptive dynamic constitutive of the community impels it to rediscover itself anew in each of the ongoing contexts where its history places it. At no point short of the end of history, however, will this process of self-constitution achieve a final cultural embodiment. There are moments in the process of appropriating the meanings and values constitutive of the community that represent permanent and irreversible achievement, and yet the process remains ongoing.

Given this condition of eschatological incompleteness—the "not yet" of Christian existence—a space opens in which to discern the gift and fruits of the Spirit operative beyond the limits of the Christian community. This gift and these fruits evidence themselves in those elements of truth and holiness that Vatican II discerned in other world religions.[19] In addition, Western colonialism brought Christ to the attention of participants in other world religions, a dynamic accelerated by contemporary globalization. One result, as Peter notes, is that several Hindus and Buddhists have reflected on the figure they have encountered, while at the same time numerous Christian theologians have been rising to the challenge that inculturation poses for Christology. Whatever the fate of Peter's proposal of an interfaith Christology, his recognition of the heuristic character of the title, Christ, and his suggestion that priority be accorded to pneumatology in negotiating the encounter of religions have, I believe, merit. Bernard Lonergan once wrote that "a religion that promotes self-transcendence to the point, not merely of justice, but of self-sacrificing love, will have a redemptive role in human society."[20] Such is clearly the criterion for authentic Christianity, which lives from the transformation of evil into good effected by the life, death, and resurrection of Jesus of Nazareth. Perhaps the cruciform character of what Christians call grace can add further specificity to the heuristic to be pursued in the open encounter of religions for which the dogmas of Nicaea and Chalcedon, I would suggest, open a space.

NOTES

1. Peter C. Phan, "Christ in the Many and Diverse Religions: An Interreligious Christology," in *Finding Salvation in Christ: Essays on Christology and Soteriology in Honor of William P.*

Loewe, ed. Christopher D. Denny and Christopher McMahon (Eugene, OR: Pickwick, 2011), 307–18. The same article, minus the concluding section on R. Panikkar, appeared under the title "An Interfaith Christology: A Possibility and a Desideratum?" in *Negotiating Borders: Theological Explorations in the Global Era. Essays in Honor of Prof. Felix Wilfred*, ed. Patrick Gnanapragasam and Elisabeth Schüssler Fiorenza (Delhi: ISPCK, 2008), 379–85.

2. Phan, "Christ," 312.

3. Colin J. D. Greene, *Christology in Cultural Perspective: Marking Out the Horizons* (Grand Rapids: Wm. B. Eerdmans, 2003).

4. Phan, "Christ," 313.

5. Phan, 309.

6. Phan.

7. Phan, 316–17.

8. Phan, 317.

9. Phan, 311.

10. Phan, 312.

11. Phan, 310.

12. Phan, 317–18.

13. Phan, 311.

14. For a sample of his comparative work, see Francis Clooney, "Theology and Sacred Scripture Reconsidered in the Light of a Hindu Text," in *Theology and Sacred Scripture*, ed. Carol J. Dempsey and William Loewe (Maryknoll, NY: Orbis, 2002), 211–36.

15. See Donald Mitchell and James Wiseman, eds., *Gethsemani Encounter: A Dialogue on the Spiritual Life by Buddhist and Christian Monastics* (New York: Continuum, 1999).

16. See E. P. Sanders, *Jesus and Judaism* (London: SCM, 1985); and James H. Charlesworth, ed., *Jesus' Jewishness: Exploring the Place of Jesus Within Early Judaism* (New York: Crossroad, 1991).

17. Frederick M. Crowe, "A Three-Fold *Kenosis* of the Son of God," in *Appropriating the Lonergan Idea*, ed. M. Vertin (Washington, DC: Catholic University of America Press, 1989), 315–23.

18. On classicism, see Bernard Lonergan, *Method in Theology* (Toronto: University of Toronto Press, 2003), 301–2 and passim.

19. *Nostra aetate*, 2.

20. Lonergan, *Method*, 55.

CHAPTER 8

Interreligious Marriage as a Way of Being Religious Interreligiously

Chester Gillis

My colleague and friend Peter Phan surely did not seek the attention of the Congregation for the Doctrine of Faith in Rome; but his work represents a different view of salvation from that of Church documents like *Dominus Iesus*—which, as its title indicates, defends the unicity and salvific universality of Jesus and Christ and the Church.[1] In particular, Phan's Asian experience has led him to conclude that religions other than Christianity play a significant role in the salvation of many people who live daily lives of faith that draw from more than a single religious tradition.

PETER PHAN'S DEFENSE OF RELIGIONS AS PART OF GOD'S SALVIFIC PLAN

This view brought unwanted attention from Rome and the American bishops.[2] In their document titled "Clarifications Required by the Book *Being Religious Interreligiously: Asian Perspectives on Interfaith Dialogue* by Reverend Peter C. Phan," the Committee on Doctrine of the US Conference of Catholic Bishops stated: *Being Religious Interreligiously* . . . defends the view that "the non-Christian religions possess an autonomous function in the history of salvation, different from that of Christianity," and that "they cannot be reduced to Christianity in terms of preparation and fulfillment."[3] Phan's book asserts: "Religious pluralism . . . is not just a matter of fact but also a matter of principle. That is, non-Christian religions may be seen as part of the plan of divine providence and endowed with a particular role in the history of salvation." Theologians who hold a view similar to Phan believe that it is necessary to go beyond the Second Vatican Council's position and to assert with Phan "that these religions may be said to be ways of salvation and that religious pluralism is part of God's providential plan."

Despite ecclesial objections, Phan's work has informed a generation of theologians who are concerned with the contemporary Christian theological response to the pluralism of religions. I, like my fellow contributors to this volume, have studied and struggled with the challenges of religious pluralism. My recent work addresses one important aspect of an increasing manifestation of religious pluralism, namely, interreligious marriage. In this chapter, I examine religious pluralism on the ground, in the most intimate and important relationship—marriage. In exogamous marriages in which Christians marry someone from another religion, religious pluralism *is* part of God's plan.

INTERRELIGIOUS MARRIAGE

One dimension that young about-to-be-marrieds no longer consider as important as previous generations is religious compatibility. Only 42 percent of young singles consider it important to find a spouse of the same religion.[4] Religion itself carries less significance. The couples want someone who shares a common spiritual interest, but this does not necessarily translate into a religion or a denomination. Religious marriages have declined dramatically in recent decades. In 1998, 75 percent of marriages in America took place in a church or synagogue.[5] In 2017, only 22 percent of marriages took place in religious congregations, with 43 percent presided over by a relative or friend in secular settings.[6]

Exogamous marriages produce complications that endogamous ones do not, and interfaith couples cannot afford to be sanguine about them. At the same time, religious difference should not inhibit couples from pursuing a relationship and marriage. Negotiating difference is never easy, and religious difference presents unique sensitivities and challenges. After all, if someone has been taught all her life that her religion is the "right" one, the implication follows that other religions are somehow, or to some degree, "wrong." Her heart may be telling her this is the right man, but her religious upbringing delivers a different message. However, *different* does not necessarily imply wrong. The theological thinking to which she was exposed in her religion no doubt centered on a single religious path to God and did not suggest that other available paths may also lead to God. In my view, God cannot be sequestered, and religions should treat one another with greater respect and encourage mutual understanding.

Religious provincialism seems to be a natural state of being for many religious communities. By separating themselves from "the other," they can more easily ensure their own doctrine. John Bowker correctly argues that religions are natively conservative and attempt to draw boundaries that separate and distinguish them from other religions.[7] The dilemma that confronts religions in the twenty-first century is not how these religions can survive on their own but how they can survive together. Concretely, the pluralism of religions in the United States means that, no matter where you live, your religion exists alongside one or several others. In some rural areas, diversity may be as confined as two Christian denominations coexisting, perhaps with one having a significant majority presence and the other a minority. In cities, one encounters multiple expressions of Christianity and perhaps a few other religions. In major metropolitan areas, the panoply of the world's religions abides in neighborhoods and is evident in the diversity of worship spaces, from gurdwaras to synagogues, churches, meeting halls, and temples.

Clearly, statistics support the notion that religious unity affords greater stability to marriages. Nevertheless, not everyone finds the love of their life at church. Social and professional circles foster contact with a wide diversity of people who come from a variety of religious backgrounds. In America, people fall in love with all varieties of people. In some nations, where marriages are generally arranged, such is not the case. Families involve themselves deeply in the negotiations that lead to marriage, and religion plays a key role in the decision-making process. The tradition of marriage for love in the United States allows greater autonomy for those who wish to pursue marriage, but its lack of restrictions also sometimes complicates the process of choosing a spouse.

In our multicultural society, some may opine that religious difference makes no difference, but this is naive. However, to suggest that religious difference erects insurmountable barriers is equally naive. Religious difference must be addressed and negotiated thoughtfully by each partner if the couple wants the relationship to evolve into a permanent union. And the wedding symbolizes a moment in this process, not an end to it. As one Lutheran minister observed: "When a couple is 'madly in love,' as the saying goes, it is extremely difficult to pay attention to all the practical aspects and potential pitfalls of married life. Being in love, however, is rarely sufficient grounds for marriage."[8] For example, religious identification or nonidentification, practice or lack of practice, children's religious affiliation, significant life markers, birth, adulthood, marriage, death, and family traditions must all be negotiated. Even those who are not religious must agree with each other to be so. Couples may not wish to admit that religious difference matters, or they may be reluctant to face the inevitable issues that religious difference surfaces. Love may conquer all, but not without a struggle. Exploration of religious identification or nonidentification does not seem the usual topic with which romances begin, but it is sometimes one at which they end and, therefore, must be taken seriously.

In many cases, one partner chooses to convert to the other's religion. This encourages harmony only when the conversion is undertaken not simply for convenience but with genuine conviction. In other cases, each partner plans to continue to practice his or her religion, respecting the religion of the other and conferring on the children a dual religious identity.[9] Others begin their religious life anew by joining a "neutral" religion that is new to each partner, thus not favoring either previous religious identification. In some instances, the couple chooses to abandon religion altogether. All these choices have inherent complications that affect the couple and confront them with decisions regarding the single religious, dual religious, or the nonreligious identity of children.

An increasing number of American Christians marry exogamously to adherents of other world religions, such as Judaism, Islam, Buddhism, and Hinduism. Though the trend toward an increasing number of interreligious marriages signals a decline in religious isolation and bigotry, it also creates complications that may not have been anticipated. For example, a minority religion like Judaism faces the debilitating effects that assimilation by marriage presents. In the 1920s, only 2 percent of Jews married Christians in America; today, that number has increased to over 50 percent.[10] Marriages between Muslims and Christians, which are now more common than a generation ago, require delicate negotiations about religious and cultural practices that affect couples and their families. The same is true for Hindus, Buddhists, Sikhs, and others who now have a significant presence in America. Marriage commitments and ceremonies often require creativity and concessions, but they represent only the beginning of interfaith decisions that multiply with child-rearing, religious practice, and social relations.[11]

One example of how interreligious marriage is received comes from the Jewish faith. The Jewish community is divided in its response to intermarried couples. At one end of the spectrum, some want to reverse the trend toward more intermarriage and insist that Jews should only marry Jews. At the other end, many argue that intermarriages are inevitable, the consequence of being accepted and living in a tolerant secular society. In the middle reside those who would prefer endogamous marriage but recognize that many couples already live in religiously mixed marriages and extend a welcoming invitation to these couples to participate in Jewish religious life to the degree to which the couples are comfortable and that interpretations of Jewish law and custom, Halakha, allow. The first group defends religious and ethnic purity, and maintains that unless Jews exclusively marry Jews, the Jewish community in America will disappear. The Conservative rabbi and religion professor Arthur Hertzberg reflected their attitude when he made the dire prediction that unless there is a reversal of the trend toward intermarriage, "American Jewish history will soon end, and become part of American memory as a whole."[12] The middle group tries to work with intermarried couples to welcome the non-Jewish partner, encourage him or her to convert to Judaism, and hopes to influence the couple to raise their children as Jews. The journalist Rahel Musleah reported in the article "Jewish Jeopardy" that "all Reform congregations today include intermarried couples who are raising Jewish children—in some cases 50 percent or more of a synagogue's members are intermarried."[13] It is the consequence for welcomed assimilation into American society. For them, Jews no longer must marry Jews because no other community accepts them, the way it was when they or their grandparents married. They have the freedom to marry anyone from all ethnic groups and any or no religious persuasion. They see this as liberating, not constricting. As Jack Wertheimer—a professor of American Jewish history at the Jewish Theological Seminary of America, and a critic of such easy assimilation—puts it: "Rather than being pressured to conform to starkly defined categories, Jews in the United States are finding that their identity can be as loosely marked as that of any other American group."[14] To some, then, intermarriage indicates that Jews have come of age in America, are treated the same as everyone else, and no longer reside in a ghetto either imposed upon them or self-constructed. Reflecting this view, Eric Yoffie—a Reform rabbi, in a speech while president of the Union of American Hebrew Congregations—observed: "Intermarriage, of course, is a product of modernity, and not of any religious stream. The only way to stamp it out would be to return the Jews to the medieval ghetto."[15]

Of course, not all couples believe that the religious dimension of marriage represents a vital aspect of married life. Substantial numbers of Americans do not take religion seriously, and it plays little to no role in their conception of marriage.[16] This ranges from outright antagonism toward religious identification to apathy. Often couples maintain a veneer of religion by having some quasi-religious ceremony to begin their married life, but the motives for this range from placating parents and relatives to a lack of another ceremonial model that is sufficiently dignified.

Whether couples are devout, religion virtually always must be considered when choosing a life partner. This remains as true for those who profess no religion at all as it does for the weekly churchgoer, because religion touches not only individuals and couples but also families and society. For some, religion represents customs and traditions that are as easily tied to ethnicity and family as they are to religious practice. Thus, even for those who do not practice their religion by going regularly to religious services, or who do so only a few times a year on widely celebrated occasions—for example, for Christians, on Christmas and Easter; for Jews, on Rosh Hashanah and Yom Kippur; or for Muslims, on Eid—religion maintains an importance that exhibits itself plainly when considerations of marriage arise. A dimension that may be in the background in daily life often comes to the foreground when considering a marriage partner. Usually, potential mates do not inquire about religious identification when they first meet for dinner or a movie. But when they establish a relationship, inevitably what religion each professes becomes known, making it a bridge or a potential obstacle. And if the couple does not broach the subject, family members surely will inquire. Parents, grandparents, siblings, relatives, and friends will exhibit a natural curiosity about a potential mate's background, family, profession, and *religion*. It may be none of their business, but that will not prevent them from asking. When a potential partner's religion turns out to be different, often it will be cause for advice, speculation, and concern. After all, if she is from New York and he is from Seattle, people will wonder where they will make a home. If she is Methodist and he is Jewish, how will they negotiate differences? In the words of the popular play *The Fantasticks*, "a bird can love a fish, but where do they make a home?"

If it were only theological differences that couples must negotiate, the task would be difficult but focused. However, religious difference implies a host of other areas of concern not limited to, but including, social, familial, cultural, and personal. What sacred days does an interfaith couple celebrate when their traditions differ? What do they serve at table when two extended families with different dietary sensitivities and restrictions sit together? What religious symbols (if any) do they display in their home? Who in the extended family is likely to be offended by their food, symbols, and religious participation or nonparticipation? For many, religion intertwines with culture such that the two become inseparable. To be Jewish, for some, may not necessarily mean being religious, but it does mean being *Jewish*. To be Muslim implies Islamic culture as well as religion. To be Hindu means that caste carries significance. To be Buddhist means that nonviolence is a way of life. For the majority of Americans, religion is important, and to deny this is to risk unanticipated consequences.

Exogamous marriages produce complications that endogamous ones do not, and interfaith couples cannot afford to be sanguine about them. At the same time, religious difference should not inhibit couples from pursuing a relationship and marriage. However, for cultural, social, or religious reasons, some may try to prevent interreligious marriages, but no one disputes their increasing presence in America. Religious communities may seek to preserve their identity, parents may discourage their children from seeing potential marriage partners from another faith, and society may look awkwardly at interreligious combinations; yet despite these disincentives, such unions are increasing, not decreasing, in the United States.

CLASHES OF THEOLOGIES

Different theologies have engendered different religious identities, identities that often pit one religious person or religious community against another. These theologies often clash into one another in awkward and painful ways when persons from different religions contemplate and/or enter into marriage. Some prefer to interact almost exclusively with their own community and protect the purity of their religious identity at all costs. However, this strategy works only imperfectly unless strict vigilance and enforcement accompany it. Even when it succeeds, it can lead to a xenophobia that separates and distinguishes the religious community even from its American neighbors. Unless the members of the community live in close proximity to one another, maintaining religious purity usually becomes problematic. Some may wish to promote exclusively intrareligious marriages for reasons of religious purity. Others may want to protect the ethnic identity of the community. Each of these objectives has an internally coherent logic as long as purity does not imply prejudice. No one faults communities for preferring "their own kind."[17] And, indeed, these congruent combinations often work best. If the preference implies denigration of those who are religiously different, then it casts a different shadow over the community. Religion provides a rich dimension of commonality for couples and thus accords a legitimate priority when seeking a spouse. Shared dimensions lay the foundation for harmony in a marriage. Differences bring novelty and often expand the horizons of each partner, but they also present obstacles.

The obstacle of religious difference must be taken seriously, but it should not be considered insurmountable. Most religious communities do not teach their adherents how to negotiate religious difference. Instead, they create theologies of separation and pastoral practices that cater to their own and largely ignore the religiously "other" or treat them as an aberration. They think and act as if God has been revealed exclusively to them, even though they know the world is religiously plural. However, those who believe differently from them are not about to disappear, and ignoring them fosters ignorance that, as we have seen time and again, leads to caricatures and misunderstanding. The time to think about religious difference is before marriage. However, the time for love is before and during marriage, and that can be the characteristic that makes all the difference.

A theological investigation of interreligious marriage needs to begin with God. However, this starting point lacks specificity and clarity, particularly when examining the broad phenomenon of religion across the spectrum of religions. Because religions do not conceive of God in identical ways, and because some conceptions seemingly contradict one another, a theological analysis requires careful accounting of how different religions describe the Transcendent.[18] A key thesis of this chapter centers on how the construction and use of theological categories and theories affect the appropriation of religion, and this appropriation in turn affects self-understanding, attitudes, beliefs, and practices of religious believers. These dispositions then affect how the believer interprets the religion of the other and how he or she relates to the religiously other person. One may be suspicious of those who do not share fundamental religious categories in an identical manner. Or one may think that they misinterpret who or what God is and how God relates to humankind. These concerns capture precisely the suspicions that complicate an interreligious marriage and can interfere easily with the ability to understand one's religiously other partner.

Most religious persons grow up believing in one well-formulated and definitive description of God. From the profoundly simple Qur'anic manifestation that "there is one God," to the more complicated theology of the Trinity in Christianity, religions fundamentally subscribe to an internally coherent and uniform definition of God or the Transcendent. Adherents of the religion usually learn the definition early in their childhood and experience reinforcement of it regularly in prayer and worship. However, they appropriate it not simply as a convenient or useful definition but also as a true one. They believe it because they think that it is not merely a suitable description but because they believe that the description is true. Thus, the Muslim believes that God is uniquely one and Muhammad is his messenger. The Christian professes that God is three persons in one: Father, Son, and Holy Spirit. The Hindu believes that the multiple manifestations of gods and goddesses all represent Brahman, the ultimate Reality. The Buddhist believes that there is no god, personal or impersonal, yet humans have the capacity for nirvana.

These descriptions of the Transcendent usually rest on revelation disclosed in a text, through a prophet, or in an epiphany. The originating texts, persons, and events occupy a privileged place in the religion's heritage and influence the construction of systems of belief. Over time, followers of the religion clarify and codify the originating elements, proposing authoritative interpretations and structuring the resulting beliefs and practices into what can be commonly described as religion. A community forms that holds certain beliefs in common and uniform practices arise that further define and solidify the community of believers. These developments enable the religion to form a distinctive character, set of beliefs and practices, and community that all separate it from other identifiable religious or social bodies. Without these evolutions, the religion likely would not survive its infancy. Forging a clear and distinct identity aids the social bonding necessary to survive. Defining beliefs clarifies ambiguities and fosters unanimity that contributes to coherence and intelligibility that further promote stability. One other important effect of this codification and development is that these initiatives bestow a distinctive identity on the followers of the emerging religion, allowing them to differentiate themselves from other religious patterns and communities and to recognize their own more easily.

The process I am describing does not occur in a matter of mere years but over decades, centuries, and generations. Those born today both reap the benefit of this lengthy process and are heirs to centuries of refinement. At the same time, however, they are hostage to sometimes-arcane formulations, historical disputes, and differing sects of the same religion. What may have started out pure gets muddy with time and human manipulation.

When a religion makes a theological claim, which is its right, it usually rejects other claims, even if only implicitly. Of course, all religions do not share identical theological categories, so the claim of one religion may be irrelevant to another. Nevertheless, exclusive theological claims on the part of one religion imply that other religions do not grasp ultimate reality properly. In the sometimes-esoteric world of academic theology, this may be viewed as arcane distinctions of little practical consequence. However, in the daily living of an interreligious marriage, it may have far-reaching implications. If one spouse believes that without accepting Jesus, the other spouse is condemned in the afterlife, this profoundly affects the relationship. If one spouse believes in an afterlife and the other does not, some mutual understanding needs to be worked out in this life, for their benefit and for the benefit of children. If one spouse maintains strict dietary proscriptions derived from his or her religion that the partner does not share, minimally a dialogue between them must occur, and likely this situation requires some form of accommodation or mutual agreement. If one spouse keenly insists on raising the children in his or her religion, the other spouse must agree, capitulate, or resist such an endeavor. If one spouse conscientiously follows the teachings of religious authorities, or even simply factors them into personal and familial decisions, the other spouse will inevitably be affected.

In other words, religious differences transcend theory and can deeply affect the quality of marital relationships. But theological theories and teachings play a key role in these situations because they ground the beliefs and practices of religious practitioners, so they should not be ignored or considered mere theories without consequence.

Religions create constituencies that generally agree on basic teachings and ethical practices. One of the by-products of this development is the ability of one religious community of believers to differentiate itself from other groups of believers from a different religion. On one hand, all this is to the good and gives the religions distinctive identities. On the other hand, it may pit one religion against another, figuratively and sometimes literally. Religions often codify their originating stories and revelations into carefully crafted epistemological claims. Originating language that may be properly characterized as confessional is developed into philosophical language that makes absolute claims. Confessional language is of the type that states "I believe that . . . ," whereas philosophical language is of the type that states "It is the case that . . ." Thus, a Christian rightly claims his or her belief that Jesus is Lord and savior. That is, the Christian *believes* that Jesus delivers salvation to humankind by virtue of his death and resurrection. Of course, the very claim of resurrection is a belief and not a simple historical fact. The Christian professes faith in Jesus and believes that his life and death were salvific and that those who confess belief in Jesus have the possibility of forgiveness of their sins and eternal life awaiting them. Properly speaking, these are beliefs held by the Christian, not certainties. However, for all intents and purposes these beliefs have come to be treated as certainties by Christian churches. By means of councils, pronouncements, and official documents, Christianity proclaims these beliefs to be true and therefore absolute. The problem arises when other religions treat their own beliefs in a similar fashion, and proclaim truths held by their constituents and believed to be valid for all.

All would be well if these faith-claims-turned-truths were identical, but as we know they vary considerably. Examples of conflicting claims abound within the religions of the world. Islam holds that God never became incarnate; Christianity proclaims that Jesus is the incarnate Son of God. Buddhism denies that persons possess an immortal soul; Christianity and Islam believe that each person has an immortal soul. Hinduism teaches the theory of reincarnation; Judaism does not believe that the soul is reincarnated. These represent examples of conflicting claims that the various religions make, and each believes that its claims are the right ones.

The problem arises when these claims confront one another in a world where religions regularly encounter one another. The claims both oppose one another and take on an absolute character. Therefore, for example, if Christians say that Jesus is the only savior, then other religions with their prophets and revelations are rendered inadequate because they do not recognize Jesus's saving character. And Muslims assert that Christians misinterpret God when they make theological pronouncements about God as triune. Buddhists reject the absolutizing character of Christianity's claims about Jesus Christ. Hindus refuse to narrow religious truths by dogmas and doctrines, as Christians have done in their history.

This chapter is directed by the principle that guidance will be more useful than resistance. Not everyone will agree with this principle, I know. For example, a battle has already been engaged within the Jewish community with those who would foster marriage of Jews to Jews exclusively—in part, because they are concerned about the shrinking Jewish community in America. Orthodox Christians have consistently and firmly resisted interfaith marriage and do not show any signs of a change in policy. Roman Catholics have complicated canonical laws that govern marriage even between Christians of different denominations, let alone marriages that involve Catholics and persons from other religions. Islam affords benefits and protections associated with marriage to men differently from those to women, and this especially complicates marriage for Muslim women who want to marry outside their faith. Hindus in America often want to maintain traditions and ties to Indian customs, and marriage between eligible Hindus accommodates this objective. Buddhists adopt a lifestyle / belief system that is tolerant but most readily engaged when couples share its teachings. Fundamentalist Christians cannot imagine accommodating someone who has not accepted Jesus as his or her personal Lord and savior. The Jain community in America keeps close ties among its members and encourages its children to preserve the integrity of the community. In short, religious communities strive to maintain their identity and to increase their faithful membership.

One exception to the strong theological and cultural insistence on cohesiveness may be the Unitarian Church, which welcomes persons of all creeds and no particular creed into its fold. Because of this open-ended theological stance, the Unitarians attract a sizable number of interreligious couples that opt for neither of their traditions but join the Unitarian community as a viable alternative that preserves a religious life without the inherent conflicts involved with the religions they left behind.

Although traditions play an important role for religions in the United States, as elsewhere, American society and culture affect, and to some degree shape, religion in America. Our laws influence how we perceive marriage, and our customs influence how religion and marriage mix. Thus, if states recognize same-sex relationships as worthy of civil and legal protections equivalent to those accorded to marriage, as has happened all over America since the Supreme Court recognized the validity of same-sex marriage, so that the states now sanction same-sex marriages, then our notions of marriage change. If cohabiters receive the same economic arrangements, from health care plans to death benefits, as married couples, then incentives to marry decrease. Many oppose such a change jeopardizing the potential permanence of these changes. Nevertheless, the notion of what type of partnership constitutes a marriage—or enjoys social, economic, and legal benefits of marriage—can no longer be identified exclusively with a heterosexual couple who has exchanged vows publicly in a religious or legal ceremony. Such changes must concern religious institutions that generally support traditional notions of marriage, but these religions find themselves embedded in culture and society and thereby cannot completely escape these influences. This results in a dialectical relationship between the religion and the culture in which each influences the other, consciously or unconsciously.

DUAL IDENTITIES

Peter Phan's work explores the potential dual or multiple religious identity that some persons hold. Thus, they are, for example, Christian *and* Buddhist, Catholic *and* Hindu. His investigation studies those who from birth have embraced two religious traditions, often without conflict. He argues that the salvific process is active in these people and in both the traditions they profess. They are drawn to the Transcendent through more than one religious lens and practice.

The Christian theological tradition has its roots in salvation history. Christians believe that God has acted in human history through the vehicle of persons and events that disclose God's presence and will. A long lineage of Old and New Testament prophets and leaders—such as Abraham, Moses, Isaiah, Jeremiah, Ezekiel, and John the Baptist—were charged with the responsibility to announce God's message and encourage the people of the region to follow God's laws. In God's name these spokespersons invited, encouraged, cajoled, and begged their contemporaries to heed their message, a message they were convinced was from God. For Christians, this message culminated in the person of Jesus as the Messiah and savior. Their salvation was intimately interwoven into human history. This dramatic unfolding of salvation within human history is well chronicled in the Bible.

For some theologians, such as Peter Phan and myself, one of the problems with salvation history is that it excludes much of the world. Persons in the Far East—for example, China—or in South Asia—for example, India—are not included in this history. This history is foreign to them. Even when the Gospel, formulated and announced within this history, is preached to them, it is not related to their experience or history. If this message is the only true means of salvation, why were they not privileged to participate in its unfolding? Further, they also have authoritative texts and traditions that they believe will lead them to salvation. Why should their history and traditions be considered less significant?

If one adopts the position that persons whose history and heritage are different from that of Christianity must forgo their history in favor of salvation history as it occurred in the biblical period, then one practices a type of Christian hegemony. If one adopts the position that peoples and cultures that have not participated in biblical history directly will find the completion of their religious tradition in biblical history and its transhistorical message, the religiously other will be considered a theologically second-class citizen of salvation.

Julius-Kei Kato, a professor at King's University College of Western University in Canada, notes that "in my survey of the work of Peter Phan (and indeed of numerous other Asian North American theologians), I was particularly impressed by the way they insisted on this practical dimension. Virtually all of them were adamant that being a person who partakes in multiple worlds necessarily produces a respect for the generous spirit of inclusion of whoever is considered 'other.'"[19] Couples who enter into interreligious marriages surely participate in multiple worlds religiously. For most of these couples in America, unlike in Asia, they have not grown up with two, or more, traditions, but experience this multiple belonging for the first time in marriage.

Therefore, they generally do not have the tools or the vocabulary to negotiate difference easily. The Church can ignore them, pressure them, or guide them. In its history, the Church has either ignored them or pressured them to adopt Christianity as their joint religion. And to some degree, this has worked. Today, however, it is increasingly less likely to work. In a society that has displaced so many interpersonal experiences with technological ones—with the bank teller being replaced by the automated teller machine and the smart-phone, and with customer service reduced to numeric sequences on the phone, just two examples of this widespread phenomenon—the increased expectations for marriage to fulfill deep personal needs place additional bur-dens on the marriage relationship.

Among the early generations of Americans, the extended family played a key role in family life. Later generations relied more exclusively on the nuclear family. Recent generations have witnessed the erosion of the nuclear family. Increasingly, the circle of affection and the reliability of relationships have nar-rowed to the couple, and although divorce has seriously damaged this fragile bond, couples continue to seek emotional, personal, and sexual fulfillment in marriage. Most Americans no longer expect their companies to be loyal to them, they wonder whether the government will fulfill its promises with Social Security, and they do not anticipate that their children will settle down next door. They look to their spouse for intimacy, trust, and understanding. This expectation does not differ from previous generations, but the notion that they often do not think that they will find these qualities in other relation-ships places a qualitatively higher emotional weight on marriage.

Not long ago, Christianity dominated the religious identity of America, with Judaism as a minority in the background. Today, the religious map of America continues to be dominated by Christianity, but a host of other reli-gions have been interwoven into the tapestry that constitutes our religious identity. In particular, Islam, Hinduism, and Buddhism have joined Juda-ism as significant minority religions, along with smaller numbers of Native American religious practitioners, Sikhs, Jains, and others. The pluralism of religions in the United States affords us a diversity unparalleled anywhere.[20] With each of these religions come unique expressions of faith and practices that sometimes set them apart from the larger culture.

Unmistakably, what people believe affects how they think and act. If one is unacquainted with the religious beliefs of another and then engages that person in courtship, if that is not too quaint an expression today, it will not take long before one bumps into a belief in the form of a practice, a value, a religiously observant relative, or some other concrete reminder. Minimally, these practices require explanation as they create difference for the couple. In order to do so, the partner who holds the belief or engages in the practice should understand why he or she does or believes something, and, addition-ally, this person should be able to explain the belief or practice in a manner that is comprehensible to his or her partner.

Sometimes people engage in practices, particularly religious ones, that reflect unconscious habits, so they can provide no lucid or compelling reason for them. Put simply, they grew up doing this just like their mother, father, aunts, uncles, and siblings. They remain tied to the practice, though it appears theologically vague to them. In such cases, the couple encounters an opportunity to learn together the rationale for a particular belief or practice. A Christian baptism or a Jewish bris, or naming ceremony, both center on an infant child, but the theological explanations differ, and it is likely that the Jewish parent has never been to a baptism and the Christian parent has never attended a bris. If a Christian and a Jew plan to marry, will they be attending baptisms or brises for their children? The question demands consideration, and the answer has significant implications for their marriage and family life. When a Muslim and a Catholic marry, will it be a sacramental union or a legal one? When a Hindu student dates a Methodist, can this lead to marriage, or will that be arranged by the parents? What happens when a Jain man falls in love with a Presbyterian woman? Will he receive the blessing of his family?

The work of Peter Phan recognizes the complexity of religious identification. Single belonging may be the norm for the Church, but for many people it is not. Forcing them to choose may alienate them altogether from religious identification. This terrain is not new. History demonstrates that for centuries, missionaries have encountered peoples of different religions, the difference being that the intention of missionaries has been to have persons from different religions abandon their beliefs and practices to embrace Christianity exclusively. As Phan has shown, this appeared to happen in many Asian countries; but in practice, people lived multiple types of religious belonging, continuing practices from their native religions while at the same time embracing Christianity. Multiple belonging complicates marriages, but it does not prevent them. Thinking through the theological implications of exogamous marriage in the United States surely is not identical to Phan's analysis of religious belonging in Asia. However, it is a condition that merits theological attention.

NOTES

1. Congregation for the Doctrine of the Faith, "Declaration 'Dominus Iesus' on the Unicity and Salvific Universality of Jesus Christ and the Church," www.vatican.va/roman_curia /congregations/cfaith/documents/rc_con_cfaith_doc_20000806_dominus-iesus_en .html.

2. For a personal chronicle of the investigation into Phan's theology, see Peter Phan, The Joy of Religious Pluralism: A Personal Journey (Maryknoll, NY: Orbis, 2017).

3. Peter Phan, Being Religious Interreligiously: Asian Perspectives on Interfaith Dialogue, (Maryknoll, NY: Orbis, 2004); Committee on Doctrine of the United States Conference

of Catholic Bishops, "Clarifications Required by the Book *Being Religious Interreligiously: Asian Perspectives on Interfaith Dialogue* by Reverend Peter C. Phan," www.usccb.org /about/doctrine/publications/upload/statement-on-being-religious-interreligiouly .pdf.

4. "Who Wants to Marry a Soul Mate?" National Marriage Project, http://nationalmarriage project.org/resources-category/marriage/.

5. Don Browning, "The Task Force of Religious Institutions in Strengthening Families," issued jointly by the Religion, Culture, and Family Project of the University of Chicago Divinity School and the Communitarian Network, https://www2.gwu.edu/~ccps/documents /1998TaskofReligiousInstitutions.pdf. In 2017, the percentage is lower with many millennials marrying in secular venues without an ordained presider, but there are no current statistics available.

6. Jacob Lupfer, "Fewer Couples Are Marrying in churches. Does It Matter?" Religion News Service, June 7, 2018, https://religionnews.com/2018/06/07/fewer-couples-are -marrying-in-churches-does-is-matter/.

7. See, e.g., *The Oxford Dictionary of World Religions*, edited by John Bowker (New York: Oxford University Press, 2000), online version.

8. Matti Terho, "Mixed Marriages: A Lutheran Perspective," *Ecumenism* 131 (1998): 32.

9. Susan Katz Miller argues for dual religious identities and chronicles families that have successfully negotiated religious differences; Susan Katz Miller, *Being Both: Embracing Two Religions in One Interfaith Family* (Boston: Beacon Press, 2013). Naomi Schaefer Riley argues the opposite, claiming that interfaith marriages undermine religious commitment; Naomi Schaefer Riley, *'Til Faith Do Us Part: How Interfaith Marriage Is Transforming Marriage* (New York: Oxford University Press, 2013).

10. Pew Foundation surveys indicate that 58 percent of Jews marry exogamously; Pew Foundation, *A Portrait of Jewish Americans*, "Chapter 2: Intermarriage and Other Demographics," October 1, 2013, www.pewforum.org/2013/10/01/chapter-2-intermarriage-and -other-demographics/.

11. Many websites and books offer advice on interfaith ceremonies. See, e.g., Interfaith Families, "The Knot," www.theknot.com/interfaith-weddings; and "Wedding Ceremony Ideas for Interfaith Couples," in *Celebrating Interfaith Marriages: Creating Your Jewish/Christian Ceremony*, by Devon A. Lerner (New York: Henry Holt, 2011), www.interfaithfamily .com/files/pdf/WEDDING%20CEREMONY%20IDEAS%20FOR%20INTERFAITH %20COUPLES.pdf.

12. Arthur Hertzberg, *The Jews in America* (New York: Columbia University Press, 1998).

13. Rahel Musleah, "Jewish Jeopardy," *Reform Judaism*, Fall 2001, 21.

14. Jack Wertheimer, "Judaism without Limits," *Commentary* 104, no. 1 (1997): 25.

15. Eric H. Yoffie, "The Triumph of Outreach," *Reform Judaism*, Fall 2001, 21.

16. Increasingly, younger Americans do not indicate any religious identification and are called "nones" in surveys asking religious identity. See books by the evangelical pastor James Emery White, *The Rise of the Nones* (Grand Rapids, MI: Baker Books, 2014); and James Emery White, *Meet Generation Z: Understanding and Reaching the New Post-Christian World* (Grand Rapids, MI: Baker Books, 2017). Also see Santa Clara professor Elizabeth Drescher, *Choosing Our Religion: The Spiritual Lives of America's Nones* (New York: Oxford University Press, 2016).

17. The Pew Research Center reports that "adults in religiously mixed marriages are, by and large, less religious than their counterparts who are married to spouses who share their

faith. They attend religious services less often, pray less frequently, tend to be less likely to believe in God with absolute certainty, and are less inclined to say religion is very important in their lives." Pew Research Center, *One-in-Five US Adults Were Raised in Interfaith Homes*, "2: Religion in Marriages and Families," October 26, 2016, www.pewforum.org /2016/10/26/religion-in-marriages-and-families/.

18. The use of the term "God," though common in Western writings, does not adequately account for the range of interpretations of a higher being, state, or power found in religions. In order to avoid a hegemonic nomenclature, I use the term "Transcendent" to refer to the reality that Christians call God. Even this more inclusive term may not be fully adequate for a philosophy like Buddhism, but at least it avoids the implicit personalism inherent in the Western use of the term "God." Sometimes, I use the term "God" because this is familiar language for believers and nonbelievers alike. But I want the monotheistic reader to understand the term to be inclusive and not exclusive of other ways of conceiving the Transcendent as found in Buddhism, forms of Hinduism, and other important religions.

19. Julius-Kei Kato, *Religious Language and Asian American Hybridity* (New York: Palgrave, 2016), 52.

20. For a thorough study of the religious complexion of America, see Diana L. Eck, *A New Religious America: How a Christian Country Has Now Become the World's Most Religiously Diverse Nation* (San Francisco: Harper, 2001).

CHAPTER 9

Peter Phan and Ecclesiology
Beyond Borders

Brian P. Flanagan

Any brief review of a theologian as significant, prolific, and varied in his interests as Peter Phan will inevitably fall short, particularly because, as this volume goes to publication, I, happily, do not expect that we have heard the last from him. And given the connections of the topics at hand and Phan's treatment of them, it is doubly challenging, and a bit unrepresentative, to abstract out from the wider corpus of his writing an understanding of Phan's overall ecclesiology. Nevertheless, the attempt is worthwhile, because, *pace* some Catholic watchdogs of doctrine, I judge Peter Phan to be a theologian of the Church, in two senses: first, as a theologian deeply grounded in the complicated, complex life of the Christian community in history, whose biography and contextual identities and commitments exemplify deep, critical love as a son of the Church; and, second, as a theologian whose work, even when not explicitly focused upon ecclesiology, always explores theological questions with an eye toward how the answers he and others give to them will affect the Church, both positively and negatively.[1] Whether in his explicit ecclesiological texts or in his treatment of other areas such as religious pluralism, migration, eschatology, and fundamental theology, Phan has always written with, for, and about the Church.

In this chapter, I hope to highlight both these aspects of Phan's theological achievements. First, I focus upon Phan as a contextual theologian—as all theologians are—who not only has a context but also has thought critically about his context and how to do theology in and for that context. Especially as an Asian American, as an immigrant, and as a Roman Catholic priest, Phan writes in and through a particular ecclesial experience, and provides a model for authenticity in doing so. Second, I focus more explicitly upon the content of Phan's distinctive ecclesiological vision, particularly by highlighting three related qualities of the Church that he has promoted in his writing: a Church and an ecclesiology that are *regnocentric*; a Church and an ecclesiology that are *dialogical*; and a Church and an ecclesiology that are *kenotic*. In all this, I hope to bring out the consonances between the theological method and conclusions that Phan has maintained throughout his career, and the kind of ecclesiology and ecclesial practice being currently promoted by a fellow migrant and Catholic priest with a similar vision, Pope Francis.

PHAN'S METHOD:
CONTEXTUAL ECCLESIOLOGY

First, I offer two comments about Phan's ecclesiological method. Like all his theology, Phan is rooted deeply in contexts, "betwixt and between" as they may be.[2] In particular, in his writings on the Church, he unsurprisingly draws deeply from the wells of Asian ecclesiology, especially as expressed in statements of the Federation of Asian Bishops' Conferences and that body's Office of Theological Concerns. Asian ecclesiological reflections on "a new way of being Church," particularly as expressed in documents of the Federation of Asian Bishops, provide *the* crucial context for Phan's reflections on the Church.

Second, from this Asian and Asian American context, one notes not only what ecclesiological topics and questions Phan (and other Asian ecclesiologists) raise for our attention, and what topics they tend to leave out. He has written about the topics most often absent in Asian ecclesiology that are often the primary focus of much European and North American ecclesiology: "papal primacy and infallibility, apostolic succession, magisterium, episcopal power, the hierarchical structure, canon law, the Roman Curia, and the like."[3] Phan does not focus solely or primarily upon these "churchy" issues, as he names them. These decisions are rooted in part in the kenotic ecclesiology I discuss below, but they also indicate something important about Phan and his valuation of different topics in theology and ecclesiology. With no disrespect intended, we might ask where Phan has been swimming. He writes in his correspondence with William Cardinal Levada over the investigation of his writings that he is "a very small fish in the theological pond,"[4] "a tiny minnow, as it were."[5] It might be better to compare him with one of those deep sea fish, those with the fortitude, the strong bones, and the thick skin to reach some of the deepest questions in ecclesiology by comparison

with those of us splashing around in the relatively shallower depths of ecclesiastical polity. Phan points theology, and the Church, away from the "easy"
questions of papal primacy and episcopal authority to the deepwater ecclesiological question of what the Church is and what it is called to be in the
service of the reign of God.

In many ways Phan's work therefore parallels, from the beginning, the
working ecclesiology of Pope Francis. In the preconclave speech he gave
before his election, Pope Francis famously critiques not only a theology but
a Church that spends too much time talking about itself instead of about its
mission to the world. According to notes released after his election as pope,
he said: "When the Church does not come out from itself to evangelize, it
becomes self-referential and gets sick (one thinks of the woman hunched
over upon herself in the Gospel). The evils that, in the passing of time, afflict
the ecclesiastical institutions have a root in self-referentiality, in a sort of
theological narcissism."[6]

Phan, anticipating Pope Francis's call, has in his theology always placed
the mission of the Church and its broad role in the making whole of humanity
and creation at the heart of his theology; attention to the details of ecclesiological organization, important and necessary as they may be, have taken
second place to focus upon the Church's mission. Phan refers to this "new
way of being Church," and I would argue of doing ecclesiology, as "a sort of
Copernican revolution" that "de-centers the church in the sense that it makes
the center of the Christian life not the Church but the reign of God."[7] This
Copernican revolution helps to locate his theology as contextual, as all theologies are but of which not all theologies are aware, rooted not only in Phan's
individual biography but also in the contexts, churches, and ways of being
religious of the Asian and Asian American communities in and from which
Phan has pursued his scholarly and pastoral career.

THE CHURCH AND ITS MISSION

One way of thinking systematically about this Copernican revolution in
Phan's ecclesiology can be derived from a concept developed by the ecclesiologist Neil Ormerod that is helpful in explaining the importance of Phan's
work. In his book *Revisioning the Church*, Ormerod draws on Bernard Lonergan and Robert Doran to discuss "integrator" and "operator" functions in
the Church—that is, the institutions, symbols, and narratives that point to
the conservation of past values and establishment of identity, and those that
push ahead and outward, and are focused less on what the community is

supposed to be and what the community is supposed to do.[8] Helpful, if simplifying, shorthand for the ecclesial "integrator function" might be "ecclesial identity," while for the operator function we might use "ecclesial mission." We have a rich ecclesiological vocabulary to talk about ecclesial identity, and, in fact, many of the "churchy" issues that dominate European and North American ecclesiology are questions about integration, identity, and conservation. Ormerod identifies the interaction between the two as a dialectic, a dynamic, transformative system in which the operator function, what the Church does, defines and redefines—or ought to define and redefine—what the Church is.[9] But "real" ecclesiology is often reduced to questions regarding the nature of the Church, communion ecclesiology, the structures of ecclesial authority, and other "integrator" topics. Why?

Some of this is no doubt historical—an accident of the particular vagaries of Western European history, a luxury of working in a primarily Christian society, a by-product, for Catholics, of the ultramontanist strategies of survival of the nineteenth century. But for today, I would also add that the particular anxieties for identity and connection, for "integration" into a community in a more-than-technical sense, have a particularly strong hold in places like the North American and European contexts in a late capitalist, consumerist "secular age." Among other things, consumerist culture fosters increased concern about who you are, where you stand in relation to others and to the wider community, and what you can/should do in that situation to improve your odds of finding yourself and finding your ideal partner or community of belonging. It does that because it wants to sell you the products that will either fulfill that need for identity or need for community (and the two are closely related), and continues to stimulate anxiety about the validity of those identities because if you stop attempting to find yourself or find your ideal community, you stop consuming quite so frenetically.

Christianity, as well as other religious traditions and serious nonreligious forms of human pursuit, rightly presents a pathway to an alternative source of identity beyond consumer consumption; an identity and a community that cannot be bought and sold can be a way off the carousel of late capitalist anxiety. And yet, as Vincent Miller argues in *Consuming Religion*, the structures of consumer society run deeply not only in "the world," "out there," but also in the Church, that is, in us.[10] In this context, our contemporary hunger for identity and for community can, providentially, be satisfied by the new identity in Christ given freely rather than purchased, and by the communion of the Church rooted in an open table rather than a VIP section. The shadow side of this positive good in this particular context, however, is that because identity is received as a providential, even miraculous, deliverance, there is a greater temptation to focus upon the integrator function of the Church rather than the operator function. In other words, the joy of being given identity and community in Christ in a consumer culture tempts us to focus upon *what the Church is* rather than *what the Church is called to do*, upon integrator over operator, upon identity over mission. A quick look at what Church people—and particularly ecclesiologists—spend their time writing about and arguing about suggests that this is true across many of the ideological, traditional/progressive divisions we find within our Church.[11]

A REGNOCENTRIC CHURCH

A focus upon the operations of the Church rather than the question of its integration as a community characterizes both Peter Phan's ecclesiology and the "Copernican revolution" in ecclesiology that he identifies in the contexts of the Asian Church and Asian American Church. Three of his major characteristics help to summarize the way we might think about and promote a Church and ecclesiology that are *regnocentric*, a Church and ecclesiology that are *dialogical*, and a Church and ecclesiology that are kenotic.

The call of the Church to be "regnocentric"—that is, to make the reign of God rather than the Church itself the focus of Christian life and work— is, on its face, uncontroversial. Fifty years after the Second Vatican Council, the idea of distinguishing the Church from the reign of God, and of understanding the Church as but "the initial budding forth" of the reign of God (Lumen Gentium 5) or as the kingdom "now present in mystery" (Lumen Gentium 3) is, in most areas of the Church, happily received. But such a distinction comes with consequences, particularly with regard to understanding and studying the Church primarily in terms of its providential function in the history of salvation rather than by questions of its identity. As Phan writes, "What the Church is, is determined by what it must do; its essence is defined by its function."[12]

In his work, Phan, as an ecclesiologist, points us gently away from the integrator function of the Church to the operator function—as does, conveniently, Pope Francis. A regnocentric Church and a regnocentric ecclesiology foster a "moving away from the Church *ad intra* to the Church *ad extra*, from self-absorption to mission."[13] Such a regnocentric Church is by nature missionary, that is, is directed outward to the world, and is missionary not primarily *to* the world, or to the peoples of Asia in which this concept is most elaborated in Phan's work, but missionary *among* and *with* the world, its peoples, and its religious traditions.[14] Focusing on the Kingdom of God as a shared center of gravity opens up space for the forms of "being religious interreligiously" and for collaborating in our work for the kingdom with other religious communities and believers, and others of goodwill. From within this context, the mission of the Church "is not to expand the Church and its structures . . . in order to enlarge the sphere of influence for the Church, but rather to be a transparent sign and effective instrument of the saving presence of the reign of God—the reign of justice, peace, and love—of which the Church is a seed."[15]

Phan has written much on how this regnocentric vision has major implications for our understanding of other religious communities and other people of goodwill, and for the continuing path of dialogue in the Church to be addressed below. Rooted in the Asian context, in which Christianity is a minority community in the pluralistic and complex "multilingual, multiracial, multiethnic, multicultural, and multireligious world of Asia," Phan's theology has opened up major pathways for thinking about religious pluralism, multiple religious belonging, and interfaith dialogue.[16]

At the same time, however, that such a regnocentric vision changes how we think of other religious believers, it also fundamentally challenges how we think about the Church. It especially influences the practical life of the Church when, in the messiness of actual historical life, choices must be made about what programs, forms of institutions, and activities best serve the reign of God. Phan leaves open a question that should challenge those of us who spend time studying or strengthening the integrator functions of the Church. He writes, "Real life does not always allow an easy choice between Church and reign of God, and not every decision in favor of the Church promotes the reign of God. When push comes to shove, what is to be favored, the reign of God or the Church?"[17]

One can find a similar vision in the working ecclesiology of Pope Francis. Throughout his papacy, he has taught and attempted to embody in personal and collective action his vision of a Church that places itself at the service of the reign of God. Echoing Phan's idea of a "Copernican revolution" that decenters the Church, Pope Francis writes in *Evangelii gaudium* that "I prefer a Church which is bruised, hurting and dirty because it has been out on the streets, rather than a Church which is unhealthy from being confined and from clinging to its own security. I do not want a Church concerned with being at the center and which then ends by being caught up in a web of obsessions and procedures."[18] His oft-repeated image of the Church as a "field hospital" indicates some sense of a Church that is radically embedded in the lives of the people that it serves, especially at the margins, rather than isolated or, worse, placed above that experience, out of the fray.[19] A regnocentric ecclesiology, and regnocentric ecclesial practice, decenter the Church in two ways, locating the reign of God and the Gospel of Christ at the center of the Church's life, and locating the Church at the peripheries, the margins, of the complex and pluralistic world of real life, especially where life is most threatened.

A DIALOGICAL CHURCH

This rethinking of our priorities and of the Church's location leads to the next characteristic of the Church that Phan highlights, the Church as *dialogical*. Phan's concept of the Church as dialogical, like his concept of a regnocentric Church, is again, on its surface, relatively uncontroversial, given that promoting dialogue, even if sometimes observed only in the breach, has been a constant of ecclesial vocabulary for at least the past fifty years. But, again, Phan has gone deeper in exploring the ecclesiological implications of what such an ecclesiological move entails. In this, Phan's work maintains its particular contextual origins within pluralist Asian and Asian American contexts. Phan draws upon the "triple dialogue" developed within Asian Catholic theology—that is, "dialogue with the Asian people, especially the poor; with their cultures; and with their religions."[20] He takes this further, connecting the reality of the multiple forms of dialogue with the "churchy" topic of the *magisteria* (plural) of the Church. In addition to the episcopal magisterium of the bishops of the Church, and the theological magisterium often claimed or reclaimed by academic theology, he highlights three additional *magisteria*: the magisterium of the lay faithful, the magisterium of the poor, and the magisterium of believers of other religions. In addition to the classical topic of *sensus fidei/fidelium* that arises in discussing a lay magisterium, he writes movingly of the special role of the poor as "teachers of the faith." He draws on liberation theologians to argue that "it is the 'magisterium of the poor'—Christians and non-Christians—that can teach us, more effectively and persuasively than any other Church magisterium, how to be a disciple of Jesus today."[21] "Without the magisterium of the poor, Christian as well as non-Christian, who are the living icons of Jesus the Crucified and the object of God's preferential love, the teachings of bishops and theologians about God and the Crucified will be no more than a noisy gong and clanging cymbal."[22]

Dialogue has relevance not only within the communities that compose the Church, especially those most often neglected or voiceless, but also for the Church's dialogue with other religious traditions and with the wider world. Based upon the emphasis on real dialogue found in the Asian context,

Phan suggests that the Church has something to learn from believers of other religions: "Those who accept with humility and gratitude the magisterium of the *pagans* can bear witness to their goodness and holiness of life, the truth of their teachings, the nobility of their ethics, and the transformative power of their spirituality."[23] His reimagination of the multiple *magisteria* of the Church encourages real, multiple dialogues within the Church, rather than a carefully disguised monologue or an impoverished dialogue between two groups of competing theological experts.

Again, key elements of Pope Francis's working ecclesiology and practice are foreshadowed in Phan's priorities. "Dialogue" is one of the key terms and concepts thus far of Francis's entire magisterium. As he himself said in a 2017 speech, "If there is one word that we should never tire of repeating, it is this: dialogue. We are called to promote a culture of dialogue by every possible means and thus to rebuild the fabric of society."[24] A major section of *Evangelii gaudium* treats the role dialogue plays in conversation with the society, with other Christian churches, and with other religious traditions;[25] the encyclical *Laudato si'* is premised upon the fruitfulness of dialogue for the healing of our environmentally and economically damaged common home, and includes major suggestions for future dialogue at the international, national, and local levels.[26] At the level of Pope Francis's basic conception of the life of the Church, he conceives of a Church that "lives by dialoging" in ways that deeply resonate with Phan's idea of a church committed to patient, respectful, and charitable dialogue with its communal and religious neighbors.[27]

A second key aspect of Pope Francis's idea of a dialogical Church that relates to Phan's ecclesiology is Francis's emphasis upon encounter in general, and on encounter with the poor in particular. If the Church is to listen to the "magisterium of the poor," as Phan suggests, then the church needs to be "a Church which is poor and for the poor," in Francis's vision.[28] Francis continues, with Phanian emphases:

> They [the poor] have much to teach us. Not only do they share in the *sensus fidei*, but in their difficulties they know the suffering Christ. We need to let ourselves be evangelized by them. The new evangelization is an invitation to acknowledge the saving power at work in their lives and to put them at the centre of the Church's pilgrim way. We are called to find Christ in them, to lend our voice to their causes, but also to be their friends, to listen to them, to speak for them and to embrace the mysterious wisdom which God wishes to share with us through them.[29]

Learning from the poor, not from a distance but through encounter and spiritual closeness, is a crucial aspect of living as a dialogical Church, in which the magisterium of the poor is heard and received as a privileged expression of the *sensus fidelium*.

A KENOTIC CHURCH

From this, we can turn to the third, and arguably the most interesting and challenging characteristic Phan highlights, the Church and its ecclesiology as *kenotic*. Though Phan is distinctive in the way he expresses the previous two characteristics, calls for the Church to be focused on the Kingdom of God and to be dialogical are relatively commonplace. The same cannot be said for what Phan terms a "kenotic ecclesiology," that is, a Church that in its service to the kingdom and missionary dialogue has the courage to imitate its Lord by dying to itself so that the reign of God might live. Writing about the Church in Asia, Phan states: "It is only by bearing witness to and serving the reign of God among the Asian peoples, and not by expanding its membership and sociopolitical influence, that the Church will truly become Asian. To be truly church, the Asian Church, paradoxically, must cease to be 'Church,' that is, it must 'empty' itself and cease to exist for its own sake for the service of a higher reality, namely, the Kingdom of God."[30]

What Phan says about the Church in Asia can arguably be said about the Church, period: "To be truly Church, the Church, paradoxically, must cease to be 'Church,' that is, it must 'empty' itself and cease to exist for its own sake."[31] Here I think we see the more radical ecclesiological engine that is driving much of the rest of Phan's conception of the Church and its characteristics. To return to Ormerod's terms, here we see the possibility of a Church whose operator function, whose mission, *is* its only integrator function. Is this desirable, or even possible?

At a first instance, one can raise numerous problems that such an understanding raises. First, one could argue that this is not how human institutions or societies work—even if, historically, we may have overemphasized the formation of identity over mission in the service of the Kingdom, it is possible for a community to serve the Kingdom without having some form of identity, some form of integrating reality, however minimal or "weakly" claimed. Second, the idea of a Church that loses itself runs headlong into a history of the Church in which the claim to institutional identity and power has defined epochs of Church history and seemed crucial to generations of bishops, theologians, and the lay faithful whom Phan believes should teach us. It seems possible (and possibly providential) that only in the Asian context, where the Church is such a stark minority, could one even conceive of a Church that helps the Kingdom appear through its own disappearance. Third, in the secular age of the Global North, this trajectory runs against some of the major fears for identity, community, and stability that fracture life in our modern consumerist societies.

And yet, here Phan's work points to a possibly new insight into the mystery of the Church, where the paradox of the kenosis of Christ might yet help us understand the paradox of a kenotic Church. It is possible that the Church is called to lose its life so as to save it, and that by taking on John the Baptist's faith it may be called to state that "we must decrease, that the kingdom must increase." A resource here might be some of the eschatological imagination discussed earlier, or von Balthasar's explorations of the Word of God losing its identity on Holy Saturday almost to the breaking point so as to receive its identity anew as the Risen One.[32] It is difficult to know what this would look like, and how deeply it would change the way in which we, not only in Asia but here in North America, "do church."

Once again, Phan's vision seems to be deeply resonant with the ecclesiological thought and practice of Pope Francis. Phan himself highlights the similarities between the kenotic ecclesiology developed within his own thought and Asian ecclesiology more broadly, and Pope Francis's statement in *Evangelii gaudium* that he "prefers a Church which is bruised, hurting, and dirty because it has been out on the streets."[33] As Judith Gruber suggests, the images Francis uses for the Church as a pilgrim people and as leaven within humanity in *Evangelii gaudium*'s paragraphs 111 and 114 point to this kenotic ecclesiology: "Both metaphors resist the idea of a Church as a self-contained, independent, autonomous body in clear delineation from the world, and instead imagine a Church open in terms of both time and space; they picture a Church in the midst of the world."[34] Further, Gruber writes, "Kenotic theology . . . therefore does not allow for clear-cut definitions of Church and world, but makes for blurred, leaking, and shifting borders between them. God's kenotic revelation, in short, results in an instable Church."[35] Such instability of identity, in contrast to the almost overdetermined security of identity that has been a hallmark of modern Catholic ecclesiology and self-understanding, might be the cause, one suspects, of some of the traditionalist backlash to Pope Francis's prioritization of mission over communion, of operator function over integrator function. The blurring of borders, perhaps even the blurring of religious borders in the complex realities of "being religious interreligiously" and multiple religious belonging that characterize Phan's ecclesiology, similarly press forward to a vision of a Church that is *for* and *with* rather than *against* or *above* other cultural, sociopolitical, and even religious communities.

CONCLUSION

These resonances between the ecclesiology of Peter Phan—with his focus on a Church that is regnocentric, dialogical, and kenotic—and Pope Francis's ecclesiological thought and practice, suggest that Phan, swimming in the deep waters of basic ecclesiological questions, has outlined over the course of his career a theology being realized today in the renewal of the Catholic Church. We owe an ironic debt of gratitude, notwithstanding the real suffering involved, to the Congregation for the Doctrine of the Faith and the US Bishops' Committee on Doctrine for providing him the bittersweet stimulus for expanding these ideas in greater depth, most recently in *The Joys of Religious Pluralism*. And, finally, particularly in relation to the question of what a truly kenotic Church might look like, there are both room and a need for the continuation of Phan's project, in the exploration of the complexity of identity in a Church that recognizes its connections with other religious traditions and its internal diversity, and that puts the reign of God rather than itself at the center of its self-reflection. The migrant Church, and its ecclesiologists, are hereby challenged to walk in the pathways that Phan has suggested for us.

NOTES

1. Peter Phan, "How It All Began: History of Two Investigations of an Obscure Book," in *The Joy of Religious Pluralism*, by Peter Phan (Maryknoll, NY: Orbis, 2017), 1–19.
2. Peter Phan, "Betwixt and Between: Doing Theology with Memory and Imagination," in *Journeys at the Margin: Toward an Autobiographical Theology in American-Asian Perspective*, ed. Peter Phan and Jung Young Lee (Collegeville, MN: Liturgical Press, 1999), 113–33.
3. Phan, "A Church in the Service of the Reign of God," *Zeitschrift für Missionswissenschaft und Religionswissenschaft* 95 (2011): 105.
4. Phan, *Joy of Religious Pluralism*, 189.
5. Phan, x.
6. Quoted by Sandro Magister, "'The Last Words Before the Conclave," March 27, 2013, www.chiesa.espressonline.it.
7. Peter Phan, *Christianity with an Asian Face* (Maryknoll, NY: Orbis, 2003), 176.
8. See Neil Ormerod, *Revisioning the Church* (Minneapolis: Augsburg, 2014), 66–67.
9. See Ormerod, *Revisioning*, 68.

10. Vincent Miller, *Consuming Religion* (London: Bloomsbury, 2005).
11. See also Brian Flanagan, "Communion Ecclesiologies as Contextual Theologies," *Horizons* 40 (2013): 53–70.
12. Phan, *Joy of Religious Pluralism*, 133.
13. Phan, 132.
14. Cf. Phan, 146–59.
15. Phan, *Christianity with an Asian Face*, 176.
16. Phan, *Being Religious Interreligiously: Asian Perspectives on Interfaith Dialogue* (Maryknoll, NY: Orbis, 2004), 117.
17. Phan, *Joy of Religious Pluralism*, 134.
18. Pope Francis, *Evangelii gaudium*, §49.
19. See Antonio Spadaro, "A Big Heart Open to God: An Interview with Pope Francis," *America*, September 30, 2013; and Blaise Cupich, "Field Hospital," in *A Pope Francis Lexicon*, ed. Joshua J. McElwee and Cindy Wooden (Collegeville, MN: Liturgical Press, 2018), 72–74.
20. Phan, *Joy of Religious Pluralism*, 137.
21. Phan, 43.
22. Phan, 43.
23. Phan, 45.
24. Pope Francis, "Address," Conferral of the Charlemagne Prize, May 6, 2016, www .vatican.va/content/francesco/en/speeches/2016/may/documents/papa-francesco _20160506_premio-carlo-magno.html.
25. Pope Francis, *Evangelii Gaudium*, §238–58.
26. Pope Francis, *Laudato si'*, §163–88.
27. Pope Francis, "General Audience, October 22, 2016," quoted by Roberto O. González Nieves, "Dialogue," in *Pope Francis Lexicon*, 40.
28. Pope Francis, *Evangelii gaudium*, §198.
29. Pope Francis.
30. Phan, *Joy of Religious Pluralism*, 133.
31. Phan, "Church in the Service of the Reign of God," 106.
32. Cf. Hans Urs von Balthasar, *Mysterium Paschale* (London: T & T Clark, 1970).
33. Pope Francis *Evangelii gaudium*, §49, quoted by Phan, *Joy of Religious Pluralism*, 132.
34. Judith Gruber, "'The Lord, Your God, Is in Your Midst' (*EG* 4): *Evangelii Gaudium*—Francis's Call for a Kenotic Theology," in *Pope Francis and the Future of Catholicism*, ed. Gerard Mannion (Cambridge: Cambridge University Press, 2017), 70.
35. Gruber.

CHAPTER 10

Dialogue in a Multireligious and Political Ecosystem: Understanding Catholic Relations with Other Religions in Mainland China

Stephanie M. Wong

How can we best understand the work of Chinese Catholics in interreligious dialogue? Our understanding must account for three major factors that profoundly shape Christianity in mainland China: the minority status of Christians as a demographic group, the plurality and multiple religious belonging common to Chinese religious life, and the political power of the state managing religious groups and their relations for state ends like social stability and harmony. As Peter Phan has noted, however, such religiosocial dynamics are hardly new:[1] early communities of Jewish Christians / Christian Jews arose in a pluralistic religious context, and the Jesus movement took shape under the wary eye and legislative hand of the Roman Empire. Therefore, to understand interreligious dialogue in China today is not to pursue an idiosyncratic case study irrelevant to the rest of the worldwide Church. Rather, it can help us gain insight into conditions that have shaped Christian conversation, service, and witness from the start.

In this chapter, I draw upon insights from sociologists to set the Catholic Church's dialogic ideals within the social patterns of religious life in the mainland. At the moment, there are two main models for understanding the dynamics of religious groups in China: the "religious market" model and the "religious ecology" model. My hope is that if we view Catholics as belonging to social and discursive matrices—in other words, in the reality of being already embedded in a multireligious environment, and one that is not laissez-faire but curated by the state—then we can more concretely understand the likelihood, challenges, and possibilities for dialogue.

THE STATE OF CATHOLIC INVOLVEMENT IN INTERRELIGIOUS DIALOGUE IN CHINA

In general, the question of whether to engage in interreligious dialogue has been answered in the affirmative by the Catholic magisterium. Since Vatican II, Church documents have endorsed interreligious dialogue as an important and even "integral element" of the Church's mission (*Redemptoris missio*)[2] and an "integral dimension of human life."[3] Nonetheless, Catholic participation and interest in formal interreligious dialogue efforts today are generally low in mainland China, even in comparison with nearby Catholic communities in Hong Kong, Macao, and Taiwan. As the Jesuit Benoît Vermander, a professor at Fudan University in Shanghai, has put it, "Interreligious dialogue in China is still at a nascent stage. Religions coexist more than they dialogue and collaborate."[4] What are the reasons for this?

First, if we focus on formal, ecclesiastically organized interreligious dialogues, then it is true such events are rarely organized at the diocesan or parish level. This is for the very practical reason that clergy and vowed religious are extremely busy. If they are to be the ones spearheading such efforts, then this is made difficult by the fact that the ratio of Catholic religious ministers and the ordinary faithful is so low in the mainland. On average, for every Catholic priest or sister, there are more than a thousand Catholics, though of course local ratios vary considerably.[5] Priests and vowed women are stretched to the limit trying to serve the pastoral needs of their Catholic communities. Their work leaves little time and energy for activities, like interreligious dialogue, which are still perceived to be secondary.

Second, Chinese Catholics often interpret the faith with a highly ecclesiological view of salvation that can make it seem pointless or even dangerous to venture out into the non-Catholic religious landscape. Many Chinese Catholics have maintained the conservative tenor and hierarchical understanding of the faith that was normative in the global church before Vatican II. As the sociologist Richard Madsen puts it, the Chinese Catholic Church was formed by a "pre-Vatican II, Counter Reformation theology" that was keen to reinforce the authority of the hierarchical church and suspicious of pluralism.[6] Over the last few decades, conciliar and postconciliar teachings on interreligious dialogue slowly entered into Chinese conversation through a number of avenues: through translations of key documents, courses taught by foreign theologians, and study abroad programs for Chinese seminarians. Nonetheless, most ordinary Catholics continue to view the Church primarily on a vertical access, as the arbiter of salvation and guardian of moral order in the world.

This theology has strengthened the community in hard times, but it can situate dialogue with non-Catholics as peripheral to the faith. For Chinese Catholics who maintain what Madsen calls a strong "hierarchical imagination," the hope of belonging within a divine and eternal community is closely tied to participation in the Church's displays of hierarchy.[7] Thus, the case must be made for why one should arrange lateral dialogues with people outside the ecclesial community. For instance, in an interview with Father Edward Chau of the Diocesan Commission for Interreligious Dialogue in Hong Kong, a lay Catholic woman readily acknowledges the practical good in, for example, teaming up with Buddhists to care for the elderly. But she also asks with some bafflement about the usefulness or liability of dialogue events for her faith life: "If I were to go to those interfaith activities how would they help in my salvation? What would they do for the salvation of my soul? Why should I take part? I should think that doing less would result in fewer mistakes!"[8] This remark captures a common hesitancy about engaging in interreligious dialogue among Chinese Catholics.

Third, if we consider state-organized religious dialogues, then Catholics' hesitancy to engage may come from fears of the dialogue being instrumentalized by the state. After all, in the People's Republic of China, there are both religious and political interests at play in Chinese interreligious dialogue efforts. The United Front Work Department (which has directly managed religious affairs since 2018, when the State Administration for Religious Affairs was brought more directly under the Central Committee of the Chinese Community Party) promotes interreligious dialogue for state-defined social goods.[9]

According to the Fudan University professor Xu Yihua, at a 2016 event sponsored by the State Administration for Religious Affairs in Hamburg, there are four sociopolitical reasons why the officially atheist government considers interreligious dialogue necessary for the stability of Chinese society:[10] (1) the rapid growth of Chinese religious beliefs across religious traditions, (2) the acceleration of economic and social mobility and migration putting different groups into contact with each other, (3) for combating religious extremism and ethnic separatism, and (4) for foreign relations, to facilitate cultural understanding in the Belt and Road Initiative. In this way, state-sponsored interreligious dialogue is a means to stabilize Chinese society at home and promote Chinese soft power abroad.

The state's stated desire for social harmony is not necessarily at odds with the Catholic rationale for dialogue. For instance, Wang Zuo'an, the former director of the State Administration for Religious Affairs and now vice minister of the United Front Work Department, wrote in a 2010 paper titled "Religious Harmony" that "all religions should enhance mutual understanding and empathy through dialogue. . . . It is imperative to promote the principle of 'harmony without uniformity' and learn to respect each other and jointly shoulder social responsibilities."[11] Understanding, empathy, and social responsibility are values also upheld by the Church.

Nonetheless, because of historic tension between the Church and the Communist government, some Catholics are suspicious of any interreligious dialogue effort that comes from the state because it comes from the state. Top officials of the Catholic Patriotic Association participate in the state's institutions for dialogue—for instance, the Joint Conference of National Religious Organizations (全国性宗教团体联席会议), which was established to serve as an ongoing mechanism for exchange and cooperation between religious groups. However, as Vermander notes, some religious groups may react with a "natural tendency to stress their specificity rather than letting other faith experiences resonate with their own" because they are loath to appear as pawns in any government initiative.[12]

Finally, a fourth reason for the low levels of activity in interreligious dialogue may simply be the narrowness of our starting focus on formal dialogues. To expand the definition of dialogue is in keeping with the Catholic Church's own teaching on what constitutes dialogue. The Pontifical Council for Interreligious Dialogue acknowledges multiple possible modes: It is not limited to the "dialogue of theological exchange," in which elite specialists discuss matters of doctrine. The Council also recommends the "dialogue of life" as Christians strive to live in an open and neighborly spirit; the "dialogue of action," in which Christians collaborate with others for the integral development and liberation of people; and the "dialogue of religious experience," where practitioners might share spiritual practices like prayer and contemplation.[13] In affirming these multiple dialogues, the Church acknowledges that religions are not only sets of beliefs to be talked about but also lived traditions in dynamic engagement with their wider societies. My intention in this chapter is to explore the dynamics of interreligious dialogue in this wider sense of lived interreligious relations.

THEORIZING INTERRELIGIOUS DIALOGUE: ITS DESIRED "WHAT" AND SITUATIONAL "HOW"

To understand interreligious dialogue in China, we must consider both the desired "what" of interreligious exchange and its situational "how." In academia, scholars of religious diversity in the West have identified heuristic and spiritual goals for interreligious dialogue. In the last few decades, their ideals have included learning about other religions to advance toward an ultimate reality or truth that transcends any one religious system (e.g., John Hick);[14] using conversation with others to work through religious world-views in hopes of transformed meanings (e.g., Martin Forward);[15] clarifying presuppositions to gain better understanding of where commonalities and differences lie, and then sharing these learned insights with a wider audience (e.g., Francis Clooney);[16] offering a witness to the truth in one's own tradition so that religious riches are not left at the door but are humbly and compel-lingly shared (e.g., Catherine Cornille);[17] and cultivating epistemic humility to reduce the absolutist claims to truth and hermeneutics of hostility that can lead to religious violence (e.g., Leonard Swidler and Leo Lefebure).[18]

These theorists acknowledge, of course, that social and political context will play an important role in promoting friendly exchanges.[19] Nonetheless, these discussions tend to define the conditions for dialogue in terms of per-sonal dispositions, like humility about one's own truth claims and generous hospitality toward the other. The emphasis on humility is understandable, given the regrettable aspects of Christian dominance in the West and in colonizing missions in the Global East and South. Insofar as this literature envisions dialogue as a meeting of distinctly religious figures and their reli-giospiritual commitments, this makes sense in a context like the United States, where religions(s) are culturally and legally construed in a private sphere separate from the state.

At the same time, others scholars have stressed the already-plural and inevitably political character of religious life in places like Asia. This is not to deny the good of achieving greater understanding. Rather, it is to situate that effort in the historical dynamics whereby, for better or for worse, religious groups have related to each other. This can lead to both more and less opti-mistic assessments of what interreligious dialogue can achieve.

For instance, Raimon Panikkar points out how, in a globalized world, interreligious encounters can and do arise from any corner of life and society. He insists that the "religious encounter must be a truly religious one," not instrumentalized for other agendas. Yet he sees the world as ripe for creative engagement because of its pluralism. For instance, where dialogue is not limited to formal ecclesiastical endeavors but arises through more organic encounters in religiously diverse societies, its potential to be meaningful is heightened—though its success will depend on whether there is mutual trust among the parties.[20] Perhaps historical patterns—such as the hybrid reli-gious belonging expressed in the principle "the unity of the three teachings [Confucianism, Daoism, and Buddhism]" (*sanjiaoheyi*, 三教合一)—merit optimism that the norm could be one of trusting coexistence. For this reason, Phan points out that the expression "multiple religious belonging" may even be a misnomer in Asia, insofar as the borders between religions are often not distinct. Religions in much of East Asia are not separate monoliths but have often played specialized functions in the life of a person.[21]

In a more negative assessment, the Korean American theologian Anselm Min has expressed doubts about interreligious dialogue in the fraught religiopolitical context of Asia. He warns that "not all religions are equally ready for a genuine dialogue with other religions." And because genuine dialogue "requires a certain sense of equality among the participants; . . . there cannot be a dialogue between an oppressor and an oppressed religion."[22] For Min, there is an even more urgent goal than gaining understanding: building the solidarity by which communities of dignity and justice can be realized. For this reason, Min urges Christians not to adopt a knee-jerk posture of hostility to the state but to take seriously the state's capacity to improve human lives and serve the public good on a scale beyond our individual capacities.[23] Also for this reason, Min urges theorists and practitioners of interreligious dialogue to strive for their religions' visions of loving, just, and peaceful societies without making this contingent on epistemic gains. In an essay on Panikkar, Min emphasizes the religious challenge to "love one another without understanding the other," because "we cannot postpone loving members of other religions as fellow citizens and fellow human beings until we can understand and agree with them."[24] This sense of urgency is one that Peter Phan shares. For minority Christians in Asia, religious pluralism is not an abstract intellectual question but very often "literally a matter of life and death."[25] Of course, how this plays out is very particular to the local setting.

RELIGION IN MAINLAND CHINA: RELIGIOUS MARKETS AND RELIGIOUS ECOLOGIES OF "SHENG" AND "LING"

This brings us to the basic question of how religions relate in modern mainland China. Here, I would like to briefly map out the insights of three sociologists: the *sheng/ling* polarity identified by Kenneth Dean, the religious market framework of Yang Fenggang, and the religious ecology framework developed by Mou Zhongjian. Their substantive and functionalist accounts of Chinese religions can help us think more concretely about interreligious relations.

First of all, Kenneth Dean has proposed that Chinese popular religion operates between "the polar attractors of *sheng* (Confucian sagehood) and *ling* (spiritual power) by the attraction and mutual repulsion of these centers."[26] In this multipolarity, Chinese religiosity is multivalent. In the pull toward *sheng*, practitioners are encouraged toward the sorts of virtues that make them loyal citizens contributing to a harmonious society. In the pull toward *ling*, Chinese religions affirm ecstatic practices, spirit possession, charismatic leadership, and what Richard Madsen calls "the disruptive reconfiguration of the terms of social order."[27] By pointing out these two poles, Dean helps us see that Chinese religiosity is perhaps not best understood in terms of a unidirectional quest (e.g., along the lines of John Hick's imagination of each religion grasping for a transcendent truth). The meaning of a Chinese religion arises in the creative and dynamic configurations of the cosmos and the individual, which take shape in the immediate "contests of power" in the local context.[28]

This multipolarity and creative tension in Chinese religious life is useful to keep in mind when considering Catholicism as a Chinese religion among others. Discourses about Catholicism in China tend to suffer from a kind of absolutism about the status of the Church: Registered or unregistered? Persecuted or free? These narratives often treat the Chinese case as exceptional and abnormal, as though religion is, properly speaking, a-political and untouched by social tensions and power negotiations. However, if Dean is right about Chinese religions, then we should expect a fully inculturated Chinese Catholicism to take part in the dynamism between *sheng* and *ling*, complicated though this may be. As for how this plays out *between* Chinese religions, there are two main frameworks for understanding interreligious relations.

The Religious Market

On one hand is the religious market theory developed by Yang Fengang of Purdue University. The basic idea is that religious groups and their activities compete in a religious market to attract adherents and offer spiritual and moral resources. Yang's work strives to show how socialist ideals and regulations have shaped China's religious economy. First, he identifies three types of markets in mainland China: a red market of officially permitted religious organizations, a black market of officially banned religious groups, and a gray market of religious actors with ambiguous status.[29] He therefore classifies the Chinese system as a "religious oligopoly," where the government permits a limited set of religious groups to operate while others are banned or repressed. Here, Kenneth Dean's heuristic is helpful for seeing that the state typically permits those religious expressions that encourage *sheng* values of loyalty and harmony but sometimes suppresses those that tend toward the unpredictability and disruption of *ling*.

In attending to the role of government regulation, Yang points out the "supply-side" shortage of religion in the mainland: "China, unlike the over-supply of religion in the US, is a seller's market, with chronic shortage of supply: so the religious economy of China is a shortage economy under an oligopoly, in which only a few religions are deemed local and placed under restrictive regulation."[30] In Yang's assessment, this puts pressure on religious groups but is more likely to reshape and redirect religiosity than actually expunge it. He projects that with increased religious regulation, participation in formal religious organizations may decline, but other forms of religiosity will persist or even gain energy. Yang's market framework has been especially helpful in explaining the rapid growth of independent and charismatic Protestant Christian groups in China. In the last decade, other scholars have employed the framework in other ways. For instance, Li Xiangping has used the market framework to highlight the importance of rational choice if China is to gradually transform into a more pluralistic civil society.[31] Adam Yuet Chao has also employed the market framework to explain the provision and consumption of rituals.[32]

For the theorization of interreligious dialogue, the benefit of market theory is that it helps us overcome the (Western) conception of religions as organizational wholes. Heuristically, it can account for the way that religions in Asia often have had specialized functions according to the different needs and circumstances of a person's life—as Peter Phan puts it, operating through "a division of labor, as it were."[33] In an adage attributed to Emperor Xiaozong of the Song Dynasty, society has "Confucianism for managing the world, Daoism for managing the body, and Buddhism for managing the heart-mind."[34] Yang's economic theorization gives us second-order language for talking about these functions. Insofar as state actions affect financial economies, the financial metaphor also helps us see how extrareligious factors like regulation do shape the form and flow of religious identities and activities.

However, the downsides of market theory for interreligious dialogue are twofold. First of all, does this simply reproduce on the theoretical level a consumeristic postmodern attitude toward religion? Peter Phan has worried about the type of multiple religious belonging in which people act like consumers and look upon various religions as a supermarket from which to choose doctrines, practices, and rituals ad hoc to suit their preferences, "without regard for their truth values and mutual compatibilities."[35] If market theory is used reductively to suggest that religion is fundamentally about consumption, then it would be clearly at odds with the hopes of scholars and practitioners for interreligious dialogue to foster deep learning of religious traditions.[36] Second, any market theory of religions posits a fundamentally competitive relationship between them. This assumption also seems at odds with the normative aspirations of interreligious dialogue for mutual enrichment and peace.

Of course, the main normative debate raised by the market economy model is whether one believes a market is better left laissez-faire or better managed for certain ends. It is not immediately obvious which might be more conducive to interreligious dialogue. Though the theorists of comparative theology and interreligious dialogue typically stress the open-ended and freely conversational nature of true dialogue, they also do have normative goals in mind, like avoidance of religious conflict and the peaceful coexistence of religions in a pluralistic society. Though practitioners of interreligious dialogue might hope to achieve certain goals for understanding and collaboration, they also must remain open to the unpredictability of interreligious encounter. Hence, to speak of "religious markets" is not merely a descriptive discourse; it also immediately raises questions of control and freedom in the religious economy.

Religious Ecology

Conversely, scholars like Mou Zhongjian and Chen Jinguo have employed an organic framework of religious ecology. As a scholarly heuristic, the basic idea is that religions exist together in a shared environment. Mou explains that

> [religious ecology is] seeing the religious and secular cultures within a relatively independent community (such as a nation, a state, or a region) as a social life system, which maintains internal structural data and external interactions with the social-cultural system of the larger context. Through adjustment and contentions, the system survives and develops through internal, continuous renewal and external interactions. Therefore, religious ecology is the study of the dynamics of religion as a life system, a theory viewing religion as live culture and aiming at promoting religious harmony.[37]

In this school of thought, the ecological system may experience periods of stable coexistence but also may experience conflict if ecological equilibrium is disrupted. No religion can be understood without attention to contextual factors: the fertility of the land, the entry of new species into the ecological space, and the possible role of various gardeners tending to it all. This ecological metaphor mitigates against seeing religion in a vacuum, drawing attention to how religious groups respond to each other and to external social factors.

One of the first instances of an ecological explanation of religion was the Hong Kong theologian Leung Ka-lun's proposal that the Communist Party's suppression of popular religion had removed an obstacle to Christian proselytization, enabling Christianity to grow much more quickly.[38] Then, in 2006, Mou Zhongjian of Minzu University called for more full-fledged "religious cultural ecology studies" (宗教文化生态学).[39] He offered a typology of three types of religious ecologies:

1. The unitary dominant type, where a society has one strongly dominant religion (e.g., Islam in Pakistan, Catholicism in Poland, Buddhism in Thailand).
2. The plural contentious type, where a society has multiple religions engaging in conflict with each other (e.g., Sunni vs. Shia in Iraq, Protestantism vs. Catholicism in Northern Ireland).
3. The plural harmonious type, where multiple religions coexist in peace (e.g., China, South Korea, Japan, and Singapore).[40]

Mou's point was that the third type was a civilizational achievement, distinctive to the Sino-sphere, which China ought to recover. Because the government's twentieth-century political campaigns against China's traditional religious culture had unwittingly damaged China's religious ecology, public policy must now seek to restore a balance.

So, too, the religious ecology scholar Chen Jingguo, of the Chinese Academy of Social Sciences, has employed religious ecology theory to promote the rehabilitation of Chinese popular religion. In his view, domestically indigenous popular religion long served as a key carrier of cultural identity and was the traditional "glue that held local society together."[41] Abroad, this heritage can serve an asset of Chinese soft power in cultural exchange. The policy implications are then clear: to encourage ecological arrangements that reaffirm the prime place of indigenous religioethical traditions in China and to curate harmonious stability among religions, so that an authentically "Chinese" ecological balance can be maintained.

It should be noted that not all scholarship using the lens of ecological systems is so explicitly geared toward public policy. For instance, the sociologist Anna Sun of Duke University has used a Weberian understanding of Confucianism and Daoism constituting an interconnected whole to discuss "the ecological dynamics of the Chinese religious system." She and other social scientists have mapped the locations of temples in a given locality, for instance, to see how people and ritual practices move between these temples. There, the goal is not primarily parsing the interactions between religions and the state but investigating the "rich tapestry of practices, beliefs, and ethics that give meaning to people in their everyday lives."[42] In this scholarly mode, religious ecology is a more neutral framework for attending the interreligious patterns of daily lived religion, not on the civilizational or national scale but in very particular localities.

For interreligious dialogue, the benefits of the religious ecology model are twofold. First, the ecology approach is theoretically open to harmony and not just competition, taking seriously the possibility of harmonious coexistence that interreligious dialogue promotes. Second, it is methodologically oriented toward seeing where interreligious dynamics already are. People do not simply emerge out of an undefined fog of society to arrive at the table of interreligious dialogue. They are often already embedded in a multireligious local environment. In China (and also increasingly in diversifying societies like the United States), the most common form of dialogue is not a formal ecclesiastical or academic affair. More likely, the interreligious exchange takes the shape of daily interactions at the temple, the market, or a relative's home. The interlocutor is probably not a stranger representing an unknown-until-studied tradition. He or she might be even one's relative, given the frequency of interreligious marriages. Once again, the Pontifical Council for Interreligious Dialogue has encouraged a "dialogue of life," and religious ecology theory is one way of foregrounding this.

Nonetheless, the downside is the easy instrumentalization of this heuristic for state visions of an ecology that can, at times, seem more strategic than truly organic. Lai Pan-Chiu points out that the discourse of a harmonious "equilibrium" of religions does not mean "equality" among them. Rather, it is a "hierarchical plurality," in which diversity is strategically regulated.[43] For this reason, the theory's main detractor, Li Xiangping, has questioned whether it is really a theory of "religious ecology" or simply a framework for "power ecology."[44] Where the state distinguishes between a healthy and disturbed religious ecology, this can very quickly become a polemical assessment of traditional Chinese religions as indigenous and legitimate species, versus foreign religions (Protestantism, Catholicism, Islam, and sometimes Buddhism) as invasive ones to be contained. For instance, the anthropologist Chen Xiaoyi has done fieldwork in Guizhou using the religious ecology model in order to analyze the persecution of Catholics in Qingyan in 1861.[45] In investigating the nature of the destabilization of the local religious ecology, she concluded that the Catholics brought it upon themselves by behaving in disharmonious ways. Notwithstanding that Christians in China have sometimes acted in self-serving or antagonistic ways bound to create conflict with neighbors, this raises a troubling question about the framework's usage: Is the discourse of harmony and disruption used for a descriptive or judgmental purpose? This is important for theorists of interreligious relations to consider, because one of the main stated goals of dialogue has been to forestall the cycles of blame that so often characterized the wars of religion in the West.

As in the market paradigm, the main normative debate raised by religious ecology is whether one believes that ecosystems are better left to develop on their own or best managed and cultivated for certain ends. This is, of course, a question of religious and state authority.

CONCLUSION: CONSIDERATIONS FOR PARTICIPATION IN INTERRELIGIOUS DIALOGUE

The social setting of interreligious relations in China, and the theoretical discourses around it, raise important questions about how the Catholic Church can best engage in dialogue. I am of the opinion that interreligious dialogue is in fact a pressing task for the Church. After all, the fact that China is already a religiously hybridized society does not mean that there is no work to be done in Catholics coming to understand and work in solidarity with people of other religious traditions. Nor is the politically fraught discourse about interreligious relations a reason to desist from pursuing them on the ground.

In a related issue of President Xi Jinping's campaign to Sinicize religion, Benoît Vermander, SJ, has noted that there are two risks in the Catholic response to the government's call to make the Church more Chinese: One risk is that Catholicism could be instrumentalized by the state.[46] And the other one is that Catholics might wholly reject the call to inculturate simply *because* it comes from the state.[47] The same is true in the case of interreligious dialogue. Christian participants in dialogue should not be naive about the fact that dialogue is a domain and a discourse involving more than just religious practitioners and academics; it is also a state campaign and rhetorical discourse that quite openly puts interreligious relations at the service of state goals. Yet that fact should not lead Christians to eschew interreligious dialogue entirely. For if the Church is to be *of* rather than just *in* China, it must pursue those areas of common ground where Christian hopes for society intersect with the aspirations of other groups in that society.

The sooner we can accept that lived religion is both already multireligious and inevitably political, the easier it will be to see the potential for true harmony between religious groups and to find ethical common ground between them and the state. The conditions and discourses surrounding interreligious dialogue in China may be complicated, but is there an alternative to nonetheless trying to foster positive relations? Does not the pursuit of common goods necessitate some coalition work? As the late Anselm Min puts it, "There is no human dignity without human solidarity because we cannot produce the historical, economic, political and cultural conditions that will protect and promote human dignity, except in collaboration and solidarity with one another. There is no human solidarity without the integrity of human dignity because only a mode of collaboration in solidarity that serves human dignity can preserve its moral justification."[48] Diverse groups must work together for shared aspirations, and religions have an important role in continually insisting that those aspirations are worthy ones.

The necessary line to discern and walk has been articulated well by the Federation of Asian Bishops' Conferences:[49] "Religions have a prophetic role in public life. They should not become victims either of those who seek to keep them apolitical and private, or of those who seek to instrumentalize them for political and communal ends."[50] This means that Chinese Catholics cannot ignore the call to work for better understanding and solidarity in whatever formal and informal dialogue opportunities they might have. It is important to not become cynical about concepts like interreligious harmony, because there are theological and missional reasons to keep pursuing it as part of the Church's witness to the Kingdom of God. At the same time, Jesus's commission to engage the world with both the innocence of a dove and wisdom or shrewdness of a serpent (Mt. 10:16) is important here. Discourses about interreligious dialogue do not belong solely to the domain of religious interests, but there are also political stakes.

Engaging in interreligious dialogue with goodwill and wisdom is no easy matter. As Jonathan Tan has noted, the minority status of Christians in much of Asia means they "always struggle as *puillus grez*, the 'little flock' in the sea of Asian plurireligiosity."[51] Nonetheless, this experience, though perhaps different from that of Christians in the early modern West, is hardly unknown to the Church. Just as the early followers of Jesus came to be the Church in a context that was religiously pluralistic and politically tensive, so too Chinese Catholics live in dialogue with the world.

NOTES

1. Peter Phan, "Multiple Religious Belonging: Opportunities and Challenges for Theology and Church," *Theological Studies* 64, no. 3 (2003): 504.

2. Pontifical Council for Inter-Religious Dialogue, "Dialogue and Proclamation: Reflection and Orientation on Interreligious Dialogue and the Proclamation of the Gospel of Jesus Christ," Vatican website, www.vatican.va/roman_curia/pontifical_councils/interelg/documents/rc_pc_interelg_doc_19051991_dialogue-and-proclamatio_en.html. For a fuller compendium of documents on interreligious dialogue, see Francesco Gioia, ed., *Interreligious Dialogue: The Official Teaching of the Catholic Church from the Second Vatican Council to John Paul II* (Boston: Pauline Books and Media), 2006.

3. Theological Advisory Commission of the Federation of Asian Bishops' Conferences (FABC), "Seven Theses on Interreligious Dialogue: An Essay in Pastoral Theological Reflection," Thesis 1, *International Bulletin of Missionary Research*, July 1989, 109.

4. Benoît Vermander, SJ, "Prospects for the Development of Interreligious Dialogue in China: Lessons from Neighboring Asian Countries," *Lumen* 1, no. 1 (2013): 137.

5. It is estimated that as of 2016, there are about 9 to 10.5 million Catholics in China, counting both registered and unregistered communities. Meanwhile, there are only several thousand priests (3,800, according to the Holy Spirit Study Centre in Hong Kong; or 3,100, according to the Catholic Patriotic Association); the numbers of sisters are slightly higher (4,561, according to the Holy Spirit Study Centre, or 5,800, according to the Catholic Patriotic Association). Even taking the higher estimates for religious personnel (priests and sisters), this still works out to more than 1,000 Catholics per religious minister. These data were collated from the Holy Spirit Study Centre in Hong Kong and from the Chinese Catholic Patriotic Association, represented at the Ninth National Assembly of Representatives of the Chinese Catholic Church in 2016, published by China Zentrum in Sank Augustin, Germany. Katharina Wenzel-Teuber, "Statistics on Religions and Churches in the People's Republic of China: Update for the Year 2016," *Religion & Christianity in Today's China* 7, no. 2 (2017): 26–53.

6. Richard Madsen, *China's Catholics: Tragedy and Hope in an Emerging Civil Society* (Berkeley: University of California Press, 1998), 140.

7. Madsen, 28.

8. Interview with Fr. Edward Chau on "Harmony in Diversity" (周景勳神父談：和而不同), Fountain of Life (生命恩泉), https://fll.cc/video/harmony-in-diversity.

9. Nanlai Cao, "Chinese Religions on the Edge: Shifting Religion-State Dynamics," *China Review* 18, no. 4 (2018): 1–10.

10. Xu Yihua, "拆墙搭桥——宗教对话在中国 徐以骅" [Tearing Down Walls: Religious Dialogue in China], speech presented at the 中德宗教对话——和平与共享 [Sino-German Religious Dialogue: Peace and Sharing Conference], sponsored by State Administration for Religious Affairs and Protestant Church of Hamburg, May 9, 2016.

11. Wang Zuo'an, "Religious Harmony: A French Concept in the Age of Globalization," selected papers from Beijing Forum 2010, *Procedia: Social and Behavioral Sciences* 77 (2013): 210–13.

12. Vermander, "Prospects," 137.

13. These four dialogues were first made explicit in "The Church and Other Religions: Dialogue and Mission," by Secretariat for Non-Christians, June 1984, and then reaffirmed

by Pontifical Council for Inter-Religious Dialogue, "Dialogue and Proclamation," section 3, art. 42, May 1991, www.vatican.va/roman_curia/pontifical_councils/interelg/documents/rc_pc_interelg_doc_19051991_dialogue-and-proclamatio_en.html.

14. John Hick, *An Interpretation of Religion* (New Haven, CT: Yale University Press, 1989).

15. Martin Forward points out that *dia* is a Greek preposition meaning "through," and thus "dia-logue" signifies worldviews being argued *through* to significant and potentially transformative conclusions, for one or more participants." Martin Forward, *A Short Introduction: Inter-Religious Dialogue* (Oxford: OneWorld, 2001), 12.

16. Francis Clooney, *Comparative Theology: Deep Learning Across Religious Borders* (Hoboken, NJ: Wiley Blackwell, 2010); Francis Clooney, "Comparative Theology and Inter-Religious Dialogue," in *The Wiley-Blackwell Companion to Inter-Religious Dialogue*, ed. Catherine Cornille (Hoboken, NJ: John Wiley & Sons, 2013), 51–63.

17. Catherine Cornille, "The Role of Witness in Inter-Religious Dialogue," in *From World Mission to Interreligious Witness*, ed. Linda Hogan, Solange Lefebvre, Norbert Hintersteiner, and Felix Wilfred (London: SCM Press, 2011), 61–69.

18. Leonard Swidler, *After the Absolute: The Dialogical Future of Religious Reflection* (Minneapolis: Fortress Press, 1990), 5–21; Leo D. Lefebure, *True and Holy: Christian Scripture and Other Religions* (Maryknoll, NY: Orbis, 2014), 10.

19. Catherine Cornille, "Conditions for Interreligious Dialogue," in *The Wiley Blackwell Companion to Inter-Religious Dialogue*, ed. Catherine Cornille (Hoboken, NJ: Wiley Blackwell, 2013), 20; Lefebure, *True*, 10.

20. Raimon Pannikar, *The Intra-Religious Dialogue* (New York: Paulist Press, 1999), 68–69, 70.

21. Peter Phan, "Multiple Religious Belonging," 498.

22. Anselm Min, "The Role of Religions in the Dialectic of Public Space in Asia," in *Interactive Pluralism in Asia: Religious Life and Public Space*, ed. Simone Sinn and Tong Wing-sze (Leipzig: LWF Studies, 2016), 32.

23. Min, 24.

24. Anselm Min, "Loving Without Understanding: Raimon Panikkar's Ontological Pluralism," *International Journal for Philosophy of Religion* 68 (2010): 59–75.

25. Peter Phan, "Review of *Introducing Theologies of Religion*, by Paul Knitter," *Horizons* 30 (2003): 117.

26. Kenneth Dean, *Lord of the Three in One* (Princeton, NJ: Princeton University Press, 1998), 58.

27. Richard Madsen, "Religious Renaissance in China Today," *Journal of Current Chinese Affairs* 40, no. 2 (2011): 24.

28. Dean, 60–61.

29. Yang Fenggang, "The Red, Black and Grey Markets of Religion in China," *Sociological Quarterly* 47, no. 1 (2006): 97.

30. Yang, "Oligopoly Dynamics: Consequences of Religious Regulation," *Social Compass* 57, no. 2 (2010): 199.

31. Li Xianping, "宗教生态," 还是 "权力生态" 从当代中国的宗教生态论思潮谈起 ["Religious Ecology" or "Power Ecology" in Contemporary Chinese Religious Ecology Theory], 上海大学学报 18, no. 1 (2011): 124–40.

32. Adam Yuet Chao, "A Different Kind of Religious Diversity: Ritual Service Providers and Consumers in China," in *Religious Diversity in Chinese Thought*, ed. Perry Schmidt-Leukel and Joachim Gentz (New York: Palgrave Macmillan, 2013), 141–55.

33. Phan, "Multiple Religious Belonging," 498.

34. The Buddhist scholar Liu Mi [刘谧] (1271–1368) attributed this to Emperor Xiaozong in his text *Sanjiao pingxin lun* [三教平心论], https://ctext.org/wiki.pl?if=gb&chapter= 839945.

35. Phan, "Multiple Religious Belonging," 497.

36. In fact, Yang himself does not take such a reductionist view. On the contrary, he has sometimes been criticized for adopting what some social scientists view as a too-theological definition of religion as "belief in the supernatural." Yang, "Exceptionalism or Chinamerica: Measuring Religious Change in a Globalizing World," presidential address to the SSSR, *Journal for the Scientific Study of Religion*, 2016, 11.

37. Mou Zhongjian, "宗教生态论" [On Religious Ecology], 宗教生态论 [*World Religious Culture*] 1 (2010): 1–10, at 2.

38. Leung Ka-lun, "改革开放以来的z红过农村教会" [The Popularity of Rural Churches since the Reform and Opening Up] (Hong Kong: Jiandao Shenxueyuan, 1999).

39. Mou Zhongjian, "宗教文化生态的中国模式" [The Chinese Model of Religious Cultural Ecology"], in 中国民族报, no. 5367, 2006.

40. I have reproduced this condensed summary from Philip Clart, "'Religious Ecology' as A New Model for the Study of Religious Diversity in China," in *Religious Diversity*, ed. Schmidt-Leukel and Gentz, 188–89.

41. Clart, 190.

42. Anna Sun, "Thinking with Weber's *Religion of China* in the Twenty-First Century," *Review of Religion and Chinese Society* 7, no. 2 (2020): 250–70.

43. Lai Pan-Chiu, "Religious Diversity and Public Space in China: A Reconsideration of the Christian Doctrine of Salvation," in *Interactive Pluralism in Asia*, ed. Sinn and Wing-sze, 46.

44. Li Xiangping, "宗教生态," 还是 "权力生态" 从当代中国的宗教生态论思潮谈起 ["Religious Ecology" or "Power Ecology" in Contemporary Chinese Religious Ecology Theory], 上海大学学报 18, no. 1 (2011): 124–no. 1.

45. Chen Xiaoyi, 中国式宗教生态: 青岩宗教多样性个案研究 [Chinese Religious Ecology: A Case Study of Religious Diversity in Qingyan] (Beijing: 社会科学文献出版社, 2008).

46. In 2016, Xi Jinping gave a speech expressing the role of the state in actively guiding the adaptation of religions to socialist society through Sinicization, and then also reiterated this plan to the Nineteenth Communist Party Congress. Xi Jinping, "全面提高新形势下宗教工作水平- 新华网" [Comprehensive Improvement of Religious Work in the New Situation], Xinhua Net, April 23, 2016, www.xinhuanet.com/politics/2016-04/23/c _1118716540.htm.

47. Benoît Vermander, "Making Christianity More Chinese: Pastoral Perspectives," *La Civiltà Cattolica*, May 14 2018, https://laciviltacattolica.com/making-christianity-more -chinese-pastoral-perspectives/.

48. Anselm Min, "The Role of Religions in the Dialectic of Public Space in Asia," in *Interactive Pluralism in Asia*, ed. Sinn and Wing-sze, 21.

49. The bishops of the Chinese Church do not belong to the FABC, but the federation's assessment of the way ahead seems relevant for mainland China as well as the rest of Asia.

50. Theological Advisory Commission of the Federation of Asian Bishops' Conferences, "Seven Theses," 109.

51. Jonathan Tan, "Dynamics of Interfaith Collaboration in Postcolonial Asia," in *Postcolonial Practice of Ministry: Leadership, Liturgy, and Interfaith Engagement*, ed. Kwok Pui-Lan and Stephen Burns (Lanham, MD: Lexington Books, 2016), 176.

PART III

ESCHATOLOGY

CHAPTER 11

Migration and Eschatology
in Hebrews

Alan C. Mitchell

Peter Phan has coedited three books on migration and has written a chapter in each of these books.[1] Whereas he refers to a text of Hebrews in one of those chapters, the essay that is most relevant to the topic of "Migration and Eschatology in Hebrews" is Peter's contribution to the most recent of those books, *Christianity in Migration: The Global Perspective*, where his offering— "Christianity as an Institutional Migrant: Historical, Theological, and Ethical Perspectives"—is the book's first chapter.[2] After tracing the history of Christianity as a migratory and global religion, Peter rightly concludes that Christians have been migrants throughout their history, that migration produced "world Christianity," and indeed, that migration is so constitutive of the Church that its fifth mark—in addition to one, holy, catholic, and apostolic—is migrant. This fifth mark expresses the Church's eschatological nature.[3]

Importantly, in this chapter, Peter shows how Christianity inherited its migrant character from Judaism. He makes good use of the Acts of the Apostles in charting the spread of Jesus Messianism to show how Luke viewed its spread from Jerusalem to Samaria, Phoenicia, Cyprus, and Antioch as the first migration.[4] Shortly thereafter, a second migration after 70 CE occurred with five destinations, first to Mesopotamia, then to Greece and Asia Minor, followed by movement to the western Mediterranean, then to Egypt, and finally to South Asia, namely, India.[5] In its earliest years, Christianity became ever migratory and increasingly global. Using Acts gives the basic outlines of the migration, which is very helpful; but it does not provide us with information about the social realities those Jesus Messianists faced. Agreeing with Peter's views on the migratory character of the Jesus Messianist movement, and supporting his valuable insight about that movement's essential migratory character, I would like to focus on another New Testament book, Hebrews, which will corroborate his views on how migratory the Jesus movement was, and how its migratory status helped to define its eschatology.

I understand Hebrews to be what its author describes it as being (in 13:22): "a word of exhortation" or "a word of encouragement"; this same expression finds itself in Acts 13:15, where Luke used it to describe a synagogue homily. And so, like many commentators, I take Hebrews to be a sermon. Furthermore, I believe it was addressed to a mixed community in Rome, made up of Jews and Gentiles shortly after 70 CE, a time when there was not yet a separation between Judaism and Christianity. This community sees itself as part of Judaism. And so, you can imagine what it would have been like for them to be living in the wake of the defeat of Judea in the Jewish war with Rome, the destruction of the Temple, the end of the priesthood and the cessation of sacrifice. Some members of the community may have fled from Judea to Rome. Doubtless, all felt socially dislocated, to say the least.

Josephus recounts the sufferings of Jews in Rome after the war. He vividly describes the triumphal victory processions of Vespasian and Titus through the streets of Rome, where pictorial representations of the various campaigns were so realistically re-created on stages that the war was relived by those who had not witnessed it first-hand, as though the events were unfolding before their very eyes.[6] He says further that the most conspicuous of the spoils were those taken from the Jerusalem Temple, including a copy of the Torah.[7] Included in the procession were captives from Judea, among whom was a general, Simon son of Gioras, who was then publicly executed.[8]

Is it not, then, interesting that the author of Hebrews describes himself and his readers as "we who have taken refuge" (Heb. 6:18), or as refugees? Some commentators read this description metaphorically, as referring to those without a homeland, or eschatologically, as those who seek a heavenly destination.[9] Luke Timothy Johnson underscores this identity by noting that verb καταφύγειν can allude to Abraham and other Hebrew ancestors wandering as aliens in search of a homeland, but that the Septuagint context of the verb strongly suggests the nuance of "fleeing to find refuge."[10] In either case, he says, the characterization "provides a sharp image of readers who are *not* sure of their place in the world and are in need of what is stable and secure."[11] And so, I think the text could also refer to the actual situation of the audience, as refugees, people who have lost hope and are bereft over the loss of the legacy they have received from Judaism in postwar Rome, after 70 CE. Therefore, one need not choose between metaphor and eschatology when one combines them to describe the real situation of the recipients of Hebrews. In response to their social dislocation, the author of Hebrews encourages his readers to take hold of hope, likened to an anchor of the soul, sure and steadfast. Refugees, after all, lack security, as we know all too well from the circumstances of refugees in our world today. As in other New Testament letters, he presents this hope as something to attain, a goal (see Rom. 8:24–25; Gal. 5:5; Phil. 1:20; Col. 1:5; and Titus 2:13).

In its context, the exhortation to attain this eschatological goal is situated within a larger section of hortatory material in the sermon that runs from Hebrews 5:11–6:20, comprising three smaller sections: Hebrews 5:11–6:3, 6:4–12, and 6:13–20.[12] The author addresses the lassitude of the community as a result of its wavering faith, waning love, and withering hope, all most likely linked to the difficulties it faces as refugees. Regarding faith, he notes that his audience is not as far along as they should be. And so he encourages them to move from elementary matters to those that characterize a more mature faith (Heb. 5:11–6:3). The difficult teaching in Hebrews 6:4–8 regarding the impossibility of a second repentance is hortatory, designed to prevent a loss of what they have already received in baptism. The author identifies them as those "who have once been enlightened, and have tasted the heavenly gift, and have shared in the Holy Spirit, and have tasted the goodness of the word of God and the powers of the age to come" (Heb. 6:4–5). The author uses the impossible to encourage his audience to what is possible by reminding them of what was inceptive in their baptism, the heavenly gift, a share in the Holy Spirit, the goodness of the word of God, and the powers of the age to come.[13] This description of what they have already received calls attention to their present situation and enables their perseverance. It may be that the author intends to offset their social dislocation in post-70 Rome with encouragement and an exhortation for them to persevere toward their goal.

After acknowledging that they have become sluggish, in Hebrews 5:11 (νωθρός), the author tells his audience that he knows they are capable of much more than that because they possess the things of salvation (Heb. 6:9). Moreover, he reminds them of God's justice on their part, and how God will not forget their work and love that continues in the service they offer one another (Heb. 6:10). Having spoken of their faith and love, he arrives at what is most important for those who have taken refuge: encouraging them "to realize the full assurance of hope to the very end" (Heb. 6:11), so they might not become sluggish (νωθρός) by imitating those "who through faith and patience inherit the promises" (Heb. 6:12).[14] The adjective νωθρός literally means sluggish. Interestingly, for a first-century-CE author, Babrius, who compiled a version of Aesop's Fables, the adjective modifies the word "hope" to render the meaning of dashed hopes (νωθραῖς ἐλπισιν), waiting for some-thing that will not happen. Given the centrality of hope in this exhortation, it is tempting to think that the author refers to the audience's dashed hope for the fulfillment of the promise they await. Like many refugees, they lack hope, or they believe that what they hope for, the release from the uncertainty of their status as refugees, will not be realized. How can the author restore their hope? He does so in the final section of the exhortation by invoking the example of God, who guaranteed the promise made to Abraham by swearing an oath. This is the reason why he and his audience "who have taken refuge" can be encouraged "to seize the hope set before them" (Heb. 6:13–20).[15]

The example of God's fidelity to Abraham is a boon to the audience because it speaks of steadfastness and commitment on God's part not to abandon Abraham, who in the biblical narrative is a wanderer without a land, a homeland, or descendants. More pointedly, in Hebrews Abraham is counted among those "who confessed that they are strangers and foreign-ers on the earth" (Heb. 11:13). The author goes on to note that people who describe themselves thus are those who seek a homeland and a better country, a heavenly one. It is for them that God has prepared a city (Heb. 11:14–15).

In the final chapter of the sermon, the author exhorts his audience to remember to practice hospitality, where the Greek, φιλοξενία, means liter-ally "love of the stranger" (Heb. 13:2). There follows the poignant reminder of Abraham, who unwittingly entertained angels through his own hospitality (Gen. 18:2–15). For the author of Hebrews, Abraham is capable of offering hospitality to strangers because he shares that status with them. It is not acci-dental that the next two exhortations, to remember those in prison and those who are mistreated, are motivated by compassion and empathy in sharing their plight as though they were in prison and mistreated with them (Heb. 13:3). It is this very solidarity with the disenfranchised of society that the author of Hebrews wishes to instill in his audience the compassion and empathy of Christ, of which he wrote in Hebrews 2:17–18, that enabled him to help others in their suffering because he himself was so intimately acquainted with human suffering.

According to Genesis 12:1–3, God promised Abraham that he will have a land, a name, numerous descendants, and a blessing for the families of the Earth. The oath referred to in Hebrews 6:13–20 reprises this earlier prom-ise and adds the assurance of God's veracity, by having God swear an oath that the promise will be fulfilled. In Hellenistic Jewish literature, the mat-ter of whether it was necessary for God to swear an oath was debated.[16] The reason humans swear oaths is because it is possible for them not to honor their promises and commitments. With God, however, such an impossibility does not exist. Therefore, the reason God swears an oath is for the sake of Abraham, to reassure him that he will realize what God promised him. For the readers of Hebrews, the assurance of God's oath has a similar function to remind them that God is trustworthy, and that they have every reason to continue to hope for the fulfillment of God's promise in their lives.[17]

Very importantly, hope functions in this section of the sermon as a transitional metaphor that anticipates what follows, where the author presents Jesus as a heavenly high priest. Personifying hope itself as a high priest who "enters the interior place behind the curtain" in Hebrews 6:19, helps the author to demonstrate this transition to his audience. Hope becomes Jesus himself in Hebrews 6:20, 9:12, and 24–25, the pioneer of their salvation who opened up the way to God.[18] The image of an anchor moving into the Holy of Holies (Heb. 6:19) concludes an exhortation against becoming sluggish and in favor of persevering and resisting the despair that comes from the feeling that what they once had was now lost for all time. The reason the anchor of hope provides this encouragement is because Jesus himself has entered the sanctuary as the "forerunner" on behalf of the recipients. The author has effectively made Jesus the anchor and the object of their hope, as the high priest the recipients have. Thus, he addresses their concern for the loss of that figure from their Jewish heritage, while offering them the hopeful image of Jesus as a high priest who leads them to the security they seek as refugees.

When hope is the antidote to the insecurity of the refugee, it naturally becomes an eschatological concept. Commentators are unanimous on the strong eschatological focus of the sermon, which sees its readers as a people "moving," or, as Ernst Käsemann would have said, "wandering."[19] In relation to this notion, I recall that Philo, in his tractate *On the Migration of Abraham*, says the name "Hebrew" means migrant (περάτης).[20] Since the seventeenth century, scholars have noticed the affinities in the thought and vocabulary of Philo and Hebrews, notably the Platonic worldview both share.[21] The sermon's title, "To the Hebrews," has stumped scholars for centuries, and so it is tempting to think that the riddle of the title may be solved with the help of Philo. Its author viewed his readers as migrants. After all, throughout the sermon the audience is reminded that it is on a journey that has not yet ended. They are moving toward their goal, which is sometimes described as rest (Heb. 4:1, 6, 9, 11), as a heavenly city (Heb. 12:22), or as an unshakable kingdom (Heb. 12:28). Remarkably, the last two destinations are apprehended in the present, because the audience has already come to this heavenly city and finds itself at the moment of receiving the unshakable kingdom. And yet they are reminded that they have no lasting city here (Heb. 13:14) and that they yearn for a heavenly country (Heb. 11:16), perhaps echoing Paul in Philippians 3:20, "our citizenship is in heaven," where the Greek word πολίτευμα, or citizenship, suggests that it is a place where they belong, while they feel displaced on Earth. Thus, Hebrews combines present and future eschatology in a way that asks the refugee to live in an interim state that is marked by a tension between the present and the future.

Taking a spatial perspective of the sermon's eschatology, we see that the present/future tension in Hebrews is also one between Heaven and Earth. In the sermon, the tension is bridged by the specialized use of the word "today," as in "but exhort one another every day, as long as it is called 'today,' so that none of you may be hardened by the deceitfulness of sin" and "today if you hear his voice harden not your hearts" (Heb. 3:13–15, 4:7). In these texts, "today" is a definite period of time, in which the readers must prepare for their ultimate destination. And so, in Hebrews, migration and hope are constitutive elements of eschatology.

I was pleasantly surprised to discover that Peter Phan explicitly made the connection between migratory movement and hope to eschatology in the second book he coedited on migration. In "Embracing, Protecting, and Loving the Stranger: A Roman Catholic Theology of Migration," the fifth chapter in that book, he wrote: "Movement and hope are precisely the two essential elements of Christian eschatology."[22] As he points out, hope is more than just a wish or a desire or a passive expectation: "In contrast, hope is vigilant, standing on tiptoe, a longing expectation, a leaning forward, and above all, hope is embodied in actions to bring about or at least prepare for and anticipate, the coming of the reality that is hoped for."[23]

Even though he does not refer to Hebrews in his definition of hope, he has defined it in terms that the author of Hebrews would have embraced. For this author sees hope as an act. I want to recall that in the earlier text, already discussed, Hebrews 6:18, readers were encouraged to seize hope. In Hebrews 6:11, he writes, "And we want each one of you to show the same diligence so as to realize the full assurance of hope to the very end." Again, in Hebrews 10:23, "Let us hold fast to the confession of our hope without wavering, for he who has promised is faithful."[24]

Peter's analysis of the eschatological nature of the migrant's hope calls attention to what really is the ground of that hope. Whereas this hope looks to the future, it also looks for assurances in the past: "Thus, eschatological hope is deeply rooted in the past. However, this remembering (*anamnesis*) is not just a private mental act, a nostalgic hankering after the good old days in the old country. Rather, God's past deeds and faithfulness are celebrated here and now in the community in the community of migrants, by word and sacrament, so that together they can look forward (*prolepsis*) to the eschato-logical future that God promises."[25]

The final part of the last text I referred to (Heb. 10:23) stresses that the readers of Hebrews are capable of holding on to the confession of hope, pre-cisely because their faith is grounded in the promises of God, who is faithful; and, as Peter notes, the readers' hope for the future is grounded in the past.

What I have tried to show in this chapter is that Peter's understanding of the migratory identity of Christianity, expressed in its eschatology, has real support in Hebrews. The author of Hebrews wrote to a Roman community shortly after the destruction of Jerusalem, bringing an end to the war that the Romans pressed to suppress the Jewish rebellion against Roman occu-pation. The community included both Jews and Gentiles, suffering social dislocation, as the vanquished in Rome. They "sought refuge" in the escha-tological hope of a heavenly homeland and a heavenly city, and they may have grown sluggish in awaiting hope's fulfillment. The author of Hebrews sought to encourage them to maintain hope by seizing it and holding fast to it. His encouragement called his readers to actively participate in their hope with perseverance and steadfastness, as well as with the assurance of God's fidelity, which makes hope real. It seems to me that this is exactly what Peter means in what he has written about hope, which is so essential to the expe-rience of migration.

As you may know, scholars have little information on the author of Hebrews. Even the great Origen, after considering several possible candi-dates, expressed exasperation that only God knows who this author was. Wrestling with this question in my commentary, I had to conclude that the author remains anonymous. But now, after comparing Hebrews with Peter's work on migration and hope, I think I know the author's identity. It is Peter Phan in another life.

NOTES

1. Peter Phan, "The Experience of Migration as Source of Intercultural Theology," in *Contem-porary Issues of Migration and Theology*, ed. Elaine Padilla and Peter C. Phan (New York: Palgrave Macmillan, 2013), 179–209; Peter Phan, "Embracing, Protecting and Loving the Stranger: A Roman Catholic Theology of Migration," in *Theology of Migration in the Abrahamic Religions*, ed. Elaine Padilla and Peter C. Phan (New York: Palgrave Macmillan, 2014), 77–110; and Peter Phan, "Christianity as an Institutional Migrant: Historical, Theo-logical, and Ethical Perspectives," in *Christianities in Migration: The Global Perspective*, ed. Elaine Padilla and Peter C. Phan (New York: Palgrave Macmillan, 2016), 9–35.
2. Peter refers to the figures of Abraham and Sarah as "strangers and foreigners" (Heb. 11:13–15), in "Embracing, Protecting and Loving the Stranger," 77.

3. Phan, "Christianity as an Institutional Migrant," 22.

4. "Jesus Messianism" is a term coined by the Australian New Testament scholar Brendan Byrne, SJ, to describe Jews who believed that Jesus was the Messiah. Brendan Byrne, *Lifting the Burden: Reading Matthew's Gospel in the Church Today* (Collegeville, MN: Liturgical Press, 2004), 2. I would include Gentiles among these Jesus Messianists.

5. Phan, "Christianity as an Institutional Migrant," 13–16.

6. Josephus, *War* 7, 145–46.

7. Josephus, 148–52.

8. Josephus, 155.

9. See Craig R. Koester, *Hebrews: A New Translation with Introduction and Commentary*, American Bible 36 (New York; Doubleday, 2001), 328–29, 334.

10. Later in the sermon, at 11:34, the author includes among the heroes of faith those who had "fled (ἔφυγον) the edge of the sword."

11. Luke Timothy Johnson, *Hebrews: A Commentary* (Louisville: John Knox Press, 2006), 171.

12. Harold W. Attridge, *The Epistle to the Hebrews: A Commentary on the Epistle to the Hebrews* (Philadelphia: Fortress Press, 1989) 156.

13. See Koester, *Hebrews*, 331.

14. *The Aesopic Fables of Babrius in Iambic Verse*, ed. Ben Edwin Perry, Loeb Classical Library 436 (Cambridge, MA: Harvard University Press, 1965), 27.

15. Alan C. Mitchell, *Hebrews*, Sacra Pagina 13 (Collegeville, MN: Liturgical Press, 2007) 131–37.

16. Philo of Alexandria, *Sacrifices of Cain and Abel*, 91–94; *Allegorical Interpretation*, 3.203–8.

17. Mitchell, *Hebrews*, 135–37.

18. Mitchell, 134.

19. Ernst Käsemann, *The Wandering People of God: An Investigation of the Letter to the Hebrews* (Minneapolis: Augsburg, 1984).

20. Philo, *On the Migration of Abraham*, 20. This occurrence of περάτης is *hapax* in Philo. It also occurs in the LXX at Gen. 14:13, where it is apposite to the name Abraham, and is also *hapax*. The Hebrew Bible has Abraham the Hebrew (יִּרְבְעָה). Philo most likely took the word "migrant" from the LXX.

21. James Thompson, *Hebrews* (Grand Rapids: Baker Academic, 2008), 23–24.

22. Peter Phan, "Embracing, Protecting and Loving the Stranger," 103.

23. Phan, 104.

24. God's fidelity to God's promises was also the cause for the restoration of the audience's hope in Heb. 6:13–20, where the promise to Abraham was guaranteed by a God sworn oath.

25. Phan, "Embracing, Protecting and Loving the Stranger," 104.

CHAPTER 12

Waiting Outside Time?
The Intermediate State

Brian M. Doyle

Peter Phan explains in his book *Journeys at the Margin* that

> eschatology is Christology conjugated in the future tense by means of
> the imagination. Thus, far from being a harmless appendix of system-
> atic theology to be treated at the end of the theological curriculum,
> or a treatise providing answers to our curiosity about when the end of
> the world will come or how long purgatory lasts, eschatology or apoc-
> alypticism is, in Ernst Käsemann's memorable phrase, "the mother of
> all Christian theology," without which the Christian faith would be
> robbed of its forward-looking and world transforming thrust.[1]

Another festschrift for Peter Phan demonstrates that we are one closer to
the number his theology deserves. I am honored to call Peter professor and
friend and thus am honored to contribute to this volume on Peter's theology.
Our joy is tempered by our recollection that the two-day symposium honoring Peter was organized by Gerard Mannion, whose untimely death still
leaves a void in our world, Church, and hearts. Gerard asked me to present
on Peter's eschatology because "someone needs to do that and it sure as hell
won't be me."

The question before us is typical of Christian theology—it is essential
to the life of the Church, but a clear answer is unknowable. To put it simply,
what happens to me when I die? Will I experience the fullness of my eternal
fate at the moment of my death, or must I wait until the general resurrection
of the dead? This question concerns the Catholic teaching of the intermediate

state: "By the intermediate state is meant the intervening 'temporal' period between the death of a human person, it takes place before the general resurrection and the final consummation of human history and the universe, a period in which the soul continues its existence apart from the body (the doctrine of the *anima separata*)."[2] The questions concerning the teaching of the intermediate state relate to metaphysics, anthropology, and Christology. This chapter looks briefly at a few biblical texts pertinent to the conversation before turning to the theological works (and arguments) of Joseph Ratzinger, Karl Rahner, and Gisbert Greshake. Peter Phan's contribution to this conversation is essential, in that his traditional anthropology, influenced by his experience of Eastern religions, enlightens and moves this conversation away from the logjam in which it found itself in the 1970s.

THE BIBLICAL WITNESS

The Old Testament includes Jewish eschatologies that develop as the Jewish people encounter the religious imaginations of their neighbors and conquerors.[3] The eschatology of the intertestamental period was influential for the imaginations of the biblical writers, but so was the dualistic thought of the Greeks, especially the dualism of Plato. A complete review of biblical eschatology, even if we restricted ourselves to the New Testament, would be onerous and misleading. Our questions about the intermediate state are, primarily, postbiblical; yet there are four specific pericopes functioning as arguments in favor of the teaching of the intermediate state. Thus we are not addressing the eschatological discourse of the Gospel of Mark, the discussion of hell in Matthew, or the Last Supper in the Gospel of John. Paul's eschatology develops, but we will restrict our study to 1 Corinthians and then examine two stories from Paul and a specific part of the Book of Revelation.

Paul's eschatological vision(s) is spread throughout his letters—usually contextualized by a call to a moral change in his audience. First Corinthians 15 is a theologically dense chapter that follows Paul's exhortation on the gifts of the Holy Spirit in chapter 14. Chapter 15 begins with Paul affirming the resurrection of Christ by informing/reminding his audience that the risen Christ appeared to Peter, the twelve (not the faithful eleven), James, more than five hundred disciples, and finally to Paul, who is most unworthy. Verses 12 and 13 provide a circular argument regarding resurrection: "But if Christ is preached as raised from the dead, how can some among you say there is no resurrection of the dead? If there is no resurrection of the dead, then neither has Christ been raised."[4] Thus Paul, rightly, ties our theology of the resurrection of the dead to the experience of Christ's resurrection. Christian eschatology is, at its very core, Christological. After affirming this point, Paul presents his Adam typology in its fullest form, in that Jesus Christ undoes the sin of the first man. This theology is followed by a rejection of the Roman lifestyle and a call to the strict morality of Paul's Christianity. Obedience to this morality leads to resurrection, but what is this resurrected body like?

First Corinthians 15:36–49 is Paul's explanation of the relationship of the earthly/natural body (that of Adam) and the spiritual body (given by Christ). Using the analogy of a seed, Paul notes the corruptibility of the natural body, which like a seed must die, and the glory of the spiritual body, which is raised. It is in the spiritual body that we hold the image of Christ in us. Paul continues, "Just as we have borne the image of the earthly one, we shall also bear the image of the heavenly one" (1 Cor. 15:49). Notice Paul's use of the future tense in describing our bearing of the divine image. Paul uses the future tense for all Christians, including those who have "fallen asleep." And though this is certainly not a specific argument in favor of the intermediate state, one can argue that Paul sees a radical change in the Christian when resurrection is experienced—which seems to be some "time" after death: "Behold, I tell you a mystery. We shall not all fall asleep, but we will all be changed, in an instant, in the blink of an eye, at the last trumpet. For the trumpet will sound, the dead will be raised incorruptible, and we shall be changed." Paul distinguishes the resurrection of the dead from the individual's experience of death.[5] These verses are followed by a call for hope in the resurrection of Christ. The literary and theological context is important for a fair interpretation of this text—Paul is providing a carrot and a stick for his audience to act with morality and have hope in their future with Christ. First Corinthians allows for the possibility of a teaching on the intermediate state, but it does not teach it.[6]

The Gospel of Luke provides two pericopes that are used to argue for a biblical faith in the intermediate state. The first is the Parable of the Rich Man and Lazarus (16:19–31). In Jesus's parable, unique to Luke in the New Testament, Lazarus is a poor man who dies and is carried to the bosom of Abraham by angels. The unnamed rich man is sent to the netherworld to be punished. The rich man sees Lazarus and asks Abraham if Lazarus can dip his finger in cool water to relieve the torment of the rich man. In this story, then, after their deaths, the two men experience their just rewards—pleasure and torment, respectively. Lazarus is with Abraham, not with the Lord—leading some commentators to argue that he is in an intermediate state. Yet the point of the parable is the reversal of fortunes of the two men, echoing the theme of the Sermon on the Plain. The righteousness of God vindicates the poor and punishes the wealthy, especially the uncaring rich. This is not an eschatological text; it is a parable: "It must be kept in mind that precisely a parable is a poor basis for deciding the pro's and con's of such a doctrinal question. In this case this is especially true since the material for this parable is apparently taken from popular tales of Jesus' days."[7] Regardless, theologians employ this text in support of their belief in the intermediate state.

The second Lukan text is the communication Jesus has with the two criminals executed with him (Lk. 23:39–43). After asking his Father to forgive those crucifying him, Jesus is reviled by one of the criminals. The other criminal rebukes the first and then asks Jesus to remember him when he came into his kingdom. Jesus replies, "Amen, I say to you, today you will be with me in Paradise" (Lk. 23:43). The key word in this sentence for our purposes is "today." Jesus seems to be telling the penitent criminal that the two of them will be entering the kingdom on that Good Friday. Yet, Jesus will not be raised until Sunday, communicating a distinction between the final glory of heaven and the paradise open to the faithful at the time of their death. Luke's Gospel is unique with the inclusion of this conversation as he is with the statement regarding forgiveness for the crucifiers and the Centurion's proclamation of Jesus's innocence. Commentators argue about the authenticity of Jesus's conversation with the criminals, given its absence from the other gospels. Moreover, Jesus's followers were standing "at a distance" (Lk 23:49). The question of authenticity is difficult to answer, but if it is authentic to Jesus, this eschatological statement should be understood in a Jewish context that the penitent criminal wanted to be with the Jesus in the messianic age.[8] If this line develops later, it can be read within the theology of the early Church, which saw the salvation of all as intimately tied to Jesus's resurrection, not the cross. In either case, the emphasis of the chapter is soteriological. To share in the paradise of Christ, the Messianic kingdom, one must be allied with Jesus. This relationship with Jesus must begin *today*, for Luke. Thus Jesus's promise to the penitent criminal is about the urgency of the need for conversion. The Lukan Jesus is not explaining to us the eschatological reality of our experience of death.

Our final biblical book is Revelation. This apocalyptic book, claimed to be a dream of John's written on the island of Patmos, is full of imagery of the end times. However, given its apocalyptic genre, it does not lend itself well to doctrinal formulations. What could be interpreted as a prophecy of the last days may be a statement about the lost churches of modern Turkey.[9] The specific text at which we must look is from the sixth chapter, where the lamb is opening the seals and unleashing great suffering onto the world. Then John watches as the lamb opens the fifth seal:

When he broke open the fifth seal, I saw underneath the altar the souls of those who had been slaughtered because of the witness they bore to the word of God. They cried out in a loud voice, "How long will it be, holy and true master, before you sit in judgment and avenge our blood on the inhabitants of the earth?" Each of them was given a white robe, and they were told to be patient a little while longer until the number was filled of their fellow servants and brothers who were going to be killed as they had been.

John sees these righteous martyrs who have died but are still waiting for final judgment upon those that are wicked. The lamb cautions them to be patient, for it seems their reward is coming.

Is Revelation positing an intermediate state? The greater eschatology of the book is a realized eschatology that looks to the past to understand the present more than it looks to the future.[10] These martyrs are assured glory after their virtuous deaths, but they are not in full glory yet. The white robes they are given signify this glory and eternal life; yet they cannot be perfected as long as their brethren suffer on Earth. It is easy to affirm an intermediate state here if we assume these to be Christian martyrs who were killed in defense of the Christian faith. Yet that is not clear in the text. If we read these verses as if the martyrs were Jews who stood up to the Roman assault on their faith (including the Temple), then the waiting was for the Messiah and the age the Messiah brings.[11] There were few Christian martyrs at this point, but many faithful Jews who could call out to Christ "in a loud voice." Their salvation may be now that the Lamb of God is present, echoing the theology of the Fourth Gospel. So this text is the most supportive of a theological argument for the intermediate state but, as Hanhart argues, "the veiled language of Revelation and the many problems facing the exegete make a definite conclusion rather hazardous."[12]

GISBERT GRESHAKE

Most of the theologians discussed in this chapter have been translated into English or write in English. Our exception is Gisbert Greshake, a German theologian who has taught dogmatic theology at the University of Vienna, at Albert Ludwig University in Freiburg, and as a permanent visiting professor at the Gregorian University in Rome. His contributions to Catholic systematic theology are in the areas of eschatology and Trinitarian theology, though his influence primarily has been in continental schools of theology.

The 1969 publication of his book *Auferstehung der Toten* marked an important step in Greshake's theological career. *Auferstehung der Toten* examined the theological presentation of the resurrection of the body as found in Barth, Bultmann, and Moltmann. Greshake presented these theologians' differing understandings of Christ's resurrection, the death of the individual, and the general resurrection of the dead. After this examination, Greshake turns to the Scriptures and the different conceptualizations of resurrection found within the Bible. After examining the concepts of resurrection of the dead found in the Hebrew Scriptures, the Pauline corpus, and 2 Peter, Greshake presents his systematic interpretation of the resurrection of the dead.

Greshake's conclusions asserted in the final sections of *Auferstehung der Toten* are repeated and refined in many of his subsequent works.[13] Our question of the intermediate state is foremost on Greshake's mind as he argues that at death, the person rises into the Body of Christ (eschatological salvation). When a person dies, he or she steps directly into the last day and the final judgment. The intermediate state between a person's death and the general resurrection of the dead is only perceived by those of us who have yet to die. The dead move immediately into resurrection and, one hopes, salvation: "The resurrection can be placed at death and not only the last day."[14] Related to this is the issue of the corporeality and the relationship of the created body of history to the experiences of bodiliness for the individual. Greshake speaks of the resurrection of phenomenological body by claiming, "Matter in itself (as an atom, molecule, organ, etc.) is not able to be perfected."[15] One can witness movement on this point in Greshake's career, but he does not waver on death being the walk into salvation. He flatly denies the traditional teaching of the intermediate state, which leads to a decade-long theological dispute with his countryman Joseph Ratzinger.[16]

This "new" view, first posited by Greshake with Gerhard Lohfink, rejects the traditional thesis on metaphysical, biblical, and anthropological grounds.[17] First, metaphysically, it does not make sense to "wait" in eternity.[18] These two theologians assert that when the soul leaves the body, it leaves history and, therefore, time. To wait outside time is an oxymoron. They ask: "How can a soul in eternity await a future?"[19] All is present in eternity.[20] Moreover, our theological discussions of the future of God are in relation to the future of this time–space continuum. Greshake and Lohfink argued that Christian metaphysics argues that, for God, all reality and history are present. There is no past or future for the origin and end of all things. Time is a construct of the created world. When all things are subject to God and God is all in all—this is the end of time, the end of history. This is the fullness of eternal life. So the death of the individual is the movement from created time to uncreated eternity, that is, to the eternal God.

Second, Lohfink and Greshake find the biblical texts wrestling with resurrection to support their position. As we have seen, there is no scholarly consensus on the eschatology of the New Testament, let alone of Jesus. However, Greshake finds that the letters of Paul, especially the later letters, are evidence of an individual's ability to experience salvation immediately upon death, including 1 Corinthians 15:35–44, the text examined above. Greshake also examines Philippians 1:23–24: "I am caught between the two. I long to depart this life and be with Christ, [for] that is far better. Yet that I remain [in] the flesh is more necessary for your benefit." Second Corinthians 5:1–4 also supports Greshake's theology:

> For we know that if our earthly dwelling, a tent, should be destroyed, we have a building from God, a dwelling not made with hands, eternal in heaven. For in this tent we groan, longing to be further clothed with our heavenly habitation if indeed, when we have taken it off, we shall not be found naked. For while we are in this tent we groan and are weighed down, because we do not wish to be unclothed but to be further clothed, so that what is mortal may be swallowed up by life.

Also convincing is Jesus's statement to the criminal crucified with Him: "Truly I tell you, *today* you will be with me in Paradise" (Lk. 23:43). Thus the biblical witness does not contradict Greshake's position regarding resurrection. Moreover, the Greek distinction between the body and the soul is foreign to the Jewish / early Christian authors of the Bible.[21] Thus their eschatology, Greshake reasons, must affirm the constant unity of the person and the immediate enjoyment of salvation upon death. For Greshake, the eschatology of the New Testament does not leave room for an intermediate state.

Third, Greshake rejects any anthropology that allows for such a stark distinction between body and soul. Many of Greshake's eschatological claims are based upon a well-developed anthropology that does not allow for this type of division within the human person.[22] For Greshake, death must be an event that flows into resurrection. One dies into the Body of Christ. This maintains the integrity of the human person and Christian anthropology: "Death finalizes what the human subject has internalized in freedom during that person's lifetime, such that the human person in death 'is not a worldless spiritual subjectivity, but a freedom that has become what it is through its ecstasy in corporeality and world.'"[23] It was this aspect of Greshake's eschatology that proved persuasive to Rahner, Küng, and others.[24]

KARL RAHNER

Rahner was nearly thirty years older than Greshake and was a significant influence on the younger theologian's views of the Trinity and priesthood. We present the men in this order, however, because Rahner's view on the intermediate state shifts through his career, and he credits this change to the work of Greshake.[25] The theology of death was in Rahner's regular teaching rotation, so we are not surprised to find books and articles on eschatological topics throughout his career. It would be imprudent to summarize Rahner's eschatology in a few paragraphs (it took Phan 269 pages!), but several specific contributions will best set the stage for my examination of Ratzinger's response, as both as theologian and prefect.[26]

The first contribution of Rahner is to open the possibility of the discussion of the intermediate state: "My intention here is not to deny the doctrine of the intermediate state. I should only like to point out that it is not a dogma, and can therefore remain open to the free discussion of theologians."[27] In 1336, Pope Benedict XII declared in *Benedictus Deus* that the Beatific Vision was experienced by all those saved as they waited for the general resurrection of the dead. The papal bull is only three paragraphs long, but its influence on our theology of the Beatific Vision and the intermediate state warrants its quotation here:

> According to the general disposition of God, the souls of all the saints who departed from this world before the passion of our Lord Jesus Christ and also of the holy apostles, martyrs, confessors, virgins, and other faithful who died after receiving the holy baptism of Christ.... All these souls, immediately [*mox*] after death,... already before they take up their bodies again and before the general judgment, have been, are and will be with Christ in heaven, in the heavenly kingdom and paradise, joined to the company of the holy angels....
>
> Since the passion and death of the Lord Jesus Christ, these souls have seen and see the divine essence with an intuitive vision and even face to face, without the mediation of any creature by way of object of vision; rather the divine essence immediately manifests itself to them, plainly, clearly and openly, and in this vision they enjoy the divine essence. Moreover, by this vision and enjoyment the souls of those who have already died are truly blessed and have eternal life and rest. Also the souls of those who will die in the future will see the same divine essence and will enjoy it before the general judgment.[28]

This papal bull affirms the intermediate state. Rahner's argument is that the intermediate state is not the theologically or dogmatically binding aspect of this proclamation. Rahner claims that this pronouncement argues that the glorification of the body is not simultaneous with death. The argument by Greshake does not claim that these are simultaneous experiences of the body and soul. Rahner argues that the intermediate state can be seen as an "intellectual framework or a way of thinking."[29] Thus Rahner claims that a theologian can question this teaching without entering the sphere of heresy.

Rahner has two concerns with the intermediate state. One is metaphysical—he does not recognize the possibility of waiting outside time. This concern he shares with Greshake. His second concern is anthropological, and this is his greatest contribution to this conversation. The concept of the *anima separata*, the separated soul, is found as early as Aristotle and is addressed specifically by Thomas Aquinas.[30] Rahner sees the theological teaching on the intermediate state to be dependent upon the idea that the soul can be separated from the body. But Rahner's theological anthropology is centered on the unity of the body and soul.[31] As we will see, Ratzinger and the Catholic Church never deny the unity of the body and the soul; but Rahner argues that the intermediate state cannot make sense without a rending of soul from the corporeal body: "That is why, for Rahner, even empirical evidence of the corpse in the grave is not per se a proof against the fact of the resurrection."[32] Rahner argues that glorified body can only be understood in union with the perfected soul, and vice versa. So though Rahner insists he is not denying the Church's teaching on the intermediate state, he concludes that "it may be said that, in view of its understanding of unity of man, modern metaphysical anthropology can never . . . consider that an intermediate state, or an absolutely non-material mode of existence on the part of the spiritual subject, is possible."[33] After an affirmation of the dogma of Mary's Assumption, Rahner makes his point clear: "The idea of the intermediate state contains a little harmless mythology, which is not dangerous as long as we do not take the idea too seriously and do not view it as binding on faith."[34]

JOSEPH RATZINGER

In many ways, the theology of Ratzinger stands in a unique place in this chapter and Christian theology. Ratzinger's career as a theologian began before Vatican II, where he served as a consultant to Josef Cardinal Frings. His academic career and professional arguments were typical during his time as professor and priest. In 1977 Ratzinger was named bishop of Munich and

Freising. Then in 1981, John Paul II named him prefect of the Congregation of the Doctrine of the Faith. He served in this role for a nearly quarter
century before changing jobs, clothes, and his name, becoming Pope Benedict XVI. Throughout this time, he wrote much theology, including his specific interest in eschatology. His views on these topics change little, but the
authority with which he writes does. During his time as prefect, the congregation published *Some Current Questions in Eschatology* (1992).[35] It has
been argued that the primary onus of this document was to protect the theology of the intermediate state.[36] In 2007, he penned the encyclical *Spe salvi*,
in which he again affirms his eschatological argument for the intermediate
state.[37] Given this consistency of thought, we will, with apologies to ecclesiologists, treat all these writings of Ratzinger as equal contributions to his
eschatological thought, ignoring the ecclesial authority with which each is
written. Ratzinger fully affirms Christianity's teaching on the intermediate
state and falls just short of making it official Catholic dogma. We will look
at Ratzinger's arguments against Rahner and Greshake, highlighting their
differences, especially their use of the Scripture and tradition, the understanding of the relationship of body and soul, and the use of philosophy and
anthropology in eschatological statements. Finally, Ratzinger makes a final
point, barely acknowledged by others, about the role of the liturgy and rituals of the Church.

Ratzinger examines many of the same biblical texts as his adversaries. He
does so critically, using the work of biblical scholars to uncover the historical, literary, and theological contexts of the pericopes. However, his interpretations fit his theological position. First, he insists that the New Testament
does not speak of the immortality of the soul, but is focused on the resurrection of Christ as the perfect example of our future resurrection: "The proper
Christian thing, therefore, is to speak, not of the soul's immortality, but of
the resurrection of the complete human being and of that alone."[38] The hope
of the New Testament message is based on resurrection on the last day, not
an individual soul's trip to heaven.

Greshake and Rahner believe the Jewish teaching of Sheol is inappropriate to the Christian eschatology of the early Church because there is no
resurrection, no hope in Sheol. Ratzinger sees Sheol and the eschatology of
the Old Testament as the building blocks of the eschatology of Jesus and the
Gospel writers. He does not go so far as to equate Sheol with the intermediate
state; but this is the kernel that blossoms in the New Testament, especially in
the thought of Paul and Luke. Ratzinger finds both passages of Luke fruitful
for our conversation. Again, he does not equate Abraham's bosom with the
intermediate state, but Luke is asserting that a final judgement exists after

one's death.[39] Moreover, Jesus promises the penitent criminal that he will join him in paradise. Though other authors argued that the "today" of Jesus's sentence affirmed their eschatology, Ratzinger highlights Jesus's "with me." Jesus is the way to salvation. It is here that Ratzinger demonstrates the care needed in a Christologically centered eschatology. Jesus's death does walk him into resurrection. Jesus's descent into Sheol is his intermediate state. As a direct rebuke of Greshake, Ratzinger argues, "One can hardly ignore the fact that the message of the resurrection 'on the third day' posits a clear interim period between the death of the Lord and his rising again."[40]

As noted above, one of the significant points of disagreement between these two theological perspectives is the relationship of the body and soul. Greshake and Rahner insist on the unity of the body and soul, arguing from Thomas Aquinas and modern anthropology that the separated soul contradicts the Christian (and Thomistic) insistence of their unity. We must note that Ratzinger agrees. The body and soul can only be understood in their relationship to the other. And the individual soul can only be understood in its relationship to others: "The soul in the Christian sense cannot be conceived as an isolated individual, but rather as obtaining in fellowship, first and foremost with God, but also with humanity. What continues after death is the person in relation, not an isolated *anima separata*."[41] Ratzinger is affirming the communal nature of the totality of the human person. As my earthly existence is only understood through my relations in the community here, so my salvation must be tied to the salvation of this community: "Man is by nature always 'fellowman' at the same time, and if man as man is to be brought to salvation, this must happen in community with his fellow men, who together with him build up the full totality of humanity."[42] Thus the individual's experience of salvation at death is already the Beatific Vision, but it is not yet the fullness of communion with God because we wait for those in history.

Greshake's argument that one cannot wait outside time is rhetorically successful, but Ratzinger worries that this concept misrepresents history and dismisses its significance. First, he argues that the individual soul cannot enter into eternity upon death because the soul cannot be eternal. The soul has a beginning, so though it can be united with the eternal God, nothing can become eternal, especially because the "eternity" of the soul is claimed to begin with death.[43] Christian theology must protect the significance of history, for two reasons. First, Christ and the grace of God are experienced within temporal history. Second, salvation history cannot be removed from eternity or we risk treating history as an illusion.[44] History transcends physical, temporal limits and becomes the condition for the sacramental experience of God's grace.

The Christian tradition has long recognized in its prayers and liturgy the effectiveness of the prayers of the living for the dead. As Pope Benedict, Ratzinger writes, "The belief that love can reach into the afterlife, that reciprocal giving and receiving is possible, in which our affection for one another continues beyond the limits of death—this has been a fundamental conviction of Christianity throughout the ages and it remains a source of comfort today."[45] Part of Ratzinger's theological insistence on the intermediate state stems from the spirituality and ritual of the Church. In *Some Current Questions on Eschatology*, the author argues that the denial of intermediate state undermines the theology of the Communion of Saints, intercessory prayer, and our prayers at funerals.[46] Most Catholics tear up at the prayer of "Eternal rest grant unto them, oh Lord, and let perpetual light shine upon them. May their souls and the souls of all the faithful departed, through the mercy of God, rest in peace." Ratzinger sees the doctrine of the intermediate state as a concept that brings comfort, peace, and hope to those still bound in the suffering of history. For him, the preservation of this doctrine is theologically appropriate and pastorally necessary: "The definitive fulfillment of this body, which is accomplished at the end of the ages in the Last Judgment, does not merely signify an external addition of a blessedness that has long since been completed, but, rather, creates its real, final perfection for the first time."[47]

PETER PHAN

The theological debate on the intermediate state stalled out. Rahner's position was clear and influential, while Greshake continued to publish books and articles on eschatology, convincing Kasper and others. Yet, Ratzinger's authority in the Church increased and functioned to end the debate. Peter Phan continued to study and write on eschatology, always addressing the issue of the intermediate state. As he claims in his most recent book on eschatology (2014), "Eschatology has been a constant concern of my scholarly endeavor. Indeed, my first doctoral dissertation deals with the eschatological vision of the Russian Orthodox theologian Paul Evdokimov, and my second with that of the German Catholic theologian Karl Rahner. Even my third deals with aspects of eschatology."[48]

Phan insisted on the unity of the body and soul and the emphasis on the interdependence of each human person. His eschatology and his position regarding the intermediate state most resemble those of Rahner, but with several important contributions that deserve attention.

First, Phan insists that each human life is to be seen as life-in-community, as interdependent with other human beings and with the world itself. To exist is to coexist in mutual relations in a community.[49] This view marks Phan's anthropology, which is communal in nature. One's humanity is only properly understood as the acts of freedom done in a material and social world that are done for or against another. Our relationships, especially our relationships of love, are definitive of us.[50] The theological value of the doctrine of the Communion of Saints is the ever-communal characteristics of the human person.

Death is the ripping asunder of the person, but the person is a unity of body and soul. For Rahner, and thus for Phan, death is a final act of freedom. Our freedom (fundamental option) is brought to a conclusion. This act of freedom is final, definitive, and irrevocable: "Dying is the privileged moment of human freedom in which the person has the power to make a decision that is of eternal validity."[51] It is the moment that we claim who it is we have become. Our process of becoming has ended, our constitutive acts are complete. We are now saying to God, this is who I am. In this way, it is the most isolated and individual act and experience of a person's life. But death is also always interpersonal. For Phan, death's enormous personal aspect makes it that much more interpersonal. We lose our freedom to participate in our spiritual and material relationships.[52]

Phan fills a lacuna of the arguments of Greshake and Rahner. Both scholars investigate the Scriptures and discuss Thomas Aquinas regarding the soul, but do not trace their theology through the theological tradition. Phan argues his anthropology of the continuity of the body and soul through Justin Martyr, Irenaeus of Lyon, Origen, the Cappadocian Fathers, Tertullian, Augustine, and Aquinas.[53] Ratzinger assumed the attack on traditional eschatology began with Oscar Cullmann in 1964. Phan demonstrates that this conversation has a long and rich history that deserves greater attention. Ratzinger claims his view is protecting traditional theology, but it is Phan who argues in the traditional Catholic theological method—with the voices of the past.

It is also noteworthy that two of Phan's eschatological books are written for a popular audience. I appreciate Ratzinger's defense of liturgies and prayers that mean so much to me and others who have lost loved ones. But with the exception of a long encyclical, his arguments are meant for other scholars. Phan recognizes the pastoral responsibility of the theologian to write to the Church as well as the academy. In this vein, Phan continually discusses the *Catholic Catechism* to help his audience see the teachings of the Church and their complexity. By way of an example of this, and quite pertinent to our argument, Phan references the teaching on the soul: "The Church teaches that every spiritual soul is created immediately by God—it is not 'produced' by the parents—and also that it is immortal: it does not perish when it separates from the body at death, and it will be reunited with the body at the final Resurrection."[54] This sets up a dualism of body and soul—body from parents, soul from God. Body as corruptible, soul as eternal. Yet the preceding paragraph argues the opposite: "The unity of soul and body is so profound that one has to consider the soul to be the 'form' of the body; i.e., it is because of its spiritual soul that the body made of matter becomes a living, human body; spirit and matter, in man, are not two natures united, but rather their union forms a single nature."[55] Phan recognizes that when the body and soul are separate, the "person" does not exist. Her freedom does not exist. Demonstrating that this is a tension, even for the official teaching of the Catholic Church, helps the readers navigate their own path and belief.[56]

Phan's Christian anthropology is rooted in the theology of Karl Rahner, but Phan recognizes the dynamic aspects of our views of ourselves. He argues that our understandings of the self, the unity of body and soul, and even our understanding of history and time must be informed by modern thought: "Formulated on the basis of these authoritative sources, these answers should be enriched by contemporary scientific, psychological, philosophical, and theological insights of anthropology."[57] Even if a theologian can demonstrate that the Scriptures and all of the Christian tradition agree on the meaning of the human body, this does not make it a revealed truth because human self-understanding is always dynamic and bound to the worldview in which it was articulated. In this case, many of these sources on the intermediate state are from a prescientific world.

A theme of Phan's eschatology is to raise the issue of reincarnation. The *Catechism* and most Christian theologians, including Rahner, dismissed a compatibility of Christian eschatology and the eschatology of the East—especially Hinduism and Buddhism. Phan argues that this is not exclusively a theology of the Orient, but can be found in Plato.[58] Moreover, the concept of Karma shares theological concepts with purgatory, a theme we chose to avoid in this chapter. Two salient points must be made here. First, Phan insists that Christian eschatology must be done in an interfaith context. We may not and should not claim exclusive understanding of a person's experience after death:[59] "Is it theologically plausible to maintain that there are people whose eternal destiny God has refused for all eternity to permit to be also the finality of their act of freedom through no fault of theirs?"[60] The faithful of many religions share imagery and symbols of death and the afterlife. The second point is that the dialogue about reincarnation within

Christian theological contexts is done, not to dismiss the reality of hell but to emphasize the mercy and patience of God. This dialogue should continue while respecting the stark contrasts between Christianity and Hinduism and Buddhism.

In the final paragraphs on his article on eschatology, Phan insists that four specific approaches must inform our Christian eschatology.[61] Liberation theology insists that eschatology, and specifically the doctrine of purgatory, must take into account the need for justice and peace in this world. Does the teaching of the intermediate state dismiss the suffering of this world, or does it amplify those cries of pain caused by systemic oppression? Feminist theology criticizes traditional theology for ignoring the immortality of the whole of humanity. The experience of women and their (quite different) theology of death must be heard in this conversation. Ecological theology reminds us that we cannot support a dualism of Earth and heaven, history and salvation history. Humanity belongs to the cosmos, and all creation grows and prospers as it returns to the creator. In the penultimate paragraph of his essay on eschatology, Phan notes that many of these concerns can be addressed by process theology. Process theology lifts up all humans—regardless of religion, gender, race, or socioeconomic status. Moreover, "it lifts up three themes of Christian eschatology, namely, that in the reign of God there is forgiveness of sins, reversal of oppressive structures, and renewal of the Earth."[62] Perhaps this "new" theological approach to God and time can overcome the argument over the intermediate state. Maybe all history can be viewed as the intermediate state.[63] It would be nice to see Phan pick up this challenge to eschatology and run with it, but I fear this will be left to us, his students, colleagues, and friends. Or so he has told us: "Finally, to those friends who were worried about my—in their view—morbid interest in death and dying and urged me to get a life (if a bit late), I promise I won't write another book on 'eschatology.'"[64]

NOTES

1. Peter Phan, "Betwixt and Between: Doing Theology with Memory and Imagination," in *Journeys at the Margin: Toward an Autobiographical Theology in American-Asian Perspective*, ed. Peter Phan (Collegeville, MN: Liturgical Press, 1999), 128.

2. Peter Phan, *Eternity in Time: A Study of Karl Rahner's Eschatology* (Toronto: Associated University Press, 1988), 116.

3. Donald Gowan, *Eschatology in the Old Testament* (New York: T&T Clark, 2000).

4. Biblical quotations are taken from the *New American Bible* (Washington, DC: US Conference of Catholic Bishops, 2002).

5. Karel Hanhart, *The Intermediate State in the New Testament* (Franeker, Netherlands: Franeker, 1966), 131.
6. Hanhart, *Intermediate State,* 174.
7. Hanhart, 191.
8. Hanhart, 201.
9. Craig Koester, "Revelation," in *The Anchor Bible* (New Haven, CT: Yale University Press, 2015).
10. Hanhart, *Intermediate State,* 225.
11. Ernst Lohmeyer, *Die Offenbarung des Johannes: Handbuch Zum Neuen Testament,* (Tübingen: J. C. B. Mohr, 1953), 16.
12. Hanhart, *Intermediate State,* 233.
13. Gisbert Greshake, *Naherwartung, Auferstehung, Unsterblichkeit,* with G. Lohfink (Freiburg: Herder, 1975); "Die Alternative 'Unsterblichkeit der Seele' oder 'Auferstehung der Toten' als ökumenisches Problem," *Theologisch Praktische Quartalschrift* 123 (1975): 13–21; *Stärker als der Tod: Zukunft, Tod, Auferstehung, Himmel, Hölle, Fegfeuer* (Mainz: Matthias-Grünewald, 1976); *Tod:Und dann?* (Freiburg: Herder, 1988); *Resurrectio Mortuorum: Zum theologischen Verständnis der leiblichen Auferstehung,* with J. Kremer (Darmstadt: Wissenschaftliche Buchgesellschaft, 1992).
14. Gisbert Greshake, *Auferstehung der Toten: Ein Beitrag zur gegenwärtigen theologischen Diskussion über die Zukunft der Geschichte* (Essen: Ludgerus, 1969), 387.
15. Greshake, 386. For an excellent study of the resurrection of matter in Ratzinger and Greshake, see Terrence Ehrman, "Joseph Ratzinger's Debates with Gisbert Greshake: An Argument for the Resurrection of Matter," *Modern Theology* 36, no. 2 (2020): 239–58.
16. The controversy between Greshake and Ratzinger is presented and analyzed by Gerhard Nachtwei, *Dialogische Unsterblichkeit: Eine Untersuchung zu Joseph Ratzingers Eschatologie und Theologie* (Leipzing: St. Benno, 1986), 70–180.
17. Cf. Pamela Kirk, *Tod und Auferstehung innerhalb einer anthropologisch gewendeten Theologie: Hermeneutische Studie zur individuellen Eschatologie bei Karl Rahner, Ladislaus Boros, und Gisbert Greshake* (Munich: Bad Hoffen, 1986).
18. Greshake, *Naherwartung,* 19–21, 95–96.
19. Greshake, *Naherwartung,* 20.
20. Cf. Peter Phan, *Eternity,* 116–34; note the endnotes to appropriate discussions by Aquinas and others.
21. Cf. Oscar Cullmann, *Immortality of the Soul or Resurrection of the Dead? The Witness of the New Testament* (London: Epworth Press, 1958).
22. For the most specific articulation of the relationship of eschatology and anthropology in Greshake, cf. *Auferstehung der Toten,* 360–78.
23. Ehrman, "Joseph Ratzinger's Debates," 245 (translation his, from *Auferstehung der Toten*), 385.
24. Karl Rahner, "The Intermediate State," in *Theological Investigations,* vol. 17 (New York: Herder & Herder, 1981); Hans Küng, *Eternal Life?* (New York: Crossroad, 1996), 138–40. Cf. Walter Kasper, "Individual Salvation and Eschatological Consummation," in *Faith and the Future: Studies in Christian Eschatology,* ed. John Galvin (New York: Paulist Press, 1994), 12–16.
25. I first learned of this shift in footnote 102 of Phan's *Eternity:* "In the foreword to Zucal's *La Teologia delle Morte in Karl Rahner,* 6, Rahner explicitly said that he had abandoned

the theory of pancosmicity of the soul and adopted rather the view proposed by Gisbert Greshake in his book *Naherwartung, Auferstehung, Untesblichkeit.*"

26. Further examination into Rahner's theology of death as he wrestles with the relationship of body and soul in light of the questions raised here reaps great rewards. We see the beginnings of these questions in Karl Rahner, *On the Theology of Death* (New York: Herder & Herder, 1972), 16–22.

27. Rahner, "Intermediate State," 114.

28. Cf. Pope Benedict XII, "*Benedictus Deus*: On the Beatific Vision of God," 1336, www .papalencyclicals.net/ben12/b12bdeus.htm.

29. Rahner, "Intermediate State," 115.

30. Question 76 of the "Prima Pars" of the *Summa Theologiae.*

31. Cf. Karl Rahner, *Hearer of the Word: Laying the Foundation for a Philosophy of Religion* (New York: Continuum, 1994).

32. Phan, *Eternity*, 119.

33. Rahner, "Intermediate State," 121.

34. Rahner, 123.

35. International Theological Commission, "Some Current Questions on Eschatology," 209–43, www.vatican.va/roman_curia/congregations/cfaith/cti_documents/rc_cti_1990 _problemi-attuali-escatologia_en.html.

36. Peter Phan, "Eschatology: Contemporary Context and Disputed Questions," in *Church and Theology* (Washington, DC: Catholic University of America Press, 1995), 246.

37. Benedict XVI, *Spe salvi*, 2007, #44, www.vatican.va/content/benedict-xvi/en/encyclicals /documents/hf_ben-xvi_enc_20071130_spe-salvi.html.

38. Johann Auer and Joseph Ratzinger, *Eschatology: Death and Eternal Life* (Washington, DC: Catholic University of America Press, 1988), 105. Cf. Joseph Ratzinger, "Zwischen Tod und Auferstehung," *Internationale katholische Zeitschrift* 9 (1980): 209–26.

39. It is worth noting that Ratzinger discusses whether this parable ought to be considered as the authentic voice of Jesus, deciding that its authenticity is moot. This text demonstrates early Christian eschatology rooted in the eschatology of Judaism. Ratzinger, *Eschatology*, 124.

40. Ratzinger, 111. Ratzinger quotes Greshake as the "exegete" who ignores aspects of the text.

41. John Gavin, "On the Intermediate State of the Soul," *Nova et vetera* 15 (2017): 925–39. Gavin includes an extended quotation from Joseph Ratzinger, *Introduction to Christianity* (San Francisco: Ignatius, 1990). The German original of that text was written in 1968.

42. Joseph Ratzinger, *Dogma and Preaching* (San Francisco: Ignatius Press, 2011), 269. Cf. *Spe salvi* #14–15, which argues for "communal salvation" and a community-oriented vision of the blessed life.

43. Auer and Ratzinger, *Eschatology*, 109.

44. Cf. Gavin, "On the Intermediate State," 934–36.

45. Benedict XVI, *Spe salvi*, #48.

46. International Theological Commission, *Some Current Questions*, 229–31.

47. Ratzinger, *Dogma and Preaching*, 269.

48. Peter Phan, *Living into Death, Dying into Life* (Hobe Sound, FL: Lectio, 2014), viii.

49. Phan, *Living*, 19.

50. This is true of Phan's theology but also of his mode of being. The next time you pick up one of his books, read the dedication and you will sense how important friendships are to him.

51. Peter Phan, *Responses to 101 Questions on Death and Eternal Life* (Mahwah, NJ: Paulist Press, 1997), 55.

52. Phan, *Responses*, 54.

53. Phan, 57–61.

54. *Catechism of the Catholic Church*, paragraph 366, www.vatican.va/archive/ENG0015 /_INDEX.HTM.

55. *Catechism of the Catholic Church*, paragraph 365.

56. Phan, *Living*, 54.

57. Peter Phan, "Eschatology," in *Church and Theology: Essays in Memory of Carl J. Peter*, ed. Peter Phan (Washington, DC: Catholic University of America Press, 1995), 259.

58. Phan, *Living*, 63

59. Phan, "Eschatology," 271.

60. Phan, 268.

61. Phan, 271–74.

62. Phan, 274.

63. Cf. Joseph Bracken, ed., *World Without End: Christian Eschatology from a Process Perspective* (Grand Rapids: Wm. B. Eerdmans, 2005).

64. Phan, *Living*, 269.

CHAPTER 13

On Religions, Peter Phan, and Christian Expansivism

Keith Ward

There have been many Christians convinced that only members of their own church held unchangeably true beliefs that were inscribed infallibly in the Scriptures. Only those who held these beliefs would live with God forever, while all others were probably condemned to an eternity of misery in Hell. There are probably many Christians who still hold these beliefs, and they are unlikely to be moved by argument. But many other Christians disagree with such beliefs, and it is important to ask why this is.

On December 8, 1864, Pope Pius IX issued his "Syllabus of Errors," listing eighty errors that had apparently become increasingly current around that time.[1] The syllabus was an appendix to the encyclical *Quanta cura*, and has always been controversial, both within and outside the Roman Catholic Church. The syllabus is largely concerned to affirm the rights of the Roman Catholic Church, to oppose "rationalist" or secular philosophy, and to uphold the moral teachings of the Catholic Church. But also opposed are "progress, liberalism, and modern civilization" (error 80), as well as socialism and biblical societies (described as "pests"). Error 15 is to think that "every man is free to embrace and profess that religion which, guided by the light of reason, he shall consider true." Error 17 is to think that "good hope at least is to be entertained of the eternal salvation of those who are not at all in the true Church of Christ." It is apparently wrong even to hope that those not in the true Church can be saved. And to make clear what the true Church is, error 18 is committed by those who affirm that "Protestantism is nothing more than another form of the same true Christian religion."

This document, of course, never was infallible, and it is often regarded as applying only to specific historical situations like those in Spain; nevertheless, it does reflect a papal view that was held in 1864. Times have certainly changed. In the encyclical *Redemptor hominis* (1979), Pope John Paul II wrote: "The human person—every person without exception—has been redeemed by Christ, . . . even if the individual may not realize this fact."[2] And in *Redemptoris missio* (1990), John Paul II wrote: "God loves all people and grants them the possibility of being saved" (1 Tim. 2:4).[3]

It is possible to try to reconcile these seemingly very different views by holding that the "true Church" consists of all those who, if they had realized the truth, would have become members of the Church (they are, however, invincibly ignorant). Or one can say that it consists of all who would have been baptized if they had had the chance. I doubt that this is what Pius IX had in mind; and in any case, it depends upon the truth of a counterfactual conditional—if people knew the truth or had the opportunity to be baptized, they would have acted in a specific way. There is no way of knowing whether such statements about what people would have done had things been different are actually true. In fact, that rather seems to be a "good hope" than a known truth. If people are truly free, who knows how they might have acted in circumstances that never actually existed?

An assertion that all people *actually* have the possibility of being saved, or that they *actually* have been redeemed by Christ, is very different from an assertion that if things had been different (not actually as they are), people would have had a chance of salvation. Moreover, saying that people have been redeemed already does not seem to be the same as saying that they have the possibility of being saved. If you have the possibility of being saved, this implies that you are not yet saved.

It could be said that God has, in Christ, done all that is necessary for salvation—in Christ God has united human nature to the divine nature—though it is up to individuals to play their part, and either accept or reject this change of state. In that case, God has not actually already fully redeemed everyone. But God has done something that makes redemption actually possible for everyone, whereas before or without that, salvation was not a human possibility. Now all humans have to do is accept what God has done, which is very different from achieving salvation by one's own acts alone.

Perhaps this does capture the sense of recent papal statements. Salvation can only be finally achieved if you realize what God has done and consciously commit yourself to accepting the new role you have been given. You can hardly be saved if you do not believe there is a God who has done anything, or if you turn down what God has offered you. At some point atheists must come to believe in God and accept the offer of God's love, before they can actually be saved. In fact, that is what salvation, in Christian understanding, is—the grateful acceptance of the love of God that has been freely offered, and the fulfilled and happy life with God that will result from this. If this is so, there must at least be a point at which they realize who God truly is, so that they can no longer maintain honest doubts about God's existence. Salvation in the Christian understanding cannot be actual for anyone unless and until they come to know the truth about God and the right relationship with God.

Some Christians think that such a point may come at the moment of death. There are Christian theologians who think the moment of death is a point of supreme significance, at which one is finally faced with a choice of accepting or rejecting God, and therefore at which one is confronted with an undeniable knowledge of God, in the sense of an awareness of God's presence. At that moment, one might make the decisive choice to accept life with God or reject it.

This view seems to be very implausible. Suppose you are a committed Buddhist, who has no belief in God, but have been devoted for many years to cultivating universal compassion. At the moment of death, you believe that you may obtain release from the round of rebirth and suffering, and you lose your sense of egoistic individuality altogether. Does it seem likely that at the very last moment a God in whom you have not believed will appear to you and offer you a continuance of your individual self in relationship to this personal Lord? All your beliefs will be upset in an instant, and you are asked to choose something you have never before considered, and that you have regarded with some disfavor, without time for further reflection or consideration—and your whole future, for eternity, depends upon it.

Or consider the case of someone who dies after being in a long coma, or when Alzheimer's Disease has changed the personality to a great extent. It can hardly be thought that clarity of mind will come at the moment of death. It seems, therefore, that if there is to be a real possibility of salvation for everyone, and if actual salvation entails awareness of the true nature of God and the ability to accept or refuse God's love, then for huge numbers of people, at some time after death such awareness must come to exist, together with a real freedom of choice.

I do not think this is a view that is radically different from some biblical suggestions about life in the world to come. Samuel was able to speak to the Witch of Endor,[4] Elijah and Moses were able to converse with Jesus on the mountain of transfiguration,[5] Jesus preached to the dead after his crucifixion,[6] and Paul seems to accept without critical comment that Christians baptized dead people.[7]

It seems most unlikely that by the time they die, most people will have wholly correct ideas about the nature of God and Jesus. It is therefore reasonable to assume that there will be a learning process in which people come to know more about these things. This implies a temporal continuance of life after the death of the physical body, and a possibility of developing consciousness and freedom in that afterlife.

Whatever your view of the afterlife is, there will be a large number of other views that contradict yours, so you must regard them as mistaken. If there is an afterlife, we will presumably discover the truth. There will be a truth about whether the afterlife is timeless or temporal, whether there is development of our personality or whether there is a possibility of repentance for those who have hated God, and whether we will be able to act and choose in some way. Most of us, perhaps all of us, will receive new information; and many will be considerably surprised at what they find.

Most Christians will hope to come to know Christ much more clearly and adequately after they die, though I suspect this will take quite a lot of development and change on their part, as they gradually dispel mistaken ideas and learn new truths. But I can see that Buddhists will not expect to encounter Christ. If a Christian view is correct, they will have to learn much of which they are now ignorant, about their past lives and the course of their future lives. The truth they expect to see more fully is not God but an indescribable state of bliss and knowledge, a state beyond individual personality or possibility of change. If all have the possibility of salvation, that entails a stage beyond death when all will come to see the truth. But it also entails that vast numbers of people do not now know the truth. In a sort of reversal of one common theme in interfaith dialogue, we might say that we are all wrong to some extent, but some are more wrong than others, and maybe even that one church has the privilege of being absolutely wrong.

If one adopts such a perspective, then to say that all have the possibility of salvation is to say that virtually all will go through a time of learning and development, and gradually come to see the truth about God and human nature and destiny.[8] Of course, there is always a possibility, logically speaking, that we may remain in ignorance; locked into hatred, pride, and greed; and perhaps never come to know the truth, which would require a transformation of character we might refuse to accept. Perhaps Hell is filled with souls who refuse to learn the truth, and live in a fantasy world constructed by their own perverse desires. But even then, salvation must remain a possibility for them, for it hardly seems compatible with the love of God to say that once they have had just one chance, they are condemned to misery forever.

That, however, is precisely what many Christians have said, and underlies the thought that, as Dante put it, over the door of Hell is written, "Abandon hope, all ye who enter here." If God has redeemed all, or made salvation possible for all, it can never be right to abandon hope, for what God has done can never be undone. "If I make my bed in Sheol, you [O God] are there" (Ps. 139:8).

Within the Roman Catholic Church, perhaps Karl Rahner has argued most effectively for the thesis that Christ has redeemed all humanity. Strangely, however, his written views on the afterlife do not seem to allow temporality to play an important role in supporting this thesis.[9] The doctrine of Purgatory, about which Rahner apparently felt some difficulties, does give a temporal dimension to the afterlife, and entails that there can be development and purification. It could be true, then, that, as Robert Cardinal Bellarmine is reputed to have said, Catholics are bound to believe that there is a Hell but are not bound to believe that there is anyone in it.

If we think about the afterlife, it is clear that there is an objective truth about what will happen. Either we will be reincarnated or not; either we will go on learning or not; either we will fulfil our personalities or leave them behind. When an assertion of truth is made, that necessarily entails that there exists a possible contradictory thesis that must be false. It is a simple matter of logic that not all views of the afterlife can be true.

To take just one example, many Jews believe that there is a life in the world to come, and such a belief is enshrined in Maimonides's quasi-creed (which has no official status). But many Jews believe that there is no afterlife at all, and that what matters is how one lives in this life. Contradictory beliefs can be held by different members even of one religion—sometimes not openly declared, but present nevertheless. One set of beliefs is true; the others are false. They are not all more or less equally true. With regard to these questions of truth about the afterlife, there is only one set of truth claims that can be true. It is possible that we do not know any members of that set, or that we know very few members of it. But it is clear that contradictory claims cannot both be true. A pluralistic view of truth, that different sets of truth claims can all be more or less equally true, is incoherent, unless it is speaking of claims that are not contradictory. In that case there may be diverse truth claims, but they cannot refer to exactly the same data to which the one true set refers. That would entail that the true set is not complete, and that is a plausible assumption, because it is unlikely that any human being could know the complete set of truth claims about such an obscure topic.

It is possible that different religions could contain different truths about the afterlife, stressing different but complementary aspects of it, that no religion has the whole truth, and that all religions contain some mistaken claims about the afterlife. I suppose one could call that a sort of pluralism. But it would not be a view that all religious claims about an afterlife are "more or less equally" true.[10] It would rather be a view that in all known religions some claims are false, and some different claims are true, though perhaps all claims are inadequate in some way, and no religion has the complete truth. All known religions contain many fallible, inadequate, and incomplete truth claims. In that case we might need to look at a range of religions to get a more adequate set of truths, though we would almost certainly still think that one religion (at least on one interpretation of it) has some fairly distinctive truths that are considered to be very important or even vital.

Christians usually believe that there is a moral judgment after death, that progress is possible after death (e.g., in Purgatory), that continuance of personal identity is important, that there will be relationships with other people, and that the goal is a loving relationship with God and with others and freedom from hatred and egoism. Yet many Christians may also believe in reincarnation (as John Hick latterly did), and deny some once-central Christian beliefs, such as belief in eternal Hell or the denial that one can repent after physical death. Much can be learned from Buddhist characterizations of Nirvana and selflessness, and from Jewish insistence that it is what one does in this life that really counts. In other words, Christian views can be expanded by a sympathetic knowledge of what is important in other traditions, and by an attempt to understand why they are important.

If I had to choose a word for this, it would be "expansivism"—my initial religious (or nonreligious) beliefs need to be expanded by knowledge of the global range of developed religious and philosophical traditions. That will probably cause a development of my own prior beliefs. It would be presumptuous to try to predict how religions may change in the far future, or to try to understand the whole range of world faiths and philosophies. It is enough, starting with one's initial position, which was taught by others in a specific culture and language, to deal with specific problems as they arise from actual and often inevitable encounters with different views, each of which is historically influenced and capable of various interpretations.

It is such encounters that inform the work of the important Roman Catholic theologian Peter Phan. He writes as an Asian Catholic. Beginning from an informed Catholic viewpoint, he is keenly aware of the situation that Asian Catholics face, as small minorities in predominantly Buddhist, Hindu, or communist countries. After many years of missionary activity, Catholic Christianity has not attracted more than a tiny minority of Asians. That is partly because they already had access to sophisticated and well-loved traditions older than the Christian one, and because their general attitude toward religions was not one that made exclusive claims to complete truth, but one that often combined different religious practices and concepts in various ways. A new religion associated with a Western colonialist culture and making exclusive claims to superiority seemed alien to their natural ways of thinking.

In this situation, Peter Phan uses a definition of pluralism rather different than the one I have so far mentioned (that many religions are more or less equally true). He says, "All religions are valid paths leading, each in its own way, to salvation."[11] To say that there is a path leading to salvation does not entail that every proposition to be found on that path is true. If Pope John Paul II is to be believed, the Catholic Church has already moved to a position affirming that all could be saved by Christ, even if people did not realize who Christ truly was. I have argued that such a view is coherent only if change and development after death are postulated. Phan goes further, and supposes that each religion is a different path, which of itself leads to salvation (so it may not be the case, as Rahner said at one point, that Buddhists, for example, ought to convert to Christianity when they see what it really says).[12] This supposition raised the ire of conservative Catholic bishops, but their criticisms partly miss the point, because Phan is not actually speaking of ultimate truth but of the possibilities of salvation.[13]

It is important to distinguish questions about the truth of propositions from questions about the possibility of salvation. If salvation consists in a life fulfilled by conscious and transforming relation to a spiritual reality of supreme value, then such a transformation may be brought about even if many of one's religious beliefs are false. In other words, salvation may be possible for people who believe many false propositions, even about religious matters. We all have reason to hope this is true, because many of us may unknowingly believe many propositions that are false. For instance, I believe that there is a temporal dimension to the divine being, whereas many other theologians think that God is essentially timeless and changeless. Some of us are wrong, but I hope it is possible for all of us to be saved. Many religions may be paths to salvation (to fulfillment in relation to supreme value), while they incorporate many false beliefs—but of course there are limits. Those on a path to salvation cannot deny a supreme spiritual value or the possibility of human fulfillment. The fact that I may be wrong about divine temporality is not relevant to my achieving a fulfilling relation to supreme value, even if my theoretical description of that reality is in error in some ways.

This means that the possibility of salvation does not depend upon people now or even during their earthly lives believing the complete set of true propositions about religion (supposing there is such a set and that it is possible for humans to know it). If a path to salvation is a path that leads one nearer to actually being saved, then there may, as Peter Phan says, be many paths to salvation.

There is a problem, however, which is that some religious paths are not interested in what Christians call "salvation," and would deny that such a state is their goal. Some Buddhists think that the idea of personal immortality is not a desirable one, and that it should be renounced as a goal. If salvation is construed as personal immortality in a conscious relation to a personal God, such a Buddhist path, it may seem, could hardly be said to be a path toward salvation.

Does this mean that such Buddhists can be saved despite their religious beliefs, or because of them? Phan opts for the latter alternative, and that is probably what worried the American Catholic bishops. How can Buddhists achieve a goal that their path denies is a desirable one? At that point, we need to take a step back and reflect on the nature of religious language. I have said that propositions are true if they reflect what is objectively the case. But all truths are stated in human language, and human language has definite limits. Some languages are incapable of stating objective truth in some areas. The case is perhaps clearest in the case of mathematics, where the proof of Fermat's last theorem, for example, could not even be stated (in the way that the mathematician Andrew Wiles stated it) without the development of sophisticated mathematical concepts that have only been available in the last century. In physics, too, the idea of a "superstring" could only exist when a whole range of concepts have been developed that enable such ideas to be expressed (and even then, they will only be intelligible to a tiny minority of the human population).

If this is true of mathematics and physics, it is even more likely to be true of language about a God who exists beyond our space and time. Writers from many religions have agreed that the ultimate reality of which they speak is incomprehensible.[14] True things may be said of it, but those truths will not mean exactly what they mean in ordinary contexts of use, and the whole truth is probably inexpressible in any human language. So language about the ultimate objects of religious practice are usually said to be analogical (i.e., inadequate attempts to grasp an infinitely greater reality) or metaphorical (using words in an undefined sense different from but suggested by their primary usage).

This is likely to be true both of the ultimate goal of human spiritual practice (which few, if any, have actually attained) and of the ultimate spiritual reality with which religions are concerned (with which few would claim acquaintance). For instance, if "salvation" is construed as a personal relationship with a personal God, most theologians would admit that the senses of "personal" and "relationship" in this statement are either analogical or metaphorical or both. This does not mean that the statement is not true, but it means that the statement is almost certainly an inadequate and partly symbolic way of stating an objective truth that the human mind is unable to grasp in its fullness.

This is perhaps why Phan objects to the claim that the "full and complete truth" about God is revealed in Jesus. It is wholly orthodox to say that no purely human mind can ever grasp the full and complete truth about God. Phan puts this by saying that the full truth may be revealed in Jesus, but probably nobody has understood it fully. I am sure he would say that what is absolutely and finally revealed in Jesus is that God is love. But that is after all a very vague statement, even for those who believe it is completely true, and what such "divine love" is and implies remains a project to be worked out through perhaps centuries of human reflection and practice—and the churches have not been very good at it.

The thing about analogies and metaphors is that when they differ, they do not necessarily contradict. If a Christian says that we will be bound in a mutual union of love with God forever, and a Buddhist says our sense of self will pass over into a boundless state of compassion and bliss beyond individual personhood, then, if taken literally, these statements will be contradictory. But if we take these as inadequate symbols of a state beyond the present comprehension of most of us, things are not so clear. Both statements deny that individuals are annihilated after physical death. Both commend the practice of love, compassion, and selflessness as ways to attain some final state that is thought to be of supreme value. Both condemn egoism, pride, hatred, and greed, and both say that in the ultimate state such tendencies will cease to be. It seems that both postulate a goal of supreme value, to be attained through disciplines aiming at a state of being beyond our present suffering and sorrowful existence. They are obviously not identical, but it would be correct to say that both aim to foster spiritual welfare, as Phan puts it.[15] It is in that sense that both may be "paths of salvation," increasing awareness of a spiritual reality of supreme value that both exists now and also lies ahead as a goal of spiritual practice.

Peter Phan's aim is to say this while maintaining the traditional Christian position that Christ is the only savior of the whole world. This is a coherent position, I suggest, if one says that many (certainly not all) different religious paths increase awareness of a supreme spiritual reality that fosters "justice, peace, reconciliation and love."[16] But (probably sometime after death) it will be seen by all that the most adequate symbol for humans of this reality is the Trinitarian model of one supreme Spirit who is transcendent creator, incarnate redeemer, and sanctifying Spirit.

This looks like the "inclusivist" thesis that one religious view has a more adequate conception of God as self-giving love and of salvation as a communion of love than any religion that lacks such concepts, though many others contain important elements that are true. It is not like the form of "pluralist" thesis that says all religions are more or less equally conducive to salvation, even when salvation is seen in its final and fully achieved form. It is pluralist, however, on Phan's definition because it claims that many religions are paths to salvation—which does not entail that they in themselves have a wholly adequate and correct understanding of what final salvation is. At one point he calls his view an "inclusivist-pluralist" thesis. This seems to me a coherent view, which is compatible with saying that while there are many paths leading to salvation, some of them, and perhaps only one of them, affirm truths that truly define what salvation ultimately is, as opposed to giving accounts of it that are in some respects mistaken or are at least less adequate.

Peter Phan goes further than this, however. Writing as a Roman Catholic theologian, he thinks that we should not say that the Roman Catholic Church contains the fullness of truth. The terms "unique, absolute, and universal," when used of the Christian set of truths, should, he suggests at one point, be jettisoned.[17] This was bound to raise some hackles among more conservative Catholic thinkers. However, each of these terms can be interpreted in more than one way. I think that in one sense they would be quite appropriate. But in another sense, they would not. It is this latter sense, which is a sense in which some people do take it, that Phan questions.

It is quite possible to say that, for instance, "God is love" is the fullness of truth. It is, Christians may think, the most adequate statement about God that humans can formulate, and it is unequivocally true. In this sense, it is "absolute." Nevertheless, virtually every major Catholic theologian would agree that this phrase is very difficult to spell out, and that to understand it fully would need complex and difficult reflection. I have already argued that no human is capable of knowing all the things that are true of God, and, in this sense, no one will know the fullness of truth about God. Even a "true definition" of salvation will be inadequate in some ways and liable to be misunderstood. If one speaks of "absolute truth," one must be aware that all language about the divine is inadequate and symbolic in some ways. The form of words we use, with the best of intentions, is probably not "absolutely" true—truly conveying exactly what God is in full detail and in the divine nature itself. The best that might be said is that it is the most adequate formulation that we humans can understand.

The word "unique" might suggest—and has suggested to some—that only explicit knowledge of Jesus conveys truths about God. But one can hold that there are other great spiritual teachers who convey important truths about a spiritual reality of supreme value, and there are other Scriptures that do the same and could well be seen as inspired by what Christians may call the Holy Spirit. Christian truths are thus not unique, in the sense that no other faith contains anything like them. "God is love" could be affirmed by devotees of Krishna and by many Jews and Muslims. But they are unique in their specific reference to the life and teaching of Jesus, and in giving a specific context for understanding what the love of God is and implies.

With regard to the term "universal," Christians generally believe it is true that Christ is the savior of everyone, and in this sense is the universal savior. But if it is said that everyone must now, in their present state of knowledge and historical context, believe this, that shows a lack of charity and understanding toward those whose training and reflection have led them to the different views they hold. If a Christian says to a Jew or a Buddhist that their views about spiritual fulfillment are "gravely deficient" and that they can only be saved if they turn to Christ during their lifetime, then that sounds, and is, offensive and patronizing. Phan insists that we should not regard all religions as "preparations" for the Catholic truth, as it is expressed by some individual or institution at a particular time, which fulfills and supersedes them, rendering them obsolete. They are, as just explained, "ways of salvation," by which their followers are saved.

Naturally, Christians will and should attempt to bring all people to Christ. The point is that if we meet, for example, a devout Muslim who is convinced of the truth of his or her faith, who lives a life of piety and charity, and who cannot agree with some Christian claims, we should respect, and not deplore, their faith. More controversially, it may be in the providence of God that their faith should exist, because it may stress some elements that our tradition has neglected, and that may be helpful in correcting some deficiencies in the way we have interpreted our own faith.

We need to bear two things in mind. First, the Catholic Church has been and to some extent still is, insofar as it is a human institution, very imperfect, even harmful, in some ways (in some of the political machinations of the medieval papacy—or, e.g., in its treatment of women and animals). It does not always look an attractive prospect when compared with the universal compassion and renunciation shown by some Buddhist monks. We might correctly say that these things do not show the Church as it is meant to be.

But it is helpful to be aware of how we, as the actual Church, might look to those who judge the faith by our conduct. We should not confuse our attempts to get others to believe what we believe with the saving work of the Holy Spirit in the lives of others. We cannot know how the Spirit operates, but we should be sure that God always works for good, sometimes through us and sometimes despite us.

Second, if development is possible after death, then there is ample time for all to come to an understanding of saving truth, and it is up to God, not up to us, whether and how they will have the opportunity to do so. What is important in this life is for people to follow their consciences in seeking a good and spiritually fulfilled life. If they are Jews or Buddhists, this will usually mean following their own path toward such fulfillment. Any claim like "My savior is superior to your enlightened teacher" will sound hollow when uttered by a comfortable, well-fed priest to a Buddhist monk who has renounced all worldly goods. Christians must show by example what a God of self-giving love is like, rather than announcing that everybody ought to agree with their beliefs. Jesus Christ is the universal savior because he serves the world in love, not because he sought to impose a specific set of truths on everybody.

There is another way in which it could be misleading to speak of the Roman Catholic faith as "universal." That happens if it is claimed that, ideally, only the Roman Catholic Church should exist (something that Pius IX believed). Against such a view, Peter Phan claims that the existence of many religions is part of God's plan for the world. The reality of God is so rich and unlimited, and the understandings of humans are so limited and liable to corruption by the manifold temptations of power and domination, that many diverse ways of understanding may be needed to criticize, correct, and complement each other.

Nothing of what I have said entails that we should be content to let all religions (including our own) remain just as they are. Often there is a felt need to reform or even to oppose specific forms of religion. I suppose some Roman Catholics would say that the development of the hierarchical Church centered on the sacrifice of the Mass was a necessary correction and development of the Jewish priesthood. It does not have to condemn Judaism as obsolete, but it could have reason to offer a new form of religious life, in fact to offer an offshoot of Judaism for Gentiles. Some Protestants would say that the Reformation's criticism of the Roman Church was necessary if the purity of the Gospel message was to be preserved. Again, Protestants do not have to (though many of them did) regard the Roman Church as irremediably corrupt, but it could feel a need to offer a different form of Christian discipleship. Perhaps, since Vatican II, a time has come when Catholics and

Protestants can seek to learn from each other, for instance about the importance of reading the Scriptures in the vernacular, and about the centrality of the Eucharist to Christian spirituality. In the wider ecumenical context of world faiths, there may be similar possibilities for renouncing old hostilities to other faiths and interacting in a more positive way with them.

If there is any providential direction in history, and if the many religions are not just evil or perverse, one would think that God must in some way be able to include a diversity of religions in the divine purpose for the world. It is indeed hard to see what this purpose is, in any detail; but it is not hard to see that the many religions, as they actually exist, have much to learn from each other. As Peter Phan says, "Each in their own way contribute to the kingdom."[18]

We can thus see a positive reason for the existence of a number of religions and general worldviews, insofar as we can see human understanding developing by means of a creative interaction of viewpoints. We might even see such a thing as suggested by the fact that Christians have four Gospels, not just one. The differing viewpoints of the four Gospels cannot be collapsed into one another, but together they provide a picture of Jesus wider than that which only one Gospel would depict. There may not be contradictions there, but there are certainly differing perspectives on the person of Jesus. We could see in this the need for human knowledge to be expanded by critical and reflective encounter with others, as we grow nearer to that fullness of truth that still lies ahead of us.

What Christians can do in the complex, multifaith world in which we live is to offer the positive vision of a spiritual reality of self-giving love, which can be seen in Jesus, and which can live, as the Spirit, in the hearts of those who submit to it in love. This is not saying, "My set of truths is correct, and yours is wrong." It is saying, "Here is a way of living in love that is a response to a supremely attractive divine love." Of course, Christians think this persuasive assertion is based on truth, the truth that God is self-giving love, seen in the life of Jesus, whose Spirit of love is in human hearts. This truth is, though central and important, in many ways rather general and unspecific, allowing various interpretations and capable of many sorts of overlap and influence with other spiritual traditions. It does not support the claim that there is one human institution that possesses a wholly correct set of truths, that has the authority to censor thoughts with which it disagrees, and that can impose belief in the truth by decree, by pressure, and sometimes even by force.

One might, then, be skeptical of claims that any religious tradition possesses the fullness of truth. One might think it unhelpful to regard traditions other than one's own just as preparations for one's own, which fulfills them all. Perhaps our tradition, too, is a preparation for something greater and wiser and more loving (Christians call it "the Kingdom of God"), for which our tradition is a seed or imperfect foreshadowing. One could still believe that, absolutely speaking, there is just one truth. One might believe that one's own tradition states some of the central truths about ultimate reality and final human destiny in a way that is as adequate as our human situation allows. But one could still think that other traditions exist, in the providence of God, to lead us into a deeper understanding of truth.

Whether this is termed inclusivist-pluralism (Phan's phrase) or expansivism, or whether it is better not to decide on a catch-all terminology, the label does not matter so much as the underlying thought that no one is ever excluded from the love of God, that no one ever has a totally complete grasp of the truth about God, that many religious paths lead toward God, and that the Christian perception of God as self-giving and invincible love, expressed on Earth in the person of Jesus, is an authentic and trustworthy approach to the truth about God.

NOTES

1. Pope Pius IX, "Syllabus of Errors," available in many editions; trans. by R. Walker (London, 1865).
2. John Paul II, *Redemptor hominis*, March 4, 1979 (London: Catholic Truth Society, 2002), para. 14.
3. John Paul II, *Redemptoris missio*, December 7, 1990 (London: Catholic Truth Society, 2003), para. 9.
4. 1 Sam. 28.
5. Mt. 17:1–8.
6. 1 Pet. 4:6.
7. 1 Cor. 15:29.
8. This seems to be the view of Gregory of Nyssa, as set out, e.g., in his treatise "On the Soul and Resurrection," trans. by A. H. Williams in *The Nicene and Post-Nicene Fathers* (Grand Rapids: Wm. B. Eerdmans, 1988).
9. See Karl Rahner, *Foundations of Christian Faith* (New York: Crossroad, 1995), 436: "It is necessary to avoid clearly and from the very beginning the impression that we are dealing with a linear continuation of man's empirical temporality beyond death."
10. The claim that religious beliefs about the afterlife are more or less equally true appears in the version of pluralism of John Hick, *An Interpretation of Religion* (London: Macmillan, 1989), chap. 14.
11. Peter C. Phan, *The Joy of Religious Pluralism: A Personal Journey* (Maryknoll, NY: Orbis, 2017), 115.
12. Karl Rahner, "Christianity and Non-Christian Religions," in *Theological Investigations*, vol. 5 (London: Darton, Longman & Todd, 1964).

13. The Response of the Congregation for the Doctrine of the Faith, dated July 20, 2005, to Peter Phan's book *Being Religious Interreligiously* (Maryknoll, NY: Orbis, 2004), is appended to his later book *The Joy of Religious Pluralism*.

14. Such a case is powerfully argued by the Catholic philosopher Denys Turner in the book *Silence and the Word* (Cambridge: Cambridge University Press, 2002).

15. Phan, *Joy of Religious Pluralism*, 130.

16. Phan, 157.

17. Peter Phan, *Being Religious Interreligiously*, 144.

18. Phan, *Joy of Religious Pluralism*, 114.

PART IV

THE LEGACY OF
PETER C. PHAN

Decentralizing Theology: Peter Phan and the Second Vatican Council

Debora Tonelli

This chapter focuses on the decentralization of theology—that is, on the inclusion of Christian traditions rooted outside the West, within a worldwide community, having as reference the prophetic vision of the Second Vatican Council. This theme lends itself to an ecclesiological analysis, but I deal with it from a political perspective *interested* in the complexity of the new challenges of contemporary theology, and also in their social and political consequences. The legitimacy of this perspective is grounded—first of all—in the Christian tradition, which over the course of the history has influenced not only the religious sphere but also every area of human life, and especially the political. Second, I argue that the solutions and approaches to this issue will be both theological and political, because whenever we face the theological challenges, this will influence the sociopolitical order, whether directly or not. Third, though not pretending to resolve the question of the decentering of theology, I hereby attempt to frame and restate the term of the issues at hand.

Vatican II was an epochal event both for its ability to understand the demands of the time and for its ability to give them a voice. In fact, a "prophet" is not one who foresees the future but rather one who is able to grasp the signs of the times, understanding the issues at stake and imagining new solutions that can indicate new paths to follow. Vatican II was certainly able to grasp and understand the signs of the times and to take an effective stand in order to trigger a process of intra-ecclesial change, that is, a dialogical approach, while avoiding the elaboration of a formal doctrine. As Gerard

Mannion explains: "Vatican II was not a council where such definitive and fixed agreement could be achieved, given the differences of opinion represented there. Indeed, the council fathers quite wisely avoided definitive pronouncements on a wide range of issues where they realized that dialogue was to be preferred, quite literally, to pontification."[1] Vatican II was therefore an expression of true "concord," that is, the ability to think together, without having the same opinion, a constant invitation to action, to the maintenance of a certain of "order"—both as continuity with tradition and attention to the differences among local churches—in the face of conflicting opinions.[2] Notwithstanding divergences, there was convergence in the recognition of the importance of the dialogue. This convergence and the resultant consensus were rooted in the ecclesiastical institution and brought together by centripetal forces. The Council Fathers were operating in a time of great theological rethinking, and they understood that it was more important and wise to be open to dialogue, to find a method, before finding a doctrine: Mannion calls attention to "the importance of *dialogue*, seen as an all-embracing priority and as a method for the enhancement of the church and the human family. Hence dialogue is seen as the *practical extending* of Christian charity. And the call to dialogue is one that throws open the doors of the Church to the world."[3]

Peter Phan's reading of Vatican II comes from an original perspective, because for decades the most scholarly interpretations of Vatican II came from Western theologians.[4] Over the years, Phan's thought has proved increasingly timely. The themes he reflects on include dialogue with Asian theology and the relationships among cultures, the theology of migration, Christian pluralism as a theological resource, and the need for the decentralization of theology. Phan's work encourages reflections on how the Church could implement her vocation to universality. In his writing, his formation and experience are intertwined and become the source of his original point of view, which is able to put different cultural worlds in dialogue.

In this chapter, starting with suggestions urged by Phan, I deal with the decentralization of theology, that is, the need to shift the core of theological thinking from the West to the world, from what used to be the "heart" to the peripheries. This decentralization is necessary for the Church to realize her prophetic vocation and to be really "universal."[5] Being "universal" is not so much a matter of expanding oneself and incorporating others into our cultural identity, but rather a matter of building a common and universal identity, through dialogue—an identity that is inclusive. This means that there is not a "model" to adapt to, there is not an established way "we should be"; but we are included just "as we are," with our differences. There is not a "center" that establishes how things should be and a periphery that needs to adapted itself to such a "center."[6]

My reflection on the issue is subdivided into three sections. In the first one, I question the common narrative of Christianity as "Western religion," given that Christianity was born in Palestine, came to Rome, and then spread throughout the whole world. As Charles Taylor argued, "religion" is a polysemic word, but here I mean a set of behaviors and beliefs, related to the sacred (i.e., what is separated from the common life).[7] Such beliefs and practices unify all those who adhere to a "religion" into a single moral community called a "church."[8] Such a definition conceptualizes the "religious" on the basis of its social effects. In this first section, a short discussion of the common historical narrative is useful to distinguish among historical facts and our perception and interpretation of them. As we will see, history shows that Christianity was born from the combination of several cultures. A monocultural vision of Christianity—that is, European or Western—betrays its essence. In his work, Phan shows that Christianity has in itself the resources to open up to the world. Even though Western Christianity has been dominant in recent centuries, it is inculturated as the Asian or African one—that is, it is not "pure"—so we need to distinguish historical from essential characteristics. In order to understand this, it is useful to question the common historical narrative: it is a mix of facts—of specific points of view, interpretations, and purposes—like any other narrative. The rereading of history can be a good strategy to build our narrative, rediscovering the resources that we have available to imagine the future.

I continue my treatment of the issue by showing the importance of recovering the variety of cultures within Christianity: faith in Christ ought not be the monopoly of a culture, and neither should the criteria of judgment and thought be culturally and historically limited. We should avoid all forms of cultural colonialism. Christianity will really be itself if it is able to be prophetic and to grasp the signs of the times. It must be "inclusive" and respond to the appeals coming from the cultures that constitute it and actualize it: "our understanding of the church–world relationship today requires a renewed acknowledgment of the pluralistic nature of that world."[9]

For this reason—and this is the third part of my argument—the contemporary Church, in continuity with the instances expressed by the Vatican Council, needs to welcome the challenges of "other" cultures, specifically of those subjected by European colonialism and previously considered "inferior." Their diversity with respect to Western culture is a very important resource for the vitality of Christianity—a Christianity not reduced to doctrine but able to welcome contemporary challenges.

CULTURAL PLURALISM:
THE LIFEBLOOD OF CHRISTIANITY

The history of recent centuries has accustomed us to a one-way vision of Christianity that has spread all over the world from Europe. In many countries, the expansion of Christianity went hand in hand with colonialism and, therefore, the association of colonialism, of imperialism with missions, is quite common; as Peter Phan notes, "One of the bitter ironies of Asian Christianity is that though born in Asia, it returned to its birthplace, and is still being regarded by many Asians as a Western religion imported to Asia by Portuguese and Spanish colonialists in the 16th century, and later by other European countries such as Britain, France, Germany, Denmark, and the Netherlands, and lastly by the United States."[10]

From this perspective, the universality of Christianity is a form of expansion from what is considered its center to the periphery. Phan radically criticizes this narrative:

> The conventional narrative of Christianity as a Western religion, that is, one that originated in Palestine but soon moved westward, with Rome as its final destination, and from Rome as its epicenter, spread worldwide, belies the fact that in the first four centuries of Christianity, the most active and successful centers of mission were not Europe but Asia and Africa, with Syria as the center of gravity. But even Asian Christians outside West Asia can rightly boast an ancient and glorious heritage, one that is likely as old as the apostolic age.[11]

However, it should be specified that the "conventional narrative" is in some way rooted in the Acts of the Apostles and in the Pauline-Petrine churches. That is probably because some centralization and normative harmonization are necessary to bring different cultures into contact and create a stable political atmosphere for dialogue to take place, but having as its precise purpose dialogue and not centralization. So the story is very complex from all points of view, and each historical narrative and geographical route highlights different aspects within the Christian tradition.[12]

Historical vicissitudes then diversified the concentration of Christianity into other areas and, subsequently, into Rome and Europe, favored by various factors and historical events. From the Roman Rite's perspective, it will gradually be possible to distinguish between a Christianity "of the center" and a peripheral one. The conventional narrative of the Roman-European center of Christianity is called into question by historical evidence that describes a geographically diverse and complex path.[13]

Furthermore, the whole body of biblical texts shows numerous contacts between Judaism and the cultures of the Ancient Near East and the Greek world. Above all, the idea of the existence of a "pure" culture—uncontaminated by other cultures—is not credible. Such cultures do not exist. In the Gospels, the action of Jesus was aimed at rediscovering the meaning of the ancient Jewish religion. Jesus did not want to found a new religion, but to rediscover the heart of his own. The Acts of the Apostles and the Letters tell us about an itinerant nascent Church, born of mission and dialogue with different cultures, concerned with questions about how to embody faith in Jesus in cultures other than the Jewish one. After AD 70, with the destruction of the Temple, Palestinian Temple Judaism as a cultural and political religion was destroyed and something different from Judaism was born. What could possibly be the "root culture" of Christianity: The Jewish culture? The Mediterranean pagan culture? The culture of Asia Minor or of North Africa?

The evangelical figure of Jesus highlights the importance of opening up Judaism to other cultures and the cultural pluralism of Christianity. The purpose was not "to preserve Jesus's culture" or any another one. The purpose was to live the faith in Christ, recognizing him as Messiah. Believers of the new religion used their old cultural and religious practices to celebrate their new faith. Some Christian celebrations have their roots in others religions, other were new. One example is Christmas: many cultures of the Mediterranean area celebrated the birth of the Sun on December 21. The messianic Church transformed it into celebration of the birth of the Sun of Justice, Jesus. Using symbols of Greek-Roman culture to celebrate their own new religion, Christians evangelized that Greek-Roman culture.

The origins of Christianity are multicultural and polyphonic, but sometimes we forget this.[14] The conventional narrative speaks of a Christianity that gradually spread from the West to the rest of the world. This contributed to the idea that the Western version of the faith was the standard of Christianity, a pure Christianity. To understand the tension between narration and the progression of historical events, it is very useful to refer to what Massimo Faggioli calls "institutional memory," which recalls an epochal event (in this case Vatican II, but it is also useful for any other historical event, and therefore also for Christianity itself): "It is indeed clear that 'institutional memory' is often not the contrary, but the companion of its counterpart or the other side, of 'institutional amnesia'—the need for institutions to forget some aspects of their past in order to maintain integrity and cohesion."[15]

It is therefore a selective memory, aimed at preserving the institution and not at reconstructing the event: "On the other hand, memory is not always helped by the process of 'memorialization,' that is, the culture of constructing festivities, rituals, monuments, and memorials supposed to help us not just remember but also shape our national and political identities around a given interpretation of major events of our recent history."[16] The narration of this memory serves to answer questions of the present, those for which it is useful to "remember," and therefore memory contributes to forming the present consciousness and political identity.

The pluralism intrinsic to Christianity is from its origins, but it requests a complex narrative and dialogue among cultures. For many centuries not only Christian missionaries, but also the political and military hegemony of Europe, contributed to the spread of Christianity; and the two aspects, religion and politics, have been interwoven. Unfortunately, in most of the cases dialogue was not the main tool of cultural exchange.[17]

With this awareness, I continue my reflection by discussing the importance of cultural pluralism within Christianity. After centuries of expansion, cultural inclusion as a social practice is a challenge for both theology and religion.[18] The identification of Christianity with a specific culture contradicts its intrinsic pluralism. The Christian tradition has gradually been conceived of as one, but it remains substantially pluralist. The fact that there is "only one" Catholicism does not mean to say that it is just "one thing" (identifiable with only one culture). The Church is both a spokesperson for the "Good News" and an expression of human religious experience, with all its questions and doubts that are answered in the kerygmatic announcement and with all the cultural variety that characterizes it. Therefore, real faith requires that we welcome the requests coming from the various cultures in which it is rooted and incarnated. Contemporary Christianity must rediscover and fully experience the pluralism that is intrinsic to the Christian faith.

CONTEMPORARY CHALLENGES: AN INCULTURATED CHRISTIANITY

I have shown that Christianity was pluralist from the beginning and that a "pure" Christianity cannot exist: wherever it is planted, it will either take root in that culture or remain encapsulated in the culture of those who implanted it. This places Western Christianity on the same level with Asian, African, and Latin American Christianity. At the same time, this shifts the issue from religion to cultures.

With the official end of colonial experience and the growth of the autonomy of countries that were once colonized, the Church has also rethought missionary experience.[19] Too often, over the centuries, some missionaries have supported the colonial and imperialist enterprise, feeling empowered to "make disciples of all nations," and causing Christianity to be perceived as the religion of the colonizers.[20] The selective institutional memory has exacerbated an increase in this perception, talking about Rome and the West as the center of the Church and forgetting to underline the fact that many Church Fathers came from different regions.

In addition to the historical question, there is the theological one: a theology—that is, a reflection on God and faith—that does not take into account the variety of cultures can hardly be the expression of these cultures. If, in the past, the perception was constructed of a Christianity that reached the "periphery" from a "center," today—in the so-called globalized world—it would be desirable to encourage "mobility," that is, the possibility that a periphery becomes a center, and vice versa.[21]

Each culture has its own way of accepting and interpreting faith in Christ and of expressing it so that it is consistent with its identity.[22] The end, at least officially, of the colonial age has called into question a series of monopolies, including the cultural one.[23] However, today difficulties still emerge in combining the Christian tradition and non-European cultures, despite the fact that Christianity is growing in Asia and Africa and, though remaining a "minority" in some countries, the number of Asian Christians exceeds that of European and North American Christians.[24] The reasons are many, and I am not able to deal with them here, but Phan's reflection on this is very important, because he experienced this historical passage firsthand and thematized the need of an inculturated Christianity. Phan's experience of living "in between" two cultures, Vietnamese and that of the United States, makes his theological thought particularly interesting.

The attempt to combine the Christian tradition and non-Western cultures poses several issues, namely, those involved in distinguishing and harmonizing what is essential from what is culturally contingent. For instance, the document *Faith and Inculturation* (1988) from the International Theological Commission speaks about the evangelization of cultures.[25] Another issue concerns engaging in an equal dialogue between the theological tradition and non-Western cultures, that is, the decentralization of theology in order to build a really universal Christianity.

These questions arise from the need to interpret the present through new categories and approaches. In his work *Being Religious Interreligiously*, Peter Phan deals with the issue of religiosity within the horizon of religious pluralism.[26] The title of this book is an excellent synthesis of the contemporary issue of religion in a context where we cannot be indifferent to pluralism, both inside and outside Christianity. The pluralism within Christianity, in fact, has to do with the plurality of cultures, by the coexistence of multiple Christian voices and, often, also of other religions:

> Asia is the home of many different Christian ecclesiastical traditions, rites, and denominations, so that it is more accurate to use "Christianities" (in the plural) to denominate them. Due to its past extensive missions in Asia, Roman Catholicism is the largest church. Older than the Roman Catholic Church is the Malabar Church of India ("Saint Thomas Christians"). The Orthodox Church also has a notable presence in China, [South] Korea, and Japan. The Anglican Church (including the Anglican Church of Canada) is well represented, especially in Hong Kong, India, Malaysia, and Pakistan. Various Protestant Churches have also flourished in almost all Asian countries, e.g., the Baptists (especially in North India), the Lutherans, the Mennonites, the Methodists, the Presbyterians (especially in Korea), and the Seventh-Day Adventists.[27]

This is a wide and complex context. The role of Asian Christianity is essentially pastoral and faces significant challenges, including those posed by ethnicity and language, poverty, the colonial heritage, the fact of being a religious minority, and extensive human mobility in the region.

Both the interreligious dialogue and pluralism within Christianity are crucial for living together within the Asian world. "Interreligiously" means—first of all—that we need to consider religions different from our own (Roman Catholic), and we must try to build a kind of relationship with them. This relationship is more than religious, because it influences politics, culture, and society.[28]

Therefore, religious pluralism and interreligious dialogue need to consider the multiple levels of interaction: religious and social practices and beliefs, including political beliefs. Practices cannot be said to be fully religious and Christian if they are not seen in relation to the theological tradition—that is, a set of reflections made on God's Revelation, on sacred texts, and on the foundations of religious practices and beliefs. At the same time, theology needs to speak to different cultures. Both practices and reflection tell us something essential about the religious experience of a believing community. The ecclesial community is therefore in constant dialogue with the past from which it comes and with a pluralist present, and this dialogue raises new questions. Through dialogue, the ecclesial community vivifies and updates the tradition. I could claim that each cultural community is "in between," which is reminiscent of Hannah Arendt's thought—and the quality of the dialogue in which each community is engaged makes a difference; at best, a dialogue to which all can contribute is both in continuity with tradition and also welcoming contemporary challenges.[29] This capacity for dialogue triggers important changes. In fact, it is not possible to engage in dialogue on equal terms with someone without experiencing—even if only for a short time—a change of perspective, and this also changes the way of living in between different cultures. Belonging and origins intertwine with each other, blurring differences, triggering novelties. Looking to the future, we could imagine a global believing community, in which geographical and cultural differences are not decisive to determine the "center" and the "periphery" and the common belief is increasingly the result of their interaction. Peter Phan's work makes a significant contribution in this direction, reflecting on an inclusive Church that is increasingly the result of a meeting between equals and not a one-way expansion.

THE THEOLOGICAL DECENTRALIZATION: DECOLONIAL THEOLOGY

Starting from a decentralized point of view, Phan's theological thinking helped raise the profile of the Church's prophetic character. But what does it mean to be prophetic?

The prophet sees the present so clearly as to have a key to imagining the future, and so is able to propose an alternative future.[30] Imagination is one of the most important gifts of theologians and politicians. It is the ability to look beyond and to create something unexpected: "The early Church used an imagination for mediating and reconciling by inculturating the Jewish Jesus into Greco-Roman culture. . . . It did it again in a more significant way at Chalcedon, articulating the human nature and the divine nature of Christ without confusion or separation. At the origins of our faith and our Church, there is a reconciliation through imagination. Who wouldn't want to continue it?"[31]

Imagination—and, even more, a prophetic imagination—allows us to look "beyond" and to find new paths. The prophets use their imagination, but this does not mean that they are unable to reason. Their imagination may seem crazy to those who are unable to understand it. I think that the analysis of "foolish wisdom" provided in the first chapter of *Being Religious Interreligiously* is not accidental. In fact, Phan states that "the purpose of this chapter is not to provide an account of how foolish wisdom or the wisdom of folly has functioned in diverse fields of human endeavor but to show how this peculiar way of knowing, which is distinct from mythos and logos, can, if properly practiced, lead to recovery of the love of wisdom."[32] In some way, Phan's prophetic imagination is foolish, because it breaks all plans, introducing a new point of view, that is, a new understanding of both the present and the future: it is the result of combining together the Christian tradition and Asian culture. A Christianity that has solid roots in Asia, and in any case outside the West, is an intrinsically pluralist Christianity, one that brings to the fore many contextual challenges and needs.[33]

Phan's idea of religious pluralism is based on an idea of human experience, which is not ideal but real. Starting with daily life, its wealth, and its needs and cultures, not using Western criteria of judgment, he looked to the future with new eyes and imagined a theology that permeates the meaning of the present. Moreover, how is it possible to be part of the Church if it does not know my language and my needs? Today, starting from reality means looking at cultures free of colonialism, even if colonial influences are still active in the economy and in some aspects of politics. By virtue of military and political supremacy, the colonizers were able to impose their own criteria of judgment and evaluation and to classify cultures different from their own (i.e., all the others) as inferior.[34]

Sometimes theologians suffered from the same prejudice, legitimizing missionary forms in a way close to imperialism.[35] The colonial heritage makes it necessary to decolonize theology.[36] That is, it is necessary to deconstruct the conventional modes of representation and the interpretative frameworks, which during the colonial period established the superiority of one culture over others:

> [The epistemological "decolonial turn"] consists in becoming critically aware of Eurocentrism, from the view point of the post-colonial world, of Eurocentrism as the setting of discourse (*locus enunciationis*). This is a generalized *habitus* of the thinker, the scientist, the philosopher, which penetrates so deeply into the subjectivity of the theoretical and the objectivity of theories (and the human and social sciences), that it is practically impossible to free oneself from its limitations, which are unanimously accepted by all.... That makes it practically impossible to go beyond its narrow deforming limits.[37]

The process of raising awareness cannot be limited to a single area. In fact, it emerged from a very complex theoretical framework that refers to José

Carlos Mariátegui and Frantz Fanon: On one hand, postcolonial reflection (philosophical, sociological, historical, etc.), subaltern studies (among historians of India), and postmodernism (in Europe and the United States) were criticized. On the other hand, issues were developed that led to the rise of the theory of addiction (in the 1960s), the criticism of the capitalism of the centered (compared with a peripheral one), and the theology of liberation.[38]

It is from this cultural ferment—of centripetal forces, of criticism, and of new proposals, that dialogue emerges as the main tool of comparison and the construction of a new vision of the future. Dialogue, as I said above, was a novelty of Vatican II, an opening that marked a very significant change of pace, because it legitimized its interlocutor. Dialogue has the power to make us listen to things that we would not otherwise know, to help us put ourselves in the perspective of the other, to modify or consider our positions and beliefs in a different way. If the purpose of dialogue is really inclusive— that is, the spreading of the Good News and making sure that as many people as possible benefit from it—everything should be simpler, theoretically. The goal, in fact, would not be to defend a position but to implement a common project from different perspectives.

CONCLUSION

The purpose of this chapter has been to discuss the decentralization of theology, in continuity with the prophetic vision of Vatican II and suggestions by Peter Phan. This decentralization is not only theological but also political, considering the complexity of contemporary challenges. Furthermore, the decentralization is strongly interwoven with colonial and postcolonial heritage, and with their idea of the "center of power" and his geographical location.

The comparison among historical narratives highlighted the importance of pluralism within the Christian tradition. On one side, the conventional narrative tells of a "Western" Christianity; on the other side, Phan and other authors focus on the intrinsic pluralism of the Christian tradition. Of course, the issue at stake is not the historical narrative in itself but its role in the legitimation of theological positions and their political consequences. The discussion of historical narratives opens onto other issues: the dialogue between Christianity and cultures, colonial and postcolonial issues, the issue of religious identity that is also social and political, and mobility between the "center" and "periphery." Trying to solve the issue of historical narrative and of pluralism, we discover many other problems, which require a synergistic approach between theology, religious practices, and political thought.

However, the purpose is incontrovertible: the need for the "Good News" to speak both *to* and *within* all cultures. With this purpose, the building of a new common historical narrative could be a step in the dialogue. In fact, the aim of the dialogue is not "to be right" or "to prevail" but to move beyond the alternative between "us" and "them" and to promote thinking together. This is a way to implement the prophetic vocation of the Church; that is, it is a performative vision to the degree that it illuminates reality with a new and unexpected light and directs it onto an unexpected path.

The prerequisite for dialogue is the existence of multiple voices and experiences, all recognized as equally significant in the realization of the prophetic vocation of the Church. A constructive communication can be useful to balance contrasting points of view, in order to rethink cultural and religious frameworks: the center and the peripheries need to become enriched by each other's experiences and pool their efforts. The quality of their relations and the possibility of their mobility can make the difference. We need to transform what divides us into a resource and to think about "cultural diversity" and "inculturation" in a more sophisticated manner. The issue at stake is not the defense of a political and spiritual monopoly but the instrument of the Gospel of love and salvation that makes no distinction between human beings. Understanding this and implementing it will truly allow us to create a different, pluralist but cohesive, and truly global humanity with no center other than Christ.

NOTES

1. Gerard Mannion, *Ecclesiology and Postmodernity: Questions for the Church in Our Time* (Collegeville, MN: Liturgical Press, 2007), 110.
2. Cf. Cicero, *Laelius de amicitia*, par. 23. For Aristotle, concord is a joint deliberation and the will to implement things decided together; cf. *Ethica Nicomachea* IX, 6, 1167a 25. For the history of this concept in the ancient times, see Ryan K. Balot, ed. *A Companion to Greek and Roman Political Thought* (Oxford: Blackwell, 2009).
3. Mannion, *Ecclesiology*, 114–15.
4. "For Asian Christians Vatican II remains a point of departure of a journey, a journey which they themselves should make. More than individual texts, it is the overall spirit and orientation of the council which matters for the Asian Churches to build their future in conversation with their contexts." Felix Wilfred, "Christianities and Asian Theologies Through the Lens of Postcolonialism," *Concilium: The International Journal for Theology* 1 (2018): 15–26.
5. See *Lumen gentium*, 23; Carmelo Dotolo et al., eds., *Enchiridion sull'inculturazione della fede* (Rome: Urbaniana University Press, 2019).
6. This could sound ingenuous, but it would likely be provocative. No human space is perfectly flat. There are always primary and secondary loci, even in the most decentered

and pluralistic universes. As I explain later in this chapter, the problem is when there is no mobility. When there is no possibility that a periphery becomes a center and vice versa. In an ecclesial context, there are authorities outside the sphere of dialogue (e.g., Scripture, Tradition) that place constraints on the communicative exercise. Not all rational opinions are equal; subversive voices should be allowed, but not given the same prominence as those most faithful to the fundamental truths that are constitutive of the communicative community itself. The complexity of the situation requests rules of communication in order to realize a constructive communication. There need to be rules so that the communication does not degenerate into pure emotional games of persuasion and manipulation. Only voices that can provide reasons for their claims, in a language that is comprehensible to everyone participating, should be allowed.

7. Charles Taylor, "Che cos'è la religione? La polisemia di un concetto contrastato," *Annali di studi Religiosi* 20 (2019): 9–22; this is the translation of Taylor's conference by Institut für die Wissenschaften vom Menschen in Vienna, on May 17, 2018, titled *The Polysemy of "Religion."* See also Peter Van der Veer, *The Modern Spirit of Asia: The Spiritual and the Secular in China and India* (Princeton, NJ: Princeton University Press, 2013). Jenny Daggers reflected on the birth of new concepts of religions in modernity; see Jenny Daggers, *Postcolonial Theology of Religions: Particularity and Pluralism in World Christianity* (London: Routledge, 2013), 13–31.

8. This is Durkheim's definition of religion, intended to explain it starting from its social effects. In one of his most famous works, Durkheim researched Australian religion, considered the simplest and most primitive then known: Émile Durkheim, *The Elementary Forms of Religious Life* (New York: Free Press, 1995).

9. Mannion, *Ecclesiology*, 118.

10. Peter C. Phan, "Reception of and Trajectories for Vatican II in Asia," *Theological Studies* 74 (2013): 302–20, at 306–7.

11. Phan, 306.

12. Other authors argue for a more radical narrative: "Historians of Christianity agree that before the end of the first century, Christianity had spread to as far as India and China. Historical records show that a certain Theophilus was sent by Emperor Constantius to 'other parts of India' in 354 and found a Christian group listening 'to the reading of the Gospel in a sitting posture,' which he found repugnant to his Arian taste. Or, in 635, Alopen arrived in the Kingdom of Ta-ch'in and was warmly welcomed by the T'ang emperor, whose tolerant government accepted Christianity. Alopen was not the first Christian to step on Chinese soil, because many of them were already doing business along the Silk Road a long time earlier. However, this Asian trajectory is little understood, because the dominant historiography of Christianity has always been Eurocentric. The majority of historical texts used in seminaries divided the subject into three historical periods: ancient (Jewish-Greek), medieval (European), and modern (colonial expansion). The last of these corresponds to the "new age of world mission," in which Latin America and Asia make their appearance in the Christian narrative." Daniel Franklin Pilario et al., eds., "Asian Christianities," *Concilium* 54, no. 1 (2018): 7–11, at 7. See also Enrique Dussel, "The Epistemological Decolonization of Theology," *Concilium* 2 (2013): 21–31. Dussel highlights that during the Middle Ages, Latin-German Europe was peripheral and isolated by the Asian-African Mediterranean system. All of a sudden, Latin-German Europe started to expand, and the Modern Age was characterized by the "death of the Mediterranean Sea" and by the "birth of the Atlantic Ocean."

13. We should distinguish between the political center of Christianity and the places of its theological ferment. The Apostolic Letter *Africa Terrarum* of Pope Paul VI to Africa is an example: "For continually there occur the names of the great doctors and writers of the Church: that is of Origen, St. Athanasius, of St. Cyril, who were the luminaries of the so-called School of Alexandria; on the other shore of North Africa, the names of Tertullian, of St. Cyprian, and above all of St. Augustine stand out, who is to be thought of as the brightest light of the Christian people. I could mention the famous and holy hermits, Paul, Anthony, Pachomius, the initial founders of monastic life, which thanks to their brilliant example has been spread throughout the Eastern and Western regions. Last I cannot pass over in silence St. Frumentius, known as Abba Salama, who raised to the rank of bishop by St. Athanasius, was the apostle of Ethiopia." I, 3, www.vatican.va/content/paul-vi/la /apost_letters/documents/hf_p-vi_apl_19671029_africae-terrarum.html.

14. R. S. Sugirtharajah, *Postcolonial Reconfigurations: An Alternative Way of Reading the Bible and Doing Theology* (Danvers, MA: Chalice Press, 2003).

15. Massimo Faggioli, "Vatican II: The History and the Narratives," *Theological Studies* 73 (2012): 749–67, at 749.

16. Faggioli, 749–50.

17. For the "dialogue" as ecclesial tool proposed by Pope Paul VI during the time of Vatican II, see *Ecclesiam suam*, numbers 70, 75–76.

18. "Relying on the conviction that 'the incarnation of the Word was also a cultural incarnation,' the pope [John Paul II] affirms that cultures, analogically comparable to the humanity of Christ in whatever good they possess, may play a positive role of mediation in the expression and extension of the Christian faith." International Theological Commission, *Faith and Inculturation*, "Introduction," 5, 1988, www.vatican.va/roman_curia /congregations/cfaith/cti_documents/rc_cti_1988_fede-inculturazione_en.html.

19. See Marion Grau, *Rethinking Mission in The Postcolony: Salvation, Society and Subversion* (New York: T&T Clark, 2011); Jonathan Ingleby, *Beyond Empire: Postcolonialism and Mission in a Global Context* (Milton Keynes, UK: AuthorHouse, 2010); and Desmond van der Water et al., *Postcolonial Mission: Power and Partnership in World Christianity* (Claremont, CA: Sopher Press, 2011).

20. For the relation between Christian missions and colonialism in Africa, see Musa W. Dube Shomanah and Gerald O. West, eds., *The Bible in Africa: Transaction, Trajectories and Trends* (Leiden: Brill, 2000); and Itumeleng J. Mosala, *Biblical Hermeneutics and Black Theology in South Africa* (Grand Rapids: Wm. B. Eerdmans, 1989). For Asia, see Linda A. Newson, "Old World Diseases in Early Colonial Philippines and Spanish America," in *Population and History: The Demographic Origins of the Modern Philippines*, ed. Daniel F. Doeppers and Peter Xenos (Quezon City: Center for Southeast Asian Studies, 1998), 17–36; and Bryan S. Turner, "Globalization, Religion and Empire in Asia," in *Religion, Globalization and Culture*, ed. Peter Beyer and Lori G. Beaman (Leiden: Brill, 2007), 145–66.

21. The evangelization of culture is a dynamic process and not the imposition of uniformity. No center should abuse its role in order to maintain a central position or, again, we should distinguish between a political center and the places of theological ferment.

22. Sacred Congregation for the Doctrine of the Faith, *Mysterium Ecclesiam*, Rome, June 24, 1973, www.vatican.va/roman_curia/congregations/cfaith/documents/rc_con_cfaith _doc_19730705_mysterium-ecclesiae_en.html; International Theological Commission, *Faith and Inculturation*, Rome, 1988, www.vatican.va/roman_curia/congregations /cfaith/cti_documents/rc_cti_1988_fede-inculturazione_en.html.

23. "Culture consists in the extension of the requirements of human nature, as the accomplishment of its end, as is especially taught in the constitution *Gaudium et spes*: "Man comes to a true and full humanity only through culture, that is through the cultivation of the goods and values of nature.... The word 'culture' in its general sense indicates everything whereby man develops and perfects his many bodily and spiritual qualities." Thus the domain of culture is multiple: "He strives by his knowledge and his labor, to bring the world itself under his control. He renders social life more human both in the family and the civic community, through improvement of customs and institutions. Throughout the course of time he expresses, communicates and conserves in his works, great spiritual experiences and desires, that they might be of advantage to the progress of many, even of the whole human family." International Theological Commission, *Faith and Inculturation*, 1.4. For Felix Wilfred, the issue at stake is not the dynamic between subjectivity and universality but that between subjectivity and pluralist diversity; see Felix Wilfred, "Cristianesimi e teologie asiatici attraverso la lente del postcolonialismo," *Concilium* 54, no. 1 (2018).

24. Cf. Julius Bautista and Francis Khek Gee Lim, eds., *Christianity and the State in Asia: Complicity and Conflict* (London: Routledge, 2009), 1; Dyron B. Daughrity, *The Changing World of Christianity: The Global History of a Borderless Religion* (New York: Peter Lang, 2010); and Dyron B. Daughrity, *Church History: Five Approaches to a Global Discipline* (New York: Peter Lang, 2012).

25. International Theological Commission, *Faith and Inculturation*, "Introduction," 7.

26. Peter C. Phan, *Being Religious Interreligiously: Asian Perspectives on Interfaith* (Maryknoll, NY: Orbis, 2004).

27. Peter C. Phan, "Reception of and Trajectories for Vatican II in Asia," *Theological Studies* 74 (2013): 308; Scott W. Sunquist, ed., *A Dictionary of Asian Christianity* (Grand Rapids: Wm. B. Eerdmans, 2001).

28. Nevertheless, in the Western secular and postsecular contexts, too often "religion" and "theology" are not able to participate in social political debates. "Religion" becomes a subject of discussion as a "question" or as "abstract concept," without adequate consideration of its daily vitality and its ability to give a meaningful horizon to the believers.

29. Hannah Arendt, *Vita Activa: The Human Condition* (Chicago: University of Chicago Press, 1958). The political thought of Arendt is based on the importance of human relationships: human beings live among their fellows. This common space is an "infra," very dynamic and characterized by a dialogical approach and by the building of common goals. Taking part in this political dialogue contributes to the full realization of human being. Similarly, living in between, members of an ecclesiological community realize the "believing community."

30. Cf. Walter Brueggemann, *Prophetic Imagination*, 2nd ed. (Minneapolis: Fortress Press, 2001).

31. N. Steeves, *Grazie all'immaginazione: Integrare l'immaginazione in teologia fondamentale* (Brescia: Queriniana, 2019), 13.

32. Phan, *Being Religious Interreligiously*, 4.

33. I cannot develop this here, but globalization is one of those phenomena that prevent overlooking the challenges that arise from places other than the West, provided that it is not another form of universalism in disguise.

34. Cf. Edward W. Said, *Orientalism* (New York: Pantheon Books, 1978). In Said's view, Orientalism is not simply about the study of the East; it is also about the West having power

over the Orient by representing, codifying, and classifying knowledge about other cultures. The Western study of other cultures and production of oriental knowledge was not an innocent activity, and it was not free from political ramifications.

35. In 1537, in the bull *Sublimis Deus*, Pope Paul III recognized the Indios as rational human beings, but the theologians of Salamanca (1539) highlighted the civilizing role of the Europeans with regard to the people across the ocean, because they were incapable of governing themselves. Under the pretext of making them fit for civil society, the destruction of their culture was legitimated. For Asian postcolonial theology, see R. S. Sugirtharajah, *Postcolonial Reconfigurations: An Alternative Way of Reading the Bible and Doing Theology* (Danvers, MA: Chalice Press, 2003).

36. David Joy and Joseph Duggan, eds., *Decolonizing the Body of Christ: Theology and Theory after Empire* (New York: Palgrave Macmillan, 2012).

37. Enrique Dussel, "The Epistemological Decolonization of Theology," *Concilium* 2 (2013): 21–31, at 26.

38. Walter D. Mignolo and Arturo Escobar, eds., *Globalization and the De-Colonial Option* (London: Routledge 2009).

CHAPTER 15

Peter Phan and the Congregation for the Doctrine of the Faith

Charles E. Curran

This chapter discusses the interaction between the Congregation for the Doctrine of the Faith (CDF) and Peter C. Phan, the Ignacio Ellacuria, SJ, Professor of Catholic Social Thought at Georgetown University. With a cover letter dated July 20, 2005, Phan received from the CDF a seven-page document titled "Some Observations on the Book by Rev. Peter C. Phan *Being Religious Interreligiously: Asian Perspectives on Interfaith Dialogue* (Orbis Books, New York, 2004)." The document alleges that there are "serious ambiguities and doctrinal problems in the book."[1] This chapter explores this interaction in three steps: (1) the process used by the CDF in the investigation of Phan; (2) why the CDF dropped this investigation; and (3) why the process itself does not meet the accepted understandings of justice today.

THE PROCESSES OF THE CDF IN THE PHAN CASE

The "Regulations for Doctrinal Examination" to be followed in the investigation of theologians was issued by the CDF in 1997 and updates to a degree the earlier 1971 version.[2] Writings of a theologian are brought to the attention of the CDF (the author is deleted). If, after a number of interoffice investigations (including some consultation with the consultors of the CDF), the conclusion is that problems exist, then the formal process begins. The ordinary form of the formal process (the one usually used and also used in the Phan case) first involves an internal phase, which takes place in secrecy.

Two or more experts examine the writings and a *relator pro auctore* (advocate for the author) give reports, and the official consultors of the CDF vote to determine if there are "doctrinal errors or dangerous opinions" (Article 13). Article 17 refers to "erroneous or dangerous propositions." If so, a second phase occurs. Through the bishop or religious superior, a document is sent to the individual involved with a list of the erroneous or dangerous propositions and the reasons supporting such conclusions, with the theologian given three months to respond. If this response is not acceptable, the matter is then referred to an ordinary session of the CDF, which involves all its members (mostly cardinals and a few bishops) who happen to be in Rome. The ordinary session decides what form the proper action should take. As a matter of fact, these actions can include a set of further questions for the theologian, the publication of an essay in a theological journal (which is to be vetted by the CDF) clarifying the author's position, or a brief public declaration of one's adherence to Church teaching.

WHY PHAN?

History shows that in the post–Vatican II era, hot button issues have drawn the attention of the CDF, with early special emphasis on liberation theology and moral theology and with a focus on sexuality and marriage. The issue of the salvific role of non-Catholic religions came to the fore at the end of the twentieth century. In response to that, the CDF in 2000 published its declaration *Dominus Iesus*.[3] This declaration pointed out that non-Christians can be saved, but non-Christian religions are gravely deficient in comparison with Christians who have the fullness of salvation. In a 1996 address to Latin American bishops, Cardinal Ratzinger criticized by name Paul Knitter, then at Xavier University in Cincinnati and the author in 1985 of *No Other Names? A Critical Study of Christian Attitudes Toward the World Religions*. Ratzinger concluded that the pluralism proposed by Knitter is basically relativistic.[4]

In 1997, the Jesuit Jacques Dupuis wrote *A Christian Theology of Religious Pluralism*. After some conversation and negotiations, the CDF issued a public notification in 2001 about the problems with the book but did not take any action against the author as such.[5] In 2004 after correspondence and negotiations, the CDF issued a notification that Roger Haight's 1999 book *Jesus, Symbol of God* contained serious doctrinal errors and concluded that until such time as these serious doctrinal errors are corrected, Haight may not teach Catholic theology.[6]

Within such a climate, Peter Phan's 2004 book *Being Religious Interreligiously: Asian Perspectives on Interfaith Dialogue* came to be investigated by the CDF. Father Phan, a Vietnamese refugee, came to the United States in 1975 and actually worked first as a garbage collector. He then taught theology at the University of Dallas and the Catholic University of America, and then was offered the chair he currently holds at Georgetown University. In 2001, he served as the president of the Catholic Theological Society of America. His earlier writings involve issues of systematic theology, such as Karl Rahner and eschatology. However, he then soon began his dialogue and study of Asian theology and Asian religions.[7]

As a result of his prominence and respected standing as a Catholic theologian in the United States, it was almost inevitable that his work would come to the attention of the CDF. The seven legal pages of observations from the CDF assert that the book is confused about a number of points of Catholic doctrine and contains serious ambiguities. It is in open contrast with almost all the teaching of *Dominus Iesus*.[8] The letter sent from the secretary of the congregation to Charles Grahmann, Phan's bishop in Dallas, instructs the bishop to ask Phan to correct the problematic points by means of an article, which after first being submitted to the CDF within the next six months would then be published in an appropriate theological journal. He is also to direct Phan to inform his publisher that this book is not to be reprinted.[9]

On September 19, 2005, Phan wrote to Bishop Grahmann saying that he had only received the text on September 19, 2005, and because of many previous obligations he would not have sufficient time to comply with the deadline for writing the article. He respectfully requested that the deadline be extended to March 20, 2006.[10] Phan heard nothing from the CDF about this and then wrote a letter to William Cardinal Levada, the prefect of the CDF, on April 4, 2006. In this letter, he requested that three things be done so that he could write the article. First, he asked the prohibition to reprint the book be revoked because such a prohibition presumes his guilt before having the opportunity to defend himself. Second, he requested clarification about the nature and scope of the article that the CDF envisages. Third, as a matter of justice, he requested the CDF to consider a fair and just remuneration for the work that he would have to do in writing the article.[11]

Phan never heard back from the CDF. On May 15, 2007, William E. Lori, the bishop of Bridgeport and the head of the Committee of the US Bishops on Doctrine, wrote a letter to Phan saying that the CDF had requested that the Committee on Doctrine now examine the book.[12] My chapter is dealing only with the interaction between Phan and the CDF, so it will not discuss the interaction with the Committee on Doctrine of the US bishops.

But the obvious question arises: Why did the CDF stop its investigation of Phan's book? This was a very unusual action that contrasts sharply with the approach taken to the works of Dupuis and Haight.

WHY DID THE CDF STOP ITS INVESTIGATION OF PHAN?

What explains the CDF's decision to drop the investigation of Peter Phan? Recall that the CDF gave the case to the doctrinal commission of the US bishops. There are no easy answers to this question. The CDF's processes are ultimately known only to it. All must agree that such processes are not transparent. One can only surmise what explains its action, or rather inaction, on the basis of the very limited knowledge we have of how it acted in other cases. It is, however, important to raise this rather significant question and to try to answer it in a tentative manner based on the limited knowledge we have. I propose two reasons that help to explain why the CDF did not follow through on the investigation of Phan—first, the condition that Phan proposed in his response to the CDF; and second, the fact that the CDF realized there was very little it could do to him in his present situation. I quickly add that these are at best conjectures, for it is impossible to know for certain what was the basis for the CDF's decision.

First, in his response, Phan insisted on a number of conditions for his acceptance of the CDF's call for him to write an article that the CDF would vet before it was published. He asked for a fair and just remuneration for the time and work it would take him to write such an article. Unlike curial officials, priests engaged in pastoral ministry, and religious, he must earn his own salary, and in addition supports his mother financially. He asked the CDF to pay for half his annual salary, because the CDF had given him six months to write the article.[13]

In discussing this condition, Phan appears a little defensive of his demand. He reports that some have "tut-tutted" at his request for financial assistance, and suggested that he had been in the United States so long that he was now "inculturated" in the capitalistic ways of this country. However, he insisted that payment is a matter of justice, and not only for himself. He proposed a scenario of a lay theologian (and they are becoming ever more numerous), whose salary from teaching helps to support self and family. To respond to the request of the CDF with a truly scholarly approach, the individual would need to take unpaid leave from teaching in order to prepare a suitable scholarly article. Should the accuser not be obliged to pay for the time necessary to respond to the accusation? In addition, there is also the psychological damage that such a charge can do to the individual theologian. Church officials think that theologians are at their beck and call, but many theologians today are not celibate and religious. Phan concludes that at the end of the day, the charge of money grabbing, though utterly offensive, might have served to draw the attention of celibate Church authorities to basic issues of justice and fairness. Such clerics and religious are accustomed to have their material needs taken care of, but this is not the case for those who must work to supply their needs.[14]

In my opinion, this condition was a superb tactic that put the congregation between a rock and a hard place. However one evaluates the justice of the condition, all must appreciate the canniness of Phan in proposing it. The CDF was never going to pay him to write the article they demanded. And Phan was not only canny but also very creative. No one before apparently had ever proposed such a condition to the CDF. If the CDF accepted his condition, it would logically have to do it for all others. (In fairness, the CDF has a comparatively small budget and would not be able to provide such a payment, but advocates of justice still would not see that as a justification for not paying.) Conversely, one can readily understand why the CDF would not want to publicly say that it would not meet the demands of justice and pay for the time and work necessary to prepare the article. Such a response would be a *bruta figura*, which is a cardinal sin for Vatican curialists. The most logical solution was to drop the hot potato and not even respond to Phan's letter to the CDF.

The second reason is the pragmatic one, that the CDF is not going to take action against a theologian if the action is not going to have any effect. Your authority is lessened if your authoritative action accomplishes nothing. Compare the case of Phan with those of Jacques Dupuis and Roger Haight, both of whom were to some extent dealing with the issue of religious pluralism. Dupuis and Haight are both Jesuits. Their exchange with the CDF came through the Jesuit general in Rome, and there was much back and forth in these cases. The fact of the matter is that in the present structure of the Church, the CDF can be effective in the actions it takes against members of religious communities by working through their religious superiors. In the end, there was very strong Jesuit support for Dupuis and the CDF took no punitive action against him personally. The CDF's notification maintained that there were notable ambiguities and difficulties on important doctrinal points in his book that could lead his reader to erroneous or harmful opinions. Dupuis agreed to adhere to the theses proposed by the CDF and to include the notification in any subsequent reprinting, further edition, or translation of the book.[15]

The action taken against Haight was quite severe. As mentioned above, the 2005 notification from the CDF maintained there are serious doctrinal errors in his book on Jesus and concluded that until his positions are amended, he was barred from teaching Catholic theology. Subsequently, it came out after further negotiations that Haight had been stopped from publishing and teaching Catholic theology, even at Union Theological Seminary.[16] However, Haight has continued in another capacity at Union and has published significant books on spirituality.

I was glancing through the letters to the editor in the July 30, 2007, issue of *America*, the Jesuit journal in the United States, and was startled to find the following. The headline was simply: "Clarification." Then it said, "I personally give religious assent to the Church's teaching regarding the intrinsically evil acts as proposed in Pope John Paul II's encyclical *Veritatis splendor*. I personally give religious assent to the Church's teaching regarding homosexuality contained in the *Catechism of the Catholic Church*." The clarification goes on to assert that giving religious assent to three other Vatican documents dealing with homosexuality. The clarification is signed by Edward Vacek, SJ.[17] Vacek at the time was teaching at the Weston School of Theology, a Jesuit theologate. The clarification had nothing to do with anything Vacek or any other person had written about in *America*. Those familiar with the practice of the CDF knew right away where the clarification came from. Vacek had written an earlier article disagreeing with the Church's teaching on homosexuality.[18] Bradford Hinze, in his discussion of the disciplining of Catholic theologians by the CDF, refers to two other Jesuits—John R. Sachs, SJ, and Paul Crowley, SJ—who also gave clarifications about their position on homosexuality after negotiations with the CDF. Hinze points out that Crowley and Stephen Pope, a lay theologian from Boston College, both wrote on homosexuality in *Theological Studies* in 2004. Crowley's essay itself did not call into question the official position on homosexuality, but he was investigated by the CDF and issued a clarification. Pope, a layperson from Boston College, actually raised critical issues about the teaching of the Church on homosexuality but was not investigated or punished in any way by the CDF.[19]

This context might shed some light on the case of Paul Knitter, a resigned priest who, as mentioned above, was explicitly named and condemned for his approach to religious pluralism and the unique salvific role of Jesus Christ in an address by Cardinal Ratzinger, then the prefect of the CDF, to the bishops of Latin America. But there is no public record that Knitter was ever condemned or punished by the CDF. Hinze mentions, without any reference, that Knitter was contacted by the CDF in 1988.[20] He retired somewhat early from the Jesuit Xavier University in Cincinnati, but the reality is that no public action was ever taken against Knitter by the CDF. One can only conclude that the fact he was neither a priest nor religious nor teaching at a Catholic institution meant that the CDF apparently decided not to proceed against him, because it would really not have any effect. Of course, here one could raise the question about what Xavier University would have done if some sanction against Knitter's teaching had been given by the Vatican and he was still teaching there.

There is no public evidence that any action was taken by the CDF against a Catholic theologian teaching at the major institutions of Catholic higher education in the United States. Again, one can only surmise that the reason was because such universities would in no way allow the Vatican declaration to have any effect on the continued teaching of one of their faculty members after any penalty or punishment given by the CDF. The best known and large Catholic institutions of higher learning firmly proclaim their adherence to academic freedom, which means that no outside authority of any type, including the Church, can interfere with what goes on within the university itself. Thus, one can surmise, obviously without certitude, that the CDF decided not to proceed in its investigation against Phan, because they did not want to respond to his condition and because whatever they did to him would have no effect whatsoever on his teaching at Georgetown University.

In his one response to the CDF in his own shrewd way, Phan reminded them of his Georgetown professorship. Phan pointed out that he was averse to publicity and tried his best to keep the investigation secret. The only people he informed were "those who must know"—John J. DeGioia, president of Georgetown University; Jane McAuliffe, dean of Georgetown College; Chester Gillis, chair of the department of theology; and the administrators of Orbis Books.[21] Thus, in a very subtle way, Phan reminded the CDF that he was a tenured and chaired professor at Georgetown.

ARE THE CDF'S PROCEDURES JUST AND FAIR?

The Phan investigation on the basis of the CDF's "Regulations for Doctrinal Examination" occasions questions about the justice and fairness of the process itself. I was the first theologian in the United States to be investigated in accord with the CDF's earlier regulations of 1971, which are quite similar to the later version. At the same time, however, the CDF took another action about theological errors in the United States. Under the date of July 13, 1979, the CDF with Franjo Cardinal Šeper as prefect, in a covering letter to Archbishop John Quinn, the president of the US bishops, sent "observations" about the book *Human Sexuality,* a study commissioned by the Catholic Theological Society of America and written by Father Anthony Kosnik and others. The US bishops had previously pointed out the errors in the book, but now the CDF wanted to add its own observation about the errors and problems with the book.[22] Note that there was no investigation of Kosnik as such, only the publication of these observations.

In a fascinating coincidence, and maybe more than a coincidence, under the same date of July 13, 1979, I received a letter from Cardinal Šeper saying I was under investigation by the CDF and including a long list of observations (ten pages in printed book form), to which I was to respond within a "working month" but also with a recognition that more time might be needed. I began my response of October 26, 1979, by stating that the procedures are "seriously flawed in terms of the protection of the rights of the individual involved." They do not incorporate the elementary principles that are involved in contemporary legal structures. One has a right to know who are the accusers, what precisely are the charges, and to have an advocate of one's own choosing.[23]

On March 20, 1980, in a preliminary response to my October 1979 letter, Cardinal Šeper, at the beginning of his letter, addressed my criticism of the procedures. My objection presupposes the model of a court trial, but the *ratio agendi* is not a trial but a procedure designed to guarantee a careful and accurate examination of published writings. There are no "accusers," only public writings; no "charges," only the results of a careful examination with a request for clarifications; and the "representation" is furnished by the author himself.[24]

Since that time, many have addressed the injustice and unfairness of these procedures. Richard A. McCormick and Richard P. McBrien reported the positions of others and concluded in a 1990 article that "it is all but universally acknowledged that the judicial process that prevails in the Congregation for the Doctrine of the Faith is woefully inadequate in the contemporary world." In brief, the institutional structures and procedures are unfair to start with. Investigations conducted within these structures are bound to be unfair.[25] Among the problems that have been pointed out are the fact that the CDF plays the roles of prosecutor, defense attorney, and judge; the author is not informed in the first stage of the investigation; has no access to the documents touching on the charges; does not have the same rights as the accuser in making one's own defense; and has no right of appeal.

Ladislas Örsy, the distinguished canonist, has discussed the CDF's procedures in an article that he later incorporated as a chapter in his book *Receiving the Council: Theological and Canonical Insights and Debates.* He describes in some detail the problems that have already been mentioned but begins by pointing out that justice demands a precise definition of the offense. The two offenses indicated in the regulations are "erroneous doctrine" and "dangerous doctrine." These two are very broad and imprecise. Catholic teaching has traditionally recognized many different types of doctrine or teaching. The bishops of Paris and London judged Thomas Aquinas's doctrine to be dangerous. Galileo was condemned because his theories were dangerous. To make ill-defined or underdefined definitions a juridical ground for condemnation is to endanger the very aspect of justice itself.[26]

In my judgment, another major problem does not concern the regulations as such but the selection of the consultors who play such a significant role in the process. These consultors basically come from the theologians teaching at the various pontifical faculties in Rome.[27] They are not truly representative of the worldwide Catholic theological community. These theologians belong to what has been called "the Roman school," which takes a very conservative approach to the understanding of Catholic theology. As a result, it is difficult for theologians coming from different theological schools to get a fair treatment of their work.

There is also a further problem that I have noted on a few occasions when theologians who are being investigated have shared their observations with me. I said to one friend that I could have written a set of observations from the perspective of the CDF that would be much more complete and much more critical than the observations that were received from the CDF. In fairness, the CDF is a comparatively small operation; but even so, its observations could be much more complete and critical than they sometimes are. On those occasions, I have had the impression that the CDF was really not familiar with all the publications of the person under investigation. This might explain why, lately, the CDF condemns one particular book.

My own experience bears out this criticism. The original letter to me from Cardinal Šeper said that "several" of my articles and writings had been called to the attention of the CDF. I pointed out in response that nowhere in the observations, which were dealing primarily with the fundamental question of dissent from noninfallible teachings, was there any mention of the book *Dissent In and for the Church,* which was collegially written by myself and my colleagues at Catholic University who dissented from *Humanae vitae.* This book represents the materials that we submitted to the faculty committee that investigated our dissent. I then enclosed the list of all my books and said that if the CDF does not have copies of them, I would be most happy to forward them.[28] In a response to me, J. Hamer (Archbishop Jerome Hamer), the secretary of the CDF, said it has at its disposition the books you included on your publications list. "Nevertheless, I would be pleased to accept your offer to send us a copy of *Dissent In and for the Church*."[29] There is some tension, if not outright contradiction, between these two sentences. On the basis of a few such observations, I have come to the conclusion that the work done in preparing the observations could be much more thorough and complete, let alone fairer.

The discussion of the Phan case and its relation to similar cases raises another important aspect of injustice in carrying out the procedures. Similar cases are not always treated in a similar manner. Those who belong to religious orders or are priests are treated differently from those who are not. Those who teach at well-known and highly regarded Catholic institutions of higher learning with a strong commitment to academic freedom have not been subject to the procedures. The CDF appears not to act if their action will have no effect. Such a system is not in practice a just system.

FURTHER PROBLEMS OF INJUSTICE

In addition to the injustice involved in the very process itself and the further injustice in how the process has been employed and handled in different cases, there are also the pain and suffering that the accused individual has personally experienced. In this context, one commentator recalled the observation of the French Dominican Humbert Clerrisac that it is easy to suffer for the Church, but the difficult thing is to suffer at the hands of the Church.[30]

Without a doubt, no one has openly talked more about personal suffering than Jacques Dupuis. There was a feeling even among some of Dupuis's Jesuit confreres that he focused too much on his own angst.[31] All must recognize, however, that Dupuis's own experience well illustrates the suffering that many have experienced to some degree as a result of being under investigation by the CDF.

Jacques Dupuis, mentioned above, was a Belgian Jesuit who taught for many years in India and dealt with the relationship between the Catholic Church and world religions. He lived with the investigation by the CDF for twenty-nine months. On October 2, 1998, Dupuis, through the Jesuit general was given a nine-page, single-spaced document from the CDF explaining the "serious errors or doctrinal ambiguities on doctrines of divine and Catholic faith" concerning revelation, salvation, Christology, and the Trinity found in his book *A Christian Theology of Religious Pluralism*.[32] In

December 1998, Dupuis sent a lengthy response to the CDF. In July 1999, the CDF responded, saying nothing about its mistakes that Dupuis had pointed out in his response and giving him three months to reply to the new document. In November 1999, Dupuis sent a sixty-page response. On September 4, 2000, he was given a fifteen-page notification on his book (already approved by the pope), which was to be published and invited to a meeting with Cardinal Ratzinger, the prefect of the CDF, on September 4. As a result of this meeting—including the Jesuit General Father Kolvenbach and Gerard O'Collins, SJ, who served as Dupuis's advocate—the original proposed notification to be published was taken off the table. In December 2000, Dupuis received a revised short notification that the CDF asked him to sign and return so that it could be made public. This notification did not imply that Dupuis held false views on Catholic faith but softened matters to "serious ambiguities and difficulties," while maintaining that independently of the author's intention, the book could lead others to adopt erroneous or dangerous opinions.

In December 2001, Dupuis signed the second notification. The CDF finally published the notification on February 26, 2002, but without informing Dupuis, added a paragraph saying that Dupuis's signature showed his agreement with the thesis of the notification and that in his future theological activities and publications, he would follow the doctrinal contents contained in the notification. Dupuis was quite upset by this abusive addition that could be held over his head and used against him in the future.[33] This has been a brief account of the bare facts but does not include many of the traumatic experiences that Dupuis went through in conjunction with the investigation.

What effect did the process have on Dupuis? In those late years of his life (he died at eighty-one on December 28, 2004), his health had not been good. He went to the hospital several times for different ailments in the twenty-nine-month period. The whole trial deeply affected his person and his mental health. He experienced periods of dejection and times when he felt alone and disowned. Thanks to God's grace, his faith was never severely tested during his investigation. But he did often raise questions, such as, Why was God allowing this to happen? Perhaps it was because of his sins in general or his pride in the work that he had done as a theologian. His relationship to the Church is a very different question. The Church is not the Roman Curia and its bureaucracy, but the people of God gathered around Jesus, its master and Lord. The Church is truly divine but also human, and is also sinful. We all share at once in the Church's holiness and sinfulness and are all responsible for the work of striving to make the Church ever more a reflection of the reign of God. He was never seriously tempted to leave his vocation as a theologian, Jesuit religious, and member of the Church, but there were moments of doubt and uncertainty.[34]

In February 2001, the CDF published a "Notification" with regard to the writings of Father Maciano Vidal, especially on his three-volume work *Moral de actitudes*. Vidal, a Spanish Redemptorist priest-theologian, is recognized as the leading contemporary Spanish moral theologian. In a preface to the "Notification," the CDF describes a process very similar to the one followed in the Dupuis case. On December 13, 1999, the congregation sent what it called a "contestatio" to Vidal about his writings and asked him to respond. There followed a subsequent document from the CDF and another response by Vidal. In addition, there was a meeting at the congregation. The final "Notification" maintains that *Moral de actitudes* does not sufficiently stress the vertical dimension of the Christian life and the Christian themes of redemption, the cross, grace, and other theological aspects. Vidal also gives insufficient attention to the Church's magisterium. He does not accept the traditional doctrine of intrinsically evil acts and absolute norms. On specific moral issues—such as masturbation, homosexuality, in vitro fertilization, and others—while informing the reader of the teachings of the Church, his own solutions differ from that teaching. Vidal accepted the doctrinal judgment formulated by the CDF along with the formal obligation to revise his writings according to the instructions given. (Vidal himself subsequently decided not to publish any revised editions of his writings.) However, the "Notification" is not meant as a judgment on the person of the author, on his intentions, on the totality of his work, or on his ministry as a theologian but solely on the works examined.[35]

In an interview with an Italian theological journal, Vidal very briefly talks about his reaction to the whole process. The process was difficult in itself and also because of its long duration (December 1997–May 2001) and because of the amount of work he had to do in conjunction with it. Particularly difficult for him was the moment when he was asked to sign the "Notification" that was to be published. He was upset that his three-volume *Moral de actitudes* could not be used for theological formation, but he was willing to sign the "Notification" because it did not impugn his intention, the totality of his works, or his theological ministry. He accepted the role of the magisterium as the magisterium itself affirms it.[36] (One sees here a somewhat vague statement that can be interpreted in a number of different ways.)

The Catholic theologian does theology for the good of the Church. Those who are accused by the CDF, as exemplified in the cases of Jacques Dupuis and Marciano Vidal, must live with the fact that the very Church one is trying to serve rejects their work. Such a tension constitutes a very difficult existential situation. From a more practical viewpoint, perhaps the biggest anxiety for those under investigation concerns what the final outcome will be. The CDF has taken various actions in the past. Will the CDF declare that the theologian can no longer teach Catholic theology? Will the condemnation refer to the major work of the theologian in question? What happens if the CDF requires the theologian to sign a public notification? Can one sign such a statement in good conscience?

In conclusion, this chapter has dealt with issues raised by the CDF's investigation of Peter Phan. Only the CDF itself knows exactly why this investigation was started and why it ended. No one else will ever know with certitude exactly what happened here. This chapter, on the basis of available public actions taken elsewhere by the CDF, has tried to explain why it started the investigation of Phan and also why it decided to stop it. In addition, a final section of this chapter deals with the injustice of the procedures used by the CDF in examining the works of theologians.

NOTES

1. This text is found in *The Joy of Religious Pluralism: A Personal Journey*, by Peter C. Phan (Maryknoll, NY: Orbis, 2017), 175–84. An appendix to this book contains the correspondence between the Congregation for the Doctrine of the Faith and Phan and also the correspondence with the Committee on Doctrine of the US bishops. For convenience's sake, I will cite the appropriate documents as found in this book.

2. Congregation for the Doctrine of the Faith (CDF), "Regulations for Doctrinal Examination," June 29, 1997, www.vatican.va/roman_curia/ ... /rc_con_faith_doc_19970629 _ratio-agendi_en_html. Commentaries on this document include Bradford Hinze, "A Decade of Disciplining Theologians," *Horizons* 37, no. 1 (2010): 97–101; Ladislas Örsy, *Receiving the Council: Theological and Canonical Insights and Debates* (Collegeville, MN: Liturgical Press, 2009), 91–96; and Paul Collins, *The Modern Inquisition: Seven Prominent Catholics and Their Struggles with the Vatican* (Woodstock, NY: Overlook Press, 2002), 32–45. The Hinze article has by far the most complete listing of theologians who have been disciplined by the CDF, local bishops' conferences, and individual bishops.

3. CDF, "Declaration *Dominus Iesus*: On the Unicity and Salvific Universality of Jesus Christ and the Church," August 6, 2000, www.vatican.va/roman ... /rc_con_faith_doc _20000806_dominus_iesus_en.html.

4. Joseph Cardinal Ratzinger, "Relativism: The Central Problem for the Faith Today," *Origins* 26 (October 31, 1996): 309, 311–17.

5. CDF, "Notification on the Book *Toward a Christian Theology of Religious Pluralism* (Maryknoll, NY: Orbis, 1997) by Father Jacques Dupuis SJ," January 24, 2001, www .vatican.va/roman_curia/ ... /rc_con_faith_doc_20010124_dupuis_en.html.

6. CDF, "Notification on the Book *Jesus Symbol of God*, by Father Roger Haight SJ," December 13, 2004, www.vatican.va/ ... /rc_con_faith_doc_20041213_notification-fr-haight_en.html.

7. For Phan's curriculum vitae, see the appendix to this book.

8. Phan, *Joy of Religious Pluralism*, 175.

9. Phan, 174.

10. Phan, 185.

11. Phan, 186–90.

12. Phan, 191.

13. Phan, 189.

14. Phan, 11–13.

15. CDF, "Notification to Dupuis."

16. John L. Allen Jr., "Rome Orders Haight to Stop Teaching, Publishing," *National Catholic Reporter*, January 5, 2009, www.ncronline.org/print/news/Rome-Orders-Roger-Haight-Stop-Teaching-Publishing.

17. Edward Vacek, "Clarification," *America*, July 30, 2007, 37–38.

18. Edward Vacek, "A Christian Homosexuality?" *Commonweal*, December 5, 1980, 681–84.

19. Hinze, *Horizons* 37, no. 1 (2010): 104–5.

20. Hinze, 107.

21. Phan, *Joy of Religious Pluralism*, 189.

22. CDF, "Observations about the Book 'Human Sexuality.' A Study Commissioned by the Catholic Theological Society of America, Rev. Anthony Kosnik Editor," July 13, 1979, www.vatican.va/roman_curia/ … /rc_con_faith_doc_1979013_mons-quinn_en.html.

23. I have published the full correspondence between the CDF and myself in *Faithful Dissent*, by Charles E. Curran (Kansas City: Sheed & Ward, 1986). This particular passage is found on pp. 143–44.

24. Curran, 165.

25. Richard A. McCormick and Richard P. McBrien, "L'Affaire Curran II," *America*, September 8, 1980, 128–29.

26. Örsy, *Receiving the Council*, 97–102.

27. Hinze, *Horizons*, 94.

28. Curran, *Faithful Dissent*, 139–41.

29. Curran, 142.

30. Maura Anne Ryan, "Search and Witness," *America*, July 31, 2006, 35.

31. John Allen, "The Word from Rome," *National Catholic Reporter*, January 7, 2005, www.nationalcatholicreporter.org/word/word010705.htm.

32. Gerard O'Connell, *Do Not Stifle the Spirit: Conversations with Jacques Dupuis* (Maryknoll, NY: Orbis, 2017), 56–146. See also William R. Burrows, *Jacques Dupuis Faces the Inquisition: Two Essays by Jacques Dupuis on Dominus Jesus and the Roman Investigation of His Work* (Eugene, OR: Wipf & Stock, 2012); also see Gerald O'Collins, "A Look Back at Dupuis' Skirmish with the Vatican," https://www.ncronline.org/news/people/look-back-dupuis-skirmish-vatican.

33. O'Connell, *Do Not Stifle the Spirit*, 142–43.

34. O'Connell, 150–55.

35. CDF, "Notification Regarding Certain Writings of Fr. Marciano Vidal, CSsR," www.vatican.va/roman_curia/ … rc_con_faith.doc_20010515_vidal_en.html.

36. Benjamín Forcano and José Antonio Lobo, "Intervista a M. Vidal," *Rivista de Teologia Morale* 137 (2003): 120–22.

CHAPTER 16

Being Honestly
Pluralistically Religious

John Borelli

The "Document on Human Fraternity for World Peace and Living Together" states:

> Freedom is a right of every person: each individual enjoys the free-
> dom of belief, thought, expression and action. The pluralism and the
> diversity of religions, colour, sex, race and language are willed by God
> in His wisdom, through which He created human beings. This divine
> wisdom is the source from which the right to freedom of belief and
> the freedom to be different derives. Therefore, the fact that people are
> forced to adhere to a certain religion or culture must be rejected, as
> too the imposition of a cultural way of life that others do not accept.[1]

This simple, seemingly self-evidently true statement of religious faith
and human rights caused quite a stir when it was released not very long ago
at all. It is the second of twelve convictions in the "Document on Human
Fraternity for World Peace and Living Together," an agreed statement bearing the names of Pope Francis and the Grand Imam of Al-Azhar, Ahmed
el-Tayeb. The pope and the grand imam, who was representing the Muslim
Wise Men Council, signed and released this document on February 4, 2019.
This occurred when Pope Francis traveled to Abu Dhabi on the history-
making, first papal trip to the Arabian Peninsula.[2] This was also the first such
agreement of religious convictions by a pope and a Muslim religious official; and, remarkably, it calls Muslims, Christians, and all people of goodwill, with or without religious faith, to practice something greater than mere

tolerance—that they join one another in building human fraternity and accompanying one another in seeking world peace and life together.

This agreed statement had its origins almost two years earlier, during the April 28–29, 2017, apostolic journey of Pope Francis to Egypt, where he had a private conversation with the Grand Imam of Al-Azhar and delivered an address at the Al-Azhar Conference Centre in Cairo. Pope Francis did not make public the substance of his private conversation with Sheikh Ahmed el-Tayeb, but his address at the International Peace Conference on April 28 is public.[3]

Bishop Miguel Ayuso, now cardinal and president of the Pontifical Council for Interreligious Dialogue, reminded me of the significance of this papal speech at Al-Azhar several months before the "Document on Human Fraternity" appeared. He directed me to two paragraphs in that address while we were discussing plans for an upcoming conference at Georgetown University on the future of interreligious dialogue. Here is that passage:

> Precisely in the field of dialogue, particularly interreligious dialogue, we are constantly called to walk together, in the conviction that the future also depends on the encounter of religions and cultures. In this regard, the work of the *Mixed Committee for Dialogue between the Pontifical Council for Interreligious Dialogue and the Committee of Al-Azhar for Dialogue* offers us a concrete and encouraging example. Three basic areas, if properly linked to one another, can assist in this dialogue: *the duty to respect one's own identity and that of others, the courage to accept differences,* and *sincerity of intentions.*
>
> *The duty to respect one's own identity and that of others,* because true dialogue cannot be built on ambiguity or a willingness to sacrifice some good for the sake of pleasing others. *The courage to accept differences,* because those who are different, either culturally or religiously, should not be seen or treated as enemies, but rather welcomed as fellow-travellers, in the genuine conviction that the good of each resides in the good of all. *Sincerity of intentions,* because dialogue, as an authentic expression of our humanity, is not a strategy for achieving specific goals, but rather a path to truth, one that deserves to be undertaken patiently, in order to transform competition into cooperation.[4] (emphasis in the original)

In these paragraphs, Pope Francis lays out his approach to dialogue and helps us understand the principles leading to the "Document on Human Fraternity," which is the fruit of interreligious dialogue. Note especially how

Pope Francis views authentic religious and cultural differences as genuine gifts offered by fellow travelers and genuine dialogue as a communal search for the truth and not a strategy for ulterior motives.

The "Document on Human Fraternity" states: "The pluralism and the diversity of religions, colour, sex, race and language are willed by God in His wisdom." This observation firmly supports the agreed statement's second conviction: "Freedom is a right of every person." When I first read this observation about the diversity of religions, I thought of the Qur'an, recalling a comment I had often heard in dialogue with Muslim participants, "The many religions are willed by God." The words have a Qur'anic ring. For example, in Surah 5 (Al-Ma'idah): 48, we hear, "If God so willed, He would have made you one community, but He wanted to test you through that which He has given you, so race to do good: you will all return to God and He will make clear to you the matters you differed about."[5] There is also this message in Surah 2 (Al-Baqarah): 148, "Each community has its own direction to which it turns: race to do good deeds and wherever you are, God will bring you together. God has power to do everything." And later, in verse 2:56, we hear, "There is no compulsion in religion: true guidance has become distinct from error, so whoever rejects false gods and believes in God has grasped the firmest hand-hold, one that will never break. God is all hearing and all knowing." The agreed statement's second conviction echoes the message in that last verse, "Therefore, the fact that people are forced to adhere to a certain religion or culture must be rejected, as too the imposition of a cultural way of life that others do not accept."

The Qur'an is quite direct about religious pluralism and divine wisdom. In the Bible, the passages acclaiming religious pluralism are more indirect and subtler, but they exist. For example, we read in the Acts of the Apostles these words that Saint Paul preached in Athens: "I see how extremely religious you are in every way; I found among the objects of your worship an altar with an inscription 'to an unknown God,' what therefore you worship as unknown, this I proclaim to you" (Acts 17:22ff). Or, in the First Book of Kings, we hear Solomon at prayer in the new temple he had completed, suggesting that experiencing the presence of God cannot be confined to a multitude of places: "But will God indeed dwell on the earth? Even heaven and the highest heaven cannot contain you, much less this house that I have built" (1 Kings 8:27).

Perhaps this directness in the Qur'an regarding religious pluralism caused some of the reactions to Pope Francis entering into this agreement with the grand imam that included the presumption that the diversity of religions is divinely willed. Raymond Cardinal Burke, one of the pope's familiar public critics, was quoted to say "that the plurality or diversity of religions is good, that's a mistaken notion and it's certainly confusing for the faithful regarding salvation, which comes to us through Christ alone."[6] Gerhard Cardinal Müller, the former prefect of the Congregation for the Doctrine of the Faith and whom Pope Francis did not renew at the conclusion of his first five-year term, was probably the most reputable critic of Pope Francis on this matter. Cardinal Müller issued his "Manifesto of Faith" four days after the Abu Dhabi document was signed and released. Citing the *Catechism of the Catholic Church*, Müller's Manifesto affirmed two leading Christian teachings: "The distinction of the three persons in the divine unity marks a fundamental difference in the belief in God and the image of man from that of other religions. Religions disagree precisely over this belief in Jesus the Christ."[7]

These indeed are true statements by Cardinal Müller for Christians, but they are not the whole truth, as Walter Cardinal Kasper pointed out in response. Cardinal Kasper, also retired but emeritus president of the Pontifical Council for Promoting Christian Unity, observed that Cardinal Müller's objection is an example of firmly pointing out a truth, one also definitely held by Protestants, but leaving the other half of the truth obscured— namely, similarities with the Jews and the Muslims in the belief in the one God. And are not these similarities today fundamental to peace in the world and in society? He concluded: "Half the truth is not the Catholic truth!"[8] Cardinal Kasper also observed that some of the blanket statements in Cardinal Müller's "Manifesto" require nuancing, others need contextualizing for special pastoral needs, and still other statements amount to a "Manifesto of Theological Opinion" and not a "Manifesto of Faith."[9] Cardinal Kasper did not accuse Cardinal Müller of confusing the faithful, just of not giving them the whole teaching.

The Pontifical Council for Promoting Christian Unity is heir to the Secretariat for Promoting Christian Unity, which produced the "Decree on Ecumenism," the "Declaration on Religious Liberty," and the "Declaration on the Relation of the Church to Non-Christian Religions" at the Second Vatican Ecumenical Council (1962–65). This latter declaration is a significant source for valuing religious pluralism, for it employed the term "religions" in 1965 in a positive way: "One expects from the various religions answers to the profound enigmas of the human condition, which today, even as of old, deeply stir human hearts." The final paragraph of that declaration contains this little gem relevant to a discussion of religious liberty: "The Church reproves, as foreign to the mind of Christ, any discrimination or harassment of men or women because of their race or color, condition in life or religion." At Vatican II, the Catholic Church for the first time in the history of its universal councils employed the terms "religion" and "religions" as positive references to what those who are other than Catholic believe and practice, and for the first time endorsed the principle of religious liberty as a fundamental human right.

In a similar spirit, the introductory paragraph of the 2019 "Document on Human Fraternity" begins this way: "Faith leads a believer to see in the other a brother or sister to be supported and loved. Through faith in God, who has created the universe, creatures and all human beings (equal on account of his mercy), believers are called to express this human fraternity by safeguarding creation and the entire universe and supporting all persons, especially the poorest and those most in need."

The "Declaration on the Relation of the Church to Non-Christian Religions" (*Nostra aetate*) concludes with equal sympathies: "We cannot truly call upon God, the Father of all, if we refuse to behave as sisters and brothers with anyone, created as all are in the image of God. The relation of man and woman to God, the Father, and their relation to their fellow human beings are linked to such a degree that Holy Scripture says, 'Whoever does not love does not know God'" (1 Jn. 4:8).

Up until Vatican II, the only time the subjects "religion" and "religions" appear in documents of a universal council of the Catholic Church was at Vatican I (1869–70). In the documents of Vatican I, we find references to "true religion" and to the "Christian religion" as synonymous terms and to "false religion," which is what those espouse who have not embraced Catholic truth.[10]

The first positive reference to "religions" in the Vatican II era appeared in the address of Pope Paul VI at the opening of the second of the four periods of the council, September 29, 1963, when he asked the council fathers to look "beyond your own sphere and observe those other religions that uphold the meaning and the concept of God as one, creator, provident, most high, and transcendent, that worship God with acts of sincere piety and upon whose beliefs and practices the principles of moral and social life are founded."[11] He had already marveled at how God showers his favors on everyone. He reiterated and extended his positive view of other religions in his August 6, 1964, agenda-setting encyclical on the Church and dialogue, *Ecclesiam suam*:

> But we do not wish to turn a blind eye to the spiritual and moral values of the various non-Christian religions, for we desire to join with them in promoting and defending common ideals in the spheres of religious liberty, human brotherhood, education, culture, social welfare, and civic order. Dialogue is possible in all these great projects, which are our concern as much as theirs, and we will not fail to offer

opportunities for discussion in the event of such an offer being favorably received in genuine, mutual respect.[12]

Paul VI not only encouraged a positive view of other religions, which was a radical shift from the policy of the Catholic Church, but also fully supported the radical shift for ecumenical and interreligious dialogue of his predecessor, Pope John XXIII, who had convoked Vatican II. This shift inherently implied appreciating other Christians and the followers of other religions for who they are and what they do as believers.[13]

Nostra aetate, the declaration on interreligious dialogue, used the term "religion" once in its fourth-draft form, as presented for debate on the council floor in September 1964. It appeared in an initial draft of that final paragraph, cited above, rejecting discrimination. Here it is in that earlier form: "It is therefore necessary that all of goodwill, especially Christians, must refrain from any discrimination or harassment of men and women because of their race, color, condition in life, or religion." This same fourth draft also includes these lines:

> In obedience to the love for our brother and sister, we ought to pay great attention to the opinions and teachings which although they differ from our own in many ways, contain nevertheless many rays of that Truth which enlightens everyone in this world. . . . This applies above all to the Muslims who adore the one God, personal and judge, and they stand close to us in a religious sense and they draw near to us with many expressions of human culture set before us.[14]

Once the debate on the draft had concluded, the secretariat realized that it needed to expand the text and say more about the value of religious pluralism. During the ensuing month, October 1964, the expertise of scholars of Islam and of missionaries from Asia and Africa, sharing a firm desire for a more positive approach to other religions, was brought to bear on the text, such that the November 1964 draft, the first to begin with the actual words "*Nostra aetate*" ("In our time"), contained several positive references to other religions. For example, the final text of *Nostra aetate*—promulgated on October 28, 1965—rejected "nothing that is true and holy in these religions" and exhorted Catholics "to recognize, preserve, and foster the good things, spiritual and moral, as well as the socio-cultural values found among the followers of other religions."

Other documents of the council followed *Nostra aetate* by referring to the religions or the followers of other religions in positive ways. Unlike

Nostra aetate, these documents also retained that other use of "religion," in the sense of the true, perhaps now implying the best, religion. For example, this controversial passage, demanded by a minority reluctant to endorse any viable notion of religious pluralism, was inserted into the "Declaration on Religious Liberty," which the drafters were loath to have in the text but was needed to allay the fears of those uncertain of the wisdom of such a positive approach to other religions: "We believe that this one true religion continues to exist in the Catholic and Apostolic Church, to which the Lord Jesus committed the duty of spreading it among all men when he said to the apostles: 'Go therefore and make disciples of all nations, baptizing them in the name of the Father and of the Son and of the Holy Spirit, teaching them to observe all that I have commanded you' (Mt. 18: 19–20)."[15]

Valuing other religions does not require lessening one's enthusiasm for one's own religious beliefs, practices, and way of life. Recall the three principles that Pope Francis outlined at Al-Azhar in April 2017, which summarize the encouragements of *Nostra aetate* fifty-two years after Vatican II: the duty to respect one's own identity and that of others, the courage to accept differences, and sincerity of intentions. The challenge for appreciating religious pluralism today is to apply more widely these three principles reiterated by Pope Francis and to move away from the language of "either this religion is true or that religion is true," from a position of "either/or" to "mine/yours and ours together," if you will.

The documents of Vatican II left many questions open—for example, on the relationship between dialogue and mission and on the salvific status of other religions. Theologians and scholars of religions have produced an abundance of literature on these topics over these last five decades. The Vatican's Pontifical Council for Interreligious Dialogue produced two very helpful documents on mission and dialogue amid religious diversity.[16] As the most visible sign of the commitment of the Catholic Church to dialogue and religious diversity, Pope John Paul II invited other religious leaders to join him in prayers for peace in Assisi, Italy, three times during his pontificate (1986, 1993, and 2002); and in his Christmas Address to the Roman Curia in 1986, he called that first World Day of Prayer for Peace at Assisi "a clear sign of the profound unity of those who seek in religion spiritual and transcendent values that respond to the great questions of the human heart, despite concrete divisions (cf. *Nostra aetate* 1)."[17] In his 1990 encyclical on mission, *Redemptoris missio,* celebrating the twenty-fifth anniversary of the Vatican II "Decree on Missionary Activity," Pope John Paul reassured Catholics that we respect other religions because God works through them to teach all humanity: "In Christ, God calls all peoples to himself, and he wishes to share with them the fullness of his revelation and love. He does not fail to make himself present in many ways, not only to individuals but also to entire peoples through their spiritual riches, of which their religions are the main and essential expression."[18]

Still, a debate on religious pluralism persisted in the Church. At some point between 2002, when Jacques Dupuis, SJ, published his second book on the theology of religious pluralism, and December 28, 2004, when he passed away, he penned "The Theology of Religious Pluralism Revisited: A Provisional Balance Sheet."[19] This last essay, provisional as it was, did not appear in print until 2017, when it was appended to a book of conversations with Dupuis by Gerard O'Connell.[20] In this final reflection, Dupuis carefully defined his position as "religious pluralism in principle," different from his use of "pluralism *de iure*" in his 1997 book that was investigated, a term some had interpreted in an equivocal manner, confusing his approach with the nonattachment some felt was required for all religions to have equal legal standing within a secular state. Dupuis wanted to give positive theological meaning to the existence of many religions, and so he reasoned this way: "The fundamental reason for the affirmation of a religious pluralism in principle is the fact that, before representing the search for God on the part of [humanity], the religions are 'the ways' through which God has sought [humanity] throughout the history of humankind."[21]

O'Connell's book is a lengthy set of reflections by Father Dupuis after his debilitating ordeal of the investigation of his 1997 book *Toward a Christian Theology of Religious Pluralism*, stretching over three years (October 1998–February 2001). Overseeing the Congregation for the Doctrine of the Faith at the time that it undertook the investigation was Joseph Cardinal Ratzinger, who became Pope Benedict XVI in April 2005. The nearly insufferable demands placed on Father Dupuis included necessitating a book-length set of responses from him to the inquiries and personally stirring him to salvage an entire life's work by refashioning the 1997 book under investigation into yet another volume, *Christianity and the Religions: From Confrontation to Dialogue* (2002). When it was all said and done, the congregation could charge him with no more than "notable ambiguities and difficulties on important doctrinal points, which could lead a reader to erroneous or harmful opinions," despite admitting his "attempt to remain within the limits of orthodoxy in his study of questions hitherto largely unexplored." The book was not condemned, nor his ideas, nor any of his previous work.[22]

At Christmastime in 2005, in his first year as Pope Benedict XVI, Joseph Ratzinger delivered a rather tortured, complex address to the Roman Curia, making the case for balancing the principles of continuity and discontinuity while interpreting the documents of Vatican II. At that point, forty years after the close of Vatican II, he recalled how the Church faced difficult challenges implementing the council's new attitude toward other religions, using the analogy of Saint Basil's description after the first Council of Nicaea of "a naval battle in the darkness of the storm." Although it is true that "the situation that the Council [Vatican II] had to face can certainly be compared to events of previous epochs," his reduction of the new approach of Vatican II to a recurrence of the age-old "dialogue between reason and faith, particularly important today, found its bearings on the basis of the Second Vatican Council," is inadequate to account for the 180-degree turn in Christian attitudes toward Jews, the exuberant opening up to the richness of interreligious encounters through dialogue, and the radical shift in missionary policy from conversion to mutual understanding and accompaniment.

To make his case, Pope Benedict acknowledged that modernity, for its valuing of pluralism, required the bishops at Vatican II to do three things:

1. to redefine a relationship between faith and modern, including social, sciences;
2. to give a new definition to the relationship between the Church and the modern state for citizens of various religions and ideologies to have an orderly and tolerant coexistence; and
3. to create a new definition of the relationship between the Christian faith and the world religions and, in particular, between the Church and the faith of Israel.[23]

His phrasing of the issues is seriously problematic, by implying that Christian faith stands opposite "world religions," as though religions, with his exception for Jewish faith, are cultural entities entirely defined as objects of historical-critical methods. Pope John Paul II had carefully stated that God is "present in many ways, not only to individuals but also to entire peoples through their spiritual riches, of which their religions are the main and essential expression." Instead, focused on the effects of religious studies for a long time, Pope Benedict worried about the implied relativism of beliefs as a consequence of leveling the field of study. Equal standing before the law for those in public dialogue and being equal partners in interreligious dialogue raised fears of an ideology of religious pluralism, which vouchsafed dialogue as "an exchange between positions which have fundamentally the same rank and therefore are mutually relative."[24]

Although *Nostra aetate* referred positively to religions, it more precisely addressed relationships between believers as persons and urged dialogue and collaboration to recognize, preserve, and foster spiritual, moral, and sociocultural values; to promote mutual understanding and esteem; and to cooperate for social justice, moral welfare, and peace and freedom for all. Building upon these proposals, one can acknowledge that God is working in wisdom in the lives of all people, not abstractly but concretely, through word and spirit in their daily engagements, through forming their deepest values in their profound decisions. The interplay of the diversity of religious experiences is a celebration of the mercy of God rather than judgment about the status of various religions. *Nostra aetate* urged Christians to pursue this "with prudence and love and in witness to the Christian faith and life."

In the Abu Dhabi text, when Christians read "willed by God in his wisdom," they look at the world from a faith that is shaped by the Bible and the Church. God's wisdom is at work in our lives and in the lives of all. This is what Pope Francis intends by the metaphor of accompaniment when applied to interreligious relationships. As companions on the journey, as Jesus invited disciples to join him on his journeys, each of us, being authentic to our own religious traditions, believes that God is directing us together to what is good. The wisdom of God becomes more and more evident to us along the way of accompaniment in fraternity and living together.

Because of the lingering fear of relativism, the Congregation for the Doctrine of the Faith, after Cardinal Ratzinger had become pope, undertook an investigation of Father Peter Phan's 2004 book, *Being Religious Interreligiously: Asian Perspectives on Interfaith Dialogue.* The congregation sent him a list of criticisms in summer 2005, indirectly through the apostolic nuncio and then through his bishop, Charles Grahmann of Dallas. Father Phan replied in April 2006, first criticizing the injustice of the process, especially the congregation's demand that the book not be reprinted even before he prepared a response, then pointing out certain unrealistic and even preposterous comments by the congregation, yet fully expressing his willingness to compose a lengthy article but with stipulations, including financial remuneration to compose the lengthy article because he would need to take leave of his position at Georgetown University.[25] Father Phan could not stop and devote his full attention to this immoderate request as the Jesuit Father Dupuis was fated to do because their academic and personal circumstances were quite different. Phan's response to the congregation seems to have caused significant embarrassment, for the congregation eventually passed the case to the US Conference of Catholic Bishops and its Committee on Doctrine.

In 2007, the Committee on Doctrine sent its own multipage set of concerns asking for a lengthy article in reply, and Phan replied with the same willingness but with stipulations. In the end, the committee issued a set of required "clarifications" on December 17, 2007, because Phan's book, *Being Religious Interreligiously*, had "pervading ambiguities and equivocations that could easily confuse or mislead the faithful" and statements deemed in need of clarification. Unlike Father Jacques Dupuis, who was seventy-seven years old when the "Notification" concluding his case was issued and thus was unable to return to teaching and research, Father Peter Phan has continued with his work, teaching, writing, publishing, and speaking.[26] Subsequent to Phan's investigation, Pope Francis ushered in a new era for the Catholic Church, reaffirming the Vatican II model of the Church of dialogue.

As with his book that was investigated, Phan draws attention in his work to authentic Asian perspectives on interreligious dialogue, and notably the nature of Asian Christian points of view. In his *Asian Christianities*, published several years after the investigation was closed, he helps us understand the gifts of that perspective under the rubric of "world Christianity." For example, he observed: "In the West, at least since the eighteenth century, the primary experience for theology consists of such cultural shibboleths as secularism, atheism, agnosticism, and relativism, against which Christian thinkers have devised a whole array of philosophical arguments in defense of theism and objective truth." Different from this North Atlantic perspective, which has some influence as well across the globe, he continues, theology in Asia, Africa, and elsewhere arises from the "massive and dehumanizing material poverty and oppression bolstered by economic and political structures." For Christian theologians in Asia, the major issue is how "the destructive legacy of Western colonialism has been enormous, and now, insidious and manifold forms of neocolonialist capitalism" are destroying the environment, reducing more and more people to poverty, and causing large-scale migrations.[27] These are, of course, the same concerns that Pope Francis has promoted in his papacy.

Consequently, promoting liberation, inculturation, and interreligious dialogue is essential for Christian theology to be effective not only in Asia but globally. These three overarching themes invigorate Phan's analysis of the significance of *Nostra aetate* more clearly in the wake of his investigation, especially in "Holy Pagans in Other Holy Religions," chapter 5 in *The Joy of Religious Pluralism* (2017). While aware of the document's role in the "revolution" in Church life and teaching that Vatican II represented, Phan sees its shortcomings more plainly from that Asian perspective. His constructive critique, by reading the text "in reverse"—that is, detecting the vestiges of the superior, universalistic, privileged perspective that brought it into being—he draws out deeper implications for interreligious dialogue that is integral to one's daily experience and thus is integrated into one's theological view.

What Phan is now accomplishing was predicted. On October 15, 1965, after the first round of final voting on *Nostra aetate*, Thomas F. Stransky, CSP, who had helped move the document through Vatican II, wisely commented at a news conference: "What is said in the declaration may seem naive in centuries to come, but at the present it would be difficult for the council to come up with any more than it has."[28] Phan, by following a self-emptying (kenotic) approach learned from Asian interreligious experience, can identify what could not be so easily stated fifty years ago at the council: "It does not seem contrary to the faith to suggest that non-Christian religions can function as 'ways of salvation' to their adherents in the sense that if and when non-Christians are saved, and this possibility has been affirmed by Vatican II, they are saved *through* and *by means of* their religions, not *in spite of* them."[29]

The title of Phan's account of his personal journey toward interreligious coexistence, *The Joy of Religious Pluralism*, was inspired, at least partially, by Pope Francis's remarkable magisterial documents: *The Joy of the Gospel* (2013), *The Joy of Love* (2016), and, we might add to Phan's list, *Rejoice and Be Glad* (2018). He gladly affirms "that under the pontificate of Francis, there has been in the Catholic Church a movement, however imperceptible, from sadness to joy as an appropriate response to religious diversity."[30]

In the apostolic exhortation, *The Joy of the Gospel*, which sets forth the agenda of Pope Francis, he describes "an attitude of openness in truth and in love must characterize the dialogue with the followers of non-Christian religions," and then he cites the wisdom of the bishops of India promoting interreligious friendships with their neighbors as opportunities for "being open to them, sharing their joys and sorrows." Francis then concludes: "In this way we learn to accept others and their different ways of living, thinking and speaking."[31] It is a simple truth that Pope Francis identifies, but one so overlooked by those lacking interreligious experience. Francis cited this passage when he visited Wat Ratchabophit Sathit Maha Simaram Temple in Bangkok on November 21, 2019, where he made a similar testimony, about appreciating "the opportunity to appreciate and esteem one another in spite of our differences." There, in Thailand, he offered an indirect reference to the "Document on Human Fraternity": "Occasions like this remind us how important it is for religions to become more and more beacons of hope, as promoters and guarantors of fraternity."[32]

Phan was particularly struck by how Pope Francis concluded his remarkable encyclical on protecting the Earth as our shared home, *Laudato si'*, with two prayers, one to share with all who believe in God and the other to share with other Christians seeking to live the Gospel with us. He writes: "What is most significant is that in contrast to his predecessor's fear and suspicion of the possibility of religious syncretism, Pope Francis invites those who believe in God the Creator, among whom Jews, Muslims, and Hindus figure predominantly, to pray *together*, and with a prayer of his own composition to boot!" Peter Phan suggests that this invitation from Pope Francis "lays to rest official disapproval of interreligious prayer."[33] I would suggest that with the "Document on Human Fraternity," Pope Francis has equally laid to rest official disapproval of theologies of religious pluralism.

NOTES

1. "Document on Human Fraternity for World Peace and Living Together," www.vatican.va/content/francesco/en/travels/2019/outside/documents/papa-francesco_20190204_documento-fratellanza-umana.html; Higher Committee of Human Fraternity, www.forhumanfraternity.org/document-on-human-fraternity-detail.

2. The Muslim Wise Men Council came into existence in 2014 under the leadership of Sheikh Ahmed al-Tayeb and Sheikh Abdullah bin Bayyah, chairman of the Forum for Promoting Peace in Muslim Societies; see http://wam.ae/en/details/1395267856533.

3. See the pope's interview with reporters returning from Egypt on April 29, 2017: http://w2.vatican.va/content/francesco/en/events/event.dir.html/content/vaticanevents/en/2017/4/29/egitto-volopapale.html.

4. "Address of His Holiness Pope Francis to the Participants in the International Peace Conference, Al-Azhar Conference Centre, Cairo, April 28, 2017," http://w2.vatican.va/content/francesco/en/speeches/2017/april/documents/papa-francesco_20170428_egitto-conferenza-pace.html.

5. Passages from the Qur'an are taken from *The Qur'an: A New Translation by M. A. S. Abdel Haleem* (New York: Oxford University Press, 2004). See also Surah 49:14.

6. Life Site News, February 19, 2019, www.lifesitenews.com/news/cdl.-burke-popes-declaration-saying-god-wills-diversity-of-religions-is-not.

7. Catholic News Agency, "From the Bishops: Manifesto of Faith," www.catholicnewsagency.com/column/manifesto-of-faith-3978; *Catechism of the Catholic Church*, paragraph 254.

8. "Kardinal Kasper kritisiert: 'Glaubensmanifest' von Kardinal Müller," www.katholisch.de/aktuelles/aktuelle-artikel/kardinal-kasper-kritisiert-glaubensmanifest-von-kardinal-muller.

9. "Kardinal Kasper kritisiert."

10. "Dogmatic Constitution of the Catholic Faith," in *Decrees of Ecumenical Councils*, vol. II, ed. Norman P. Tanner, SJ (Washington, DC: Georgetown University Press, 1990), 808, 811.

11. *Interreligious Dialogue: The Official Teaching of the Catholic Church from the Second Vatican Council to John Paul II (1963–2005)*, ed. Francesco Gioia (Boston: Pauline Books and Media, 2006), 157; Xavier Rynne, *The Second Session: The Debates and Decrees of Vatican Council II, September 29 to December 4, 1963* (New York: Farrar, Straus, 1964), 362.

12. "*Ecclesiam suam*, Encyclical of Pope Paul VI on the Church, August 6, 1964," paragraph 108, http://w2.vatican.va/content/paul-vi/en/encyclicals/documents/hf_p-vi_enc_06081964_ecclesiam.html.

13. John W. O'Malley, *What Happened at Vatican II* (Cambridge, MA: Harvard University Press, 2008), 50.

14. This is an English translation by Thomas F. Stransky, CSP, of the original Latin text found in *Acta Synodalia Sacrosancti Oecumenici Concilii Vaticani II* (Vatican City: Typis Polyglottis Vaticanis, 1970–99), III/2, 327–29. All translations of the drafts and final text of *Nostra aetate* are by Thomas Stransky.

15. "Declaration on Religious Liberty," in *Vatican Council II*, vol. I, *The Conciliar and Postconciliar Documents*, ed. Austin Flannery, OP (Northport, NY: Costello, 1975), 799. Peter Phan observes the difference in tone between *Nostra aetate* and other conciliar documents in *The Joy of Religious Pluralism* (Maryknoll, NY: Orbis, 2017), 116ff.

16. *The Attitude of the Church Toward the Followers of Other Religions* (1984) and *Dialogue and Proclamation* (1991), www.pcinterreligious.org/pcid-documents.

17. *Interreligious Dialogue*, 562, p. 399. On the Vatican website, the speech exists only in Italian. Catholic News Service published an English translation: "The Meaning of the Day of Peace in Assisi: Address to the Roman Curia and the Papal Household Staff," *Origins: Catholic News Service Documentary Service* 16, no. 31 (January 15, 1987).

18. *Interreligious Dialogue*, 178, p. 108. The text is online: www.vatican.va/content/john-paul-ii/en/encyclicals/documents/hf_jp-ii_enc_07121990_redemptoris-missio.html.

19. Jacques Dupuis, SJ, *Toward a Christian Theology of Religious Pluralism* (Maryknoll, NY: Orbis, 1997); Jacques Dupuis, SJ, *Christianity and the Religions: From Confrontation to Dialogue* (Maryknoll, NY: Orbis, 2002).

20. Jacques Dupuis, "The Theology of Religious Pluralism Revisited: A Provisional Balance Sheet," in *Do Not Stifle the Spirit: Conversations with Jacques Dupuis*, ed. Gerard O'Connell (Maryknoll, NY: Orbis, 2017), 257–98.

21. Dupuis, "Theology," 294.

22. Congregation for the Doctrine of the Faith, "Notification on the Book *Toward a Christian Theology of Religious Pluralism* . . . by Father Jacques Dupuis, SJ"; although the "Notification" is dated January 24, 2001, the congregation did not issue it until February 26, 2001; see *Origins*, CNS Documentary Service, 30, 38, March 8, 2001, www.vatican.va/roman_curia/congregations/cfaith/documents/rc_con_cfaith_doc_20010124_dupuis_en.html.

23. "Address of His Holiness Benedict XVI to the Roman Curia, Offering Them His Christmas Greetings, December 22, 2005," www.vatican.va/content/benedict-xvi/en/speeches/2005/december/documents/hf_ben_xvi_spe_20051222_roman-curia.html.

24. These words are taken from a 1996 address of then Joseph Cardinal Ratzinger, before becoming Pope Benedict in 2005, to eighty bishops from mission territories, and published as "Relativism: The Central Problem for Faith Today," *Origins* 26, no. 20, October 31, 1996.

25. Peter Phan gives the details of the investigation and new reflections on religious pluralism in *Joy of Religious Pluralism*, 1–19, and an appendix of relevant correspondence and the final notification.

26. The case against Father Jacques Dupuis concluded in September 2001. He died on December 28, 2004.

27. Peter C. Phan, *Asian Christianities: History, Theology, Practice* (Maryknoll, NY: Orbis, 2013), 103.

28. *Council Daybook: Vatican II, Session 4, Sept. 14, 1965 to Dec. 8, 1965*, ed. Floyd Anderson (Washington, DC: National Catholic Welfare Conference, 1966), 140. Father Stransky,

at age thirty, became one of the three original staff of the Secretariat for Promoting Christian Unity in 1960, and remained on the staff of the secretariat, working on its conciliar drafts, throughout Vatican II and for decades afterward as a consultor.

29. Phan, *Joy of Religious Pluralism*, 126.
30. Phan, 165.
31. Apostolic Exhortation *Evangelii gaudium*, 250, www.vatican.va/content/francesco/en /apost_exhortations/documents/papa-francesco_esortazione-ap_20131124_evangelii -gaudium.html#Interreligious_dialogue.
32. Visit to the Supreme Buddhist Patriarch, Wat Ratchabophit Sathit Maha Simaram Temple, Bangkok, November 21, 2019, http://w2.vatican.va/content/francesco/en/speeches /2019/november/documents/papa-francesco_20191121_patriarca-buddisti-thailandia .html.
33. Phan, *Joy of Religious Pluralism*, 167.

CHAPTER 17

Counting the Uncountable:
The Contributions of Peter Phan

Leo D. Lefebure

A familiar tale describes how a number of blind persons feel an elephant from different angles and come up with very different descriptions of what kind of creature this is. I do not know if this Ella Phan was related to Peter Phan, but I do know that the dilemma is the same. Depending on the angle from which we approach Phan Dinh Cho, we find very different creatures. The many different contributions of Peter that have previously been discussed in this volume do not represent the entirety of his oeuvre. We can imagine conflicting voices debating the legacy of Peter Phan.

THE MANY IDENTITIES OF PETER PHAN

Some friends and colleagues of mine involved in the study of Eastern Christianity are not personally involved in the issues discussed in this volume, but they revere the name of Peter Phan as a distinguished scholar of the Russian Orthodox refugee theologian Paul Evdokimov, who fled his homeland after the Russian Revolution. Peter's early work, *Culture and Eschatology: The Iconographical Vision of Paul Evdokimov*, provides a vantage point for viewing the theological concerns of Peter's entire career.[1] Peter was drawn to Evdokimov as a fellow exile who fled the revolution in Russia and lived from then on betwixt-and-between different worlds. In assessing Evdokimov's vision of theology and culture, Peter stressed the importance of the *imago Dei* in all humans and in Jesus Christ, as well as the role of the Holy Spirit, the liturgy, and icons in shaping religious and cultural life, not to mention the importance of Dostoevsky. Because icons are transparent to the infinite, the divine, they make present already here and now the eschatological fulfillment. After summarizing each aspect of Evdokimov's theology, Peter sought to build a bridge between Russian Orthodox and Catholic theologies that had for too many centuries been in conflict. Peter's first contribution was as a pioneer in improving Catholic–Russian Orthodox relations—in a sense, Peter launched his career by taking up one of the most difficult relations first—that with our Chalcedonian Orthodox brothers and sisters. Then he later went on to interreligious relations.

But other voices could object: "No, no, no. You have the wrong person. Peter Phan is an important scholar of his beloved Karl Rahner. Everything he writes is informed by Rahner's sense of Holy Mystery in time and eternity."[2] Peter brought his knowledge of the Russian Orthodox eschatological tradition to his study of the eschatology of Rahner, where he found a sense of Holy Mystery in relation to the unfathomable mystery of the human persons; in a way that complements the Orthodox perspectives, Peter appreciated Rahner's vision that we are each an act of reaching out for more, for a reality greater than we can possibly imagine or grasp. Theology is a process of *reductio in mysterium*, leading all things into Mystery.

But another voice interrupts, "No, no, no, no. You must be mistaken. Peter Phan is the world's leading expert on Alexandre de Rhodes, the noted seventeenth-century missionary to Vietnam who related Catholic faith to Vietnamese culture."[3] As this voice is trying to elaborate, someone else exclaims, "No, no, no, Peter is a scholar of the fathers of the early Church; he edited a volume of patristic writings on grace and the human condition and another on social thought."[4]

Another voice again objects, "No, no, no! Coming from Southeast Asia, Peter shares his culture's concern for our relationship with their deceased loved ones, and so Peter published a commentary on pastoral guidelines for prayers for the dead, plus another book with answers to 101 of your questions about the afterlife."[5] In considering the relation of the eschatological state to this world, Peter proposes a vision of "continuity-in-discontinuity, or more exactly, more-discontinuity-than-continuity."[6] One day I read a headline in *America Magazine* that advertised his lecture series: "Personally Guided Tour of the Afterlife with Peter Phan." (I have repeatedly asked Peter about the details of how he arranges the return trip from the afterlife, but he keeps that as an eschatological secret.)

Another voice intervenes: "Peter is a scholar of Catholicism in Asia who has written on the work of the Federation of Asian Bishops' Conferences and the Asian Synod; he is a trailblazer of Asian American Christian theology."[7]

Peter has taken up the challenge of the FABC to reflect on the many aspects of religious identity in a world of many poor, many cultures, and many religions; he is an active participant in dialogues with Jews, Muslims, Hindus, Buddhists, Daoists, and Confucianists; at the last Parliament of the World's Religions, he invited his friend Rabbi David Gordis to join us in a triadic Christian-Buddhist-Jewish conversation; he and I were in Kyoto in February 2017 for another triadic conversation between Buddhists, Muslims, and Christians.

Peter is always reaching out to others. The New Testament recounts that someone else received the name of Peter (Mt. 16:18) and later came to be known as the *pontifex maximus*, the greatest builder of bridges. I propose to you that our Peter is a *pontifex in pectore*, a builder of bridges in the heart wherever he goes, looking for connections. The reason we build bridges is that what unites us lies deep below the surface, and we need a way to cross over. This is Peter's constant concern, to build bridges in the heart so we may cross over. This is at the heart of what Peter calls *missio inter gentes*.

In light of his life journey, it is not surprising that Peter became a pioneer in the theology of migration, attending to people who leave their homeland, especially those who are pushed out. Dietrich Bonhoeffer taught us that God allows Godself to be pushed out of this world, and Peter shares this perspective and the concern for those who are pushed out of their homes. From this perspective, the climax of Peter's career came with his presidential address to the American Theological Society, in which he reflected on the Holy Mystery: "Deus Migrator *est*." God is a migrant.[8]

Peter has written more books and articles and edited more works than I can count, including books on the Trinity, the Asian Synod, Christianities in Asia, Christianities in migration, and American Christian diversity, and many others. These multiple identities offer too much to take in from any one point of view. Peter has evoked the famous Scholastic distinction that was emphasized by Bernard Lonergan between "*quid sit?*" ("what is it?") and "*an sit?*" ("is it so?"). But to study Peter's countless contributions, I suspect we need a third level of questioning: "*quot sint?*" "How many are there?" When Possidius was concluding his biography of Augustine of Hippo, he pointed out that surely one individual alone would never have time to read all his works! So how could one person possibly have written them all? The same is surely true of Peter, and so we face the question: *Quot sint?* How many Peters are there?

The mystery of Peter's plural identity begins with his birth. Most of us enter the world once and have one birthday, but in Vietnam Peter's father arranged for him to have government documents demonstrating that he was born on two different occasions so that he could enter a program at a younger age than was allowed. Some people talk about being born again, but Peter's father had documents to prove it. This allowed Peter, from a very young age, to be older than he was and wiser than he appeared, so he could enter a program in Vietnam ahead of his time. I do not pretend to understand the mystery of his twofold origin. I am not going to speculate on how his dual birth evokes the mystery of the dual origin of the two natures of Jesus Christ, but surely this dual origin of Peter offers us a mystery to ponder.

Peter always insists that Christology has to be closely related to Pneumatology and the Holy Trinity, so another mystery follows on the first. Peter was not satisfied with one doctorate. We know that Germans think one has to do two doctorates to be taken seriously; but for some reason, Peter felt he had to do three, possibly in competition with Raimon Panikkar. So while remaining one undivided essence, the economic Peter Phan revealed himself in three different academic personae through his doctoral studies on Paul Evdokimov, Karl Rahner, and Alexandre de Rhodes. I will not speculate on how Peter shares in the life of the three Persons of the Holy Trinity, but in this triadic self-manifestation we find yet another mystery worthy of our consideration that leads into his lifelong study of the Holy Trinity.

EXPERIENCE SHAPING THEOLOGY

Peter insists on grounding theology in human experience, and his contribution to theology is shaped by the many distinctive angles of vision because since his youth he has always been moving around.[9] He grew up in Vietnam and studied first in French at a French school, where he learned all about French history, geography, wines, and escargots, but nothing about Vietnamese history or culture. Then he went to an island near Hong Kong, where he studied Western Scholastic philosophy without learning anything about Chinese philosophy and religion. I visited this site with Peter after a conference in Hong Kong in June 2016, and it was wonderful to see Peter revisit the buildings of his youth and reminisce about the various figures of his early life. After further studies in Rome during the years after the Second Vatican Council, he returned to Vietnam.

During this period, it was not at all in Peter's expectations to become the inaugural holder of the Ignacio Ellacuria, SJ, Chair of Social Thought at Georgetown University. But one day his life changed. One Sunday morning in 1975, instead of doing his usual practice of celebrating Mass for women in a prison, he was relaxing over a late, leisurely breakfast, at the very time that the government of South Vietnam was collapsing. One of his sisters raced up and told him quite abruptly that his family members were leaving and they wanted him to join them. He raced off on his motorcycle, saw some beggars, stopped, and to their complete amazement, he hurriedly gave away all his Vietnamese money to one of them.[10] This dramatic scene captures Peter's central lesson to us, and the link between eschatology and migration in his life: when the world that we know is coming to an end, when the old assumptions and expectations no longer apply, when no one knows what is going to happen next, and when there is no security anywhere, the proper response is to be generous and give away all you have to someone else who might be able to use it better. When Peter writes about the virtue of kenosis (self-emptying), this is what it looks like in his lived experience. His generosity with his time, his talents, and his treasure overflows beyond measure. When Peter's parents gave him the personal name "Cho," they were hoping that it would characterize his future life. "Cho" in Vietnamese means "to give." On behalf of all his friends and colleagues, I daresay their hopes have been fulfilled.

After giving away all his money, Peter went home to retrieve a change of clothes, found his family, and after much hassle eventually boarded an airplane with his family without having any idea where they were going. When he left his homeland, he had with him just a change of clothing; he left behind even his licentiate research paper on Paul Tillich—another refugee who fled his homeland. Where do we find God? Deus Migrator est; we find God among those who are pushed out of the world.

Not only was Peter a refugee from the conflicts in his beloved Vietnam; when he first came to the United States, he began his working career as a collector of garbage, working for a man Peter called "Mr. Two-Ten," because he paid his workers the minimum wage, which was $2.10 at that time.[11] Though Peter probably did not realize it at the time, this experience would give Peter what Gustavo Gutiérrez calls the "hermeneutical privilege of the poor," an angle of vision denied to most theologians. Years later, Peter would write about the magisterium of the poor as having a distinctive wisdom to teach both the magisterium of bishops and that of theologians. In making this claim, Peter, more than almost any other academic theologian I know, knew what he was talking about from his own experience; he had actually worked as a collector of garbage. I dare suggest that in the long history of Christian theology, there is no other collector of garbage who has contributed as much to theological scholarship as Peter Phan. When Peter writes about consulting the wisdom of the poor, he, far more than most theologians, knows firsthand what he is writing about. He knows the crises of poor refugees who are cast out of their homes and who earn a living by handling what others throw away; he knows how different these challenges are from those of the rich and the comfortable.

THE ACCIDENTAL THEOLOGIAN

The many twists and turns of his life have given Peter a strong appreciation for the contingency and unpredictability of life, and for its undeserved suffering and blessings. He describes himself as an "accidental theologian."[12] After his unexpected arrival in the United States, one day he went to the University of Dallas, intending to apply for their doctoral program in philosophy. To his great surprise, he was welcomed and announced as their new instructor in theology; so he did a doctorate in theology on Evdokimov. There are some scholars who are like archaeologists who find an unexplored ancient site and spend their lives digging ever deeper into it. Peter could have had this kind of career; but instead, he was restless and chose instead to be more like a satellite orbiting the Earth and turning its gaze from one area to another. He makes repeated contributions through his ability to make connections among different peoples, different religions, and different cultures in ways that repeatedly open up new perspectives.

To facilitate crossing boundaries, Peter has had a lifelong interest in hermeneutics, which takes its name from Hermes, the Greek god of crossing boundaries. In this programmatic work for Latin hermeneutics, *De doctrina Christiana*, Saint Augustine of Hippo reflects on the relation between signs and realities and gives many pointers for interpreting the Bible. Toward the end of his discussion, Augustine tells us, "The preacher's lifestyle carries more weight than his style of oratory. But for us to be listened to with obedient compliance, whatever the grandeur of the speaker's utterances, his manner of life carries more weight."[13] The greatest contribution Peter has given us—the life he has lived—is symbolized for me in that moment of giving away all his money to the beggar in Vietnam.

Peter presents himself as an accidental theologian who is always betwixt and between. What happens by accident? On the morning of my ordination, my brother gave me some verses by San Juan de la Cruz, Saint John of the Cross, which evoke something of this side of Peter's contribution to us:

Por toda la hermosura
Nunca yo me perderé
Sino por un no sé qué
Que se alcanza por ventura.

For all the beauty there may be,
I'll never lose my soul,
only for something I don't know
That one may come on randomly.[14]

Encontremos Pedro por ventura. We meet this accidental theologian acci-
dentally, "por ventura," for a venture, for an adventure, randomly, by chance;
and in this chance, we discern something of the meaning of providence, of
grace. This migrant refugee from his homeland washed up on a shore where
our paths have crossed; he began to build bridges and became a *pontifex in
pectore*, and our lives have been forever enriched. We find ourselves together
with Peter as companions on a journey, a migration into "un no sé qué, que
se alcanza por ventura." In his life, we come into contact with a Mystery we
do not know, that we encounter, as it were, by accident.

Peter is a restless wanderer, never satisfied with what he has accomplished but always heading for another destination, so I would like to invoke
an important word in Hebrew. As Jews celebrate the archetypal migration of
the Exodus, at one point in the middle of the Seder service, they pause for a
moment of reflection and thanksgiving for the marvel of what is happening.
They sing a bright, lively song, "Dayenu!" "It would have been enough for
us!" They list the various works God has performed, after each one exclaiming that if God had done only this for us and nothing else, "Dayenu!": "It
would have been enough for us!" I think it is incumbent on all of us to celebrate Peter's legacy with this word in Hebrew, exclaiming "Dayenu!" Even if
he had offered us only a small portion of his lifelong contributions, "It would
have been enough for us!" Peter, Dayenu!

NOTES

1. Peter C. Phan, *Culture and Eschatology: The Iconographical Vision of Paul Evdokimov* (New
   York: Peter Lang, 1985).
2. Peter C. Phan, *Eternity in Time: A Study of Karl Rahner's Eschatology* (Selinsgrove, PA:
   Susquehanna University Press, 1988).
3. Peter C. Phan, *Mission and Catechesis: Alexandre de Rhodes and Inculturation in
   Seventeenth-Century Vietnam* (Maryknoll, NY: Orbis, 2005).
4. Peter C. Phan, *Grace and the Human Condition*, Message of the Fathers of the Church, vol.
   15 (Wilmington, DE: Michael Glazier, 1988); Peter C. Phan, *Social Thought*, Message of
   the Fathers of the Church, vol. 20 (Wilmington, DE: Michael Glazier, 1984).
5. Peter C. Phan, "Suffrage for the Dead," in *Directory on Popular Piety and the Liturgy: A
   Commentary*, ed. Peter C. Phan (Collegeville, MN: Liturgical Press, 2005), 135–50;

Peter C. Phan, *Responses to 101 Questions on Death and Eternal Life* (New York: Paulist Press, 1997).

6. Peter C. Phan, *Living into Death, Dying into Life: A Christian Theology of Death and Life Eternal* (Hobe Sound, FL: Lectio, 2014), 159.

7. Peter C. Phan, *The Asian Synod: Texts and Commentaries,* compiled and edited by Peter C. Phan (Maryknoll, NY: Orbis, 2002); Peter C. Phan, *Christianity with an Asian Face: Asian American Theology in the Making* (Maryknoll, NY: Orbis, 2003).

8. Peter C. Phan, "Deus Migrator: God the Migrant—Migration of Theology and Theology of Migration, *Theological Studies* 77, no. 4 (2016): 845–68.

9. Peter C. Phan, "Betwixt and Between: Doing Theology with Memory and Imagination," in *Journeys at the Margin: Toward an Autobiographical Theology in American-Asian Perspective,* ed. Peter C. Phan and Jung Young Lee (Collegeville, MN: Liturgical Press, 1999), 113–33.

10. Phan, 121.

11. Phan, 124–25.

12. Phan, 116.

13. Augustine, *Teaching Christianity,* 4.27.59, ed. John E. Rotelle, trans. Edmund Hill (Hyde Park, NY: New City Press, 1996), 237.

14. John of the Cross, *The Collected Works of Saint John of the Cross,* trans. Kieran Kavanaugh and Otilio Rodriguez (Washington, DC: Institute of Carmelite Studies, 1991), 71.

EPILOGUE

Peter C. Phan

This last essay in this volume is appropriately titled "epilogue," in the literal meaning of "words added at the end," to signal to the readers that they can finally close the book and put it down, with a sigh of pleasure (hopefully) or relief. It is certainly not intended to be my detailed response to all the preceding essays. Rather my first word of the "words added at the end" is one of profound and undying gratitude to our beloved friend Gerard Mannion, whose sudden and premature death on September 21, 2019, robbed the Church and the academy of an eloquent and persistent voice for social justice and significant theological scholarship. It was he, with his trademark entrepreneurship, who conceived and organized a two-day international symposium to celebrate my theological legacy. The word "legacy," usually associated with a posthumous status, prompted a friend of mine from Australia to email me inquiring, tongue in cheek, if I had died, expecting perhaps a reply from beyond the grave. My second of the "words added at the end" is also one of deep gratitude to Leo Lefebure, my colleague whom I "stole" from Fordham University for Georgetown University, for unselfishly taking over the editorial work and to all the contributors, who certainly had better things to do than coming from far and wide to the symposium and writing for this volume. Without Leo's generous and capable shepherding and the contributors' essays, this book would not have seen the light of day.

The title of the book, taken from that of the conference, *Theology Without Borders*, is Mannion's felicitous shorthand for my life and work, such as it is, as well as the state of contemporary theology. As a foreign student in Rome and a refugee in the United States, I have spent more than fifty-five years of my life outside my native land, crisscrossing all kinds of geographical, national, linguistic, cultural, and religious borders and boundaries; as a result, my writings have transgressed the traditional disciplinary divisions of theology. First of all, like my own theological efforts, this book is properly *theology*. To use Saint Anselm's celebrated expression, it is *fides quaerens intellectum*, an intellectual activity, rooted in the Christian faith and its ecclesial community, seeking to understand systematically and critically the Christian beliefs by "standing under" theology's object, or more precisely, *subject*—namely, God. It does not intend to craft universally and permanently valid answers to questions that may arise about the Christian faith in our day.

This theology is also *without borders*, understood both literally and metaphorically. This self-conscious way of doing theology is of recent vintage, one that is made possible and urgent by borderless globalization, migration, and social media. "Without borders" implicitly and paradoxically acknowledges the existence of borders, chief among which are economic, political, social, sexual and gender, cultural, and religious ones. These borders are, in my view, artificial, mostly man-made ("man" referring specifically to males, advisedly), and must be crossed theologically, always and everywhere, so that theology today must effectively be "without borders."

Parts I through III of this book deal with a few of the borders that I have tried to cross. The first border is conveyed by the expression "world Christianity." Though not a new coinage, world Christianity signals a new approach in contemporary theology, which—according to Dale Irvin, who has taught me everything I know about this new reality—is formed by the confluence of three disciplines, namely, Christian missions, ecumenical unity, and interreligious dialogue, to which I would add church history. The borders between believers and unbelievers, between the only true Church and the false churches, between Catholic and non-Catholic Christians, and between the true religion and paganism have become so porous that a clear-cut distinction between them has become well-nigh impossible. As a result, an adequate account of one side of the above-mentioned binaries cannot be given unless the other side is also taken into due consideration, and both sides must be brought into mutual correction and enrichment.

World Christianity has invalidated, among other things, the distinction, much beloved to both secular and ecclesiastical colonialists, between the metropolis/center and the periphery/margin, with the former taking on the mantle of *mission civilisatrice* for the benefit of the latter. Today, Christianity has become polycentric, with no one center—for instance, Rome, Geneva, or Constantinople—controlling and dominating the others. More precisely, both the center and the periphery exist *within* each church, so an ecclesiology that pretends to be universal must also be particularist at the same time. This ecclesial reality has been noted, as Anh Tran points out, especially by the Federation of Asian Bishops' Conferences, perhaps because the Asian

Churches, which have long been relegated to the margins because of their numerical minority, have moved to the center thanks to their new way of being Church.

A consequence of this new ecclesial reality for theological methodology is, as Jonathan Tan notes, the necessity of both memory and imagination in theological thinking. Memory is not nostalgia for the long-gone good old days, and imagination is not hankering after the phantasmagoric things of the future. Employed together, they help us imagine a new form of Christianity, evoked by the expression "world Christianity," a reality already present here but still to come, or as German biblical scholars used to say of the Kingdom of God, *Jetzt aber noch nicht* (now but not yet).

One ubiquitous phenomenon that is truly global is migration, so much so that our time has been dubbed "the Age of Migration." This massive "people-on-the-move" phenomenon, especially the forced migration of refugees, calls for a new ethics of human dignity and human rights. Furthermore, rich nations in the West must be reminded that their hospitality toward refugees and migrants is not just an obligatory act of kindness to strangers but also a payment of the debt they owe these people, the majority of whom come from countries the West has despoiled during their past colonialist enterprise and their current neoliberal economic globalization. Gemma Cruz, herself a Filipina migrant in many countries, discusses the power of resilience sustaining migrants before, during, and after they leave their countries of origin and settle in the receiving countries. This resilience, together with hope, are nourished by the Eucharist they celebrate anywhere, anytime, anyhow in their lives as migrants.

Another border to be crossed in world Christianity is that between women and men. Whereas in Western societies, women have achieved a measure of equality with men in most areas of life, in the other parts of world Christianity, especially in cultures that still regard the male/father as superior to the female/mother, women and girls are often the victims of domestic violence. Cristina Gomez, another Filipina migrant in Australia, opens our eyes to its prevalence and its various forms, especially among migrants. She points to the biblical and theological concepts and language that have been used to justify violence against women and girls and urges the Church to work for the affirmation and realization of "women's rights."

Global migration has also challenged, if not erased, the not-so-old concepts of national borders, nation-state, national identity, and nationality, if these are taken as absolutes. I must confess that migration is my current (last?) theological research topic, as I attempt to reconceptualize the *loci theologici* of the Christian faith from the perspective of migration, arguing that the Christian God is the Deus Migrator—the Father being the Primordial Migrant, the Son the Paradigmatic Migrant, and the Holy Spirit the Power of Migration—and that without migration the Church as it is now would not have existed at all.

Part II introduces one of the most challenging borders to be crossed over today, one that has occasioned vigorous theological debates and caused much anxiety in the hierarchical magisterium. This border, known as religious pluralism, lies between the claim of the uniqueness and universality of Christ and the Church on one hand and the persistent reality of other religions on the other hand, which concretely and historically have served as ways of salvation for their adherents on the other. Of course, this border is by no means new. It has existed, as the historian John O'Malley reminds us with his customary scholarly depth, since the Renaissance, and persisted even at Vatican II. But no doubt this border has become an almost insurmountable wall, especially in Christology, marriage, and ecclesiology.

William Loewe draws attention to doctrinal aporias in my proposal for an interreligious Christology. Of course, there is no place here for a lengthy and detailed response to Loewe's critical questions, but I urge readers to pay close attention to them, especially if they themselves want to develop a Christology along the lines I have suggested. Religious pluralism also poses difficult challenges for the Christian practice of interreligious marriage, which has become increasingly common. Interreligious marriage is, as Chester Gillis has amply shown, the laboratory and stress test of interreligious dialogue and can promote a way of being religious interreligiously.

One of the difficult challenges posed by religious pluralism to theology is how to understand the Church as a bordered organization. We are challenged to rethink what the Church without borders is and does, as Brian Flanagan persuasively argues. Nothing less than a new ecclesiology is called for, the one that Mannion was urging in his *Ecclesiology and Postmodernity: Questions for the Church in Our Time*. One place where religious pluralism is both a centuries-old historical fact and a threat to the state is China. Stephanie Wong discusses interreligious dialogue in China and explains how the role of the Catholic Church in China can be viewed in the three frameworks of religion in China: Kenneth Dean's *sheng/ling* polarity, Yang Fengang's religious market, and Mou Zhongjian's religious ecology.

Part III deals with the third and final border, that between life and death, between time and eternity, between this world and the next. Truth be told, this is the only border that ultimately matters, and if a pun may be permitted, it is a life-and-death matter. It is the border that all humans cross over every day, not only at the end of one's life but in all life-transforming decisions. Eschatology has been my lifelong theological concern. Alan Mitchell, who has written a definitive commentary on the Letter to the Hebrews, throws new light on the theme of migration by linking it with eschatology in his reflections on this letter. Brian Doyle focuses on the intermediate state, on which I have offered, along with Karl Rahner and Gisbert Greschake, a somewhat controversial hypothesis of immediate resurrection after death, which Joseph Ratzinger / Pope Benedict XVI has vigorously rejected. Finally, Keith Ward, Regius Professor of Divinity Emeritus at the University of Oxford, an extremely prolific philosopher and theologian, and the *Docktorvater* of our friend Gerard Mannion, honors me with reflections on what he calls my "Christian expansivism."

The last part of this book discusses my theological "legacy." Happily, all the essays are written by my friends, so readers will not see too many well-deserved negative assessments. Debora Tonelli, an Italian Old Testament and political science scholar, places my theology within the trajectory of the Second Vatican Council. Charles Curran, a world-renowned moral theologian, examines the way I responded to the investigation by the Congregation for the Doctrine of the Faith, himself having been an object of a much more severe inquisition by the same congregation several years earlier. John Borelli, whom I call "younger brother" due to his birth a little more than a month after mine, though in the same blessed and auspicious Year of the Dog (1946), and who knows everything knowable of Vatican II's teaching on interreligious dialogue, describes what a religious pluralist can honestly do in the aftermath of Vatican II and with the theological window that Pope Francis has opened for theologians. Last but not least, Leo Lefebure uses the well-known Indian story of the elephant and the blind men's description of it to illustrate my personal and theological multisidedness and captures well the fortuitous and adventitious character of my theological career.

Several years ago, I had the opportunity to reflect in print, rather prematurely, on my theological career and described myself as "an accidental theologian," to which Lefebure refers and poetically explains. By "accidental," I mean that theology is something I stumbled upon, not a vocation that most, especially laypeople, pursue, often without great financial remuneration. If I had not migrated to the United States in 1975 and remained in Vietnam, I would never have thought of becoming a "theologian." A lack of scholarly tools and the urgent life-and-death matters in my native country in the aftermath of the Communist North's takeover of South Vietnam would not afford the luxury of *otium* that is required to do theology in an academic setting. In retrospect, however, I am profoundly thankful to Divine Providence for the opportunity to read, think, teach, and write on matters divine, and now to receive this *laudatio* and *gratulatio* from my colleagues and friends. I am happy that in my case, "legacy" does not imply having crossed the border between this life and the beyond, contrary to my Australian friend's fear, and I hope to have some time left to make myself worthy of the honor of this festschrift.

Curriculum Vitae of Peter C. Phan

Peter Cho Phan
The Ignacio Ellacuría, SJ, Chair of Catholic Social Thought
Department of Theology and Religious Studies
Georgetown University

EDUCATION

Bachelor of Philosophy, Don Bosco College, Hong Kong, 1965.
Bachelor of Arts, University of London, 1968, majoring in French, Latin, and History of Philosophy.
Bachelor of Sacred Theology, Salesian Pontifical University, Rome, 1971.
Licentiate of Sacred Theology, Salesian Pontifical University, Rome, 1972.
Doctor of Sacred Theology, Salesian Pontifical University, Rome, 1978.
Doctor of Philosophy, University of London, 1986.
Doctor of Divinity, University of London, 2000.

ACADEMIC AND PROFESSIONAL APPOINTMENTS

Academic Appointments

1965–68: Instructor at Don Bosco College, Hong Kong.
1972–75: Assistant Professor of Philosophy and Theology at Salesian College, Dalat, Vietnam.
1975–76: Instructor and Counselor at Richardson High School, Richardson, Texas.
1975–77: Instructor in Theology at the University of Dallas, Irving, Texas.
1977–79: Assistant Professor of Theology at the University of Dallas, Irving, Texas.
1980–85: Chairman of the Department of Theology, University of Dallas, Irving, Texas.
1980–85: Director of the PhD Program in Theology, University of Dallas, Irving, Texas.
1980–86: Associate Professor of Theology, University of Dallas, Irving, Texas.
1983–88: Adjunct Professor, Anglican School of Theology.
1987–88: Professor of Theology, University of Dallas, Irving, Texas.
1988–92: Associate Professor of Theology, Catholic University of America.

1992–: Ordinary Professor of Systematic Theology, Catholic University of America.

1992–1995: Chair, Department of Theology, Catholic University of America.

1997–2003: Warren-Blanding Professor of Religion and Culture, Department of Religion and Religious Education, Catholic University.

2003–: The Ignacio Ellacuría, SJ, Chair of Catholic Social Thought, Department of Theology and Religious Studies, Georgetown University.

2005: Founding Director of the PhD program in Theology and Religious Studies, Georgetown University.

2017: William Scheide Distinguished Fellow, Center of Theological Inquiry, Princeton.

Professional Appointments

1980–85: Vice President, Council of Southwestern Theological Schools.

1984–88: Member of the Board of Trustees for the School of Theology for the Laity.

1990–95: Member, Editorial Board, Catholic University of America Press.

1994–96: Member, Board of Directors, Catholic Theological Society of America.

1994–96: Member, Council on Theological Scholarship and Research, Association of Theological Schools.

2017: William Scheide Distinguished Fellow, Center of Theological Inquiry, Princeton.

HONORS

Summa cum laude for the Bachelor of Arts degree, University of London.

Summa cum laude for the licentiate thesis, "Jesus the Christ the New Being: A Study of Paul Tillich's Christology."

Summa cum laude for the degree of Doctor of Sacred Theology.

King Fellow (award for distinguished teaching and scholarship among senior professors), University of Dallas, 1987.

Best Book Award from College Theology Society for the book *Eternity in Time*, 1989.

Best Article Award from College Theology Society for the article "Experience and Theology: An Asian Liberation Perspective," 1994.

Best Article Award from College Theology Society for the article "Jesus the Christ with an Asian Face," 1997.

First Place for *Mission and Catechesis* given by Catholic Press Association, 1999.

Elected to American Theological Society, 1997.

Elected to the Editorial Board of *Theoforum*, 1996.

Elected to the Editorial Board of Studies in the History of Christian Mission, University of Cambridge, 1997.

Elected President of Catholic Theological Society of America, 1999.

Elected to the Scientific Committee of *Science et Esprit*, 2000.

Jacobsen Prize for Essay, from International Society for Universal Dialogue, 2000.

Nominated by Fulbright Scholar Program for Fulbright Distinguished Chair in the Humanities, at the University of Vienna, 2001–2.

Doctor of Theology, honoris causa, Catholic Theological Union, 2001.

Editorial Board of *Daán: A Journal of Applied Theology*, 2003.

Editorial Board of *Journal of Catholic Social Thought*, 2003.

Editorial Board of *Asian Journal of Philosophy*, 2003.
Editorial Board of *Asian Christian Review*, 2006.
Editorial Board, *Offerings: A Journal of Christian Spirituality and Practical Theology*.
Editor (with Dale Irvin) of Pennsylvania State University Press World Christianity Monograph Series.
Editorial Board, *Journal of World Christianity*, Pennsylvania State University Press.
Honorable Mention for *The Asian Synod* given by Catholic Press Association, 2003.
Honorable Mention for *Directory on Popular Piety and the Liturgy* given by Catholic Press Association, 2006.
Doctor of Humane Letters, honoris causa, Elms College, 2007.
Doctor of Humane Letters, honoris causa, Virginia Theological Seminary, 2017.
Jerome Award, Catholic Library Association, 2009.
John Courtney Murray Award, Catholic Theological Society of America, 2010.
Ethics Award, Marymount University, 2014.
Elected President of American Theological Society, 2015.
First Place for *The Joy of Religious Pluralism* given by Catholic Press Association, 2018.
First Prize for *The Joy of Religious Pluralism* given by Association of Catholic Publishers, 2018.
Doctor of Humane Letters, honoris causa, Aquinas Institute of Theology, 2019.

PUBLICATIONS

Books Written

1. *Social Thought.* Wilmington, DE: Michael Glazier, 1984.
2. *Culture and Eschatology: The Iconographical Vision of Paul Evdokimov.* New York: Peter Lang, 1985.
3. *Grace and the Human Condition.* Wilmington, DE: Michael Glazier, 1988.
4. *Eternity in Time: A Study of Karl Rahner's Eschatology.* Selinsgrove, PA: Susquehanna University Press, 1988.
5. *Responses to 101 Questions on Death and Eternal Life.* New York: Paulist Press, 1997. *Śmierć i życie wieczne: Odpowiedzi na 101 pytań.* Warsaw: Wydawnictwo Księży Marianów, 1999 (Polish translation). *E dopo?. . . 101 domande sulla morte e la vita dopo la vita.* Milan: Edizioni San Paolo, 2001 (Italian translation). *Cuoc Song Vinh Hang.* Orange, CA: Vietnam University Press, 1999 (Vietnamese translation). Chinese translation (2002). *Kematioan & Kehidupan Kekal.* Yogyakarta: Penerbit Kanisius, 2005 (Indonesian translation).
6. *Mission and Catechesis: Alexandre de Rhodes and Inculturation in Seventeenth-Century Vietnam.* Maryknoll, NY: Orbis, 1998.
7. *The Mission of God: Its Challenges and Demands in Today's World.* Quezon City: East Asian Pastoral Institute, 2002. *Memperjuangkan: Misi Allah Di Tengah Dunia Dewasa Ini* (Indonesian translation).
8. *In Our Own Tongues: Perspectives from Asia on Mission and Inculturation.* Maryknoll, NY: Orbis, 2003.
9. *Christianity with an Asian Face: Asian American Theology in the Making.* Maryknoll, NY: Orbis, 2003.
10. *Being Religious Interreligiously: Asian Perspectives on Interfaith Dialogue in Postmodernity.* Maryknoll, NY: Orbis, 2004.

11. *Vietnamese-American Catholics.* New York: Paulist Press, 2005.
12. *Living into Death, Dying into Life: Death and the Afterlife.* Hobe Sound, FL: Lectio, 2014.
13. *The Joy of Religious Pluralism: A Personal Journey.* Maryknoll, NY: Orbis, 2017.
14. *La Chiesa e il pluralismo religioso.* Rimini, Italy, 2017.
15. *Asian Christianities: History, Theology, Practice.* Maryknoll, NY: Orbis, 2018.
16. *Asian Christian Theologies.* Hoboken, NJ: Wiley-Blackwell, forthcoming, 2022.
17. *Migration and Christian Theology.* New York: Oxford University Press, forthcoming, 2022.

Books Edited

18. *Christianity and the Wider Ecumenism.* New York: Paragon House, 1990.
19. *Church and Theology: Essays in Memory of Carl Peter.* Washington, DC: Catholic University of America Press, 1994.
20. *Ethnicity, Nationality and Religious Experience.* Lanham, MD: University Press of America, 1994.
21. *Journeys at the Margin: Toward an Autobiographical Theology in Asian-American Perspective.* Collegeville, MN: Liturgical Press, 1999.
22. *The Gift of the Church: A Textbook on Ecclesiology in Honor of Patrick Granfield.* Collegeville, MN: Liturgical Press, 2000.
23. *The Asian Synod: Texts and Commentaries.* Maryknoll, NY: Orbis, 2002.
24. *The Future of the Asian Churches: The Asian Synod & Ecclesia in Asia,* with James Kroeger. Manila: Claretian Press, 2002.
25. *Many Faces, One Church: Cultural Diversity and the American Catholic Experience.* Lanham, MD: Rowman & Littlefield, 2005.
26. *Popular Piety and the Liturgy: A Commentary.* Collegeville, MN: Liturgical Press, 2005.
27. *The Cambridge Companion to the Trinity.* Cambridge: Cambridge University Press, 2011.
28. *Christianities in Asia.* Oxford: Blackwell, 2011.
29. *Contemporary Issues of Migration and Theology,* with Elaine Padilla. New York: Palgrave Macmillan. 2013.
30. *Theologies of Migration in the Abrahamic Religions,* with Elaine Padilla. New York: Palgrave Macmillan, 2014.
31. *Learning from All the Faithful: A Contemporary Theology of the Sensus Fidei,* with Bradford Hinze. Eugene, OR: Pickwick, 2016.
32. *Christianities in Migration,* with Elaine Padilla. New York: Palgrave Macmillan, 2016.
33. *Christian Mission, Contextual Theology, Prophetic Dialogue,* with Dale Irvin. Maryknoll, NY: Orbis, 2017.
34. *Raimon Panikkar: A Companion to His Life and Thought,* with Young chan Ro. Cambridge: James Clarke, 2018.
35. *Christian Theology in the Age of Migration: Implications for World Christianity.* Lanham, MD: Lexington Books, 2020.
36. *Worship and Church: An Ecclesial Liturgy,* with Sallie Latkovich. Mahwah, NJ: Paulist Press, 2019.

Journal Volumes Edited

1. *Religion in China: Past and Present.* New York: International Religious Foundation (IRF), 1990.

2. *The Trinitarian Basis of Christian Unity.* New York: IRF, 1990.
3. *God and Evolution.* New York: IRF, 1991.
4. *God and God-Equivalents.* New York: IRF, 1991.
5. *The Future of God.* New York: IRF, 1991.
6. *Hindu–Sikh Dialogue.* New York: IRF, 1991.
7. *Religious Pilgrimages.* New York: IRF, 1991.
8. *God in Cultures and Cultural Gods.* New York: IRF, 1992.
9. *Arguments for God's Existence.* New York: IRF, 1992.
10. *The One and the Many.* New York: IRF, 1992.
11. *Religious Rituals.* New York: IRF, 1992.
12. *Religions and Peacemaking.* New York: IRF, 1993.
13. *Interreligious Dialogue.* New York: IRF, 1993.
14. *Peace and the Ultimate.* New York: IRF, 1994.
15. *Evil and Religions.* New York: IRF, 1995.
16. *Inculturation: Journal of Vietnamese Philosophy & Religion* (*JVPR*), vol. I, no. 1, 2001.
17. *Veneration of Ancestors, JVPR,* vol. I, no. 2, 2001.
18. *Filial Piety, JVPR,* vol. II, no. 3, 2001.
19. *The Laity in the Church, JVPR,* vol. II, no. 4, 2002.
20. *Popular Religion, JVPR,* vol. III, no. 5, 2003.
21. *Gender and Sexuality in Contemporary Christianity, JVPR,* vol. III, no. 6, 2003.
22. *Ancestor Veneration in Vietnam, JVPR,* vol. IV, no. 7, 2004.
23. *Women in the Church, JVPR,* vol. IV, no. 8, 2004.
24. *Jesus and the Buddha, JVPR,* vol. V, no. 9, 2005.
25. *The Eucharist: Mystery of Communion and Solidarity, JVPR,* vol. V, no. 10, 2005.
26. *Christian Social Spirituality, JVPR,* vol. VI, no. 11, 2006.
27. *Asian-American Catholicism, VJPR,* vol. VI, no. 12, 2006.
28. *Intercultural and Interreligious Dialogue, VJPR,* vol. VII, no. 13, 2007.
29. *Church and Social Mission, VJPR,* vol. VII, no. 14, 2007.
30. *Journal of Ecumenical Studies,* with Jonathan Ray, vol. 48, no. 3, 2013.

Chapters in Books

1. "The Doctrine of Reparation in *Divine Principle* and Anselm's *Cur Deus Homo.*" In *Restoring the Kingdom,* ed. Deane William Ferm. New York: Paragon House, 1984, 153–63.
2. "Are There Other 'Saviors' for Other Peoples? A Discussion of the Problem of the Universal Significance and Uniqueness of Jesus the Christ." In *Christianity and the Wider Ecumenism,* ed. Peter C. Phan. New York: Paragon House, 1990, 163–80.
3. "The Dipolar God and Latin American Liberation Theology." In *Charles Hartshorne's Concept of God,* ed. Santiago Sia. Amsterdam: Kluwer Academic, 1990, 23–39.
4. "Might or Mystery: The Fundamentalist Concept of God." In *The Struggle over the Past: Fundamentalism in the Modern World,* ed. William M. Shea. Lanham, MD: University Press of America, 1993, 81–102.
5. "Woman and the Last Things: A Feminist Eschatology." In *In the Embrace of God: Feminist Approaches to Theological Anthropology,* ed. Ann O'Hara Graff. Maryknoll, NY: Orbis, 1995, 206–28.
6. "Karl Rahner in Dialogue with Judaism and Islam." In *Religions of the Book,* ed. Gerard Sloyan. Lanham, MD: University Press of America, 1996, 129–50.

7. "What Is Old and What Is New in the Catechism?" In *Introducing the Catechism of the Catholic Church: Traditional Themes and Contemporary Issues*, ed. Berard Marthaler. New York: Paulist Press, 1996, 56–71.

8. "Contemporary Theology and Inculturation in the United States." In *The Multicultural Church: A New Landscape in US Church*. New York: Paulist Press, 1996, 109–30, 176–92.

9. "Preaching Jews and Judaism in the Light of the New Catechism." In *Removing Anti-Judaism from the Pulpit*, ed. Howard Clark Kee and Irvin J. Borovski. New York: Continuum, 1996, 75–92.

10. "Asian Identity, Theology, and Theological Education." In *L'Universalité catholique face à la diversité humaine*, ed. Lucien Vachon. Montréal: Médiapaul, 1998, 291–303, 328–30.

11. "The Future of the Church in Vietnam: Reflections on the Responses to the *Lineamenta*" (in Vietnamese). In *Thuong Hoi Dong Giam Muc A Chau*. Strasbourg: Centre Nguyen Truong To, 1998, 61–72.

12. "The Holocaust: Reflections from the Perspectives of Asian Liberation Theology." In *Humanity at the Limit: The Impact of the Holocaust Experience on Jews and Christians*, ed. Michael Signer. Bloomington: Indiana University Press, 2000, 112–37.

13. "An Asian-American Theology: Believing and Thinking at the Boundaries." In *Journeys at the Margin*, ed. Peter C. Phan and Jung Young Lee. Collegeville, MN: Liturgical Press, 1999, xi–xxvii.

14. "Betwixt and Between: Doing Theology with Memory and Imagination." In *Journeys at the Margin*, ed. Peter C. Phan and Jung Young Lee. Collegeville, MN: Liturgical Press, 1999, 113–33.

15. "A North American Ecclesiology: The Achievement of Patrick Granfield." In *The Gift of the Church*, ed. Peter C. Phan. Collegeville, MN: Liturgical Press, 2000, 469–503.

16. "Jesus with a Chinese Face: C. S. Song's Jesus-Oriented Christology." In *The Chinese Face of Jesus Christ*, ed. Roman Malek. Sankt Augustin, Germany: Monumenta Serica, 2000.

17. "Alexandre de Rhodes' Mission in Vietnam: Evangelization and Inculturation." In *Theology and Lived Christianity*, ed. David M. Hammond. Mystic, CT: Twenty-Third, 2000, 99–118.

18. "The Liturgy of Life as the 'Summit and Source' of the Eucharistic Liturgy: Church Worship as Symbolization of the Liturgy of Life?" In *Incongruities: Who We Are and How We Pray*, ed. Timothy Fitzgerald and David A. Lysik. Chicago: Liturgy Training Publications, 2000, 5–33.

19. "The Social Sciences and Ecclesiology: The Use of Cybernetics in Patrick Granfield's Theology of the Church." In *Theology and the Social Sciences*, ed. Michael Barnes. Maryknoll, NY: Orbis, 2001, 59–87.

20. "A Common Journey, Different Paths, The Same Destination: Methods in Liberation Theologies." In *A Dream Unfinished*, ed. Eleazar Fernandez and Fernando Segovia. Maryknoll, NY: Orbis, 2001, 129–51.

21. "The Dragon and the Eagle: Toward a Vietnamese-American Theology." In *Realizing the America of Our Hearts: Theological Voices of Asian Americans*, ed. Eleazar Fernandez and Fumitaka Matsuoka. Saint Louis: Chalice Press, 2003, 158-79.

22. "God in the World: A Trinitarian Triptych." In *New Catholic Encyclopedia Supplement: Jubilee Volume. The Wojtyla Years*, ed. Polly Vader. Detroit: Gale Group, 2000, 33–42.

23. "Religion and Culture: Their Place as Academic Disciplines in the University." In *The Future of Religion in the 21st Century*, ed. Peter T.M. Ng. Hong Kong: Chinese University of Hong Kong, 2001, 321–53.

24. "The Future of Catholic Christianity in Asia: Challenges and Opportunities in the 21st Century." In *The Future of Religion in the 21st Century*, ed. Peter T.M. Ng. Hong Kong: Chinese University of Hong Kong, 2001, 291–320.

25. "Inculturation of the Christian Faith in Asia through Philosophy: A Dialogue with John Paul II's *Fides et Ratio*." In *Dialogue between Christian Philosophy and Chinese Culture*, ed. Paschal Ting, Marian Gao, and Bernard Li. Washington, DC: Council for Research in Values and Philosophy, 2002, 119–52.

26. "The Experience of Migration in the United States as Source of Intercultural Theology." In *Migration, Religious Experience, and Globalization*, ed. Gioacchino Campese and Pietro Ciallella. New York: Center for Migration Studies, 2003, 143–69.

27. "Liturgical Inculturation: Unity in Diversity in the Postmodern Age." In *Liturgy in a Postmodern World*, ed. Keith Pecklers. New York: Continuum, 2003, 55–86.

28. "Popular Religion and Liturgical Inculturation: Perspectives and Challenges from Asia." In *Proceedings of the North American Academy of Liturgy*. Reston, VA: North American Academy of Liturgy, 2002, 23–58.

29. "Reception of Vatican II in Asia: Historical and Theological Analysis." In *Transkontinentale Eziehungen in der Geschichte des Aussereuropäischen Christentums*, vol. 6, ed. Klaus Koschorke. Eiesbaden: Harrassowitz Verlag, 2003, 243–58.

30. "Jacques Dupuis and Asian Theologies of Religious Pluralism." In *In Many and Diverse Ways: In Honor of Jacques Dupuis*, ed. Daniel Kendal and Gerard O'Collins. Maryknoll, NY: Orbis, 2003, 72–85.

31. "Theology on the Other Side of the Borders: Responding to the Signs of the Times." *Proceedings of the Fifty-Seventh Annual Convention*, Catholic Theological Society of America, vol. 57, ed. Richard Sparks, 2003, 87–120.

32. "A New Way of Being Church: Perspectives from Asia." In *Governance, Accountability, and the Future of the Catholic Church*, ed. Francis Oakley and Bruce Russett. New York: Continuum, 2004, 178–90.

33. "Christianity in Indochina, 1815–1915." In *The Cambridge History of Christianity, Volume 8: World Christianities, c. 1815–1914*, ed. Sheridan Gilley and Brian Stanley. Cambridge: Cambridge University Press, 2005, 513–27.

34. "The New Faces of the American Catholic Church." In *Many Faces, One Church: Cultural Diversity and the American Catholic Experience*, ed. Peter C. Phan and Diana Hayes. Lanham, MD: Rowman & Littlefield, 2005, 1–11.

35. "Presence and Prominence in the Lord's House: Asians and Pacific People in the American Catholic Church." In *Many Faces, One Church*, ed. Peter C. Phan and Diana Hayes. Lanham, MD: Rowman & Littlefield, 2005, 99–116.

36. "The Church as Immigrant." In *The Many Marks of the Church*, ed. William Madges and Michael J. Daley. New London: Twenty-Third, 2006, 136–40.

37. "Eschatology." In *The Cambridge Companion to Karl Rahner*, ed. Declan Marmion and Mary Hines. Cambridge: Cambridge University Press, 2005, 174–92.

38. "Roman Catholic Theology." In *The Oxford Handbook of Eschatology*, ed. Jerry Walls. Oxford: Oxford University Press, 2007, 215–32.

39. "Jesus as the Universal Savior in the Light of God's Covenant with the Jewish People: A Roman Catholic Perspective." In *Seeing Judaism Anew: Christianity's Sacred Obligation*, ed. Mary Boys. Lanham, MD: Rowman & Littlefield, 2005, 127–37.

40. "Suffrage for the Dead." In *Directory on Popular Piety: Principles and Guidelines*, ed. Peter C. Phan. Collegeville, MN: Liturgical Press, 2005, 135–50.

41. "Religious Plurality in East Asia before 1800: The Encounter between Christianity and Asian Religions." In *Christianity and Religious Pluralism: Historical and Global Perspectives*, ed. Wilbert R. Shenk and Richard J. Plantinga. Eugene, OR: Cascade Books, 2016, 118–55.

42. "La ricerca spirituale cristiana in Asia." In *Teologia in Asia*, ed. Michael Amaladoss and Rosino Gibellini. Brescia: Queriniana, 2006, 271–86.

43. "Migration in the Patristic Era: History and Theology." In *A Promised Land, A Perilous Journey*, ed. Daniel Groody. Notre Dame, IN: University of Notre Dame Press, 2008, 35–61.

44. "A New Way of Being Church in Asia: Lessons for the American Catholic Church." In *Inculturation and the Church in North America*, ed. Frank Kennedy. New York: Crossroad, 2006, 145–62, 234–36.

45. "Christian Social Spirituality: A Global Perspective." In *Catholic Social Justice: Theological and Practical Exploration*, ed. Philomena Cullen, Bernard Hoose, and Gerard Mannion. London: T&T Clark, 2007, 18–40.

46. "Reception of Vatican II in Asia." In *The Second Vatican Council and the Church in Asia*, ed. James H. Kroeger. Hong Kong: Federation of Asian Bishops' Conferences, 2006, 107–127.

47. "'Reception' or 'Subversion' of Vatican II by the Asian Churches? A New Way of Being Church in Asia." In *Vatican II: Forty Years Later*, ed. William Madges. Maryknoll, NY: Orbis, 2006, 26–54.

48. "Asia." In *The Blackwell Companion to Catholicism*, ed. Jim Buckley, Fritz Bauerschmidt, and Trent Pomplun. Oxford: Blackwell, 2006, 205–20.

49. "Religious Identity and Belonging amidst Diversity and Pluralism: Challenges and Opportunities for Church and Theology." In *Passing on the Faith: Transforming Traditions for the Next Generation of Jews, Christians, and Muslims*, ed. James Heft. New York: Fordham University Press, 2006, 162–84.

50. "An Asian Christian? Or a Christian Asian? Or an Asian-Christian? A Roman Catholic Experiment in Christian Identity." In *Asian and Oceanic Christianities in Conversation: Exploring Theological Identities at Home and in Diaspora*, ed. Heup Young Kim, Fumitaka Matsuoka, and Anri Marimoto. Amsterdam: Rodopi, 2011, 57–74.

51. "The Church in Asian Perspective." In *The Routledge Companion to the Christian Church*, ed. Gerard Mannion. London: Routledge, 2007, 275–90.

52. "Jesus with a Chinese Face: C. S. Song's Jesus-Oriented Christology." In *The Chinese Face of Jesus Christ*. Vol. 3b, ed. Roman Malek. Sankt Augustin: Institut Monumenta Serica, 2007, 1393–1420.

53. "Migrazioni nell'era patristica: Storia e teologia." In *Missione con i migranti. Missione della Chiesa*, ed. Gioacchino Campese and Daniel Groody. Rome: Urbaniana University Press, 2007, 35–68.

54. "John Paul II and Interreligious Dialogue: Reality and Promise." In *The Vision of John Paul II: Assessing His Thought and Influence*, ed. Gerard Mannion. Collegeville, MN: Liturgical Press, 2008, 235–57.

55. "The Dragon and the Eagle: Toward a Vietnamese American Theology." In *Asian American Christianity: A Reader*, ed. Viji Nakka-Cammau and Timothy Tseng. Castro Valley, CA: Isaac, 2009, 313–30.

56. "The Roman Catholic Church in the Socialist Republic of Vietnam, 1989–2005." In *Falling Walls: The Year 1989/90 as a Turning Point in the History of World Christianity*, ed. Klaus Koschorke. Wiesbaden: Harrassowitz Verlag, 2009, 243–57.

57. "Mariologia in America Settentrionale." In *Mariologia*, ed. Stefano de Fiores, Valeria Schieffer, and Salvatore Perrella. Milan: Edizione San Paolo, 2009, 64–72.

58. "A New Christianity, but What Kind?" In *Landmark Essays in Mission and World Christianity*, ed. Robert L. Gallagher and Paul Hertig. Maryknoll, NY: Orbis, 2009, 201–18.

59. "Can We Read Religious Texts Interreligiously? Possibilities, Challenges, and Experiments." In *Postcolonial Interruptions*, ed. Tat-siong Benny Liew. Sheffield: Sheffield Phoenix Press, 2009, 313–31.

60. "Christ in the Many and Diverse Religions: An Interreligious Christology." In *Finding Salvation in Christ*, ed. Christopher Denny and Christopher McMahon. Eugene, OR: Pickwick, 2011, 307–18.

61. "A Review of Lamin Sanneh's *Disciples of All Nations: Pillars of World Christianity*." In *A New Day: Essays on World Christianity in Honor of Lamin Sanneh*, ed. Akintude E. Akinade. New York: Peter Lang, 2010, 317–19.

62. "Mission and Interreligious Dialogue: Edinburgh, Vatican II, and Beyond." In *2010 Boston: The Changing Contours of World Mission and Christianity*, ed. Todd M. Johnson et al. Eugene, OR: Pickwick, 2012, 84–109.

63. "L'Esprit Saint comme fondement du dialogue interreligieux." In *Le dialogue interreligieux*, ed. Fabrice Blée and Achiel Peelman. Montreal: Novalis, 2013, 21–41.

64. "Interreligious Majority-Minority Dynamics." In *Understanding Interreligious Relations*, ed. David Cheetham, Douglas Pratt, and David Thomas. Oxford: Oxford University Press, 2013, 218–40.

65. "Embracing, Protecting, and Loving the Stranger: A Roman Catholic Theology of Migration." In *Theology of Migration in the Abrahamic Religions*, ed. Elaine Padilla and Peter C. Phan. New York: Palgrave, 2014, 77–110.

66. "Being Religious Interreligiously: A Spirituality for Interfaith Dialogue in Asia." In *Ways of the Spirit*, ed. Darrol Bryant. Kitchener, Canada: Pandora Press, 2013, 214–20.

67. "The Where, Why, and Wherefore of Christian Mission Today: A Perspective from Asia." In *Mission for Diversity: Exploring Christian Mission in the Contemporary World*, ed. Elochukkvu E. Uzukwu, Vienna: LIT Verlag, 2015, 153–69.

68. "Christianity as an Institutional Migrant: Historical, Theological, and Missiological Perspectives." In *Christianities in Migration*, ed. Elaine Padilla and Peter C. Phan. New York: Palgrave, 2016, 9–35.

69. "Bekehrung als Ziel der christlichen Sendung in Asien." In *Evangelisierung: Die Freude des Evangeliums miteinander teilen*, ed. Klaus Krämer and Klaus Vellguth. Freiburg: Wien, 2016, 353–68.

70. "*Sensus Fidelium, Dissensus Infidelium, Consensus Omnium*: An Interreligious Approach to Consensus in Doctrinal Theology." In *Learning from All the Faithful: A Contemporary Theology of the Sensus Fidei*, ed. Brad Hinze and Peter C. Phan. Eugene, OR: Pickwick, 2016, 213–25.

71. "'Always Remember Where You Came From': An Ethic of Migrant Memory." In *Living With(Out) Borders: Catholic Theological Ethics on the Migration of Peoples*, ed. Agnes M. Brazal and María Teresa Dávila. Maryknoll, NY: Orbis, 2016, 173–86.

72. "Doing Theology in World Christianities: Old Task, New Ways." In *Relocating World Christianity: Interdisciplinary Studies in Universal and Local Expressions of the Christian Faith*, ed. Joel Cabrita, David Maxwell, and Emma Wild-Wood. Leiden: Brill, 2017, 115–42.

73. "Word of Liberation." In *Unsettling the Word: Biblical Experiments in Decolonization*, ed. Steve Heinrichs. Friesens Altoma, Canada: Mennonite Church Canada, 2018, 167–70.

74. "Communist Ideology, Secularity, and Reenchantment: Challenges for the Catholic Church in Vietnam, 1954–2015." In *The Secular in South, East, and Southeast Asia*, ed. Kenneth Dean and Peter Van Der Veer. New York: Palgrave, 2018, 191–213.

75. "Migration und Erinnerung. Eine Ethik für Migranten." In *Migration und Flucht: Zwischen Heilmatlosigkeit und Gastfreundschaft*, ed. Klaus Krämer and Klaus Vellguth. Freiburg: Wien, 2018, 171–97.

76. "Christianities in Asia in the Twentieth Century (1910–2010)." In *History of Global Christianity, Vol. 3: History in the Twentieth Century*, ed. Jens Holger Schjorring, Norman A. Hjelm, and Kevin Ward. Leiden: Brill, 2018, 396–421.

77. "A Theology of Liberation for the Asian Churches." In *The Grace of Medellín: History, Theology and Legacy: Reflections on the Significance of Medellín for the Church in the United States*, ed. Margaret Eletta Guider, Félix Palazzi, and O. Ernesto Valiente. Miami: Convivium, 2018, 167–80.

78. "Who Is Raimon Panikkar: Why This Book, and Why Now." In *Raimon Panikkar: A Companion to His Thought*, ed. Peter C. Phan and Young-chan Ro. Cambridge: James Clarke, 2018, xix–xxv.

79. "Raimon Panikkar's 'Eschatology': The Unpublished Chapter." In *Raimon Panikkar: A Companion to His Thought*, ed. Peter C. Phan and Young-chan Ro. Cambridge: James Clarke, 2018, 242–69.

80. "Popular Religion, Liturgy, and Christian Spirituality." In *Worship and the Church*, ed. Sallie Latkovich and Peter C. Phan, Mahwah, NJ: Paulist Press, 241–61.

81. "An Ecological Theology for Asia? The Challenge of Pope Francis's *Encyclical Laudato Si'* in *Ecological Solidarities: Mobilizing Faith and Justice for an Ecological World*, ed. Krista E. Hughes, Dhawn B. Martin, and Elaine Padilla. University Park: Pennsylvania State University Press, 2019, 147–65.

82. "Paul Evdokimov and *Una Sancta*: A Russian Orthodox Theologian in Search of Ecumenical Unity." *Stolen Churches or Bridges of Orthodoxy? Vol. 1: Historical and Theological Perspectives on the Orthodox and Eastern Catholic Dialogue*, ed. Vladimir Latinovich and Anastacia K. Wooden. New York: Palgrave Macmillan, 2020, 261–80.

83. "How Should the Church Teach? A Mode of Learning and Teaching for Our Times." *Changing the Church: Essays in Honour of Gerard Mannion*, ed. Mark Chapman and Vladimir Latinovic. New York: Palgrave Macmillan, 2021, 279-87.

84. "Migration and Memory: An Ethic for Migrants." In *Flight and Migration: Between Homelessness and Hospitality*, ed. Klaus Krämer and Klaus Vellguth. Freiburg im Breisgau: Verlag Herder, 2020, 127–47.

85. "Migration, Nationalism, and Ecumenical Unity: Challenges and Opportunities for the Churches." In *On Nation and the Churches: Ecumenical Responses to Nationalisms and Migration*, ed. Jelle Creemers and Ulrike Link–Wieczorek. Leipzig: Evangelische Verlagsanstalt, 2020, 173–89.

86. "Pope Francis' Encyclical *Laudato Si'* in Dialogue with Asian Religions." In *Towards Renewing Church and World: Revisiting Vatican II through the Eyes of Pope Francis*, ed. Francis Gonsalves, Arjen Tete, and Dinesh Braganza. Delhi: ISPCK, 2020, 377–97.

87. "Christian Worship in the Context of Other World Religions." In *Theological Foundations of Worship: Biblical, Systematic, and Practical Perspectives*, ed. Khalia J. Williams and Mark A. Lamport. Grand Rapids: Baker Academic, 2021, 245–59.

88. "Vietnam." In *Christianity in East and Southeast Asia*, ed. Kenneth R. Ross, Francis D. Alvarez, and Todd M. Johnson. Edinburgh: University of Edinburgh Press, 2020, 187–99.

89. "Imaging the Church in the Age of Migration: The Legacy of Avery Dulles for Asian Christianities." In *The Survival of Dulles: Reflections on a Second Century of Influence,* ed. Michael M. Canaris. New York: Fordham University Press, 2021, 22–40.

Essays in Scholarly Journals

1. "Mariage, monachisme et eschatology: Contribution de Paul Evdokimov à la spiritualité chrétienne." *Ephemerides Liturgicae* XCIII, nos. 4–5 (1979): 354–80.
2. "The Eschatological Dimension of Unity: Paul Evdokimov's Contribution to Ecumenism." *Salesianum* 44 (1980): 475–99.
3. "Evdokimov and the Monk Within." *Sobornost* 3, no. 1 (1981): 53–61.
4. "Possibility of a Lay Spirituality: A Re-Examination of Some Theological Presuppositions." *Communio* 10, no. 4 (1983): 378–95.
5. "Authority and Theological Method." *The Thomist* 47, no. 3 (1983): 421–42.
6. "Cultural Pluralism and the Unity of the Sciences: Karl Rahner's Transcendental Theology as a Test Case." *Salesianum* 51 (1989): 785–809.
7. "Gott as Heiliges Mysterium und die Suche nach 'Gottes-Äquivalenten' im Interreligiösen Dialog." *Zeitschrift für Missionswissenschaft und Religionswissenschaft* 3 (1990): 161–75.
8. "God as Holy Mystery and the Quest for God-Equivalents in Interreligious Dialogue." *Irish Theological Quarterly* 55 (1989): 277–90.
9. "Gender Roles in the History of Salvation: Man and Woman in the Thought of Paul Evdokimov." *Heythrop Journal* XXXI (1990): 53–66.
10. "Vatican II and Its Appraisal: The Catechetical Perspective." *Living Light* 27, no. 2 (1991): 162–71.
11. "The Future of Liberation Theology." *Living Light* 28, no. 3 (1992): 259–71.
12. "Experience and Theology: An Asian Liberation Perspective." *Zeitschrift für Missionswissenschaft und Religionswissenschaft* 2 (1993): 99–121.
13. "Peacemaking in Latin American Liberation Theology." *Église et Théologie* 24 (1993): 25–41.
14. "Karl Rahner the Pastoral Theologian." *Living Light* 30, no. 4 (1994): 3–12.
15. "Rahner on the Unoriginate Father: A Comment." *Thomist* 58, no. 1 (1994): 131–38.
16. "The Claim of Uniqueness and Universality in Interreligious Dialogue." *Indian Theological Studies* 31, no. 1 (1994): 44–66.
17. "Multiculturalism, Church, and the University." *Religious Education* 90, no. 1 (1994): 8–29.
18. "Pope John Paul II and the Ecological Crisis." *Irish Theological Quarterly* 60, no. 1 (1994): 59–69.
19. "Contemporary Context and Issues in Eschatology." *Theological Studies* 55 (1994): 59–69.
20. "Cultural Diversity: A Blessing or a Curse for Theology and Spirituality?" *Louvain Studies* 19 (1994): 195–211.
21. "Christian Mission in Contemporary Theology." *Indian Theological Studies* XXXI, no. 4 (1994): 297–347.
22. "Theological Research and Scholarship as a Service to Faith: A Roman Catholic Perspective." *Theological Education* XXXII, 1 (1995): 31–41.
23. "The Lesser Evil of Theodicy." *Proceedings of the Fiftieth Annual Convention, Catholic Theological Society of America* 50 (1995): 192–200.

24. "Eschatology and Ecology: The Environment in the End-Time." *Dialogue and Alliance* 9, no. 2 (1995): 99–115.

25. "Overcoming Poverty and Oppression: Liberation Theology and the Problem of Evil." *Louvain Studies* 20 (1995): 3–20.

26. "Is Karl Rahner's Doctrine of Sin Orthodox?" *Philosophy and Theology* 9, nos. 1–2 (1995): 223–36.

27. "The Christ of Asia: An Essay on Jesus as the Eldest Son and Ancestor." *Studia Missionalia* 45 (1996): 25–55.

28. "Jesus the Christ with an Asian Face." *Theological Studies* 57 (1996): 399–430.

29. "Jesus as the Eldest Brother and Ancestor? A Vietnamese Portrait." *Living Light* 33, no. 1 (1996): 35–44.

30. "Contexto y temática contemporánea en escatología." *Selecciones de teología* 36, no. 144 (1997): 327–38.

31. "Mission: Theology, History, Perspectives." *Living Light* 34, no. 3 (1998): 78–83.

32. "How Much Uniformity Can We Stand? How Much Unity Do We Want? Church and Worship in the Next Millennium." *Worship* 72, no. 3 (1998): 194–210.

33. "Kingdom of God: A Theological Symbol for Asians?" *Gregorianum* 79, no. 2 (1998): 295–322.

34. "Jesucristo con rostro asiatico." *Selecciones de teología* 37, no. 147 (1998): 181–97.

35. "Dying and Rising in Christ." *Priests & People* 12, no. 11 (1998): 397–403.

36. "Now That I Know How to Teach, What Do I Teach? In Search of the Unity of Faith in Religious Education Today." *Salesianum* LX (1998): 125–45.

37. "Human Development and Evangelization: The First to the Sixth Plenary Assembly of the Federation of Asian Bishops' Conference." *Studia Missionalia* 47 (1998): 205–27.

38. "Alexandre de Rhodes's Mission in Vietnam: Catechesis and Inculturation." *Vietnamologica* 3 (1998): 3–32.

39. "Freedom and Truth: *Veritatis Splendor* in the Light of Contemporary Theological Anthropology" (in Vietnamese). *Dinh Huong* 14 (1998): 4–27.

40. "Freedom in the Philosophical Tradition and Vietnamese Thought." *Dinh Huong* 15 (1998): 4–13.

41. "To Be Catholic or Not to Be: Is It Still the Question? Catholic Identity and Religious Education Today." *Horizons* 25, no. 2 (1998): 159–89.

42. "Asian Catholics in the United States: Challenges and Opportunities for the Church." *Mission Studies* XVI, no. 2 (1999): 151–74.

43. "*Fides et Ratio* and Asian Philosophies." *Science et Esprit* 51, no. 3 (1999): 333–49.

44. "Spiritual Direction in a Multicultural Church: Helping Others Encounter God in Their Own Cultures." *New Theology Review* 13, no. 1 (2000): 14–26.

45. "*Ecclesia in Asia*: Challenges for Asian Christianity." *East Asian Pastoral Review* 37, no. 3 (2000): 215–32.

46. "What If the World Will Never End? Living between Anxiety and Hope before the Coming of God." *Dinh Huong* 23 (2000): 117–48.

47. "Doing Theology in the Context of Mission: Lessons from Alexandre de Rhodes." *Gregorianum* 1, no. 4 (2000): 723–49.

48. "Method in Liberation Theologies." *Theological Studies* 61, no. 1 (2000): 40–63.

49. "Vietnamese Catholics in the United States: Christian Identity between the Old and the New." *US Catholic Historian* 18, no. 1 (2000):19–35.

50. "Kingdom of God: A Symbol for Asians?" *Theology Digest* 47, no. 1 (2000): 21–26.

51. *Fides et Ratio* and Asian Philosophies." *Theology Digest* 47, no. 2 (2000): 148–54.
52. "Cross-Cultural Studies: Key Themes and Writings for the Pastoral Minister." *New Theology Review* 13, no. 3 (2000): 64–70.
53. "Mary in Recent Theology and Piety: The View from the United States of America." *Ephemerides Mariologicae* 50 (2000): 425–39.
54. "Asian Catholics in the United States: Challenges and Opportunities for the Church." *Triet Dao: Journal of Vietnamese Philosophy & Religion* 1, no. 1 (2001): 7–36.
55. "The Dragon and the Eagle: Toward a Vietnamese-American Theology." *Theology Digest* 48, no. 2 (2001): 203–18.
56. "The Wisdom of Holy Fools in Post-Modernity." *Theological Studies* 62 (2001): 730–52.
57. "Reception of Vatican II in Asia: Historical and Theological Analysis." *Gregorianum* 83, no. 2 (2002): 269–85.
58. "Culture and Liturgy: Ancestor Veneration as a Test Case." *Worship* 76, no. 5 (2002): 403–30.
59. "Proclamation of the Reign of God as Mission of the Church: What For, to Whom, by Whom, with Whom, and How?" *SEDOS* 33, no. 11 (2001): 300–307.
60. "Conversion and Discipleship as Goals of the Church's Mission." *SEDOS* 34, no. 1 (2002): 19–28.
61. "Mary in Vietnamese Piety and Theology: A Contemporary Perspective." *Ephemerides Mariologicae* 51, no. 4 (2001): 457–71.
62. "Doing Theology in the Context of Cultural and Religious Pluralism: An Asian Perspective." *Louvain Studies* 27 (2002): 39–68.
63. "Catechesis and Catechism as Inculturation of the Christian Faith." *Salesianum* 65 (2003): 91–122.
64. "The Laity in the Early Church: Building Blocks for a Theology of the Laity." *Journal of Vietnamese Philosophy and Theology* 4, no. 2 (2002): 36–53.
65. "Mary in Vietnamese Piety and Theology." *Theology Digest* 49, no. 3 (2002): 244–52.
66. "Crossing the Borders: A Spirituality for Mission in Our Times from an Asian Perspective." *SEDOS* 35, nos. 1–2 (2002): 8–19.
67. "US Latino/a Theology and Asian Theology: Partners in the Postmodern Age?" *Journal of Hispanic/Latino Theology* 10, no. 2 (2002): 5–30.
68. "Theologizing in the Context of Cultural and Religious Pluralism: An Asian Perspective." *Theology Digest* 50, no. 2 (2003): 143–54.
69. "Multiple Religious Belonging: Opportunities and Challenges for Theology and Church." *Theological Studies* 64 (2003): 495–519.
70. "Cultures, Religions, and Power: Proclaiming Christ in the United States Today." *Theological Studies* 65 (2004): 714–40.
71. "A New Christianity, but What Kind?" *Mission Studies* 22, no. 1 (2005): 55–79.
72. "Popular Religion, the Liturgy, and the Cult of the Dead." *East Asian Pastoral Review* 42, no. 2 (2005): 122–46.
73. "Ignacio Ellacuría, SJ, in Dialogue with Asian Theologians: What Can They Learn from Each Other?" *Horizons* 32, no. 1 (2005): 53–71.
74. "Jews and Judaism in Asian Theology: Historical and Theological Perspectives." *Gregorianum* 86, no. 4 (2005): 806–36.
75. "Where Are We Going? The Future of Ministry in the United States." *New Theology Review* 18, no. 2 (2005): 5–15.

76. "Whose Experiences? Whose Interpretations? Contribution of Asian Theologies to Theological Epistemology." *Irish Theological Quarterly* 71 (2007): 5–28.

77. "Cultural Diversity and Religious Pluralism: The Church's Mission in Asia." *East Asian Pastoral Review* 43, no. 2 (2006): 109–28.

78. "Racism and Caste: Catholic Social Thought and Theology in the Asian Context." *Journal of Catholic Social Thought* 3, no. 1 (2006): 57–78.

79. "Cosmology, Ecology, Pneumatology: A Reading of Denis Edward's Interpretation of Karl Rahner's Eschatology." *Philosophy and Theology* 18, no. 2 (2006): 385–92.

80. "World Christianity and Christian Mission: Are They Compatible? Insights from the Asian Churches," *International Bulletin of Mission* 32, no. 4 (2007):193–200.

81. "Peacemaking and Reconciliation: Roman Catholic Teachings in the Context of Interreligious Dialogue." *Journal of Catholic Social Thought* 1, no. 2 (2006): 57–78.

82. "Global Healing and Reconciliation: Gift and Task of Religion. A Buddhist-Christian Perspective" *Buddhist-Christian Studies* 26 (2006): 89–108.

83. "Asian Christian Spirituality: Context and Contour." *Spiritus: A Journal of Christian Spirituality* 6, no. 2 (2006): 221–27.

84. "Where We Came From, Where We Are, and Where We Are Going: Asian and Pacific Catholics in the US." *American Catholic Studies* 118, no. 3 (2007): 1–26.

85. "Doing Theology in World Christianity: Different Resources and New Methods." *Journal of World Christianity* 1, no. 1 (2007): 27–53.

86. "Intercultural and Interreligious Dialogue: A Challenge to Christian Mission." *Journal of Vietnamese Philosophy & Religion* 13, no. 7 (2007): 8–36.

87. "World Christianity and Christian Missions: Are They Compatible?" *Asian Christian Review* 1, no. 1 (2007): 14–31.

88. "Popular Religion, the Liturgy, and the Cult of the Dead." *Japan Mission Journal* 61, no. 2 (2007): 101–20.

89. "At Jacob's Well: An Interfaith Encounter. A Missiological Interpretation of John 4:4–42." *Mission Studies* 27, no. 2 (2010): 160–75.

90. "Church, Social Mission, Politics: Perspectives from Vietnam." *Journal of Vietnamese Philosophy & Religion* 14, no. 7 (2007): 8–18.

91. "Un mondo fuori dal mondo: Il sinodo sull'Asia: Le chiese asiatiche portano a Roma i propri doni." *Dossier di orientamento di aggiornamento teologico* (2007): 1–9.

92. "Cultures, Religions, and Mission in Asian Catholic Theologies." *Japan Mission Journal* 63, no. 1 (2009): 37–53.

93. "Paul Evdokimov et la théologie catholique contemporaine: Une perspective eschatologique." *Contacts* 235, no. 236 (2011): 417–29.

94. "The Human Soul: A Roman Catholic View." *Journal of Vaishnava Studies* 20, no. 2 (2012): 117–25.

95. "Being Christian under Communist-Socialist Regimes." *Concilium* 1 (2011): 68–82.

96. "Teaching as Learning: An Asian View." *Concilium* 2 (2012): 75–87.

97. "World Christianity: Its Implications for History, Religious Studies, and Theology." *Horizons* 39, no. 2 (2012): 171–88.

98. "The World Missionary Conference, Edinburgh 1910: Challenges for Church and Theology in the Twenty-First Century." *International Bulletin of Missionary Research* 34, no. 2 (2010): 105–8.

99. "Cultures, Religions, and Mission in Asian Catholic Theologies." *Japan Mission Journal*, 63, no. 1 (2009): 37–53.

100. "Universal Salvation, Christian Identity, Church Mission: Theological Foundations of Interreligious Dialogue." *Japan Mission Journal* 64, no. 1 (2010): 3–20.

101. "*Missio inter gentes*: Contemporary Theologies and Practices of Mission." *SEDOS* 43 (2011): 131-44.

102. "Reception of and Prospects for Vatican II in Asia." *Theological Studies* 74, no. 2 (2013): 302–20.

103. "Interreligious Dialogue Now: Recent Journey and Future Trajectories." *Japan Journal Mission* 67 (2012): 147–58.

104. "Judaism and Christianity: Reading Cardinal Koch's Address between the Lines and Against the Grain." *Studies in Christian-Jewish Relations* 7 (2012): 1–7.

105. "Christianity in Vietnam: 1975–2013." *International Journal for the Study of the Christian Church* 14, no. 1 (2014): 1–19.

106. "As ideas e conceitos de um papa para a Asia." *IHU: Revista do Instituto Humanitas Unisinos* 470, no. 15 (2015): 80–87.

107. "Historical Scholarship on Asian Christianity, 2000–1015." *Vekündigung und Forschung* 2 (2015): 92–107.

108. "Francis, a Pope for Asia?" *Japan Mission Journal* 69, no. 3 (2015): 175–184.

109. "Reading *Nostra Aetate* in Reverse: A Different Way of Looking at the Relations Among Religions." *Studies in Christian-Jewish Relations* 10, no. 2 (2015): 1–14.

110. "Deus Migrator: God the Migrant—Migration of Theology and Theology of Migration." *Theological Studies* 77, no. 4 (2016), 845–68.

111. "World Christianities: Transcontinental Connections." *Journal of World Christianity* 6, no. 1 (2016): 205–16.

112. "*L'Église: vers une vision comune*: Une approche des Églises asiatiques." *Irénikon* 89, nos. 2–4 (2016): 163–80.

113. "*The Church: Towards a Common Vision*: A View from the Asian Churches." *Journal of World Christianity* 7, no. 1 (2017): 81–92.

114. "Teaching Missiology in and for World Christianity." *International Bulletin of Mission Research* 24, no. 4 (2018): 358–69.

115. "Insorgere contro le politiche di esclusione de Erode." *Adista*, no 26 (2018): 1–4.

116. "Die Flucht des Erinners: Zum Zusammenhang von Migration und Erinerung aus theologischer Perspective." *Forum Weltkirche: Zweitalter der Migration*, (September–October 2018): 12–19.

117. "Doing Ecclesiology in World Christianity: A Church of Migrants and a Migrant Church." *Offerings: A Journal of Christian Spirituality and Practical Theology* 3, no. 11 (2018): 3–26.

118. "Raimon Panikkar's Legacy for Catholic Theology." *CIRPIT Review* 7 (2018): 63–70.

119. "From Magisterium to Magisteria: Recent Theologies of the Learning and Teaching Functions of the Church." *Theological Studies* 80, no. 2 (2019): 393–413.

120. "Nauczanie misjologii w świecie chrześcijańskim i dla niego: Treść i metoda." *Annales missiologici posnanenses* 24 (2019): 85–99.

121. "The Salvific Role of Non-Christian Religions." *Japan Mission Journal* 74, no. 1 (2020): 38–51.

122. "Current Trends and Future Tasks of Christian Theology of Asia: In Celebration of the 50th Anniversary of the Foundation of the FABC." *Jnanadeepa Pune Journal of Religious Studies* 25, no. 4 (2021): 8–29.

123. "The Holy and Great Council of the Orthodox Church: A Roman Catholic Appraisal." *Journal of World Christianity* 11, no. 1 (2021): 39–59.

124. "Papa Franceso e l'incontro con altri credenti," *Adista* 27 (2021): 13-14.

Articles for Encyclopedias

1. "Augustine, Influence of." In *The New Dictionary of Catholic Social Thought*, ed. Judith Dwyer. Collegeville, MN: Liturgical Press, 1994, 58–63.
2. "Fathers of the Church, Influence of." In *The New Dictionary of Catholic Social Thought*, ed. Judith Dwyer. Collegeville, MN: Liturgical Press, 1994, 388–94.
3. "Apostolic Succession." In *The Modern Catholic Encyclopedia* (hereafter, *MCE*), 42–43.
4. "Creation." In *MCE*, 210–11.
5. "Indulgences." In *MCE*, 425.
6. "Infallibility." In *MCE*, 425–26.
7. "Tradition." In *MCE*, 874–75.
8. "Magisterium." In *MCE*, 536–37.
9. "Mystery of Faith." In *MCE*, 594.
10. "Indefectibility." In *MCE*, 424.
11. "Aristotle." In *MCE*, 48.
12. "Salesians." In *MCE*, 783.
13. "Articles of Faith." In *MCE*, 52.
14. "Dogmatic Theology." In *MCE*, 863.
15. "Supernatural." In *MCE*, 843–44.
16. "Plato." In *MCE*, 687.
17. "Soteriology." In *MCE*, 819–21.
18. "Alexandre de Rhodes." In *A Dictionary of Asian Christianity*, ed. Scott W. Sunquist. Grand Rapids: Wm. B. Eerdmans, 2001 (hereafter, *DAC*), 697–703 .
19. "Caodaism." In *DAC*, 115–17.
20. "Ho Chi Minh." In *DAC*, 339–40.
21. "Vietnam." In *DAC*, 876–80.
22. "Vietnam War." In *DAC*, 880–82.
23. "Han Mac Tu." In *DAC*, 323–24.
24. "Vietnamese Catholics in America." In *The Encyclopedia of American Catholic History*, ed. Michael Glazier and Thomas J. Shelley. Collegeville, MN: Liturgical Press, 1998, 1434–35.
25. "Katechese/Katechetik: Asien, Afrika, Lateinamerika." In *Religion in Geschichte und Gegenwart Online*. Heidelberg: Mohr Siebeck, 1988–2007 (hereafter, *RGGO4*).
26. "Pallu, François." In *RGGO4*.
27. "De Rhodes, Alexandre." In *RGGO4*.
28. "Reception of Vatican II in Latin America, Asia, and Africa." In *RGGO4*.
29. "Vietnamese Martyrs." In *RGGO4*.
30. "Trinitarian Processions." *New Catholic Encyclopedia*, 2nd ed., vol. 11. Detroit: Thomson / Gale Research, 2003, 733–36.
31. "Trinitarian Relations." In *The New Catholic Encyclopedia*, 2nd ed., vol. 12. Detroit: Thomson / Gale Research, 2003, 45–46.
32. "Praeambula Fidei." In *Leksyknon Teologii Fundamentalnej*. Krakow: Wydawnictwo Literackie, 2002, 948–50.
33. "Rationalism." In *Leksyknon Teologii Fundamentalnej*. Krakow: Wydawnictwo Literackie, 2002, 991–92.
34. "Missio Canonica." In *The Encyclopedia of Christianity*, vol. III. Grand Rapids: Wm. B. Eerdmans, 2003, 552–53.

35. "Viet Nam." In *The International Encyclopedia of Christianity*, vol. V. Grand Rapids: Wm. B. Eerdmans, 2003, 676-80.
36. "Abrams, Mimie." In *The Oxford Dictionary of the Christian Church*, 4th edition, forthcoming in 2022 (hereafter, *ODCC*).
37. "Alopen." In *ODCC*.
38. "Bangladesh." In *ODCC*.
39. "Bangladesh Baptist Church Sangha." In *ODCC*.
40. "Bangladesh Baptist Fellowship." In *ODCC*.
41. "Bangladesh Catholic Church." In *ODCC*.
42. "Bangladesh Church of God." In *ODCC*.
43. "Bangladesh Evangelical Church." In *ODCC*.
44. "Brunei Darussalam." In *ODCC*.
45. "Cambodia." In *ODCC*.
46. "Catholic Bishops' Conference of the Philippines." In *ODCC*.
47. "China, Catholic Church." In *ODCC*.
48. "Nguyen Truong To." In *ODCC*.
49. "Nguyen Van Thuan." In *ODCC*.
50. "Orthodox Church in Asia." In *ODCC*.
51. "Our Lady of Lavang." In *ODCC*.
52. "Pallu, François." In *ODCC*.
53. "Patronato real." In *ODCC*.
54. "Petitjean Bernard." In *ODCC*.
55. "Pieris, Aloysius." In *ODCC*.
56. "Puginier, Paul-François." In *ODCC*.
57. "Punishment." In *ODCC*.
58. "Reincarnation." In *ODCC*.
59. "Ruggieri, Michele." In *ODCC*.
60. "Shamanism." In *ODCC*.
61. "Société des Missions Étrangère de Paris." In *ODCC*.
62. "Sun Myung Moon." In *ODCC*.
63. "Tran Van Luc." In *ODCC*.
64. "Truong Vinh Ky." In *ODCC*.
65. "Universities and Seminaries in Asia." In *ODCC*.
66. "Valignano, Alessandro." In *ODCC*.
67. "Vaz, Joseph." In *ODCC*.
68. "Verbiest, Ferdinand." In *ODCC*.
69. "Schall von Bell, Johann Adam." In *ODCC*.
70. "Walsh, James." In *ODCC*.
71. "Wu Yaozung." In *ODCC*.

Popular Articles

1. "Infant Baptism." *Texas Catholic* (hereafter, *TC*), June 8, 1979.
2. "Tradition and Liturgical Changes." *TC*, June 15, 1979.
3. "The Fate of Unbaptized Infants." *TC*, June 22, 1979.
4. "The Significance of Confirmation." *TC*, June 29, 1979.
5. "Christian Teachings and the Paschal Mystery." *TC*, July 6, 1979.

 6. "The Priest and the Sacrament of Reconciliation." *TC*, July 13, 1979.
 7. "The Dogma of the Immaculate Conception." *TC*, July 20, 1979.
 8. "Sin and Scandal." *TC*, July 27, 1979.
 9. "The Anointing of the Sick." *TC*, August 3, 1979.
10. "Temptations and the Priesthood." *TC*, August 10, 1979.
11. "Historical Context of the Nicene Creed." *TC*, August 17, 1979.
12. "The Bible and Truth." *TC*, August 24, 1979.
13. "The Problem of the True Church." *TC*, August 31, 1979.
14. "The Arms Race and Disarmament." *TC*, September 14, 1979.
15. "The Deacon in the Church." *TC*, September 21, 1979.
16. "The Meaning of Episcopal Collegiality." *TC*, September 28, 1979.
17. "Christianity and Non-Christian Religions." *TC*, October 5, 1979.
18. "Miracles: Historical Events of Inventions?" *TC*, October 12, 1979.
19. "Miracles as Signs." *TC*, October 19, 1979.
20. "The Two Functions of Miracles." *TC*, October 26, 1979.
21. "The Nature and Method of Theology." *TC*, November 2, 1979.
22. "The Parish Council." *TC*, November 9, 1979.
23. "Belief in Purgatory." *TC*, November 16, 1979.
24. "Death and Dying." *TC*, November 23, 1979.
25. "The Sacramental Character." *TC*, November 30, 1979.
26. "Church as Sacrament." *TC*, December 7, 1979.
27. "Christian Hope." *TC*, December 21, 1979.
28. "Hope in the Old Testament." *TC*, February 1, 1979.
29. "Jesus Christ, Hope of the Church." *TC*, February 22, 1980.
30. "Hope and Christian Living." *TC*, March 7, 1980.
31. "The Unbelief of Believers." *TC*, March 21, 1980.
32. "Science and Faith." *TC*, April 4, 1980.
33. "God Is No Competitor of Man." *TC*, May 2, 1980.
34. "Faith, Creed, and Dogma." *TC*, June 13, 1980.
35. "The Death of Christ." *TC*, June 20, 1980.
36. "Christ's Descent into Hell." *TC*, June 27, 1980.
37. "The Experience of God." *TC*, July 18, 1980.
38. "I Believe in One God." *TC*, August 8, 1980.
39. "The Two Names of Old Testament God." *TC*, August 15, 1980.
40. "The Name of God." *TC*, August 29, 1980.
41. "The Sacrament of Penance." *TC*, September 19, 1980.
42. "Infallibility and the Magisterium." *TC*, October 31, 1980.
43. "The Non-Infallible Magisterium." *TC*, December 5, 1980.
44. "Hans Küng as a Theologian." *TC*, December 5, 1980.
45. "The Ascension of Jesus." *TC*, June 12, 1981.
46. "Sitting at God's Right Hand." *TC*, June 19, 1981
47. "Understanding the Beatitudes." *TC*, July 3, 1981.
48. "True and False Righteousness." *TC*, July 10, 1981.
49. "Faith in Ordinary Things." *TC*, July 17, 1981.
50. "Asian Catholics: Challenges and Opportunities for the American Church." *Catholic Update*, June 2000, 3–4.

51. "Escape to Freedom: 25 Years after the Fall of South Vietnam." *America* 182, no. 15 (April 29, 2000): 12–14.

52. "Under the Bamboo Cross." *US Catholic* 65, no. 7 (July 2000): 36–37.

53. "Faith in Cultures: Inculturation and Catechesis." *Evangelizing Catechesis* (National Conference for Catechetical Leadership), 2000, 1–4.

54. "This Too Shall Pass: Why *Ex Corde*'s Mandate Won't Last." *Commonweal* CXXVIII, no. 22 (December 21, 2001): 13–15.

55. "The Next Christianity." *America* 188, no. 3 (February 3, 2003): 9–11.

56. "The Preacher as Border-Crosser: Proclaiming God's Word across Cultures." *Preach: Enlivening the Pastoral Art* (May–June 2005): 26–29.

57. "Human Freedom and the Free Market Economy: Pope John Paul II's Critique of Capitalism." *Insight* (2005).

58. "Speaking in Many Tongues: Why the Church Must Be More Catholic." *Commonweal* (January 12, 2007): 16–19.

59. "Praying to the Buddha: Living Amid Religious Pluralism." *Commonweal* (January 26, 2007): 10–14.

60. "The Case against Humanity." *World & I* (Summer 2007): 87–89.

61. "Papież, który nie przyszedł nawracać." *Gazeta Wyborcza* Sobota-niedziela, September 27–28, 2014, 37.

62. "Is Francis a Pope for Asia?" *National Catholic Reporter* 51, no. 24 (September 11–24, 2005): 12.

63. "The Eternal Question." *America*, November 9, 2015, 37–40.

64. "Matthew & Migration: Reading the Birth Story of Jesus in New Light." *Nurturing Faith Journal & Bible Studies* 36, no. 6 (November–December 2018): 44–46.

General Editor

General editor of the Theology in Global Perspective series; twenty-five volumes for Orbis Books.

General editor of the Pastoral Spirituality series; twelve volumes for Paulist Press.

General editor of the Christianities of the World Series, Palgrave Macmillan.

General editor of the World Christianity series, Pennsylvania State University Press.

CONTRIBUTORS

THOMAS BANCHOFF is the vice president for global engagement and a professor of government and foreign service at Georgetown University. He previously served as the founding director of Georgetown's Berkley Center for Religion, Peace, and World Affairs.

JOHN BORELLI is special assistant for Catholic identity and dialogue to the president of Georgetown University, a position he has held since 2004. He has coauthored *Catholics and Evangelicals for the Common Good; One Hope: Re-Membering the Body of Christ; Interfaith Dialogue: A Catholic View;* and *The Quest for Unity: Orthodox and Catholics in Dialogue;* and he edited *A Common Word and the Future of Christian-Muslim Relations*. He staffed ecumenical and interreligious relations and dialogue for sixteen years as associate director of the Secretariat for ecumenical and interreligious affairs of the US Conference of Catholic Bishops. He was a consultant to the Vatican during those years as well. He has published over two hundred articles on ecumenism, interreligious relations, and related fields.

GEMMA TULUD CRUZ is senior lecturer in theology and member of Institute of Religion and Critical Inquiry at Australian Catholic University. She is author of *An Intercultural Theology of Migration: Pilgrims in the Wilderness;* and *Toward a Theology of Migration: Social Justice and Religious Experience.* She is currently writing a monograph, *Christianity Across Borders: Theology and Contemporary Issues in Global Migration;* and an edited book, *Christianity in Migration and Diaspora: Filipino Perspectives.*

CHARLES E. CURRAN is the Elizabeth Scurlock University Professor of Human Values at Southern Methodist University. He has served as president of three national professional societies; has written and edited sixty books on moral theology; has received various awards for his books, including the 2008 American Publishers Award for Professional and Scholarly Excellence in Theology and Religion; has received the highest award from three national academic societies; and in 2010 was elected to membership in the American Academy of Arts and Sciences.

BRIAN M. DOYLE is professor of theology at Marymount University, where he has served as department chair and the director of the Center for Ethical Concerns. He received his PhD from the Catholic University of America. His research interests include eschatology, theodicy, and the doctrine of the Trinity.

BRIAN P. FLANAGAN is an associate professor of theology and religious studies at Marymount University. His research focuses on ecclesiology, ecumenism, and Jewish–Christian dialogue, particularly through the Ecclesiological Investigations Network and the Ecclesiological Investigations Group of the American Academy of Religion. He teaches Marymount's foundational theological inquiry course and upper-level courses on ecclesiology, Christology, and sacramental theology.

CHESTER GILLIS, professor of theology at Georgetown University, was the initial holder of the Amaturo Chair in Catholic Studies later held by Gerard Mannion. The founding director of the Program on the Church and Interreligious Dialogue at the Berkley Center for Religion, Peace, and World Affairs, he is the author of *A Question of Final Belief: John Hick's Pluralistic Theory of Salvation* (1989); *Pluralism: A New Paradigm for* Theology (1993); *Catholic Faith in America* (2003); and *Roman Catholicism in America* (2020); and the editor of *The Political Papacy* (2006).

CRISTINA LLEDO GOMEZ is a systematic theologian and the Presentation Sisters Lecturer at BBI–The Australian Institute of Theological Education. Her role is directed at promoting women's spiritualities, feminist theologies, and ecology. She was previously the social justice coordinator for the Catholic Diocese of Broken Bay (2017–18) and chair of the Australian Catholic Social Justice Council (2019–20). She is also a Religion and Society Research Fellow for Charles Sturt University's Public and Contextual Theology Centre. Her areas of research interest are maternal-feminist theology, ecclesiology, migration, colonialism, domestic violence, and ecotheology.

DALE T. IRVIN is professor of world Christianity at the New School of Biblical Theology and an adjunct in the Department of Theology and Religious Studies at Georgetown University. He is the current chair of the

Ecclesiological Investigations International Research Network, and he has published widely in the area of world Christianity, ecumenical studies, and the history of the world Christian movement.

LEO D. LEFEBURE is the inaugural holder of the Matteo Ricci, SJ, Chair of Theology at Georgetown University. He is the author of *Transforming Interreligious Relations: Catholic Responses to Religious Pluralism in the United States*; and *True and Holy: Christian Scriptures and Other Religions*. He is the president of the Society for Buddhist-Christian Studies, a research fellow of the Chinese University of Hong Kong, and a trustee emeritus of the Council for a Parliament of the World's Religions.

WILLIAM P. LOEWE is professor of historical and systematic theology at the Catholic University of America. His teaching focuses on fundamental theology, Christology and soteriology, and Lonergan studies. His most recent book is *Lex crucis: Soteriology and the Stages of Meaning*.

ALAN C. MITCHELL is associate professor of New Testament and Christian origins at Georgetown University and is the director of the Reverend Joseph A. Fitzmyer, SJ, Institute on Sacred Scripture. He is the author of *Hebrews* in the Sacra Pagina Series (Liturgical Press, 2007), winner of the 2008 Catholic Press Association Book Award in Scripture. His most recent publication is a commentary on First Corinthians (Bloomsbury Press, 2021). He is the editor for books on Hebrews in *The Religious Studies Review*. He served for eight years on the Editorial Board of the *Catholic Biblical Quarterly*.

JOHN W. O'MALLEY, SJ, is a Jesuit priest and university professor emeritus at Georgetown University. His specialty is the religious culture of early modern Europe, particularly Italy, and he is also an expert on the Second Vatican Council. He has held a number of fellowships from the Guggenheim Foundation, the National Endowment for the Humanities, the American Council of Learned Societies, and other academic organizations. Among his many publications are *When Bishops Meet: An Essay Comparing Trent, Vatican I, and Vatican II* (2019); *Vatican I: The Council and the Making of the Ultramontane Church* (2018); *What Happened at Vatican II* (2008), now published in six languages; and *Trent: What Happened at the Council* (2012), published in five languages and winner of the John Gilmary Shea Prize in 2013. In 2016, the Graduate School of Harvard University awarded him its Centennial Medal, its highest honor.

PETER C. PHAN, who has earned three doctorates, is the inaugural holder of the Ignacio Ellacuría, SJ, Chair of Catholic Social Thought at Georgetown University. His research deals with the theology of icons in Orthodox theology, patristic theology, eschatology, the history of Christian missions in Asia, liberation, inculturation, and interreligious dialogue. He is the author and editor of over thirty books and has published over three hundred essays. His writings have been translated into Arabic, French, German, Italian, Polish, Portuguese, Romanian, Serbian, Spanish, Chinese, Indonesian, Japanese, and Vietnamese, and have received many awards from learned societies. He is the first non-Anglo to be elected president of Catholic Theological Society of America and president of American Theological Society. In 2010 he received the John Courtney Murray Award, the highest honor bestowed by the Catholic Theological Society of America for outstanding achievement in theology. He has also been awarded four honorary doctorates.

JONATHAN Y. TAN is Archbishop Paul J. Hallinan Professor of Catholic Studies in the Department of Religious Studies at Case Western Reserve University. He is the author of *Introducing Asian American Theologies* (2008); *Christian Mission among the Peoples of Asia* (2014); and *The Federation of Asian Bishops' Conferences (FABC): Bearing Witness to the Gospel and the Reign of God in Asia* (2021). He was the lead editor of *World Christianity: Perspectives and Insights* (2016); and coeditor of *Theological Reflections on the Hong Kong Umbrella Movement* (2016).

DEBORA TONELLI is Georgetown University's representative in Rome and permanent researcher at Fondazione Bruno Kessler–Centro per le Scienze Religiose. She is also invited lecturer in political philosophy, politics, and religion and theology at the Pontifical Athenaeum S. Anselmo and at Gregoriana University. She has served as visiting scholar at the Institute for Religion, Culture, and Public Life of Columbia University and at the Berkley Center for Religion, Peace, and World Affairs of Georgetown University. Her research and publications (in Italian and in English) focus on the dynamics between religion and violence and on the biblical legacy in modern political thought. Among her publications are *Il Decalogo: Uno sguardo retrospettivo* (2010); and *Immagini di violenza divina* (2014).

ANH Q. TRAN, SJ, is associate professor of theology at the Jesuit School of Theology of Santa Clara University and member of Core Doctoral Faculty at the Graduate Theological Union in Berkeley. He specializes in comparative theology and religious studies and Asian Christianity, and he is the author of *Gods, Heroes, and Ancestors* (2018); and coeditor of *World Christianity: Perspectives and Insights* (2016). He has contributed two dozen book chapters and articles in the areas of Asian contextual theology, interreligious dialogue, Confucian-Christian studies, and Vietnamese Catholicism, both in English and Vietnamese.

KEITH WARD is a canon of Christ Church, University of Oxford, and Regius Professor Emeritus of Divinity in the University of Oxford. He is a fellow of the British Academy and author of numerous works.

STEPHANIE M. WONG (黃欣慧) is a theologian and scholar of Christianity in East Asia, especially in dialogue with Chinese religious and philosophical traditions. After studying Chinese Christian history and theology at Yale Divinity School, she studied at Georgetown University because its program in religious pluralism offered the flexibility to dive deep into the study of both Catholic theology and the intellectual history and lived traditions of Chinese religions. Since becoming an assistant professor at Valparaiso University, she has been teaching a wide range of courses in Christian theology, world Christianity, East Asian traditions, and methods and theories in the study of religion. In her research, she focuses especially on the experience and theological expressions of Chinese Catholics.

INDEX

afterlife, 6, 136, 194, 196, 204–6, 214, 265
Allen, John L., Jr., 52
al-Tayeb, Ahmed. *See* Tayyib, Ahmad
Amoris laetitia [*The Joy of Love*], 7, 105n45, 260
Anglican(s), 14, 98, 226
asylum, 49, 71, 82n60, 90, 101
atheist(s), 159, 202
Augustine of Hippo, 123, 195, 232n13, 266, 269

Balthasar, Hans Urs von, 29, 154
Baptist(s), 13, 139, 226
Barth, Karl, 29, 188
Benedict XVI, Pope, 5, 101, 184, 188, 190–95, 236, 240, 245, 247, 256–58, 277
Bergoglio, Jorge. *See* Francis, Pope
Bible, 36, 85–86, 91–92, 112, 114, 140, 182n20, 188–89, 192, 201, 211, 213, 234n35, 251, 253, 258, 269. *See also* Hebrew Bible; New Testament
Buddhism, 21, 131, 137, 141, 144n18, 161, 164, 166–67, 196–97

Catholic and Apostolic Church. *See* Catholic Church(es)
Catholic Charismatic Renewal Movement, 53–54, 58, 62n37
Catholic Church(es), vii, 3, 21, 23, 32, 35, 42, 45n20, 52–54, 57, 72, 93, 97, 99, 102, 106n48, 109, 155, 157–58, 160, 168, 170nn2,5, 191, 196, 201, 205, 207, 210–12, 226, 240, 244, 252–55, 259–60, 276
Catholic University of America, The, vii, 118, 237, 243

CCRM. *See* Catholic Charismatic Renewal Movement
CDF. *See* Congregation for the Doctrine of the Faith
China, 4, 38, 40–42, 48, 55, 86, 140, 157–60, 162–64, 166–69, 170n5, 172n49, 226, 231nn7,12, 276
Christianity, vii–viii, 1–2, 5–6, 11–22, 24n7, 25nn15,18, 26nn39,40,41, 27n64, 30, 39, 41, 47–48, 51–53, 55, 57–60, 62n23, 63n44, 64n61, 66, 91, 97–99, 105n38, 124, 126, 128, 130, 135, 137–38, 140–42, 148, 150, 166, 175–76, 185, 192, 194, 197, 206–7, 221–26, 228–29, 231n12, 232n13, 256, 259, 264, 274–75
Christology (ies), viii, 1, 3, 118–22, 125–26, 183–84, 244, 267, 276
clergy, 35, 46n25, 53–56, 90, 93–94, 158. *See also* pastors
Clooney, Francis Xavier, 123, 127n14, 161
Confucianism, 21, 161, 164, 166
Congregation for the Doctrine of the Faith, 6–7, 20, 128, 155, 192, 215n13, 235–47, 247nn1,2, 252, 256, 258, 262n22, 277
Consejo Episcopal Latinoamericano. *See* Federation of Latin American Bishops' Conference
creation, 11, 75, 92, 101, 113, 147, 197, 253
CUA. *See* Catholic University of America, The

death, 5, 73, 75, 77–78, 94, 96, 98, 103, 125–26, 130, 137, 139, 162, 183–91, 193–97, 199n26, 203–4, 206–7, 209, 212, 214n9, 273, 276–77
diaspora, 50, 62n36, 81n43

Dignitatis Humanae [Declaration on Religious Liberty], 252, 255, 262n15
documented (migrant), 49
Dupuis, Jacques, 236, 238, 240, 244–46, 256, 258–59, 262n26

ecclesiology, viii, 2, 18, 23, 34, 48, 56–58, 69, 145–55, 274, 276
ecumenism, 22, 252
eschatology, 1, 4–6, 11–12, 145, 175–77, 180–81, 183–85, 187, 189–90, 192–97, 198n22, 199n39, 237, 264–65, 268, 277
Eucharist, 33, 55, 58, 72–74, 76, 213, 275
Evangelical(s), 17, 56, 98, 143n16
Evangelii Gaudium [The Joy of the Gospel], 7, 150, 152, 154, 260
evangelization, 17, 33, 37, 40, 98, 152, 225, 232n21
Evdokimov, Paul, 1, 12, 194, 264–65, 267, 269

faith(s), 3–4, 6, 14–15, 18–20, 23, 28n64, 29–30, 32, 36–37, 39, 41–43, 51–56, 58–60, 66, 72, 74, 78, 85, 100–101, 110, 119–21, 125, 128, 131, 134, 137–38, 141, 151, 154–55, 158–60, 177, 181–83, 185, 187, 191–92, 206, 211–13, 221, 223–25, 227, 235, 242, 244–45, 249, 252–53, 256–58, 265, 274, 276–77
Federation of Asian Bishops' Conference, 30, 33–36, 38, 40, 44n4, 146, 265–66, 275
Federation of Latin American Bishops' Conference, 32
feminist theology, 79n11, 197
Francis, Pope, 4, 7, 97, 98–99, 101, 105nn37,45, 109, 116, 146, 147, 149–50, 152, 154–55, 249–52, 255, 258–61, 277

Gaudete et Exsultate [Rejoice and Be Glad], 7, 260
Gaudium et spes [Pastoral Constitution on the Church in the Modern World], 33, 44, 46n24, 233n23
Germany, 109, 170n5, 222

Gospel(s), 2, 7, 19, 27n64, 31–32, 35–37, 42–43, 56, 63n47, 71, 73, 110, 114, 140, 147, 151, 170n2, 184–87, 192, 212–13, 223, 230, 231n12, 260
grace, 75–76, 91, 98, 123, 126, 193, 245–46, 265, 270
Greshake, Gisbert, 5, 184, 187–95, 198nn15,16,22, 199nn25,40

Haight, Roger, 236, 238–40
heaven, 111, 180, 186, 189–90, 192, 197, 251
Hebrew Bible, 110, 188. *See also* Bible
Hinduism, 21, 57, 60, 131, 138, 141, 144n18, 196–97
Holy Scripture. *See* Bible
Holy Spirit, 3, 115, 122, 135, 177, 184, 211–12, 255, 264, 276
homosexuality, 240, 246
hospitality, 5, 22, 52, 74–75, 161, 178, 275
humanism, 110–13

immigrant(s). *See* migrant(s)
immigration. *See* migration
injustice, 99–100, 242, 244, 247, 258
interfaith, 3–4, 44n4, 118–23, 126–29, 131–34, 138, 143nn9,11,17, 150, 159, 172n51, 196, 204, 235, 237, 258
interreligious dialogue, 12, 34, 40, 45n9, 109, 115, 118, 157–62, 164–65, 167–69, 170n2, 226, 250, 254–55, 257, 259, 274, 276–77
Islam, 15, 21, 52, 72, 131, 137–38, 141, 166–67, 254

Jesuit(s), 16, 49, 158, 236, 239–40, 244–46, 258
Jesus Christ, 3, 39–40, 42–43, 48, 56, 59–60, 63, 68–69, 74–78, 84, 93, 119–20, 123–28, 136–38, 140, 151, 157, 169, 175–76, 179, 182n4, 185–86, 189–90, 192–93, 199n39, 203–4, 209, 211–14, 223, 227, 236, 240, 245, 252, 255, 258, 264, 267
Jews, 15, 109, 111, 122, 125, 131–33, 138, 143n10, 157, 176, 181, 182n4, 187, 205, 211–12, 252, 257, 261, 266, 270

John Paul II, Pope, 33, 45n15, 49, 109, 192, 202, 207, 232n18, 240, 255, 257, 261n11
Joy of the Gospel [Evangelii Gaudium], 7, 150, 152, 154, 260
JPII. *See* John Paul II, Pope
Judaism, 15, 21, 131–32, 138, 141, 175–76, 199n39, 212, 223
justice, 6–7, 22, 42, 68–69, 71, 76–77, 90–91, 99–103, 126, 150, 162, 177, 197, 209, 223, 235, 237–39, 241–43, 247, 258, 273

Kingdom of God, 4, 23, 33, 38, 42, 125, 153, 169, 214
Knitter, Paul, 236, 240–41
Korea (includes North and South), 33, 38, 41–42, 45n11, 166, 266

Laudato si' [Praise Be to You], 152, 260
liberation, 5, 16–17, 25, 28n83, 35–36, 40, 71, 74, 151, 160, 197, 229, 236, 259
Lefebure, Leo, viii, 161, 273, 277
Lohfink, Gerhard, 188–89
Lonergan, Bernhard, 121, 126, 147, 266
Lumen Gentium [Dogmatic Constitution on the Church], 149, 230n5
Lutheran(s), 109, 115, 130, 226

magisterium, 33, 146, 151–53, 158, 246, 268, 276
Mannion, Gerard, viii, 1–2, 7, 183, 220, 273, 276–77
marriage(s), 4, 84, 91, 93, 96–98, 100, 129–36, 138–42, 143nn9,10,17, 167, 236, 276
memory, viii, 1–2, 7, 11, 47, 60, 132, 223–25, 275
messiah, 63n47, 119, 125, 140, 182n4, 187, 223
Methodist(s), 133, 142, 226
migrant(s), 2–3, 48–55, 58–60, 62n23, 63n40, 65–78, 100–102, 106n52, 175, 179–80, 275
migration, viii, 1–3, 5, 11–12, 22, 24n3, 28n83, 38–39, 48–51, 61n14, 62n23, 64n61, 65–78, 79n2, 81n43, 84–89, 100,

145, 159, 175, 179–81, 182n20, 220, 259, 266, 268–70, 274–77
missionary(ies), 14, 39, 71, 121, 142, 149, 224–25, 254, 265
Muslims, 15, 122, 131, 133, 138, 211, 249, 252, 254, 261, 266
mysticism, 77, 82n67

New Testament, 124, 139, 176–77, 182, 184–85, 189, 192, 266. *See also* Bible
non-violence, 34, 87, 134
Nostra aetate [Declaration of the Relation of the Church to Non-Christian Religions], 45n9, 46n24, 109–10, 112, 114, 252–55, 257–60, 262nn14,15

Orthodox, 11, 21, 124, 138, 226, 264–65. *See also* Russian Orthodox
orthodoxy, 30, 121, 256

pastor(s), 52, 55, 68, 73, 143n16. *See also* clergy
Paul (Apostle, Saint), 69, 91–93, 122, 123–24, 180, 184–85, 189, 192, 203, 251
Paul VI, Pope, 32, 106n50, 232nn13,17, 253–54, 261n12
Phan, Peter, vii–viii 1–7, 11–12, 19–21, 23, 27n64, 30–31, 44–47, 60, 61n14, 66, 84–85, 103, 118–23, 126–29, 139–40, 142n2, 145–47, 149–57, 162, 164, 175, 180–84, 190, 194–97, 198n25, 199n50, 206–14, 215n13, 220–22, 225, 227–29, 235–39, 241, 244, 247, 247n1, 258–61, 262nn15,25
pluralism, vii–viii, 1, 3, 6–7, 20, 22–23, 27n64, 37, 40, 58, 118, 128–30, 141–42, 142n2, 145, 150, 155, 158, 161–62, 206–7, 214, 214n10, 215n13, 220, 223–24, 226, 228–29, 236, 239–40, 243, 249, 251–52, 254–57, 259–61, 262n25, 276
Pneumatology, 1, 3, 119, 122–23, 126, 267
Pontifical Council for Interreligious Dialogue, 40, 45n19, 160, 167, 170n13, 250, 255
prayer(s), 33, 73, 76, 122, 135, 160, 194–95, 251, 255, 260–61, 265

Presbyterian(s), 142, 226
priest(s), 56, 58, 91, 97, 102, 145–46, 158,
    170n5, 179, 191, 212, 238, 240–41, 244,
    246
priestess(es), 3, 111
priesthood, 93, 176, 190, 212
process theology, 105n39, 197

Rahner, Karl, 1, 5, 12, 29, 184, 189–96,
    198n25, 199n26, 205, 207, 214n9, 237,
    265, 267, 277
Ratzinger, Joseph. *See* Benedict XVI, Pope
reconciliation, 35, 94–96, 98, 109–11,
    115–16, 209, 227
Redemptoris Missio [*Mission of the
    Redeemer*], 158, 202, 255
refugee(s), 1–3, 5, 38, 49, 68, 70–72, 75,
    85–86, 88, 90, 95, 101–3, 176–80, 237,
    264, 268, 270, 273, 275
Renaissance, 3, 110–14, 276
resurrection, 48, 78, 125–26, 137, 183–86,
    188–93, 196, 198n15, 214n8, 277
Rhodes, Alexandre de, 1, 12, 265, 267
Roman Catholic Church(es). *See* Catholic
    Church(es)
Russian Orthodox, 12, 45n22, 194,
    264–65

Sacred Scripture. *See* Bible
Said, Edward, 15, 233n34
salvation, 5, 25, 35, 74, 110, 119, 122,
    128–29, 137, 139–40, 149, 158–59, 177,
    179, 186–89, 193, 197, 199n42, 201–5,
    207–11, 230, 236, 244, 252, 260, 276
Scripture. *See* Bible
sensus fidei/fidelium, 151–53
sex, 39, 80, 83, 88, 99, 249, 251

sexuality, 21, 84, 236, 242
sin(s), 84, 91, 94–95, 98, 124–26, 137, 180,
    185, 197, 239, 245
spirituality, 74, 77, 152, 194, 213, 240

Taoism, 21
Tayyib, Ahmad, 7, 249–50, 261n2
Thomas Aquinas, 15, 112, 124, 191, 193,
    195, 243
Tillich, Paul, 29, 268

undocumented [migrant], 49, 68, 71
Unitatis redintegratio [*Decree on Ecu-
    menism*], 112, 252
US Conference of Catholic Bishops, 6–7,
    128, 258

Vatican I. *See* Vatican Council
Vatican II. *See* Vatican Council, 2nd
Vatican Council, 124, 253
Vatican Council, 2nd (1962–1965), vii–viii,
    2–3, 6, 31–35, 38, 44, 44n8, 53, 109,
    112–13, 115–16, 125–26, 129, 149, 158,
    191, 212, 219–21, 223, 229–30, 230n4,
    236, 252–55, 257, 259–60, 267, 276–77
Vietnam, vii, 1–2, 5, 12, 33, 38, 40, 42,
    45n11, 46n25, 265–70, 277
violence, 37–38, 43, 67, 83–95, 97–103,
    105nn37,38,39, 161, 275

woman or women, 3, 33, 39, 43–44, 71–73,
    83–103, 105nn37,38,39, 111, 122, 138,
    142, 147, 158–59, 197, 211, 252–54,
    267, 275
worship, 59, 74, 84, 122, 130, 135, 251

xenophobia, 2, 59, 68, 134